Song Loves the Masses

The publisher gratefully acknowledges the John Daverio Endowment of the American Musicological Society, funded in part by the National Endowment for the Humanities and the Andrew W. Mellon Foundation.

The publisher also gratefully acknowledges the generous support of the Music in America Endowment Fund of the University of California Press Foundation, which was established by a major gift from Sukey and Gil Garcetti, Michael P. Roth, and the Roth Family Foundation.

Song Loves the Masses

Herder on Music and Nationalism

JOHANN GOTTFRIED HERDER
AND PHILIP V. BOHLMAN

University of California Press

University of California Press, one of the most distinguished university presses in the United States, enriches lives around the world by advancing scholarship in the humanities, social sciences, and natural sciences. Its activities are supported by the UC Press Foundation and by philanthropic contributions from individuals and institutions. For more information, visit www.ucpress.edu.

University of California Press
Oakland, California

© 2017 by The Regents of the University of California

Library of Congress Cataloging-in-Publication Data

Names: Herder, Johann Gottfried, 1744-1803, author. | Bohlman, Philip V., 1952- editor, translator, writer of added commentary. | Container of (expression): Herder, Johann Gottfried, 1744-1803. Alte Volkslieder. English.
Title: Song loves the masses : Herder on music and nationalism / Johann Gottfried Herder and Philip V. Bohlman.
Description: Oakland, California : University of California Press, [2017] | Includes bibliographical references and index.
Identifiers: LCCN 2016026829 (print) | LCCN 2016032212 (ebook) | ISBN 9780520234949 (cloth : alk. paper) | ISBN 0520234944 (cloth : alk. paper) | ISBN 9780520234956 (pbk. : alk. paper) | ISBN 0520234952 (pbk. : alk. paper) | ISBN 9780520966444 (ebook)
Subjects: LCSH: Folk songs—History and criticism. | Nationalism in music. | National characteristics. | Herder, Johann Gottfried, 1744-1803—Criticism and interpretation.
Classification: LCC ML3545 .H47 2017 (print) | LCC ML3545 (ebook) | DDC 781.5/99—dc23
LC record available at https://lccn.loc.gov/2016026829

Manufactured in the United States of America

26 25 24 23 22 21 20 19 18 17
10 9 8 7 6 5 4 3 2 1

for Andrea and Ben
whose life journeys overflow with the
songs we together share

Gott, laß uns dein Heil schauen,
Auf nichts Vergänglichs trauen,
  Nicht Eitelkeit uns freun!
Laß uns einfältig werden,
Und vor dir hier auf Erden
  Wie Kinder fromm und frölich seyn.
—MATTHIAS CLAUDIUS, "Abendlied"
Final folk song in Johann Gottfried
Herder, *Volkslieder*

Contents

List of Illustrations	ix
Acknowledgments	xi
Note on the Text	xiv
Note on Translation and Commentary	xvii
Prologue: Again, Herder	1

PART I. THE ONTOLOGY PROJECT — 19

1. Folk Song at the Beginnings of National History: Essay on *Alte Volkslieder* (1774) — 21
   Translation from *Alte Volkslieder / Ancient Folk Songs* — 26

2. The Folk Song Project at the Confluence of Music and Nationalism: Essay on *Volkslieder* (1778/79) and *Stimmen der Völker in Liedern* (1807) — 44
   Translation from *Volkslieder* and *Stimmen der Völker in Liedern / Folk Songs* and *Voices of the People in Song* — 50
   Appendix A: Introduction to the Folk Song Texts — 71
   Appendix B: Translation from the Folk Song Texts — 74

3. Singing the Sacred Body: Essay on *Lieder der Liebe* (1778) — 105
   Translation from *Lieder der Liebe: Die ältesten und schönsten aus Morgenlande / Songs of Love: The Oldest and Most Beautiful from the Orient* — 111

PART II. THE HISTORY PROJECT 133

4. The Nation and Its Fragments: Essay on "Briefwechsel über Ossian und die Lieder alter Völker" (1773) 135
   Translation from "Briefwechsel über Ossian und die Lieder alter Völker" / "Correspondence about Ossian and the Songs of Ancient Peoples" 140

5. Songs of the Enlightenment Bard: Essay on "Homer und Ossian" (1794) 168
   Translation of "Homer und Ossian" / "Homer and Ossian" 172

6. Redemption through Sacred Song: Essay on Letter 46, *Theologische Schriften* (1780/81) 186
   Translation of Letter 46, *Theologische Schriften* / *Theological Writings* 190

PART III. THE NATION PROJECT 199

7. The Shores of Modernity: Essay on "Wirkung der Dichtkunst auf die Sitten neuerer Zeiten" (1777) 201
   Translation from "Wirkung der Dichtkunst auf die Sitten neuerer Zeiten" / "The Influence of Poetry on the Customs of Modernity" 205

8. The Epic as Nation: Essay on Herder's *Der Cid* 221
   Translation from *Der Cid* / *The Cid* 228

9. Music Transcendent and Sublime: Herder's "Von Music" (1800) 246
   Translation of "Von Musik" / "On Music" 249

Epilogue: Herder's Journey 261

Notes 285
Bibliography 289
Index 307

List of Illustrations

1. Johann Gottfried Herder, portrait by Anton Graff, 1785 — 4
2. The theological field of Herder's philosophy — 6
3. "Tres Romances del Cid," Sephardic ballad — 9
4. Johann Gottfried Herder, *Vom Geist der ebräischen Poesie*, 1787 — 11
5. Title page of Moses Mendelssohn, *Shir ha-shirim*, 1788 — 14
6. Weimar circa 1830 — 35
7. Estonia and Latvia, mid-eighteenth century — 63
8. "An die Jungfrau Maria" / "To the Virgin Mary," from Johann Gottfried Herder, "Stimmen der Völker in Liedern," 1807 — 99
9. Map of the world, circa 1807 — 103
10. Title page of Johann Gottfried Herder, *Lieder der Liebe*, 1778 edition — 109
11. Title page of Johann Gottfried Herder, *Von deutscher Art und Kunst*, 1773 — 136
12. Nicolai Abraham Abildgaard, *Ossian's Swan Song*, ca. 1782. — 142
13. Johannes Brahms, "Ballade," op. 10, no. 1 — 158
14. Title page of James Macpherson, *Fingal, an Ancient Epic Poem*, 1765 — 170
15. Ximena and the Cid, woodcut from the 1869 edition of Herder's *Der Cid* — 222
16. Canto 49, "The Cid in Valencia and in Death," woodcut from the 1869 edition of Herder's *Der Cid* — 237
17. Itinerary from Herder's field notes of 1769, in his own hand — 265

Acknowledgments

Herder was there in the moment I realized my life journey would be that of an ethnomusicologist. Fall 1976, the University of Illinois at Urbana-Champaign, Music 317, "Folk Music." Bruno Nettl's introductory course was at once new, even exotic, as my first course in ethnomusicology, and familiar, even intimate, as a moment of recognition, *Erkenntnis*. I had not known that I had lived with folk music all my life, but it became clear the moment I recognized the sounds of worlds close to home and far away. Herder was there because he had given all this a name, *Volkslied*, "folk song." It, too, had always been there, just not called folk song. Herder's folk songs, too, were intimate and exotic, but in that moment of recognition they cohabited the worlds of self and other. In that moment, captured in Herder's folk songs, music changed for me. It is that moment that I attempt to capture in this book.

Herder has accompanied me on an intellectual journey of almost forty years. Beginning with ethnographic studies of the familiar—folk music in my home state of Wisconsin, which led to collections that would become the substance of my master's thesis and first publications—I traveled with Herder farther and farther into worlds that were unknown to me, to Israel and the Middle East, to the folk song landscapes of Eastern Europe, to India and beyond. If he began with folk song, Herder himself journeyed to the far shores on which it provided the ontological energy and ethnographic agency that made music far more than itself.

I have had important guides during these travels with Herder, and I acknowledge them with gratitude. Bruno Nettl first pointed me to Herder, and in one of the most recent papers that contained ideas I use in this book, the 2014 Bruno and Wanda Nettl Distinguished Lecture in Ethnomusicology at the University of Illinois, I was able to sustain the level of my indebtedness.

Over many years, my teachers and colleagues in ethnomusicology encouraged (or, more commonly, tolerated) my interests in folk music. Most of all, I was never dissuaded from recognizing that folk music was always there, be it in the anthologies and collections of Jewish folk songs that I was able to plumb at the Jewish Music Research Centre at the National and University Library of Israel, or in the Deutsches Volksliedarchiv in Freiburg im Breisgau. During those early years after my graduate studies, I benefited enormously from the guidance and wisdom of Israel Adler and Amnon Shiloah in Jerusalem, Rudolf Pietsch in Vienna, and Otto Holzapfel in Freiburg. Otto, especially, knew that folk song was always there, and in different ways, so too would he be as I expanded the musical seas across which I journeyed, not least those whose shores were recognizable through religion. I am particularly thankful that Otto continues to be a fellow traveler.

Several fellowships over the course of the past forty years have allowed me to return to Herder and the worlds of folk song and folk music that his writing and thought made recognizable. Among the most important were a Fulbright-Hays Dissertation Research Fellowship to Israel (1981–82); an Alexander von Humboldt Research Fellowship in Germany (1990–91); a Fulbright Guest Professorship at the University of Vienna (1995–96); a senior fellowship at the Internationales Forschungszentrum Kulturwissenschaften in Vienna (1999); and a Berlin Prize Fellowship at the American Academy of Berlin (2003), during which I began the translations that would come to fill the pages of this book. I am very grateful indeed for such support for my research.

Herderian topics were relatively rare in my teaching, but they were particularly important in the ways they punctuated my pedagogy. In 1984, at the University of California, Berkeley, Alan Dundes asked that I teach a course on folk music, which became the point of departure for many discussions on Herder for the two of us over many years, beginning with my first book, *The Study of Folk Music in the Modern World* (1988), which Alan commissioned, and leading in 2006 to one of the lectures that would draw my thoughts on Herder together for the present book, which I delivered at Berkeley in Alan's memory. During guest professorships in Freiburg im Breisgau, Vienna, and Berlin, folk music came to occupy entire seminars or substantial modules, which in turn led me to the other Herderian subject of this book, nationalism. For its generous support of this publication I thank the Music in America Endowment at the University of California Press; I also received an AMS Publication Grant from the John Devario Endowment of the American Musicological Society. The confluence of music and nationalism in my work has been grounded in Europe, but increasingly moves to more global shores and beyond the present. I am particularly grateful to the

John Simon Guggenheim Memorial Foundation for a fellowship that now leads me through the present Herder project to the study on music after nationalism upon which I now embark.

Students and colleagues at the University of Chicago have followed this book through a journey of many years, indulging my passion for its remarkable relevance and modernity. It would require too many pages to thank everyone at the university to whom I owe some kind of debt, but I do wish to acknowledge the students in my Herder seminar in 2010. Jennie Horton was an especially resourceful and thoughtful research assistant. Various departments of the Regenstein Library were essential for original editions from the eighteenth century, as well as for most of the illustrations in the book. Special thanks go to the staff of Special Collections and to Christopher Winters, who provided the several riches from the Regenstein Map Collection.

Herder frequently undertook publication projects that were different and even experimental in his day. He was able to do so because of colleagues willing to spend time with his ideas, critically so, and because of editors and publishers willing to place their faith in him. It is surely fitting that this project, which is rather uncommon as a monograph in music scholarship, benefited from a similar investment of trust at the University of California Press. I thank Lynne Withey for encouraging me to undertake this project in the first place, and I am particularly grateful to Mary Francis for employing a patience that simultaneously urged me to quicken my pace. Raina Polivka embraced the book with enthusiasm, and conveyed that enthusiasm to her colleagues during production, especially Zuha Khan and Francisco Reinking. Lindsey Westbrook turned keen eyes and ears toward the task of copy editing, improving the book with every suggestion and correction. The press's readers, too, responded with a thoughtfulness that inspired me to do everything possible to realize the remarkable breadth of Herder's intellectual world for twenty-first-century readers.

Of the many sea changes that we witness in Herder's writings on music and nationalism, none is more significant than his integration of music as object into the subjectivities of the collective. Song loves the masses because it grows from the agency of individuals and communities. I have always found my inspiration from music's communal ontology, from the few and the many making music together. I have been particularly fortunate, moreover, that such inspiration in the community of my family has been as abundant as it is familiar and intimate. Like folk music, my wife, Christine Wilkie Bohlman, has always been there, and my children, Andrea and Ben, always will be. I thank all three of you, with love, for just being there.

Berlin and Oak Park

Note on the Text

Song Loves the Masses is unlike other editions and translations of Herder's works in several distinctive ways. First of all, this is the first collection of Herder's writings devoted to music; second, this is the first translation of Herder's written work on music. On their surfaces, such distinctions would seem straightforward enough, justifying an obvious, if long overdue, book project. The question of music and Herder, however, is never quite so straightforward. He did write extensively, and at times in his life, notably the 1770s, intensively, about music, but with few exceptions music did not stand alone as a subject. During Herder's lifetime he published no monograph or even an extended essay on music, and when he addresses an aspect of music as a seemingly unified topic, as in the *Volkslieder* (1778/79, chapter 2 in this book), music emerges in his thought as a subject that does not lend itself to isolated treatment. Whereas other Herder translations, among them the excellent collections proximate to the two hundredth anniversary of his death in 1803, drew upon the unity of subject areas in philosophy, history, aesthetics, anthropology, sculpture, and theology, there was nothing equivalent for music. With the 2003 Herder anniversary in mind, in fact, it was my original design for the present book that it should be an anthology like the other anthologies, finally providing twenty-first-century readers with the opportunity to experience what Herder really said about music. That design, however, proved not to be the one I eventually chose.

The reader should approach *Song Loves the Masses* as the book on music that Herder would have written had he gathered the many strands of his musical thought for a single publication. The chapters chosen for the book represent his most significant writings on music, especially those he situated in the changing contexts of nation and empire in the late eighteenth century. With his writings on music Herder was responding to those contexts, which, accordingly, provide unity to the ways in which the following chapters unfold and narrate several larger processes of change. The subject "music" undergoes transformation at many different levels as Herder expands the dimensions of its global landscapes with each successive music project. The best way to read this book, therefore, is to follow its narrative arc, allowing Herder's fragments, letters, collections of songs and epics, and journeys through aesthetics and anthropology to cohere with the wholeness that was crucial to the universal history that fired Herder's musical imagination throughout his life.

Herder editions are surprisingly abundant, and they unfold as an intellectual history of their own, albeit with many directions, from soon after his death until the present day. The first attempt to gather his diverse writings with some measure of comprehensiveness was the forty-five-volume edition published by Cotta between 1805 and 1820. The initial translations into English were largely of theological writings, the first being James Marsh's American translation of *Der Geist der ebräischen Poesie* (1833). Of the several collected or complete editions, two were critical for the present book, the thirty-three volumes of the Bernhard Suphan edition, *Herders Sämmtliche Werke* (Herder 1877–1913), and the eleven volumes of *Johann Gottfried Herder: Werke in zehn Bänden* (Herder 1985–2000). With several exceptions, I use this latter modern edition (JGHW) as the basis for my translations. For the essays and anthology from Herder's folk song project in chapter 2, I use the Reclam edition (Herder 1975), which contains the expansion of the 1778/79 *Volkslieder* to the more extensive *Stimmen der Völker in Liedern*, published posthumously in 1807. For chapter 7, I use another modern edition for *Lieder der Liebe*, which fully captures the sense of Herder's work on the biblical *Song of Songs* in a single volume (Herder 1992).

Music appears almost not at all in Herder translations, and when it does, it is usually one component of a larger discussion, as for example in the essay on the origins of language, *Abhandlung über den Ursprung der Sprache* (Herder 1772). The only chapter in the book that exists in a previously translated publication is the Ossian correspondence (chapter 4), which H. B. Nisbet includes in a larger anthology of works in aesthetics and literary criticism (Nisbet 1985), but I do not use this as the source for my translation.

The opportunity to provide new and fresh translations of the important works on music has also been crucial to the ways in which I have woven the different parts into a single whole. Although Herder wrote the original works in this book for diverse purposes and readers, I have seized upon this opportunity to find common purposes and readers. In gathering the many different aspects of Herder's musical thought, I hope to have realized yet another stage of his long intellectual journey, for which his writings on music and nationalism provided some of the most significant and critical milestones.

Note on Translation and Commentary

Johann Gottfried Herder was an engaged and passionate translator throughout his life. Translation was crucial to his activities as a thinker, teacher, and writer. As both a pastor and a theologian, Herder used translation daily in the ritual practices of liturgy and the biblical exegesis that unified his theological writing. Translation provided him with one of his most important means of self-education, for example in learning Spanish for his *Cid* translation (chapter 8), and in designing schools and other educational programs (epilogue). His historical writings unfolded through the series of translations that stretched from antiquity to the present (chapters 1 and 4). Translation afforded him with the fundamental theories he developed as a philosopher of language, and from his earliest work his publications are filled with essays that address these theories of translation (chapter 4).

Herder came to understand music, too, as a process of translation. His publications of folk song grew as anthologies of translated texts (chapter 1), and it was through translation that song became the common cultural practice of the *Volk* (chapter 2). Ontologically and aesthetically, the transformation of music from object to subject, from song to singing, followed processes of translation (chapter 9). To understand Herder and his writings, it is critical to examine this pervasive role of translation in his thought. That has been one of the basic tasks of the present book: translating Herder translating (see Bohlman 2011b).

Herder was rarely a literal translator; rather, he used translating to examine a confluence of ideas. Even in his translations of religious texts, whether from the Jewish and Christian bibles (see chapters 6 and 7) or from the sacred texts of non-European religions, such as Hinduism, Herder regarded translation as a form of continuous exegesis. His translation of the *Song of Songs*, for example, remained an ongoing project, and when published as

Lieder der Liebe (see chapter 3), it included not only translations for sacred uses, but also the medieval minnesinger variants. We know also that he was willing to extend translations of original texts, for example the cantos in Spanish and French from which he spun the full epic of his *Cid*, with passages of his own creation, thus completing the process of translation.

If Herder was remarkable as a polyglot even in comparison to other translators of his age, he rarely limited himself to the reproduction of texts for exegetical purposes only. Translation was never a one-to-one replacement of words with equivalents. This is evident in the relative infrequency of his placement of the original in parentheses. Many words themselves, even those basic to Herderian concepts (e.g., *Lied* and *Gesang*, or *Volk* and *Nation*), have shifting meanings. The political and cultural conditions in which the *Volk* live, too, are described with many different terms, which reveal shifting concepts of nation and nationalism. *Nation* has a very different set of meanings when applied to Greek and Roman antiquity than when used as a description of aesthetic traditions in eighteenth-century England and Germany. The customs (*Sitten*) of the medieval Church shape society in ways quite unlike the customary ritual practices of Indigenous peoples in North and South America. The dynamic quality of translation paved the way for the very journey toward a universal history that unfolds across the chapters that follow.

Herder frequently followed translations through successive variants, adding and revising them to provide a kind of metatranslation or metatext. The newly translated texts further allowed him to translate between genres, and to employ intertextuality. Accordingly, his translation projects rarely depended on a single, authentic text, but rather drew from several variant texts to create a new, authoritative text. Herder's *Cid*, as we see in chapter 8, drew upon many different sources in several languages, which cohered only when woven into his translation. The synthetic process, moreover, was ongoing and always open to revision and expansion. We see this once again with Herder's *Cid*, which was never published in a complete version during his lifetime, but in the century after his death was the most frequently published of all his writings. An even more striking example from the present book is his *Lieder der Liebe*, in which he gathers translations of the *Song of Songs* that together become a vast historical text in which translation itself is the ontological and structural subject. This becomes clear in its third chapter, which is no more nor less than a meditation on translation.

In *Song Loves the Masses*, I too seek ways in which my translations can extend the process of transforming object to subject. My goal is to create texts from which Herder's ideas emerge, and then draw connections across a unified set of chapters that form the single text of an entire book. Herder was less concerned with readers of texts in their original languages—in many places in chapter 4 he even shows real disdain for the pedantry of such readers—than with discovering methods that would enable his publications to give ideas relevance and meaning for the readers of his own day, as well as beyond. It is significant, once again, that projects remained ongoing, as with the *Cid* and *Volkslieder*, the former never appearing in a definitive edition, the latter in an edition that could only be completed and published posthumously, three years after Herder's death. Like Herder, I seek to make my translations meaningful for modern readers.

The approach to translation that I describe above has led to a series of technical decisions that I sustain throughout the book, further enhancing its narrative unity. I am not alone in employing these conventions, many of which are used by contemporary Herder translators. First of all, I do not clutter the text with German originals, and when I feel I must clarify some aspect of the original, I do so in the footnotes. Second, I attempt to capture the flow and style of Herder's texts, which differ considerably from chapter to chapter in the book. Third, I retain the feel for poetry in song lyrics, but I do not try to find an English poetic structure that mirrors the German; I recognize the decasyllabic hemistich structure in the *Cid* translation, for instance, but I do not seek to reproduce it. Fourth, Herder uses various forms of ellipsis—single dashes, several dashes in a series, combinations of dashes and periods—to give a sense of fragments (e.g., the Ossian correspondence in chapter 4) and free-flowing thought (e.g., *Alte Volkslieder* in chapter 1), and I represent all of these with modern conventions of ellipses rather than retain Herder's dashes and their lack of consistency. Fifth, I retain Herder's own use of italics for emphasis, which range from emphasis on certain words and concepts to the identification of authors and titles. Herder means to draw attention through italics, and I retain his intent. Sixth, when Herder discusses literary figures of the past, he uses italics and last names only. Because many of these figures are not widely known to today's readers, I usually add the first name and then the birth and death dates in parentheses, usually in the main body of the chapter, thus helping the reader situate them in intellectual history.

Herder employed several voices as a writer, depending on whether he was producing more scholarly work or more popular texts. Both he and I use footnotes, but he does so only in specific instances and in certain literary genres. In many texts he uses no form of annotation; in others (e.g., *Volkslieder*) he combines footnotes with commentary. When I am the only one to use footnotes and parenthetical citations in the chapter, I do so without additional remark. When both of us employ annotation, I begin Herder's with JGH in square brackets and mine with PVB in square brackets (see especially chapter 2). When making bibliographical references in his footnotes, Herder used the abbreviated forms common in eighteenth-century citations, many of which are insufficient for modern readers wishing to find the sources. In these instances I have completed the citations, though I do not place PVB in square brackets before the parts I have added.

One of the motivations for the present book was to make important but relatively unknown texts available in English translation. These, in turn, would help us resolve some of the persistently perplexing problems of misunderstanding and confusion that have historically plagued Herder's reception. I believe such problems have also confused the ways in which some scholars and other commentators have searched for authenticity and literal meaning in Herder. For his part, Herder used writing and translating to work through ideas, to liberate them from literal meaning. The pressing question for Herder was not, for example, whether the fictional Scottish bard Ossian did or did not exist, and by extension whether the Ossian songs were real or not, but what their translatability revealed about the ways song connected the past to the present (chapter 4).

Herder was a polymath and a polyglot, and in both roles he sought to understand the difference and diversity around which larger processes of universalism coalesced. He translated in order to find difference that yielded many objects and the diversity that proliferated as multiple subjects. Songs and nations were many and diverse, and he wanted his essays, letters, song anthologies, and books, from which I have taken the texts that appear in the chapters that follow, to express these complex subjectivities. In the universal history toward which Herder was striving, music and nation had multiple and contradictory meanings. It has been my goal as translator to be as true as possible to the paradox and idealism that drew Herder to search for those meanings in the first place.

Prologue
Again, Herder

PSALM 137—"BY THE RIVERS OF BABYLON"
By the rivers of Babylon, there we sat down,
   yea, we wept when we remembered Zion.
We hanged our harps upon the willows in the midst thereof.
For there they carried us away captive required of us a song;
   and they that wasted us required of us mirth, saying.
Sing us one of the songs of Zion.
How shall we sing the Lord's song in a strange land?[1]

BE-RESHIT—BEGINNING WITH HERDER

It is particularly fitting to begin a book dedicated to the writings of Johann Gottfried Herder (1744–1803) with Psalm 137, for it was one of Herder's favorite biblical texts, and it occupied a crucial position in his own translations from and exegesis of the Bible. The psalm possessed for him deep religious meaning, and he recognized the ways it drew upon music to represent metaphors of place and time, the politics of self and other, which further defined for Herder the historical conditions of struggle for the nation (see Stowe 2016). The psalm that is known best as "By the Rivers of Babylon" represented for Herder the consummate confluence of prayer, historical narrative, and song. It was this confluence that he sought to capture in his translation of it.

> Every feeling is expressed wholly. The mourning that rises to joy, the pain that finds solace in rest, the peace that gives way to joyful trust, the story that finally abandons itself to delight, the delight that finds calm in its telling—every affect has its own expression, which fully envelops the lyrical song. It engenders the feeling of perfection. (Herder, "IX. Psalmen," *Vom Geist der ebräischen Poesie*, JGHW5 [1993], 1209)

It is in the confluence of endings and beginnings in Psalm 137 that we witness Herder's arrival at his own sensibilities of song and music. The beauty of the song, he writes, is inseparable from a peace immanent in the return from Babylon, the movement of the melody toward the sublime. The beauty of song, including its aspiration to the sublime, conveys a direct

1

political meaning, for in the collection of translations of which the psalm is a part, Herder also assigns a subtitle to the individual psalms, "Nationalgesang" (National Song), whereby he deliberately calls attention to the symbolic liberation from imprisonment (*Die Befreiung von Gefangenschaft*). Sacred song flowed together with political action in the *Spirit of Hebrew Poetry*, a volume that afforded sacred dimensions to the sublime in musical and aesthetic terms. That those dimensions further coalesced around the nation and nationalism, providing a unifying theme to writings spanning a productive career of almost forty years, is the subject of the present book.

The confluence of endings and beginnings we witness in Herder's translations affords one of the most consistent themes for approaching translation in the work of one of the most influential translators of his age. Throughout the book that follows, beginnings will appear again and again. Whereas it may seem as if there is a dissonance immanent in such juxtapositions of beginnings and new beginnings, consciously connecting the political to the musical through religious thought, that dissonance, as we shall witness throughout, was immanent in Herder's engagement with music and religion—not just his own Protestant Lutheran Christianity, but also Judaism, Hinduism, and the other world religions in which Herder, like others in the late eighteenth century, sought enlightenment. At the beginning of Herder's own philosophical and theological work, his engagement with music and religion may have been at times inchoate, but over the course of his life it was increasingly the source for reconciliation at the confluence of musical and religious thought.

The moments of confluence that return in the course of the present volume generate several sets of questions, which are posed in multiple ways in the translations and analytical interpretations. First, why do the Herders of reception history continue to reappear and have such different meanings at paradigmatic moments of change—cultural, political, and intellectual? Second, what meaning did religion and religious thought have for Herder? Third, why do the nation and nationalism acquire musical dimensions at the confluence of aesthetics and religious thought? Finally, how did his aesthetic and musical thought come to transform the way Herder understood music and nationalism and their presence in global history? In this prologue, I begin the search for a common way to connect the questions and seek methods to find answers to them through translation in the book that follows.

Translation provides me with a context for my own return to Herder in the different writings that fill the book. Following many years of work on music and nationalism (e.g., Bohlman 2011a), I now approach the translator Herder as a translator (Bohlman 2011b). Translation in ethnomusicology is for me an ontological and phenomenological question. Herder acts on the psalms, on folk songs, on Mediterranean epics, or, indeed, on the very ways music translates the nation and its history, as a translator, sustaining a tradition of repetition and transformation of a sameness that always assumes new forms. For Herder it was repetition itself that distinguished music from the other arts and invested it with the power of the sublime. His recognition of music's power increasingly distinguished his voice from those of other late Enlightenment thinkers, for example that of his former teacher, Immanuel Kant. Music crucially occupied a position in time—indeed, gave meaning to time by articulating its narrative power (see for example chapter 9 in the present volume, "On Music," from *Kalligone* of 1800).

In the chapters that follow I employ translation as a means of situating this book in a larger project on the intellectual history of ethnomusicology. Temporally and historically, the questions I pose in this prologue open a domain in which ideas and concepts return. Such return was also a concern of Walter Benjamin, for example in his concept of *Urprung* (origins) (see, e.g., Benjamin 1963). They do so by repeating and changing—seeking new beginnings. In an intellectual history of ethnomusicology, Herder thus comes to symbolize certain critical ideas "again," and these in turn adumbrate the historical moments of paradigm change that form the intellectual history of ethnomusicology. Nationalism and, by extension, the convergence of music and nationalism arise from such historical moments because of the repeated ways they form around the distinctions between self and other. As we consider the again-ness of ethnomusicology's intellectual history, we witness Herder as a symbol—repeating and changing—that signifies ethnomusicological thought.

My more ambitious aim, therefore, is to broaden the discursive field of ethnomusicology so that its history and historiography expand (see, e.g., Bohlman 2013a). Ethnomusicology does not simply emerge as a response to occasional historical moments. Rather, ethnomusicological thought—sustained and broadly constitutive—shapes a history of ideas. Herder's repeatability becomes symbolic of an ethnomusicological thought at the core of that history of ideas. Ultimately I hope to open a much broader space—globally and across different histories—for ethnomusicological thought as a means of understanding the world.

HERDER 1—THE THEOLOGICAL HISTORIAN AND THE SACRED PROJECTS

Johann Gottfried Herder was a pastor and theologian throughout his professional career. Born on August 25, 1744, in Mohrungen in the boundary region shared by East Prussia and Lithuania, he began studies in theology in

FIGURE 1. Johann Gottfried Herder, portrait by Anton Graff, 1785. Public domain.

1762 at the University of Königsberg, where he counted Immanuel Kant and Johann Georg Hamann among his teachers in philosophy. In 1764 he received his first appointment as a teacher in the cathedral school of Riga, where he served the German-speaking community in the multicultural and multi-religious metropolis for the next five years. Already during his Riga years, Herder inaugurated a prolific literary production, writing works on religion, aesthetics, and nationalism, including poetry and song (see Jaremko-Porter 2009). His first recognized work of scholarship was the *Versuch über das Sein* (Essay on Being, 1764; JGHW1, 9–21), and he followed this in the same year with an essay on aesthetics, "Dithyrambische Rhapsodie über die Rhapsodie kabbalistischer Prose" (Dithyramb-Rhapsody on the Rhapsody of Cabbalistic Prose), including music, in Jewish mystical texts, which contains smaller fragment-like sections he calls *Gesänge*, or songs (JGHW1,

30–39). He closed his Riga years with the four volumes of what would be a seminal work on aesthetics, *Kritische Wälder oder Betrachtungen, die Wissenschaft und Kunst des Schönen betreffend* (Critical Forests, or Observations Concerning the Science and Art of Beauty, 1769). In 1769 Herder embarked on a sea journey, which eventually led him to France and the German lands, but critically for our considerations of the history of ethnomusicological thought was also a transformational moment of encounter with ethnography. In the journal he kept on the journey across the Baltic and North Seas and beyond the shorelines of Europe, but never published in his lifetime, Herder sketched a plan for a new anthropology:

> For this purpose I wish to collect data about the history of every historical moment, each evoking a picture of its own use, function, custom, burdens and pleasures. Accordingly I shall assemble everything I can, leading up to the present day, in order to put it to good use. (Herder 1976 [1769], 39)

Following two years of extensive travel, Herder embarked in 1771 on a career that led him to take various positions in the religious and educational institutions of the German lands. The years of professional wandering would culminate in his arrival by 1776 in Weimar, where he would remain the rest of his life, the most public theologian in the foremost intellectual center of late-Enlightenment Germany. Even as he found himself more professionally established, however, Herder expanded the counterpoint between his theological and aesthetic/musical writings. It was in the 1770s, too, that he published his most sweeping folk song collections, *Alte Volkslieder* (1774) and the two editions of *Volkslieder* (1778/79 and 1807), which we know as foundational for the history of ethnomusicology (see chapters 1 and 2).

With the folk song collections Herder implemented a discourse about the collective singing of songs, which he was the first systematically to call "folk songs," thereby affording political and cultural dimensions to widespread musical practices. Folk songs fell into both linguistic and national categories, and the anthologies of the 1770s bear witness to the ways music might lead from the nation to nationalism. I follow the sweep of Herder's folk song projects in the early sections of this book, but I turn first in this prologue to the concern that led him to folk song, trying to understand Herder the theologian amid the aesthetic/musical projects. Accordingly, we remember first that Herder contributed notably to some of the most important philological studies of Enlightenment biblical scholarship (see Schmidt 1956). It was Herder, for example, who firmly established the order of the Gospels in the New Testament. Herder's engagement with the *Tanach*, the Hebrew Bible, was no less critical. At the very least, it grew from a much more aesthetically and musically complex interpretation of religion, surely

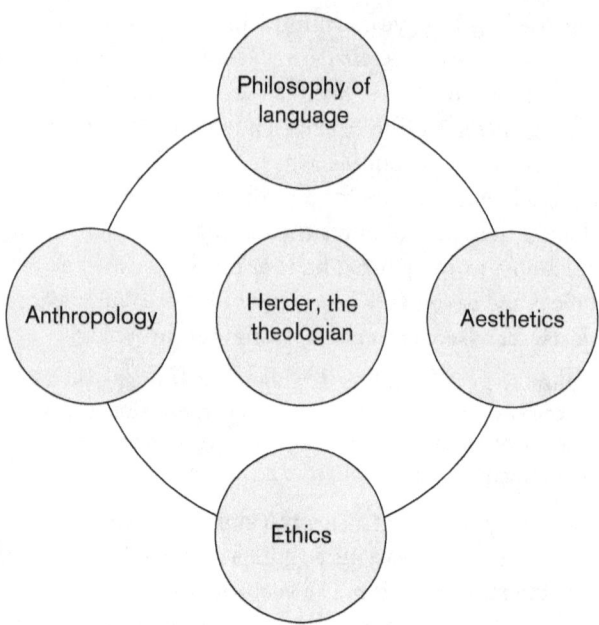

FIGURE 2. The theological field of Herder's philosophy. Figure by Philip V. Bohlman.

of Judaism. Herder's engagement with Judaism produced a considerable body of literature, which provides several of the central texts upon which I reflect in this prologue.

There are many reasons that I resist separating Herder the theologian from his other intellectual endeavors, using the metaphor of counterpoint consistently throughout the book as a means of identifying theme and variation, the repeatability and return that brings this project again and again to Herder. Thematic counterpoint was already evident in the 1770s, for it was also during this decade that Herder published some of his most aesthetically ambitious work on religion (see chapter 6) and on Jewish tradition, among them the studies of the *Songs of Solomon* (see chapter 3). Herder's religion projects took various forms. The theologian Herder employed different approaches, among them: 1) philological and textual scholarship; 2) aesthetics and poetics in sacred texts; 3) Herder the philosopher of history; 4) Herder the comparativist, as in his work on Sanskrit and the *Ṛg Veda*. Broadening the theological field to capture the different philosophical methods employed by Herder, a set of alternative and contrapuntal images might represent Herder's approach to religion, as visualized in figure 2.

The four Herders above followed intellectual paths in the projects on music and nationalism, but they continued to pass through the theological field that provided him with a central identity. To a large degree, these are the paths that I use to divide the nine chapters of this book into a series of projects, distinct from one another but linked through the more universal goals of Herder as polyglot and polymath: folk song, translation, religion, nation, and music. With an initial set of four case studies, the first on the Theologian Herder in the present section, I turn to the remaining three Herders—"again, Herder"—in search of a history of musical ideas that coalesces around them and is transmitted through them as the paradigmatic thinking on music and nationalism that emerges in the chapters that follow.

HERDER 2—HERDER'S EPIC PROJECT

It is necessary to begin with moments of beginning because they lie at the core of Herder's concept of history. That core takes shape in different ways in two of the most important Herder texts from early moments in his life, both struggling with moments of beginning: the *Journal meiner Reise im Jahr 1769* (Journal of My Sea Journey from 1769), and Herder's translation of the Iberian epic *El Cid*, begun in 1777 but never fully completed in Herder's eyes. Significantly, these were two works of beginning, but remained two unfinished projects in his lifetime. The two texts afford him different strategies to narrate beginning, the first an ethnographic history of humankind, the second a search for the transformation from myth to history, the border at which epic exposed the beginnings of the nation. The beginnings that Herder seeks to articulate, however, remain inchoate, and the presence of Jews and Jewish history remains unformed and uncertain. And for this reason, he returns to these moments again and again.

Herder's *Journal meiner Reise im Jahr 1769*, discussed briefly above and extensively in the epilogue, records his first ethnographic search for origins. Although the journal itself begins as he leaves his position as a pastor and church leader in the Protestant community of Riga, the entries depart from the biblical and exegetical style of his earlier writing. The journal signals a new direction and accordingly a new way of thinking, that of an anthropologist and a historian of religion (Bollacher 2003, 18–19; cf. Zammito 2002):

> If you seek only religion in biblical times, as well as seeking virtue, lessons, and bliss as we understand them to be, then you will preach only the virtues of *your own age*! Oh, how much must I do, that I become able to seek in such ways! How much have I achieved, however, should I seek in this way!—What a marvelous theme it would be to show how

one can be what one should be, neither Jew nor Arab, neither Greek nor uncivilized, neither martyr nor pilgrim. Rather, one can be the enlightened, lettered, noble, rational, educated, virtuous, and pleasure-loving human being that God has led to the steps of our culture. (Herder 1997 [1769], JGHW9/2, 30)

Although the Herder of the 1769 sea journey seemingly opens a broader historical field in which Jews are not bound entirely to a biblical past, there is also paradox in his early writings, which perplexes him and to which he repeatedly returns. The cultural relativism of Herder's anthropology projects is itself only partly formed, especially when it comes to the question of the nation. On one hand, Herder sees the Jewish diaspora as the bridge from the biblical past to the Europe of the Enlightenment—these are Herder's metaphors—the diaspora meaning that Jews have not yet arrived at a step or stage at which "they live according to European laws and contribute to the very best of the state" (Herder, *Ideen zur Philosophie der Geschichte der Menschheit* [1989] 6, 702). Because he never fully resolves the contradictions about Jews in the Enlightenment Europe of emergent modernity, Herder uses language that expresses prevailing themes of anti-Semitism and locates him closer to the Enlightenment of Jean-Jacques Rousseau than to the Haskala of Moses Mendelssohn (Bollacher 2003, 27).

On the other hand, it is precisely because of the *longue durée* of the diaspora that Jews had occupied a position from which they were positioned to form a nation. It is this historical moment that Herder captures with his translation of the *Cid* epic, a moment at which ethnography, poetics, and song converge (for translation from Herder's *Der Cid*, see chapter 8). Herder's *Cid* translation stands as a critical moment of ethnomusicological thought. First of all, Herder himself utilized translations over a period of almost seven centuries. Among these were those from the Sephardic *romance*, or ballad, such as the early modern print version in figure 3. Second, though Herder worked on his *Cid* translation from 1777 until his death in 1803, its incompleteness at Herder's hand did not restrict it from becoming the definitive version of the epic—in German translations—for the next century and a half, with well more than one hundred printed versions (for further discussion and images from those publications, see chapter 8). Again, Herder.

In the passages on the Jewish presence in al-Andalus, Herder seeks to find equanimity, a sort of understanding and connection, among the Abrahamic faiths. Thus he joins his Enlightenment counterparts, Ephraim Gotthold Lessing and Moses Mendelssohn, who also had explored the

FIGURE 3. "Tres Romances del Cid," Sephardic ballad. Source: Armistead and Silverman 1986, before p. 159. Public domain.

transformation from myth to history in *Nathan, der Weise* and *Jerusalem*. Toward the end of the *Cid* translation, in canto 52, the Cid himself speaks, asking forgiveness of "Israel and Benjamin," whom he addresses as "the honorable Jews," while his life approaches its end (for a full translation of canto 52, see chapter 8).

Herder's *Cid* became a critical component of the counterpoint in his much larger epic project. It completed a quartet of epics—joining his work on Ossian and Homer (see chapter 5), and, critically for a theological understanding of Herder's philosophical and musical work, the Torah, the five books of Moses—which together articulated the juncture of myth and history. For Jewish myth—biblical in the Torah, diasporic in the *Cid*—the portal to a history in the present had been sounded, "besungen," as Herder enunciates in his *Cid*, the nation of the past realizable as a nation of the future.

HERDER 3—POETICS, POLITICS, AND PSALMODY

It was Moses who would become the central figure on the stage of Herder's major work on Hebrew poesy and Jewish poetics, *Vom Geist der ebräischen Poesie* (The Spirit of Hebrew Poesy, 1787), which provides the exegetical fulcrum for Herder's work on the common aesthetic space occupied by the sacred and the secular.

The Spirit of Hebrew Poesy is an expansive two-volume work, a collection of fragments that cohere in epic proportions. The some 650 pages of the modern collected edition make it one of the longest of all Herder book projects (JGHW5, 661–1308). And yet, even as a book, *The Spirit of Hebrew Poesy* is more a work in progress, a project that never fully reaches completion. Herder employs various genres of writing and narrative, beginning with a series of "conversations" (*Gespräche*), moving through specific biblical themes, and concluding with exegesis of a number of critical texts, among the most important of which are those that he refers to as "songs" (*Lieder* and *Gesänge*). Chapter 7 of book 2, for example, has the title "Siegesgesänge der Israeliten" (Victory Songs of the Israelites; Herder 1787 [JGHW5, 1135–63]).

With *Spirit* Herder forges a larger aesthetic and musicality for the *Tanach*, the Hebrew Bible, but he also weaves them into a comparative framework with other world religions and musics, not least among them Brahmanic Hinduism, and accordingly he also creates a conceptual link to the nascent spirit of global nationalism. Herder's considerable work on India—he is sometimes called "the Brahman Herder" (Ghosh 1990)—stems also from his work as a theologian and translator, whose translations from Sanskrit predominantly center on the Vedic hymns, especially the *Rg Veda* (ibid.). Herder's translations of early Hindu texts provide one more counterpoint to his translations of Hebrew texts, not least that of Psalm 137.

It is with a chapter on "Moses" that Herder closes the first volume of *Spirit*, calling Moses to the altar of history, from which he would be the *Gesetzgeber*, the giver of laws, in which the meaning of Hebrew poetics and song emerged from the ways they afforded translation of the voice of God. The Moses of *Spirit*, then, is a political figure, the founder of a *Volk* and a nation with song. These roles—for song formed from law, given by Moses to provide narrative structure in the Torah—anchor *Spirit* in Jewish thought, history, and aesthetics, thereby rendering them whole. Herder actually ascribes three such roles to Moses, reformulating poesy as law. These three Moseses are introduced thus by Herder:

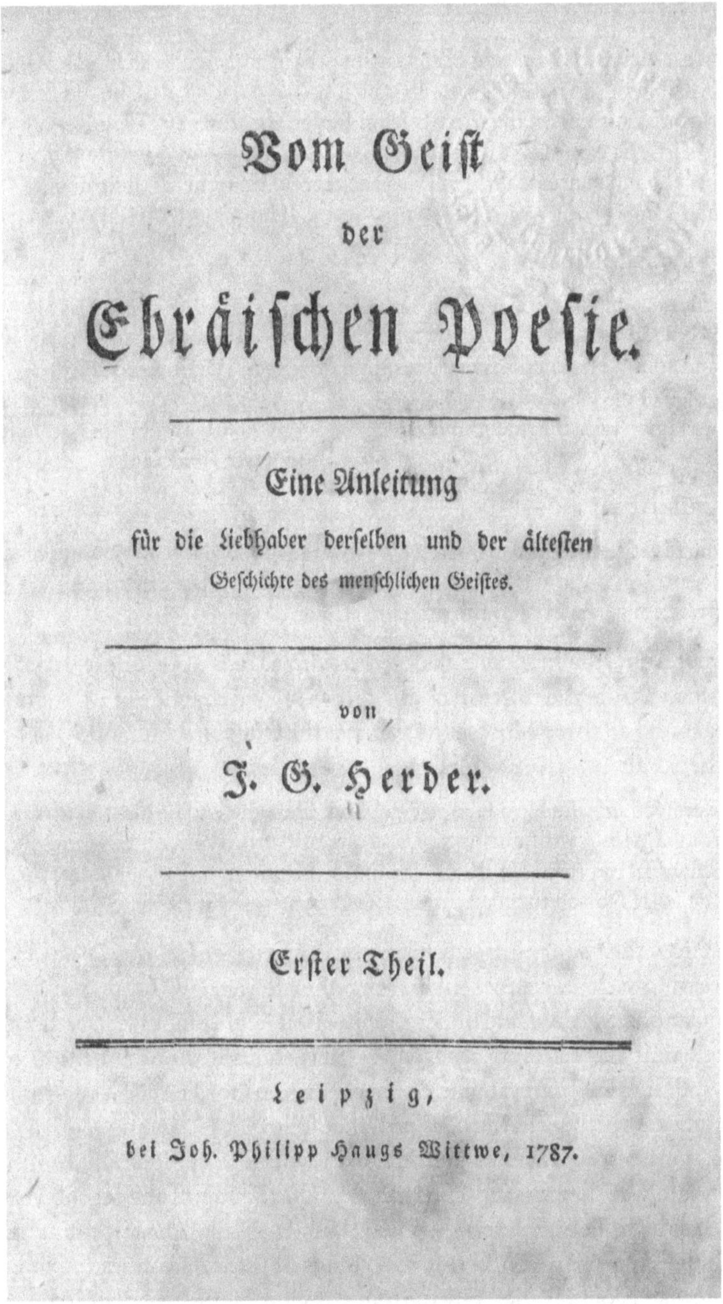

Vom Geist

der

Ebräischen Poesie.

Eine Anleitung

für die Liebhaber derselben und der ältesten

Geschichte des menschlichen Geistes.

von

J. G. Herder.

Erster Theil.

Leipzig,

bei Joh. Philipp Haugs Wittwe, 1787.

FIGURE 4. Johann Gottfried Herder, *Vom Geist der ebräischen Poesie*, 1787. Courtesy Special Collections, Regenstein Library, University of Chicago. Public domain.

(THE FIRST MOSES)

Moses shaped the poesy of his entire people and all else that was made possible in the political state in which he lived. First of all, he did this through his deeds: the exodus from Egypt, the journey through the desert, the conquest of the land, because God had laid it before the people and contested it. This was the eternal material of their images and songs about which I shall now speak. (Herder 1787 [JGHW5, 933])

(THE SECOND MOSES)

The second way in which Moses immortally shaped the poesy of his people was through the description of his deeds through his own poesy and songs. His final song ["The Song of Moses," Deuteronomy 32:1–10], as I have already explained, served as the model for the prophets: it was necessary for Israel to learn this song by heart, and to hold on to it, however hard that might be, thus uplifting itself. (Ibid., 934)

(THE THIRD MOSES)

Finally, the third means whereby Moses inspired the reawakening of sacred song in the times of decay was through the laws that he prescribed and gave to the prophets. (Ibid., 935)

Herder closes the first volume of *Spirit* with a translation of the very "Song of Moses" from the thirty-first and thirty-second chapters of Deuteronomy that bound all three Moseses together at the end of his life, at the very close of the Torah:

> Receive here the hardened, ardent, and, until the end of his life, tortured soul of Moses, still burning in his song of flame. We wish to witness what follows from his deeds, actions, descriptions, and other songs for the voices raised through poesy. (Ibid., 937)

Across the twenty-three chapters in *The Spirit of Hebrew Poesy*, Herder increasingly channels two streams together. Jewish law, Torah, provides the foundations for the state, indeed, the nation, and song gives aesthetic and ontological expression to that polity and sustains it through history, to the "I" and the "we" that establish subject positions for Herder—and for those reading his writings in the centuries that followed. Herder does not equivocate, nor does he leave his political poetics open to speculation. In his exegesis and translations of psalms in the ninth chapter of the second volume, he makes explicit that those usually known as pilgrimage Psalms 120 to 134, the *shireh la-ma'alot* (literally, songs of ascent), express the intent of the Jewish people as they return from Babylon: Herder ascribes to them the genre of *Nationalgesänge*, national songs, thereby connecting them to the volumes of folk song that he had published in the previous decade (see chapters 1 and 2 in the present volume). Writing to his Enlightenment reader in the late eighteenth century, and surely also to his Haskala reader from the Jewish Enlightenment in the same moment, Herder queries: "Could one refer to such a people as barbarian, even if they had just a few such national songs? And how many of the same kind do this people have?" (ibid., 1208).

HERDER 4—HERDER THE ANTHROPOLOGIST— ORIENTALISM AND *ANNÄHERUNG*

> King Solomon made a magnificent bed for himself,
> Of cedar from Lebanon.
> The bedposts he made from silver,
> The canopy from gold,
> The bedspreads of cardinal,
> The mattress, cushioned with love,
> For the daughters of Jerusalem.
> JOHANN GOTTFRIED HERDER—"Ein Prachtbett" /
> "A Bed of Splendor" (Stanza 2)—
> from *Lieder der Liebe* (JGHW3, 451–52)

"Jerusalem's daughters" (*die Töchter Jerusalems*) appear again and again as the allegorical leitmotif in one of Herder's most poetic, indeed, sensual, projects: his *Lieder der Liebe* (Songs of Love), an engagement with the biblical *Shir ha-shirim* (Song of Songs, or the Songs of Solomon). Part translation, part paraphrasing, part comparison with medieval contrafacts of the *Shir ha-shirim*, Herder produced his work of three lengthy chapters in three stages in 1776, 1778, and 1781, a period that encompassed the publication of his most comprehensive works on folk song, *Volkslieder* and *Stimmen der Völker in Liedern*, for which he also used the same publisher, Weygand of Leipzig (see chapter 2 in this volume). A biblical text that had undergone countless translations, as well as musical settings, from antiquity to the Enlightenment, the Songs of Solomon surely attracted Herder for many reasons, the theological and the musical among them. Critical among these reasons, however, were the ways in which a counterpoint between Jewish and Christian practice had coalesced around this particular biblical text (cf. the different translations in Timm 1982 and recordings on *Lied der Liebe* 2013; see the translations in chapter 3 of this volume).

In Jewish tradition, the allegory of *Shir ha-shirim* is most commonly between God and his chosen people, whereas the Christian allegory reflects the relation between Christ and the Church. The repeated return of the

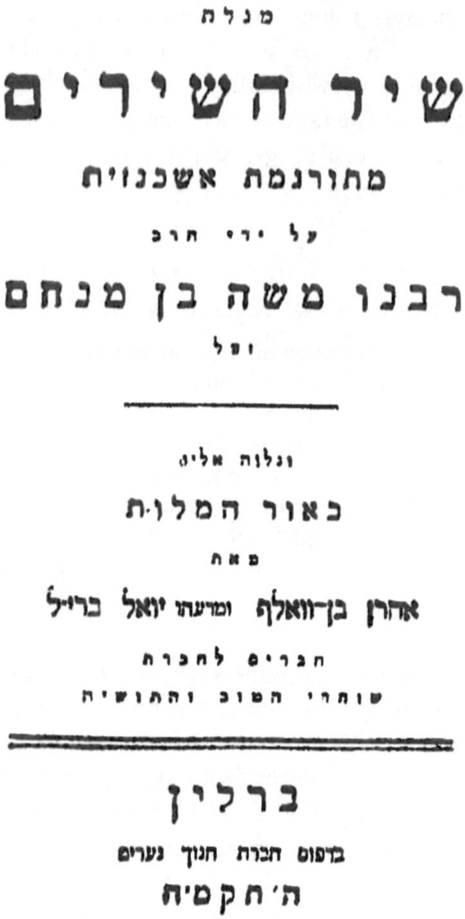

מגלת

שיר השירים

מתורגמת אשכנזית

על ידי חכם

רבנו משה בן מנחם

זצל

ונלוה אליו

באור המלות

מאת

אהרן בן-וואלף ומדעתו יואל בריל

חברים למחברת

שוחרי הטוב והתושיה

ברלין

בדפוס חברת חנוך נערים

ת'ח ק ס'ח

FIGURE 5. Title page of Moses Mendelssohn, *Shir ha-shirim*, 1788. Public domain.

"daughters of Jerusalem" thus serves as a realization of the feminine as a collective, sacred/Jewish as *Shechina*, the Sabbath bride who arrives in the synagogue on the eve of the Sabbath, and secular/Christian as in the earthly *civitas dei* (City of God) allegorically portrayed by Saint Augustine. The counterpoint weaves the sacred and the secular together as the *polis*, hence also the political, throughout Herder's writings in the final quarter century of his life. This allegorical counterpoint had unfolded musically since antiquity, and it had returned, marking significant moments of musical style at the beginning of the Baroque with the Jewish sacred work *Ha-shirim asher le-Shlomo*, by the Mantuan Jewish composer Salamone Rossi (ca. 1570–ca. 1628; see Harrán 1999), and at the close with Johann

Christian Bach (1735–1782), for example, "Mein Freund ist mein und ich bin sein," a chaconne from his *Hochzeitskantate*. Poetic translations, musical at various levels, stretch from the minnesingers through Luther to the Enlightenment and Haskala of Herder's age, with substantial works by Johann Wolfgang von Goethe and Moses Mendelssohn (see figure 5).

Why and how, we might ask, would Herder translate the Songs of Solomon again? There is no single answer to this question, which is to say, Herder himself posed the question in several ways, which together produced multiple and contradictory answers. Indeed, Herder's successive attempts to translate the Songs of Solomon illustrate the ways in which he felt the deep need to return again and again to a text in search of the elusive—and the sublime. That search unfolded as a process of drawing ever closer (*Annäherung*) to music throughout his career as a theologian and a pastor (see chapter 6 in this volume). Herder's first engagement with the Songs of Solomon dates from 1776, but never appeared as a complete version in print. We know from his notes for the first version that it was intended more strictly to be his own translation of the Hebrew original (Otto 1992). Reflecting on the songs in the 1776 version, Herder wrote: "It remains for us still irreplaceable, in its language, also in its sweetness and gentleness, and because its strength and life are for us unattainable" (cited in ibid., 168). He could only hope that his own German would possess a beauty that expressed the "inner qualities of the ancient Hebrew" (Herder 1992, 69).

For the version he published two years later, in 1778, Herder moved in a radically different direction. Rather than translate the *Shir ha-shirim*, he decided to weave paraphrases of the Luther translation into commentary about their content. He followed this section of his publication with songs from the medieval minnesinger texts and concluded the volume with a critical essay on translation itself ("Von Übersezungen desselben, insonderheit Einer in alten Minneliedern"; Herder 1992, 118–65). For reasons that remain puzzling today, moreover, he published the 1778 volume without his name or any authorial attribution whatsoever, as if the volume really was simply a translation.

What he began with the 1778 edition, Herder developed further for another edition three years later, which still contained no attribution of authorship. With this edition it became clear that he was returning to the Jewish traditions that now served as interpretive bridges to the Middle East of the present, that is, cultural understanding of difference and distinction in a Jewish poetic and musical tradition in the modern world of the Enlightenment and Haskala. This orientalist move—common also for

Jewish intellectuals of the time—introduced a new level of counterpoint, opening a historical field in which the sacred was transformed into the humanistic. This Herderian humanism could encompass the counterpoint conjoining self and other, Christian and Jew, sacred and secular, European and universal. Coeval with Herder's musical projects, the religious project enters—indeed, reenters—the history of ideas, firmly anchoring the pylons of the expanding bridge to the new intellectual history of ethnomusicology. Herder's *Lieder der Liebe*, the biblical *Shir ha-shirim*, would enter an ever-expanding counterpoint, sounded and re-sounded, again and again, until the present.

AGAIN, HERDER—TOWARD AN INTELLECTUAL HISTORY OF ETHNOMUSICOLOGY

As this prologue draws toward its conclusion, it returns to its beginning, Psalm 137, expanding the allegorical bridge across its sacred and secular confluence. There were many reasons that Herder was particularly fond of "By the Rivers of Babylon," not least among them the fact that it is a psalm, its explicit narrative of Jewish history notwithstanding, that had profound resonance for a Christianity that Herder sought to extend, for its aesthetic and ethical groundings, to a world beyond Europe. It is that resonance, moreover, that re-sounds through translation, again and again, surely in the version of Psalm 137 that Herder published in *The Spirit of Hebrew Poesy*. The psalm would appear repeatedly in translation, many of these translations widely influential, none more so than that by Martin Buber and Franz Rosenzweig in their modern translation of the Hebrew Bible in the early twentieth century (Buber 1962, 195–96). By the 1920s this translation spawned intensive debate among Jewish philosophers and theologians about the two rivers of Babylon—Mesopotamia, *Naharaim*, *Zweistromland*—which provided the modern metaphor for the Jewish diaspora. Few were more prominent and public in these debates than Hermann Cohen (1842–1918) and Franz Rosenzweig (1886–1929) (see Schulte 2003, 12, and Wiedebach 2003). Rosenzweig would use the metaphor of the confluence of two rivers, "Zweistromland," as the title for his final volume of essays (Rosenzweig 1926). Cohen, in his conversations and exchanges with Rosenzweig, would find his way to the German, Christian, modern river by returning to Herder, also in one of his final books, *Ästhetik des reinen Gefühls* (Cohen 1912). The wellsprings of Herder's intellectual history were flowing freely in the final decades of German Jewish history (Bohlman 2017). Again, Herder.

It is common to speak about reception history as a consideration of "afterlives." In the following translation and analysis of Herder's writings on music and nationalism, however, I should have found myself unhappy with the notion of a reception of afterlife, which would be far too limiting. Rather, I return to Herder in the following chapters, encountering him again, affording *new* possibilities for subject positions that we recognize as critical to the intellectual history of many fields, especially that of ethnomusicology. In each encounter with Herder—when we return to his own writing and thought in the Enlightenment, and when he returns to influence the writing and thought that shaped the history of ideas—we witness the ways in which the differences between subject and object, self and other, "oneself as another," blur and diminish (see Ricoeur 1992). The subject moves into a space of shared in-betweenness, as Jacques Lacan would say, reflected, mirrorlike, in topological subjectivity (Lacan 1989b, 1989c; cf. Nobus 2003). Sameness and difference share topological time and space precisely because they are forever repeating themselves, their confluence stretching into an ever-expanding world.

It is topological repeatability that for Herder led to a confluence of the *Zweistromländer* of the histories of religion and music, and that expanded his own contribution to ethnomusicological thought. Self and other were at once the same and different. Translation was critical to the transformation of expression in order to represent the sameness of a song as new and different. And translation is critical once again in the chapters that follow. The objects that came to be called folk songs were transformed to become the new subjectivity of an intellectual history that afforded the resonance of world music (chapters 1 and 2). Epics old and new became at once national and universal in Herder's translations (chapters 5 and 8).

These are the ethnomusicological moments that return as intellectual history. The ethnomusicological moment is one in which the past and the future are juxtaposed. As he did in his studies of song, Johann Gottfried Herder sought to sound such moments in his reflections on Judaism and Christianity, and the changing sameness of religion in musical thought. Herder's complex relation to the confluence of musical and religious thought was constantly changing, leading him to return to the waters of that confluence again and again, transforming song and music to generate ever more moments in the long history of ethnomusicological thought. In search of those moments the translations constituting the chapters of this book, too, return to Herder. Again.

PART I

The Ontology Project

1. Folk Song at the Beginnings of National History

Essay on *Alte Volkslieder* (1774)

Philip V. Bohlman

> Wen sangen die Deutschen? / Whom did the Germans sing?
> —JOHANN GOTTFRIED HERDER, *Von Ähnlichkeit*

In the beginning there were folk songs. Starting from the preface to the first of its four books, Johann Gottfried Herder's *Alte Volkslieder* (Ancient Folk Songs) possesses the character of Torah, a set of law-giving principles for hearing a nation's past and present in song. From the beginning, Herder makes the conditions of his search for "old folk songs" clear. Though beginning at least as early as the formative era of a German culture with Charlemagne, the search for songs with German character remains inchoate. It lags behind the histories of song in other peoples, those whose identity largely depends on language and culture, as well as those for whom language provides the basis for a national, political identity. Herder's admiration for the English notwithstanding, the *Alte Volkslieder* is a call to action: the old folk songs of all peoples deserve to be gathered. Together, they should be compared to understand both the distinctive character of individual peoples—and nations—as well as the universal wellspring of culture they have in common. They should be afforded a place in the present so that the character of their origins can be translated and transformed to shape the future. Herder's folk song project, at its own beginnings in 1774, becomes a bold response to this call to action.

With the *Alte Volkslieder* we find ourselves in the midst of Herder's first laboratory. He approaches song as complex empirical material, adapted for experimentation, allowing him to locate folk song in history, hence establishing several levels of narrative meaning. Herder gathers songs as fragments, particularly because of the ways they might be fitted together in different, even unexpected ways, above all at the crossroads between story and history at which identity, especially national identity, itself still inchoate in the waning Enlightenment, is forming.

The tools with which Herder approaches experimentation in *Alte Volkslieder* include the following: 1) an anthology consisting of four volumes in which folk songs from different peoples coalesce as common historical discourses; 2) the transition from oral to written tradition, with all the theoretical issues that determine that transition (e.g., translation, the core question in the second book, in "Would Shakespeare Be Untranslatable?"); 3) comparisons of texts and historical contexts, the most striking of which reflect Herder's positions on the relation of language to nation; 4) classification and categorization, which establish genre and social function; 5) translation as critical for integrating songs into the history of Germany; 6) writing with fragments, no less than including songs as fragments, often deliberately retaining their jagged edges.

Like its contents, *Alte Volkslieder* appeared in a publication project that was in many ways fragmentary. Each of the four books begins with a substantial introductory essay, which, however, stands on its own. The introductory essay was to be followed by a modest section of song texts. Herder refers to these as "the planned collection" (JGHW3, 12), and he lists most songs in that collection quite specifically, by song title or genre. There are fifteen songs each for the first two books, twelve and thirteen for the third and fourth books. The songs, which were left in manuscript form, both do and do not illustrate the specific theme of the introductory essay. The songs that would have followed pick up some themes from the introductions—some songs in the third book exemplify the similarity between English and German—but others deliberately expand the theme to broaden the foundations on which Herder's folk song project is taking shape. The "Nordic songs" of the fourth book, which Herder takes to propose a way of "approaching the songs of foreign peoples," thus provide a critical framework for a more fully developed theory of music and the nation.

The reasons that the different parts—complete introductory essays, songs left in fragmentary manuscripts—did not appear in a single publication in 1774 or soon thereafter are not entirely clear. Publication in fragments, as in chapter 4 on Ossian in the present book, was not uncommon in the eighteenth century, especially for anthologies of literary and musical works from the past (see also chapter 8 on *El Cid* in the present book). The serial publication of books, too, was widespread in the late eighteenth century, especially for publications meant to reach a broad readership. The folk song volumes of 1778 and 1779 (see chapter 2), for example, appeared serially, and then were gathered as two larger volumes (*Volkslieder* [Folk Songs] in the first edition, and *Stimmen der Völker in Liedern* [Voices of the People in Song] in the 1807 posthumous edition). The fragmentary nature of the sections of *Alte Volkslieder*, it follows, does not itself serve as evidence that Herder left this initial stage of his folk song project unfinished. Quite the contrary, the themes and songs of the four books coalesce as an increasingly focused discourse, which Herder will sustain through the folk song project of the 1770s, and throughout the writings on music in the course of his life. Both "Edward" and "Die Jüdin," for example, were to appear in the first book, even as both would assume an important position in Herder's later collections (see Bohlman 1992, 2010b).

The question of an anthology as itself providing the cultural and historical gathering point of folk song is particularly important to consider in the discourse that *Alte Volkslieder* sets in motion. There are important Enlightenment issues at work in the collection of linguistic and historical artifacts as an anthology (e.g., Denis Diderot's *Encyclopédie*). Anthology also represents a form of ontology, and this goal of the anthology would guide Herder throughout his life. Critically important for the ways folk song enters the history of ideas, *Alte Volkslieder* provides the first model for collection and anthology, which would thereafter come to underlie the entire history of folk song at one of its most critical moments, the passage from the eighteenth to the nineteenth century. Herder recognized that the anthology was a way of transforming the differences of oral tradition into the commonalities of written tradition. A folk song anthology realizes the nation by affording a presence for national language in a shared repertory. German ballads, given such an important position in book three, for example, emerged as a genre for German literary and folklore scholars, in which the texts were only in High German.

The four books of *Alte Volkslieder* are in most ways independent, each with a distinct theme of its own, but they are also linked in many ways, especially in how they move from the more universal nature of folk song to its national characteristics. Book one has no title as such, but in the "planned contents" for the book Herder refers to it as "English and German." Herder's language describing song and the nation is particularly rich with metaphors in the first book, and he uses this language to lay the groundwork for a historical understanding of folk song that grows from the soil of the past. Book two ("Songs from Shakespeare") is the best known of the four books in *Alte Volkslieder* because the introductory essay ("Wäre Shakespear unübersetzbar?") has found its way into many different areas of Herder studies. From a modern perspective, there is little in the book about folk song, for it largely contains translations of well-known passages from Shakespeare, as often without reference to song and music as with such connections. The focus of the book really is translation, and with that focus Herder locates his own critical work as a translator at the center of his musical, theological, and philosophical work.

With book three ("Englisch und Deutsch") Herder turns to the specific question of *Ähnlichkeit* (similarity). His point of departure, as evident in the title, is the linguistic similarity between English and German throughout their long histories as European literary languages. To illustrate this similarity he turns to the musical and literary genre of the ballad, signaling the establishment of narrative genres—ballad and epic—as the most broadly historical European folk song practices. Finally, with book four, "Nordische Lieder" (Nordic Songs), Herder trains the focus of *Alte Volkslieder* on music and the nation. The book is both historical and comparative, allowing Herder to move from Greek music and poesy to that of the Nordic peoples, which he claims to be more natural and hence more expressive of their way of life. Herder reaches an important conclusion about the comparison of differences that establish the cultural (and musical) integrity of what he increasingly refers to as the nation.

Herder's aim in the fourth book of *Alte Volkslieder* is to sketch a method that will allow song to provide a means of understanding cultures that contrast with the culture of enlightened selfness shared by his readers. In the course of the essay, he designates the people inhabiting these cultures with four different terms: *fremd* (literally, foreign), *unpolicirte* (literally, without political organization), *wild* (primitive), and *Natur-* (literally, living in nature, glossed a century later in comparative musicology as "primitive"). In the most general sense Herder uses these terms interchangeably, intending even to convey a sense of difference and nuance in the cultural otherness that is the subject of the essay. There are instances also in which he incorporates history into his descriptions, recognizing the ways in which language, "ways of thinking," and songs represent processes of development. Peoples that are primitive ("wild" or "Natur-") display a cultural distinctiveness endowed by nature; those who have embarked upon paths of historical development ("fremd" or "unpolicirt") have shaped their own distinctive traditions, for example, of songs.

Herder also employs several terms for describing the societies or cultures in which other peoples live: *Volk* (literally, people) and *Nation* (literally, nation). At this point in his anthropological thought, however, Herder is not trying to make the distinctions that would increasingly emerge in his later writings and then in the nineteenth century. Already in 1774, Herder recognizes and evokes a distinction between peoples who are not politically organized ("Volk") and those with a political identity determined by geography and language ("Nation"). The slippage within this distinction begins to give way to a more specific concept of culture and nation already in the fourth book of *Alte Volkslieder*, not least reflecting Herder's growing assertion that folk song forged a common space between *Volk* and *Nation*.

In 1774 Herder's terminology for otherness, however, remains unspecific and uneven, and my translations do not try to ascribe more accuracy than I believe Herder himself would have understood. It is clear, nonetheless, that Herder's sense of otherness increasingly bears witness to cultural encounter, with its concomitant contrast of self and other. In the fourth book of *Alte Volkslieder* he accounts for the encounters of both missionaries and academics, in both cases describing a goal that privileges sameness rather than tolerates difference. The vocabulary that we witness taking shape in 1774, therefore, reveals the increasingly complex anthropological perspectives that are developing around his writings about folk song.

Throughout the course of the four books Herder considers two different issues about the historical origins of folk song, particularly as these pertain to the nation: 1) Why does early song demonstrate the Germans to be different—indeed, more impoverished in their cultural history? We see here a concern with origins influenced by monogenesis, culture and history arising from a single origin. Herder's response to this question in the early books looks primarily at issues of self—German-ness as a measure of his relation to the reader—albeit in comparison with others (e.g., the question of Shakespeare's translatability). And 2) the question of similarity (*Ähnlichkeit* in book three) reflects an Enlightenment understanding of polygenesis, culture and history arising from multiple origins, and in *Alte Volkslieder* it shifts the discourse on folk song toward difference ("Lieder fremder Völker" [Songs of Foreign Peoples], in book four, translated below). *Alte Volkslieder* closes, therefore, by reflecting on otherness, concluding with an affirmation also of the selfness of each nation and its songs. Therein lies the beginning of the modern study of folk song and world music.

From *Alte Volkslieder / Ancient Folk Songs*

JOHANN GOTTFRIED HERDER,
TRANSLATED BY PHILIP V. BOHLMAN

FIRST BOOK

> All those whom I need to thank
> should still let themselves be known.
> The man who is pleased by everything
> will never hear my book. . . .
> One cannot raise an individual to feeling
> whom God has not already ordained,
> he would be more useful than am I.
> —Preface to *Sachsenspiegel*

Preface

1. There could hardly be a more patriotic wish than to gather the bards that *Charlemagne* had gathered.[a] What a treasure for the German language, poetry, customs, thought, and the awareness of the past this could be, if it only would not always remain just a *desire*! There was once a time when the latest news about the presence of these pieces was made so easy, because

---

a. [JGH] "He had made German songs from the ancient heroes of the Germans, gathering them together in a book, and many of these he set himself so that they would be remembered. Most of these, however, have been lost, so that some of them are no longer authentic, *as if they had entered the women's chamber, where the women used them as they wished to while the time away.*" Lindenbrug's *Chronik Karls*, 1593. [PVB] Herder is most likely referring here to Erpold Lindenbrug, *Scriptores rerum Germanicarum septentrionalium* (Hamburg: C. Liebe, 1706).

they were there for the taking. And now, when they are so much desired, praised, sung, and wanting for models to imitate, where are they?

I think it only right that if enough of these sought-after treasures of the fatherland could be located, they would still hardly provide us with *folk and patriotic songs* in the strictest sense. One need but look at the *Schilter* collection from the late Carolingian era to know that the language at the very least leaves no doubt. Even the grammar of the German language has changed so much over the course of many centuries that it would be all the same if we were reading poems from the old French Romanesque poets or those in German. We are always concerned about the *magical form* of previous eras, *mirrored by the scholars and through the quotations from antiquity.* These are not *folk songs of our own time*! One knows just how much the most curious readers fail to understand in the research, clarity, and artistry in this way. If they could but experience more directly with the senses, they would acquire the potential to *see with the eyes* and *understand with the heart.* They would know that what *touches the people* is the most important. Just as *Ulphila's* evangelists[b] could stir no wonder when only present in the church, so too there remains little from the *bards and their circle.* We are left only to make judgments from whatever hearsay survives, or, more maddening, might we expect something else! . . . Nothing less than an *Ossian.*

"Why not?" The most probable *answer* to this question has no place here. The word itself remains the *crux of the problem.*

2. The fortune, whereby the old can be transformed into something new that ultimately moves us the most, had already been granted to us in the second, bright period of German poetry: the *poets of the Swabian times.* This was not brighter than the source itself, except the tales of the *minnesingers,* who were the first to express *humor,* as well as some other sagas *still around,* retained from the Old German bards. They inherited the poetry as it appeared in the Codex Manesse.[c] Who is able, from all times and places, to claim that, in a *single moment* and at *very little expense,* such a *treasure trove* of *language, poetry, delightful customs, morals, and light shed on the*

---

b. [PVB] Herder is probably referring here to Georg Friedrich Heupel, *Dissertati historico-philologica de Ulphila, seu versione IV. Evangelistarum Gothica* (Wittenberg: G.W. Kirchmajer, 1693).

c. [PVB] The Codex Manesse, completed between ca. 1304 and 1340, contains manuscript sources for the songs of the approximately 135 minnesingers active between the mid-twelfth and early fourteenth centuries. The codex served as one of the most important sources of songs used by Herder for his history of German art and folk song, particularly the confluence of oral and written traditions in the Middle Ages. See also the translations in chapter 3 of the present volume.

fatherland appeared in such *volume* as in the volumes produced by *Schöpflin* and *Bodmer* from the Codex Manesse [see, e.g., Bodmer 1781]? If Schöpflin and Bodmer had done no other service to Germany, their *creative output* of sources and reprints alone would be reason to rescue them from obscurity.

I am not mistaken that this volume of precious poems for the fatherland was of great fortune for Germany, and it should have been so without great cost. Be that as it may, for those who came from the part of Germany called *Saxony*, the *sound* of the *more recent classical language, poetry, and literature*, for better or worse, found the language of this poetry still to be quite distant. The noble Swiss would require more effort to understand the language of their previous brothers, neighbors, and countrymen than a people more accustomed to it. Even the provincial dialect of the *minnesingers* used in these poems, whose content and sense mirrored a foreign ideal of love, would not sense the same impact of revolution as that in *Swabian poetry*. They did not transform them into living *folk songs*! Nor could they be thus transformed. They remain on the shelves of libraries as a *"collection of old and lovely miniature pieces"* . . . and that is where they *stay*!

3. There remains only one task left for us, as well as protecting those assumed to be of the least value: we must *seek* and *collect* the *remaining folk songs that are still alive* or survive from an earlier time in which they could still be understood and were vital. Perhaps that too would catch a spark from the spirit of the German fatherland, albeit buried in ash and rubble. . . .

What, however, does one really imagine is still possible to find? *The crude songs of a crude people! Barbarian sounds* and *fairy tales served as the most basic soup of the nation!* What do we expect might still be of *value printed and preserved* to serve the *honor of the nation and the further development of the human spirit?*

To those who would pass judgment as *privileged, educated, and totally satisfied* and who loudly condemn such an effort, I merely respond with an example from all the neighboring countries. Unquestionably the Gallic, English, and even more so the Nordic *peoples* are truly a *people!* A *people* like the German *folk!* Still, the British have every reason to be just as *privileged, educated,* and even *prouder* than we of the *masterpieces* of their *old* and *new classical writers*. Despite the strength of the national pride in our most recent literature, the British make the Germans look *more impoverished.* If they had turned away from what they had produced with their noses in the air, even avoiding the title page of what they had not seen or read, their own *Ramsey* and *Percy* would not have appeared in so many editions. Under the same circumstances we privileged and satisfied Germans would not have bothered to *collect* anything. Now let me summon everyone with feeling toward song as my witness and let me ask if nothing by *Ramsey* or in Percy's *Reliques of Ancient Poetry*[d] is worth *publishing and preserving*. Quite the contrary, these are songs, I am not ashamed to say, that have no *equal* in most recent poesy! There is nothing of the simplicity, the feeling, the stirring of the heart, the accents, and the resonance that would move the most inner soul, not to mention possess the accompanying beauty to uplift the soul! One need but compare recent experiments of this kind by poets like the *Shenstones, Masons, Malletts*, etc., with their simpler, original predecessors, and one will discover an enormous difference. The originals are full of song and sound, simplicity and impact. They will always possess the qualities of *a few isolated verses* that hang framed on the wall, *beautiful and simple*.

When one removes these songs from the paper on which they appear in order to reflect on *their context, their times, and the vital ways they touched real people*, one gains just a bit of the sense of how they might still *resonate*! One gains a sense of what the *ancient bards* meant for the earlier historians, and the impact of the *minstrels* and *Meistersingers* on more recent historians. The greatest singers and the favorites of the muses—whereby I mean *Chaucer and Spenser, Shakespeare and Milton, Philip Sidney and Selden*—all displayed *enthusiasm for the old songs*. It is not hard to find the proof for such a claim, for the *lyrical, mythical, dramatic, and epic* qualities that distinguish English poetry as *national* emerge from what has survived from the early singers and poets. In *Chaucer, Spenser, and Shakespeare* there is no question about the significance of such evidence. Also with *Dryden, Addison, and Pope*, whose works open as the tender sprouts of English poetry, producing a *loveliness* that others might imitate. More recently, the Scots, just like our more recent Germans, sought again to awaken their poetry through *re-sounding* . . . another question in its own right . . . but they did not contradict the *value* and *inner worth* of that poetry. The language, sound, and content of the old songs shape the way a people thinks, thereby leaving its mark on the nation. Those who have few or none of these qualities show they are *incapable of having anything whatsoever*. Those who make fun of them and fail to have feeling for them reveal that they are so inflated by aping the foreignness or by mimicking the cheap tinsel of the superficial that they become incapable of sensing value in the *body of the nation*. They are, thus, the offshoot of the

---

d. [PVB] Thomas Percy, *Reliques of Ancient English Poetry, Consisting of Old Heroic Ballads, Songs, and Other Pieces of Our Earlier Poets (Chiefly of the Lyric Kind) Together with Some Few of Later Date* (London: J. Dodsley, 1765).

foreign and a leaf that blows in the wind, in other words, *a virtuoso of the latest trends for all times! A thinker!*

The English, whose *national riches* exceed ours in every way, surely also exceed us when it comes to the *shabbiness of the nation* and the *acceptance of earlier times*. What kinds of poor songs was *Percy*, for example, able to include in the second part of the first volume of his *Reliques* [Percy 1765]! These are songs that our educated Germans would never have dared to print, even when the songs, whatever one's individual taste might be, would have *shed so much light on early history*! Even when they would *clarify* so much, even to the point of giving praise to God! *Nothing* of the most modest value appears. It was enough, however, that *Shakespeare knew* such songs, if just a single line, and that he integrated them in such ways that they transformed the affinity of his poetry. In a climate that is so mild, mere sprouts and buds could turn into the forests that nurtured an ancient way of thinking. In the shadow of that forest, poetry could touch those who were foreign or only *distantly related* neighbors, also bringing them joy.

The most recent English collector, of course, is at a great advantage. In part, he already has *collections at his disposal*. English libraries are *endowed* with *gifts* made by many, thus the English collector has *manuscripts* and the like at hand. Even more important, he has a discourse for thinking about the nation, that is, the *national*. The people already make up such a visible part of *the folk*, whose name is no cause for embarrassment; the folk is not something from which one needs to look away. Only the learned would choose to do that, the *learned*, that is, and all the *armchair scholars lacking any knowledge of the folk*; we are speaking here of the pedant and the critic. The English collector can focus on the *nation, the folk*, a single entity that is called the *fatherland*! He has more at his disposal for writing and collecting than we Germans (as much as we may talk, sing, or write) *have* or may ever have available to us. I might, nonetheless, take my comparison to the most impudent and bitter extremes! It is time for me to stop, however, only to say that this modest preface is intended for a *similar attempt* at a *similar collection of folk songs*, German *folk songs*, like those our brothers and forebears, who are so superior to us, the English, have already *collected*, presenting them so they will be better and more precious.

I make my case in this *impoverished way* so that I might awaken other, more precious citizens, countries, regions, libraries, and provinces! I bring with me but a *handful of water*, which is almost shameful, and I take my place at the table of my neighbor's feast, with its abundance and well-being. Would that I might find my *brothers in arms, Germans, fellow citizens, and friends of this land*, whose envy and anger I might arouse, so that they would respond, full of anger, revenge, and joy, and they might *surpass me as much as possible*! This is what I wish; this is what I hope for!

A great people with rich abundance! More to the point, the people and wealth of ten great peoples ... do you have no *folk songs*? You, a people that is so *noble, who so deeply loves virtue, shame, and tradition*, do you have no *songs that are more noble, virtuous, traditional, and full of meaning* than the *Swiss, Swabians, Franconians, Bavarians, Tyroleans, Saxons, Westphalians, Wends, and Bohemians*? Have you nothing more *natural, moving, and meaningful* than these?

I have not a moment's doubt about the answers to such questions because of my love for the nation. However, the songs lie so *deeply buried*, they are so *despised* and *held at a distance*, they stand at the edge of *extinction*. It is precisely for these reasons that I dare to undertake this project, which has the primary goal of urging others *more numerous* and with *better fortune* to take up the cause. But do so with *zeal* and *courage*, and do it *now*! We stand at the very edge of the precipice: in another hundred years it will be too late!

Each one of my readers knows the tragic or happy fate ... however it is best described ... that Germany has had since the very beginning. It is the *mother* and *servant to foreign nations*. It is their regent and law giver, deciding their fates, but almost always at the same time becoming their *bleeding slave* and *exhausted wet nurse*, who is paid almost nothing in return. I unroll the pages of history so that every German who feels something for the fatherland will take up the cause. At the same time he would unleash *joy* and *repentance*, honor and even bittersweet *lament*:

> ... truly it is a land
> no more! The marches! The island sand,
> my Germany! Already so far
> beyond its origins! In the dispersion of its people! Flowing
> far and wide! ... Jordan, Po, and Tiber
> have so often foamed with the heroic blood
> of the Germans! Filled to overflowing
> from the courage of popes and apes
>
> And German souls! Finally choked,
> O mother, Germany, on the breast
> you offer your children! Chaos
> roars, as it has so long filled
> the storms of dispute, do not prostrate yourself
> before the battles in the heavens! My Germany etc.

The German *way of thinking* and its *peaceful nature*, of course, cannot be removed from the eternal conflict, the eternal *exclusion* from foreigners, or the even more maddening *inclusion of some* foreigners into their own country! If we only truly had a history of the German national spirit ... but how, where, if only, and whereby? ... it would receive all the *rubbish and weakness* that had accumulated in the sayings of all surrounding peoples. Alas, that would say far more than I am able here to say. If the growth of a tree too quickly spreads into unruly branches that can no longer be nourished *together from a single root*, nor do they desire to be, would not the result be a relentless fate, even in the crown of the tree, truly dominated by the disadvantages of honor and misfortune? *Offshoots, saplings, and uncontrollable brush* would not be weeded out by even the gentlest hand, and the tree would forever *break apart and lose its branches*. As the old fable about "floating above the trees" says, where would the naturally healthy kinds of fruit, nourishment, and sweetness, the strength and growth of *its* roots and *its* trunk, be found? An uncontrollable, wild bush of thorns, which catches fire often, and which weakens the cedars because it tears apart everything within its reach ... this is not how I want to paint the picture of a German history with many periods shaped ceaselessly by the unforgiving law of fate.

Unfortunately, the mishmash and imitation of foreign voices, lands, and eras plague German folk song even at the origins ...

> The song of the free Germans ...
> an outcry ... an echo
> from a hundred fissures! Silent sound
> of the marshes along the Jordan and the Tiber
> and the Thames and the Seine! ...
>   Alas, it can do just that!

Hundreds of years ago, evident virtually at the beginning of *each new moment of advancement* ... *what* a miracle that the earliest European language at least contained *original content, its own material, developed in its own ways* through the spirit of the Germans over the centuries, *borrowed* from the spirit of others

> ... what other feet have trampled
> should be repeated!

How happy I should be, if I could *again truly account for recovered national fragments*! Even in this case, as it so often and usually is, the *seed*, the sprout, the branch, and the *tree full of fruit* would spring forth from the *most meager beginnings*: that would be *growth from God*!

At this moment! My German brothers, let me call out one more time! At this moment, all that survives from the ways the folk think approaches the edge of the abyss of memory as rapidly as possible! Like cancer the light of so-called culture consumes all that surrounds it! For a half century we have been embarrassed about everything that belongs to the fatherland; we dance French minuets unacceptably as German, and since the *earliest* times we sing the most obscene and crudest love songs, about whose *crude and throwaway speech, narrative, and ballad tones* nothing was known in earlier times.[e] As *Lafontaine* so often claimed for our nation:

> losing the fidelity of the arts
> consumes morality . . .

If I should truly succeed to *try* to bring back these *crude and throwaway speech, narrative, and ballad tones,* that too would be sufficient! The slovenly way of singing employed by German *ballad singers,* their droll way of imitating, without *appropriate materials* and even more so without a *true sense for the stirrings of the heart,* leads only to *mockery.* I should succeed by showing what the difference is between a *true folk song,* a *ballad given life through song,* and the most recent *sweet street songs,* which reach a dead end with outdated rhymes, *mockingly* making *choking vocal transitions, tragic-comedies, and comic-tragedies* while racing along at the dreadful pace that has recently ruined German poesy and dialect. What I offer here is just some kind of imitation. Why, you ask? Because the *ballad tones* no longer survive in our own age. Still, it is not my goal to cast aspersions on anything (even on the English songs from the translations of my friend [see the discussion of Michael Denis's translations of the Ossian songs in chapter 4]). This would be too easy, according to the most recent standards of our own poetry. The ancient fragment of this bust, if it were only still recognizable, would remain for us as *rust and decay.* If more youthful attempts were made to imitate the *rust and decay,* taking a chisel to it would not reveal what lay hidden, broken and ruined. With the proper tools we would be able to sing of the *conditions that are so natural in our own age,* with the same *noble affect and feeling* with which *folk songs in their age were sung*!

And now I should undertake a small comparison of the results that arise from an *affective,* but also *simple, if firm, brief, powerful way of thinking and meaning for a people,* through which are expressed the *finest examples* of song. In our own *unenlightened time,* this would mean the *ethereal, unfeeling morality,* which but hangs in the air before crashing down upon even the *lowliest populace.* What we know for sure is that the greatest part of our being is the *existence of our senses.* Accordingly, the primary goal of

---

e. [PVB] Herder uses *Romanze* here for the narrative genre of the ballad.

education for the folk and for children is *dedicated to the senses* and our *strongest sensual powers. Abstraction* will always arrive in abundance and of its own accord. If only its *foundations* could lie in *true materiality*. It is nothing more than the fine spirit of raw, nutritious materials. If only we could be rid of such materials! The finest art can remove nothing of the spirit; the healthiest nature can remove nothing from that which nourishes us. If only we could employ the *truly fine stories that touch upon the sensibilities of the folk,* possessing only a single moral: *true music* is that which stirs the ear with *simple* tones. If only the human soul, in its formative years, could be the *soul of the folk,* seeing and hearing, not thinking and pondering! If only *all human eyes,* like the *eyes of the blind,* would at first see and taste *everything nearby, so abundant in color and impression,* before it turned toward placating beauty and soothing experiences! There is still time enough for such alleviation. Our own lovely, enlightened century, without exciting any *power and meaning, content and deed,* so full of *beautiful words, lovely phrases, well-chosen rhymes,* and *marvelously artistic music stanzas*! Magnificent century, in which art prevails to transform the soul so that it does not weep, that it is without tears and feeling, rather it becomes a *soul formed from light and rationality*! Have you, O century, gained *substance, strength, and lasting happiness for the afterworld*? Or have you lost it?

FOURTH BOOK

Nordic Songs

> Never was there a land so directed against foreign lands as are you!
>
> —FRIEDRICH GOTTLIEB KLOPSTOCK, "Ode auf Deutschland"

Approaching the Songs of Foreign Peoples   Songs once again? And nothing else but songs? And indeed barbaric or half-barbaric peoples? . . . One should listen before one begins to damn.

It is characteristic of our age that we know more people in the world than did our forebears. How did we come to know them? What have they or we lost in the meantime? Knowledge itself burgeons, and that is good: *the map of humanity has expanded to a remarkable degree.* What was geography at the time of the Greeks and the Romans? And what is it today?

How did these earlier civilizations come to *know* the brothers of our humanity? Entirely *from the outside,* through scratches on the surface and from reports that were the same as etchings. Or *from within*? As humans

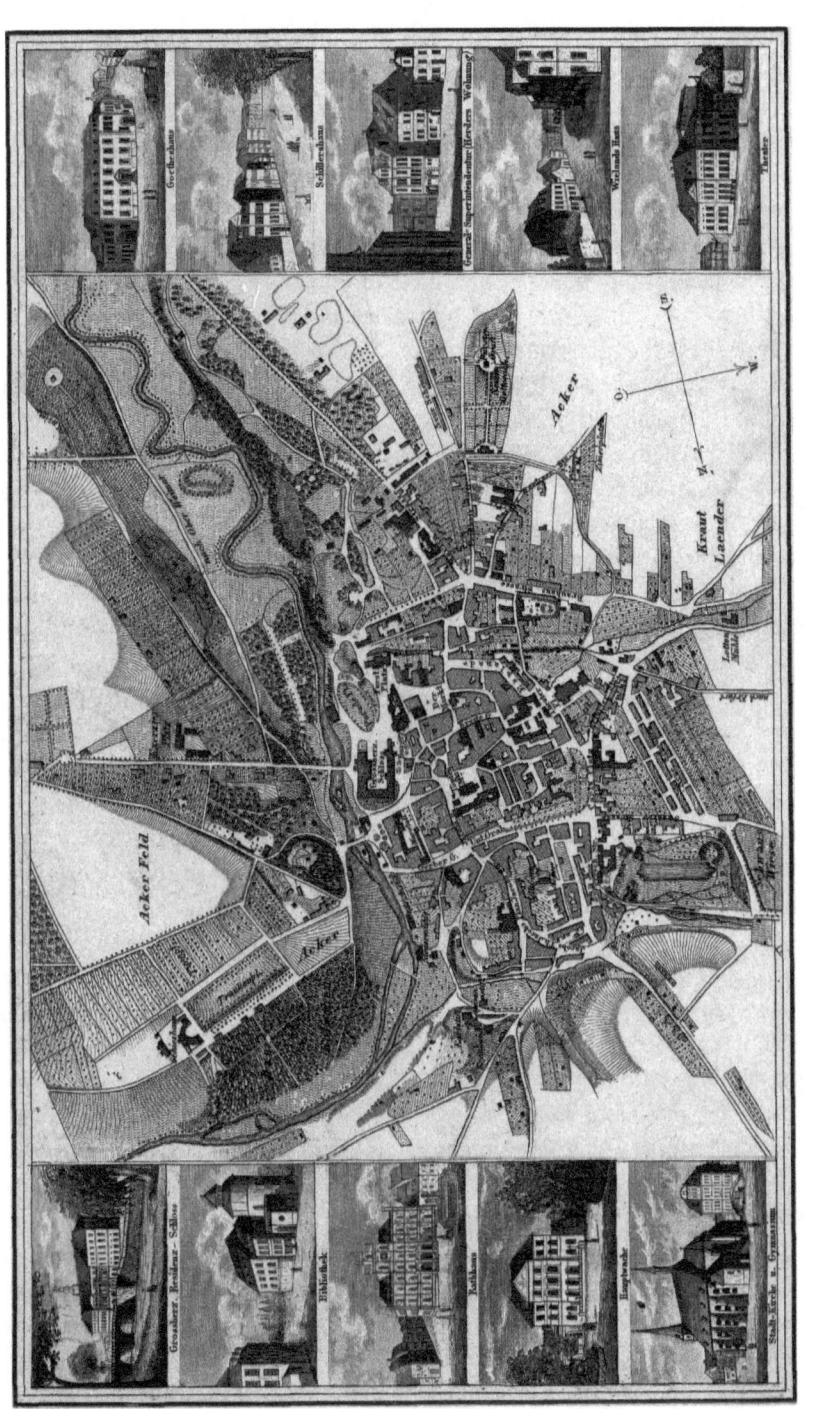

FIGURE 6. Weimar circa 1830. Courtesy the Map Collection, Regenstein Library, University of Chicago.

themselves, who possess language, a soul, and feelings? Our brothers! No one in a century of philosophy, shaped by a humanity that is acquired as it is learned and loved, will deny the *necessity* and *advantages* of such knowledge of others. And note this, my brothers in humanity! For we find ourselves where we wish to be. For we do not have to concern ourselves unduly with the appearance and shape, ... the external characteristics ... of the external way of life of those less civilized than we! We do not need to speak about what their countries produce and how they could be better if they were subjugated, used, abused, controlled, and repressed. We do not have to speak about them in negative terms ... as they are not human beings in the same way as we! Civilized nations!! And Christians!!! ... rather about *what they really are?* They provide us with a true image of their way of thinking, their sensibilities, what lies in their soul, language. They do this not as if inundated by outside influences, from all the European fools who ravage their lands, but rather in the ways they create their own *traditions* and *practices*. In this way, it follows, we arrive at their *songs!*

All nations that have yet to be organized around political systems are a *singing people*: by whatever means their songs come into being, that is how they *remain*. Songs serve as collections for all their *science, religion*, the ways the soul *moves*, the *characteristics* of previous generations, the *joys* and *sorrows* of their lives. Nature had entrusted them with the ability to console the heavy burden of human existence *with the love of freedom, the pursuit of leisure* or of *happiness*: and where everything more or less converges, that is where we find *song*. Nature has made humans *free, joyful,* singing. Artifice and forcefulness turn humans inward, removing their sense of trust, rendering them *silent*.

In the very few worthwhile travel reports that we possess, the most interesting of all passages for one seeking understanding are those about the ways of thinking and the customs of the nation, about passion and pleasure, about knowledge and speech! And these overwhelmingly also concern themselves with *songs*, and really only with *songs*. Books, the arts, cities, rationally organized societies, all these follow the appearance of song. Where nature has revealed ways of thought, it is the result of what God has granted them: *speech, sound, movement, representation, proportion, dance*. What ties all these together is one thing alone: *song*. *Warlike* peoples sing of the deeds of their ancestors, which in turn urge them on to deeds of their own. *Gentle* peoples sing *love songs* full of nature and simplicity. Those peoples with *cleverness and humor* insert puzzles into their songs and then solve those puzzles, playing with words and simile. A people with a *more creative imagination* possesses songs that contain poems, exaggerating and energizing life itself. Finally, a people that survives under the *barren, horrible conditions* of nature creates gods ... horrible gods, gods who are giants ... with songs that *negotiate* freedom and nobility. Everything from everywhere more or less flows together, expiring and becoming diluted. No image of passion, the soul, language, and thought could be truer, and yet Europeans repress such representations to show them as boring and simple, as unsophisticated superstition, and finally, the most dismissive of all, as *that in all languages, customs, and ways of thinking,* there is a total absence of concepts that recognize and understand *the masterfulness of an "Our Father!"* Remove the priest's wig from this observant individual and measure instead the heads of all tigers, lions, and elephants, and leave such observation aside ... the great natural history of the entire world! Nothing is comparable to exploring history from the perspectives of *the natural sciences*! Simply to *describe* a people through customs and ways of thought means nothing at all when compared to the possible descriptions *they themselves produce.* One cannot represent or sketch everything that lies on the surface, in other words, what is the loudest of all, or what first strikes the eye; rather, one must seek what *lies at the deepest level,* which encodes the traits with which a people are born and thus *characterizes* them most intimately. Whoever has the capacity to *take on such a task* most fully, to *arrive at the essence* most profoundly, to *describe* it with the greatest ease, to *make things familiar* for all others, that is the person who *knows* and *can represent a people,* and who does not merely *smear colors across a canvas.*

It is not my task here to determine just how quickly one encounters such noble people who are equally spread across the lands of the earth. A very fine and recent *travel enthusiast* has sketched a movable academy, which even as a stretch of imagination did not hold together, much less lend itself to provability.[f] Someone who truly knows a people must not simply *move from place to place* and write for *academies of science,* for these are necessarily required also to turn their attention toward conditions that have an *impact that is unusual in some way,* as if these very deserving men are expected in their own field to specialize in only a *single* matter. For my part, then, I am devising a plan that will include the smallest groups of people who live with us and among us.

The coastal areas of the Baltic Sea contain some peoples whose *history* is surely more enlightened than their *natural history.* Their history is the true source of their language and way of thinking. The *Wends, Slavs, Old*

---

f. [PVB] Herder is probably referring here to the idealized academy he proposes in his *Journal meiner Reise im Jahr 1769* (see the epilogue in the present volume).

Prussians, Lithuanians, Latvians, Estonians, even the *Frisians* ... these are normally contrasted with the peoples we know better, especially the *Icelanders*: Who would judge them after coming to understand their *way of thinking and language,* rather than simply comparing their epistemology to ours?

There are many scholars whose profession it is to *study the language, thought, ancient prejudices, and customs*! They surely *have studied* many of these. They *speak* about many such cultures in the third person: "They have songs! They have an incredible power of imagination, etc.!" Some scholars make such claims without really investigating *grammar* or employing *experimentation.* It could be one modest goal of the present book to awaken an interest in something more! It could provide us with a *full, accurate natural history* of cultures by fully presenting their own *monuments*! As such, this book would contain the *folk songs, myths, fairy tales, superstitions that have shaped the character of culture so powerfully.* It would not speak about such things, but rather *let them speak* for themselves. Not just ask, What was that good for? Instead, they would appear just as they are, without being made *palatable.* They would not be changed so they are acceptable to the judgment of religion or classical taste, but rather remain *as they are* ... but with faithfulness, pleasure, and love. Such representation of expressive culture would allow imperfections to be meaningful! One would report these matters and allow them to surpass what they are, just as a harvest produces seed for the future ... they acquire a *vital and real potential for theory,* a new *field* for linguists, historians, humanists, and philosophers! How *accessible and pleasing* for those engaged with such matters! Perhaps it will be a mere *description,* or the effort required for the *description* of something described long ago. Am I able to wish for this? Might I be hopeful?

I now continue with several examples, which at the very least will shed new light on some old topics.

To this point in history, it has been customary for writers to focus on a single, small part of the world whose *creations, models, masterpieces, and criteria for taste* we have extrapolated and applied to all forms of literature, poetry, and humanism, thereby *excluding all others.* Very well, for these parts of the world really were in the fortunate position of supporting the finest traditions! But also not so good, for we *blindly* accepted authority as rules, the chaff as the wheat, and the most distant similarity as the reason for empirical evidence. This is also not good if one forgets the contradictory character of art and the ways in which nature is imitated, from which every art takes its model! And if one forgets that the proper form and power of a model is something that we learn and adapt for our own purposes, such that we might slavishly apply the same attribute to a holy *Marian icon* or the *Qur'an*. Finally, a model is not good when it generates all that is *nationalistic*, hence the model for *our own* power and character, which becomes so blurred and damnable that each individual is ashamed to be who she or he is, and furthermore is unable to be something else. It seems to me that for many of us this would mean finding a path untouched by the national, which would lead to powerful medicines for healing and prevention.

The Greeks themselves were nothing more than *half civilized* because they sowed the seeds of their most beautiful plants and blossoms. Those who really read *Homer* with healthy eyes will recognize much less artistry in his writings than his rhapsodists, commentators, and translators claim: noble, blossoming nature ... just like *Ossian* has recently become as a model, and as *Wood* loudly preached against the encroachment of artificiality.[g] Do you believe that *Orpheus*, the great *Orpheus* whose service to humankind has been eternal, that this poet lives in the remnants of the entire soul of nature, that he was originally anything more than the noblest *shaman*, who was able to see the *Thracians*, who at that time were also the *Nordic Tatars*? Do you want to become acquainted with the Greek *Tyrtäus*, witnessing there a *celebration of war* and *war song* and *the singing leaders of the North Americans*! See the *ancient Greek comedies* at their earliest stages, which were still entirely, as *Horace* describes, connected through expression and dance to the same satirical games and the mummer celebrations as these uncivilized peoples! Do you want to hear a *hallelujah* sustained by a chorus!? The *Greenlanders* and the *Americans* perform a hallelujah in just this way. And there are countless other things just like these.

So profound is the respect that the really incomparable Greeks might earn, suddenly I should wish to be worthy of *earning such respect*, even if I no longer look at it with healthy eyes! We might recognize them as the human beings they were, rather than as the images painted as frescoes on a wall, grimacing about this world and the afterworld. A Greek in my own country, who would see me acting and living this way, who would look me in the eye and call out:

> ... He limps along with a Greek staff and creeps along with a Roman cane and nevertheless ...

---

g. [PVB] Robert Wood, *An Essay on the Original Genius of Homer* (London: n.p., 1769). For Herder's own comparison of Homer and Ossian, see chapter 5 in the present volume.

What is it all for, and what good does it do? It seems to me that these are nothing more than copies taken from *other people, independent people,* who really knew nothing about the Greeks and the Romans! *True people of nature!* Could they be *inventive* like the Greeks, and could they *express emotions* like the Greeks, and *paint* and *sing* like the Greeks, albeit not drawing from Greek mythology and using the Greek language? If they can, why can't *we*? Why not, a real German might call out:

> To imitate Greek song?
> Whatever pleases me should
> Not be imitated! The Greeks, too, came
> Into this world with a nose on their faces.
> What concerns me about their culture?
> I let the hen and the egg
> Lead me to mother nature!
> Their most abrasive, raw cry
> Touches me more deeply than the finest melody
> And is never absent from the person
> Who created my cousin Ossian . . .

And I believe that all free nations unfettered by civilization are the same in this regard!

Sappho sang beautifully! At any rate she sang beautifully, and even when we do not hear her, he who remains untouched will aspire to something higher, wherever he happens to be. But to imitate Sappho? Do we really believe that she has left behind an eternal form or vessel filled forever with her lovely love songs? Would we want to *adapt* ourselves with the affinity for love in nature, so that we would sing in the same way Sappho had once sung! Grounded in such beautiful poetry, and with such grace, turns, and gentle disorder in the ode, in the meter, the myths, the measurement of syllables . . . O, those who honor the Greeks and the Romans cover *Sappho* with a skirt and *Horace* with pants: this is how real men find their way to them!

The lovely Sappho once sang:

> O, dear mother, she cannot,
> Cannot weave a bit of flax!
> A beautiful boy makes me suffer,
> Evil love makes me suffer!

And she sang another time, reflecting on her beloved:

> The moon is beautiful as it rises
> Up into the stars!
> It is past midnight, and poor me,
> I still sleep alone!

And one other time:

> O, I suffer from an unfortunate love that undoes me,
> The bird sings a bittersweet song, with
> No defense against the arrow that pierces it: You were
> Once coy with me, beloved Attis! Your heart
> > Turned toward Andromeda.

And yet another time:

> Blessed youth! You have
> Now had your wedding, and now held
> Your maiden in your arms!

And yet again:

> I slept! And how I dreamt
> Of you, O Cypris!

And just how the small, tender, untranslatable remnants continue to sound forth. What, however, do we really have from them, beyond the little remains of the *impromptu* or the *fullness of passion*, in each of which the dear Sappho appears ... nothing more? And do we not have enough of that?

When they now pour out the most precious treasures of their love songs, themselves beyond translatable, we then have:

PRAYER TO VENUS

> Eternal Aphrodite, upon the throne of her kingdom,
> She who gathers her sling, daughter of Zeus, O leave me
> Not in sorrow, O let me not languish desolately
> > in the pain of love.
>
> Descend to me! O, if you could ever attend
> Tenderly to my supplication and raise me from it
> As so often before, descend as quickly as you can
> > from your father's throne.
>
> The reins for the carriage are prepared: Lovely sparrows
> Will draw the carriage! Their delicate black wings bear
> It rapidly forward, at the heights in the midst
> > of the heavenly skies.
>
> Descending ... O, you then arrived before me
> With that lovely face graced by heaven:
> "What is it you desire, my love! You have
> > called out to me.
>
> Speak, what is it that you so desire in that
> Loving heart of yours, dearest? Whom have you

> Captured in the net of love? I implore you! Who has
>   done injury to my Sappho?
>
> Who has fled from you? ... Who has scorned the gifts
> You so willingly offered? ... Such gifts he should quickly
> Have taken away! He does not love you ... he should no longer
>   be deserving of you."
>
> Come now also to me! Release my soul
> From its heavy sorrow! Under the fatigue that now
> Plagues my heart, O, help me! Goddess, come
>   to my aid in this struggle.

She seeks the *blessing of love* from the friend of her beloved, to whom she pours out her entire heart:

> Blessed! Blessed! O, blessed gods in heaven
> Who are with you, who surround you and
> See you always, who can hear that charming, sweet
>   gentle voice.
>
> Who can see you smiling! O, sweet smile, which steals
> Heart and soul from me, I saw you! Saw you,
> Ah, what am I saying: All sense and sound
>   had abandoned me.
>
> And my tongue moved silently! A powerful fire
> Rose up through my very bones!
> Night fell before my eyes! Like a dark and distant sound
>   in my fading ears.
>
> Sweat poured coldly down my body! My entire body
> Was shaking! My lips shook like the most tender
> Grasses! Reaching my innermost parts! I appeared
>   as if I were near death ...

All in all, this is a hundred times more beautifully stated and translated than what we see, than the *love of Sappho*: nothing less than the rules of love, or an ode to love heard in all four corners of the world. The young Sámi,[h] who speaks to his reindeer instead of with Venus and gives them names that portray their movement through nature, thus, flying as from *sun to sea, to trees, as the crows and the ducks,* while his beloved is always with him. ... These reindeer herders portray love with strokes seven times more believable, in other words, they create *more beautiful love songs* as

---

h. [PVB] Referring to the Sámi of circumpolar northern Europe as Laplanders, as Herder does here and elsewhere in his original text, was common until the late twentieth century.

the sweetest follower of Sappho with their artificial rules applied pedantically to poetry. The *Lithuanian maiden*, who takes leave from her entire household and portrays the world of the bride before her eyes and heart, is a far greater poet than the droll creator of a valediction, who remains glued to the very desk upon which he writes it.

If *Leibniz* failed to find the humor and wisdom of human beings more effective than a game, so too will human learning, passion, and the soul's poetic capacity never be more effectively evident and visible than at the point in which *truth* and *delight* meet and become one: And this is in *song*.[i] There is more poesy, and there are more poetic sources in *folk belief*, in *fantasy, myth, tradition, language, customs*, in the culture of all Indigenous peoples living close to nature, than in the poetics and oration of all time. Who would undertake the practical, rational collection of all kinds of *fantasy, the poetry, the prejudices, and illusions of the mind*? I am certain that it would be of great service to a deeper understanding of humankind than ten collections of the *logic, aesthetics, ethics, and politics* that were not really true to the human spirit.

How pleasant it finally is to see a people in its *naked* simplicity, the happiness with which it *was born*, and all of *nature in its most basic creative potential*. One will understand most fully after one has freed oneself from all the artificiality clinging to the heart and all the false politeness that has come to generate an inhumane sense of bourgeois life, and one finally can breathe freely. One can be free of all the rules and the traditions that bind one in a yoke and place a wall around the human heart. All this requires but a moment of *open revelation*!

---

i. [PVB] Herder refers here to Leibniz's commentary on play in Gottfried Wilhelm Leibniz, *Werke*, ed. Deutsche Akademie der Wissenschaften zu Berlin, series 6, vol. 6 (Berlin: Deutsche Akademie der Wissenschaften, 1962), 466.

2. The Folk Song Project at the Confluence of Music and Nationalism

Essay on *Volkslieder* (1778/79) and
Stimmen der Völker in Liedern (1807)

Philip V. Bohlman

> A violet in the youth of primary nature,
> Forward not permanent, sweet not lasting,
> The perfume and suppliance of a minute;
> No more.
>
> —WILLIAM SHAKESPEARE,
> *Hamlet*, act 1, scene 3[1]

How remarkable and yet how incongruous that the most widely influential work on world music prior to the late twentieth century should begin with an epigraph from *Hamlet*. Shakespeare would seem an unlikely choice for Johann Gottfried Herder to embark on his journey to gather songs of people throughout the world and publish them in a collection that would situate them in a context of their own, in which new meaning, at once human and transcendent, would accrue to the object "song" and to the subject of its creation, the "folk." Shakespeare was familiar territory in the German Enlightenment, his influence felt in rarefied intellectual circles through multiple translations. At first glance, the distance from the people and their songs might seem insurmountable. But Herder was not one to be deterred from traveling such distances. Indeed, it was by traveling the distance itself, assayed at the beginning of the 1778 first edition of the *Volkslieder* and stretching to the closing Peruvian song of the 1807 second edition, that Herder charted a folk song project that transformed the modern understanding of the relation of music to culture.

The familiarity of *Hamlet* in the German Enlightenment notwithstanding, Herder also chose his epigraph for the *Volkslieder* for its ability to unmoor readers as they joined him on his journey.[2] Herder had already devoted the second book of the 1774 *Alte Volkslieder* to "Shakespeare's Songs," and its introductory essay, "Is Shakespeare Untranslatable?," enjoyed considerable critical reception (see chapter 1 in the present volume). Adopting texts from Shakespeare's plays and sonnets, translating them, and publishing them as songs, whether they were to be sung as songs or not, whether they included references to music or not, provided essential foundations for Herder's lifelong engagement with the problems and meaning of translation. The *Hamlet* epigraph on the title page of *Volkslieder* established general connections to the historical moment, but it also was specific in the ways Shakespeare's texts and contexts provided a bridge to the objects and subjects of folk song that would follow.

Herder's choice of Laertes as the speaker in the passage from *Hamlet* was no accident. In Homer's *Odyssey* Laertes was the father of Odysseus, and in that role he not only affords Herder with a critical connection to Homer (cf. chapter 5), but represents Herder's intensifying engagement with epic as the genre of folk song that would most directly connect nation to music in the historical *longue durée* from antiquity to the nineteenth century, from Greece to Spain to India (cf. the prologue and chapter 8). Herder's decision to organize and publish the *Volkslieder* in two parts, each with three books, each of them containing approximately twenty-four songs, is also indebted to the publication of Homeric epics as anthologies.[3] Shakespeare's figure of Laertes has an even more complex presence in the epigraph, for it is Laertes who kills Hamlet in the final scene of the play. Laertes's words and actions, his dual roles in Homer and Shakespeare, provide Herder with metaphor and allegory at the moment he launches his journey into history and to the far shores from which he would gather the folk songs for his anthology.

Volkslieder encompassed both essays and the six books of folk songs, plus an appendix in the second edition of 1807. I divide the present chapter into two parts, the first containing translations from the essays, and the appendix that follows a representative anthology of twenty-four folk songs from the 1807 edition. Accordingly, the chapter serves as a microcosm of Herder's own journey into a world enunciated through folk song. Neither the essays—introductions, analyses, theoretical excursions—nor the folk songs have appeared before in a translation that captures their interrelatedness. It is my goal in the long, two-part chapter that follows to convey as much of that interrelatedness as possible.

The extensive influence and reception history of the *Volkslieder* has resulted from the availability of individual parts, especially individual songs, as fragments that could be taken from the anthology and fitted to the purposes of other anthologies and to the settings and composition of new songs. Herder's folk songs seeded the collecting activities and anthologies that would appear in the early decades of German idealism, for example Ludwig Achim von Arnim and Clemens Brentano's *Des Knaben Wunderhorn* (Arnim and Brentano 1806 and 1808), framing the publication of the 1807 second edition, *Stimmen der Völker in Liedern* (Voices of the People in Song). *Volkslieder* provided lyrics and evoked melodies directly and indirectly throughout the nineteenth century. Both Franz Schubert and Johannes Brahms would compose multiple settings of Herder's translation of the Scottish "Edward" ballad (Schubert's three settings as D. 923; Brahms's vocal setting as op. 14, no. 4, and his setting as a "Ballade" for solo piano as op. 10, no. 1; cf. Bohlman 2011a, 2011b). The circulation between folk song and art song led to the canonization of genre in both, not least in the establishment of the ballad as a critical genre of nationalism in the nineteenth century (see Gelbart 2007, throughout but especially 98–102). The publication and reception of *Volkslieder* exemplified the very paradigm shift and theoretical formation that lie at the core of Herder's folk song project: the transformation of song from object to subject.

Herder's formulation of folk song (see chapter 1) and theoretical and practical application of folk song (this chapter) meant that it would enter the histories of music and nationalism in sweeping new ways. Composers would set the folk songs in *Volkslieder* as art songs; folklorists and literary scholars would reimagine the space for music in European society; anthropologists would recognize music as a critical component of contact and exchange between and among cultures globally; and historians would introduce music into global narratives, giving those narratives aesthetic and political dimensions. These are the transformations fully set in motion by *Volkslieder* that led to the claims that Herder "invented folk song."

The first edition of *Volkslieder* (1778/79) was both a continuation and an expansion of Herder's collections of and writings about folk song earlier in the 1770s, particularly the 1774 *Alte Volkslieder* (chapter 1 in this volume) and the 1773 "Fragments" from the Ossian correspondence (chapter 4). The songs that he included in the Ossian "Fragments" appear again among the *Volkslieder*, and the songs that would have appeared in print had *Alte Volkslieder* been published are also largely present. Whereas some Herder scholars argue that the three new "books" of folk songs, published serially over the course of two years, were a response to the criticism of Herder's position in the Ossian debates and a means of completing the inchoate conceptual framework of the "ancient folk songs" (see, e.g., Maurer 2014, 108–9), a closer reading of the new introductory and analytical essays, combined with the greatly substantial increase in the contents of the collection itself, suggest that *Volkslieder* represented new directions in Herder's thinking as a philosopher, linguist, and translator, and that these new directions led him increasingly toward thinking in anthropology and musicology, inchoate as these two disciplines were in the late Enlightenment. Empirically and theoretically, that is, as an anthology of songs that together express the inseparability of musical text and cultural context, the folk song project had entered an entirely new phase for Herder and for the generations that would seize upon the paradigm shift at the core of the folk song project.

In the 1778/79 *Volkslieder*, folk songs acquire new functions, both different and distinctive. On one hand they retain Herder's goal of illustrating the historical qualities of song, with emphasis on the old and ancient. Rather than establishing these historical qualities more specifically for German and Scottish repertories, however, Herder looks beyond the historical and linguistic borders of Northern and Western Europe to establish age and oral transmission as qualities of song in cultures throughout the world. Realizing the confluence of age and oral transmission is the dynamic nature of singing—the transformation from *Lied* as object to *Gesang* as subject. Critical for this transformation is the role of the singer, the human agency that is evident in each song and its many versions. By the late 1770s the folk song project bore witness to a shift from the earlier concern for authenticity and its dependence on age, especially on the "ancient" roots of *alte Volkslieder*. Similarly, the origins of song and singing no longer depended on the theological premise of a *vox Dei* (voice of God), but rather the diversity of song spread across cultures and religions through origins as a *vox populi* (voice of the people). Rather than descending from sacred origins, song now ascended through the singing of human subjects, aspiring, as Herder makes clear for the first time in the final essay of the 1778/79 edition, to the sublime. In the first edition of the songs Herder did not yet assign a name to this shift from song as object to song as singing, but in the years leading to the preparation of the second edition in 1807, he increasingly describes the practice and agency of collective creativity of human speech and music making. The second edition, posthumously published by Johann von Müller with the assistance of Herder's wife, Karoline, appeared under the name *Stimmen der Völker in Liedern* (Voices of the People in Song). It was this conscious juxtaposition of song and singing that became the most common name of the folk song project for the subsequent two centuries.[4]

The distinctions between song and singing also provide ways for Herder to shape an analytical discourse in *Volkslieder* that encompasses two different concepts of *Volk*. The first of these concepts largely represents the *Volk* in its singular form, that is, as the individual whose creativity led to new songs and to their spread across society through performance. In the singular form, a folk song is different from an art song because the individual who created it lives in a different social world than the composer of art song. Identifying the singular *Volk* was critical for Herder and his generation in the late eighteenth century, because it shifted musical creativity away from divine sources and associated notions of authenticity to a culture constituted of human beings, for whom music could also provide agency. The folk, it followed, used song and dance to accompany rituals and rites of passage, labor and play, the everyday that was their world. The singular *Volk* is critical to Herder's choice of songs and for the songs' functions in society. In the sections on Nordic song, to take one example, Herder shifts attention from anonymous epics to the songs of the everyday bards, the *Skalden* (song 5 in appendix B to this chapter, "Morning Song during War"), and he includes Sámi styles associated with work songs (song 6, "To the Reindeer").

Herder's second context for *Volk* grows from its collective plurality. A culture, a people, a religion, and, significantly, a nation may cohere as a collective around musical practices. The emphasis of this plural form, reflected in its common use as *Völker*, is no longer on the creativity of individuals, but rather shifts to the ways in which diverse peoples live together and are therefore unlike other collectives.[5] Maintaining the distinction between self and other strengthens the formation of collective plurality, which is then sustained through common cultural practices. The songs of the plural *Volk*, therefore, are critical to who they are.

The contrastive application of the singular and the plural becomes even more critical to the paradigm shift unleashed by *Volkslieder* because the subject formations around music and nation accrue to them in different ways. The folk song of the singular has aesthetic dimensions; ontologically it expands the late eighteenth-century understanding of music. The folk song of the plural has historical and cultural dimensions; epistemologically it expands the ways in which peoples express their belonging to nations and nationalism. Herder's *Volkslieder*, as an aesthetic, historical, and anthropological framework, opened new spaces in which the subjectivities of nation and music, formed from difference and diversity, would be possible. And this is why the folk song project is no less important today than at the beginning of the nineteenth century. Music's subjectivities have critically shaped a new and modern interdisciplinarity—aesthetics, history, anthropology, and theology.

It is this new interdisciplinary subjectivity, growing from a transformation of ontologies and discourses about music and nationalism, that shapes the influences of *Volkslieder* on the following two centuries. Not all is positive about this new subjectivity, as we see in historical moments such as the period when German nationalism brutally took on the trappings of fascism, to disastrous results (see, e.g., the essays in Schneider 1994). When we celebrate Herder, we must do so accompanied by caution and criticism. In *Volkslieder*, nonetheless, we witness the first moment in which the confluence of music and nationalism has reached a point at which it would transform understandings of music and history, opening their aesthetic and ontological borders to the world, and beyond to the universal.

From *Volkslieder* and *Stimmen der Völker in Liedern* / *Folk Songs* and *Voices of the People in Song*

JOHANN GOTTFRIED HERDER,
TRANSLATED BY PHILIP V. BOHLMAN

Essays, Together with Sundry Other Pieces

PART 2

The continuation of the evidence for folk songs will follow in this part. Because, however, every good thing finds voice in two or three cases, and because even a hundred pieces of evidence would be insufficient, we want here to save paper and words. Instead, we should want to move on to that which could serve as clarification and presentation of these many poems.

There can be no question that poesy, and especially song, were originally folklike, in other words light and easy, formed from the conditions and the language of the masses, just as in the richness and fullness of nature. Song loves the masses, it loves to take shape from the common voice of the multitude: song commands the ear of the listener and the chorus of voices and souls. Song never could have come into existence as the art of letters and syllables, as a portrait of images and colors, for readers in their armchairs. More to the point, song would never have come to be what it has come to mean for all peoples of the world. Every culture and every language, especially the most ancient, shrouded ones of the Orient, produced traces for the masses from such origins, when it was necessary to lead them forward and take stock of them.

The names and voices of the oldest Greek poets already provide sufficient evidence. Do not Linus and Orpheus, Phantasia and Hermes, Musäus and Amphion . . . the names and accounts of tales and truth . . . show what was poesy at that time? Where it arose? Wherein it lived? It lived in the ear of the folk, on the lips and in the harps of living singers who sang about history, events, secrets, miracles, and signs. Poesy was the flower possessed by a people, expressed through their language and in their land, through their trade and in their prejudices, through their passions and in their pride, through their music and in their soul. We might account for as much of the tale as we wish from the poets/singers (αοιδοις), from the gathering of Greek singers. The truth, thus, remains at the base of the vessel, the same as among other peoples and ages. The most noble and liveliest of the Greek art of poetry grew from such origins.

The greatest singer of the Greeks, Homer, is at the same time the greatest folk poet. His masterful totality is not *epopee*, but rather the epic (επος), fairy tales, legends, and folktales. He did not settle on "Sammet," a heroic poem doubling twenty-four songs according to Aristotle's rules, nor, as the Muses moved him, did he write in such a way that the rules are extended, but rather he sang what he heard, he presented what he had seen and engaged in performance.[a] Homer's rhapsodies do not remain in bookstores or on stacks of paper, but rather they resound for a long time in the ears and the hearts of actual singers and audiences from which they were collected and finally, though burdened with summaries and prejudice, transmitted to us. Homer's feeling for verse, which was as extensive as the blue skies and as diversely meaningful for all who lived at his time, is no pedantic or artificial hexameter, but rather the meter of the Greeks, which was already current in their pure and finely tuned ear, and in the sound of their language, and similarly it waited as fertile soil for the figures of gods and heroes. It flows endlessly and tirelessly in gentle rapids, in repetitive poetic formulae and cadences, which were pleasing to the ear of the folk. These formulae and cadences, which become the cross borne by all famous translators and heroic poets, are the soul of harmony, the gently peaceful kiss that closes our eyes as each line comes to a close and puts our mind at ease, so that each new line powerfully awakens a new clarity and ensures that the long journey will not be tiring. Everything rose to our attention, all artificial limitations and verbal labyrinths are foreign to the simple singer; he always remains sharply attuned and thus capable of understanding. Images appear before the singer's eyes just as silver tones flow into the ear;

---

a. [PVB] Homer's *Iliad* and *Odyssey* contained twenty-four distinctive sections, called "songs," and Herder consciously organizes the three books in the first part of *Volkslieder* in the same way.

the intricate dance of both is the gait of his muse, in which there is also a goddess, which in turn serves the most humble as well as every child. One does not gladly argue in the marketplace about a matter that is secret and of the dearest pleasure; but this, it would seem to me, never occurred to Homer, who took as his model for the common pedestrian the rapidly passing cart and, for the gentle stream of his language, the clatter of a mill for a so-called heroic poesy. His pace is gentle, as is the arrival of his spirit, like Ulysses's return home to Ithaca: only he can become truly trustworthy for those who neither dismiss nor regard with shame such a humbled being.

[At this point,[b] if indeed at an inappropriate place, I should like to praise a relatively well-known gift to our language, a reprise to Homer himself, if indeed not by his friends and fellow singers, then surely by one of his noblest servants, who for many years bore Homer's harp on his behalf: I refer here to Bodmer's translation.[c] It suffers, as does every translation in the world, from comparison with the original song. One can forget this and listen with the ear rather than read with the eye, forgiving the human errors that appear here and there, which do not remain hidden even from the ear and thus announce: "This is probably not how Homer sang!" All things considered, and when one takes further into consideration every human undertaking, surely in a translation of Homer, it seems to me that one should come down on the side of an individual who lived together under the same roof with his elderly father for many years and cared for him. Like most of us, he felt especially close to the *Odyssey*, and in many of the songs he is entirely true and trustworthy. This is, in my opinion, small thanks earned for the labors of many years, other opinions and future judgments notwithstanding.]

It is much the same with Hesiod and Orpheus, in their own way. Not that I pursue the works of the latter of these two, as if they contained the original text of the ancient Orpheus; they are, rather, much later versions of very old songs and legends that have been revised and refreshed perhaps six, seven, even, in my opinion, hundreds of times. Still, it is noticeable that the ancient song or legend still shimmers through even in these versions, if I am not deceiving myself. Hesiod as well, whose authenticity is considerably greater, contains certain verses that are foreign; nonetheless, the noble

---

b. [PVB] Herder inserts this paragraph-long aside as a footnote, which I take the liberty, for the sake of continuity and because of its considerable substance, of integrating into the body of the text, in brackets.

c. [JGH] Homer, *Homers Werke*, ed. Johann Jakob Bodmer (Zurich: Bey Orell, Gessner, Füesslin und Compagnie, 1778).

folksinger, the simple shepherd who tends his flocks on the mountain of the Muses, is everywhere to be found,[d] thus the gift for the sweetest songs and their instruction that one hears in his works may have been bequeathed by the Muses. Oh, if I could but introduce into our own language something of this golden gift and the rumors of antiquity as the noblest of folk songs, in order that they might remain to some degree exactly as they were! Homer, Hesiod, Orpheus, I see your shadows before me on the island of the blessed within the masses, and I hear the echo of your songs, but I have no ship from you that allows me to transport them to my land and into my language. The waves on the sea of the return voyage quell the harps, and the wind blows your songs back, where they will never fall silent in groves that remain ever green because of the eternal dances and fests that fill them. . . .

It is the same with the Greek chorus, from which the highest form of tragedy emerges, and from which the holy flames flare out of the wood and victims rent asunder by them, at once in Aeschylus and Sophocles. Unquestionably the chorus is the ideal of folk song for the Greeks, but how does one reach such an image? Who is capable of drawing it out from the most refined of his tones and embodying it through our language? It is no less the case with Pindar's songs, from which nothing akin to foreignness has found its way into our language, perhaps not even into our ear. Like Tantalus one stands in their flow: the ringing stream moves past, and the golden fruits allude to everything they might touch. . . .

For me it is sufficient that the possibility has not been granted me to grasp the finest of these genres, but instead to be granted by the Greeks only a few brief songs, table songs, and simple melodies. I steal along the shore and allow others the high seas.

The Romans lost the old songs of the ancestors, who still sang them at their feasts in the glory days and sang them to give strength to the virtue and love of the fatherland. In Catullus and Lucretius[e] there are traces of the old songs, but it is very difficult to decipher them.

To some extent, the early songs of the Christian Church fathers have survived into eternity. Originally sung in Latin during the darkest times and by choruses in the dark temples, they were rejuvenated through dissemination into the languages of virtually every European nation. If somewhat altered in form, they continue to survive in many places. We possess

---

d. [PVB] Tradition holds that Hesiod in the eighth century BCE lived in Böotien, which lies near Mount Helikon, inhabited by the Muses.

e. [PVB] Titus Lucretius Carus (98–55 BCE).

some of them in very old translations into our own language, which are unusual, but in fact never really did belong there.[f]

. . .

Because I have not at all spoken about the lost bards, and because I shall speak about the poems of the Skalds[g] at the beginning of the second book, I thus continue here with German songs and folk songs. The earliest song we still know is probably "König Ludwig,"[h] which I present here in a quick sketch of its text, at least as much as is possible. Already when it appears as a song in 882, it is quite remarkable, and no less when we examine its inner traits.[i] Pieces from Gottfried,[j] especially verses from the preface: Ludwig, the Quick, stood at some distance from him to the side. Anno's song, a blossom in the crown of our Ludwig, however, floats away: it should be classified as a song of praise, not as a folk song.

The stream of the centuries flowed dark and dreary for Germany. Occasionally there survived a voice of the people, a song, a saying, a rhyme. More often than not it was slimy, and the waves again dragged it immediately back into the stream. I do not take Latin verse or rhymed chronicles into consideration here, for they do not really serve my purposes. There is thus very little that I have seen that bears up under comparison with the best pieces by the English, the Spaniards, or the Nordic peoples. [Johann Gottfried von] Eckhard was able to save a small fragment of an Old German novel; too bad that it was no more than a fragment, remarkable only because of its language. In Meibom's anthology[k] there is the song of the Saxon prince who was forced to sacrifice himself to the priest after losing an unfortunate battle. It is sad, but nonetheless it has only a single strophe:

---

f. [PVB] Herder refers here to Johann Georg von Eckhard's *Commentarii de rebus Franciae orientalis et episcopatus Wirceburgensis*, 2 vols. (Würzburg: H. Engmann, 1729).

g. [PVB] Old Norse epic singers.

h. [PVB] Herder provides Schilter's name only for this citation, but he most likely refers to Johannes Schilter, *Thesaurus antiquitatum teutonicarum, ecclesiasticarum, civilium, litterarum*, 2 vols. (Ulm: D. Bartholomæi, & filii, 1726–28).

i. [JGH] Just to clarify matters for those passing judgment on art, the song was not made by Opitz, but rather found and edited by him. In addition to Opitz's edition, it is found in part one of Opitz, as well as in Bodmer's unfortunately incomplete version of Opitz.

j. [JGH] Johann Gottfried von Eckhard, *Commentarii de rebus Franciae orientalis et episcopatus Wirceburgensis*, vol. 2, 864.

k. [JGH] Heinrich Meibom, *Scriptores rerum Germanicarum*, part 3 (Helmstedt: Hammius, 1688).

Soll ich nun in Gottesfronden Hände	Were I now to give myself into the hands
In meinen allerbesten Tagen	Of the priests in the flower of my youth
Geben werden und sterben so elende,	And die in such misery,
Das muß ich wohl klagen.	I must complain bitterly.
Wenn mir das Glücke füget hätte	If fortune were to proffer me
Des Streits ein gutes Ende,	A noble end to the struggle,
Dörft' ich nicht leisten diese Wette	I am no longer able to afford the punishment,
Netzen mit Blut die hiere Wände.	Attached with blood to the holy walls.

One finds old German folk songs and dances in sources other than German chronicles, and some of these possess lines and verses that are particularly good. I should like to mention here a few of them that come to mind, for even those that do not serve my purposes well might be valuable for another, especially if it is not all the same for anyone attempting to provide a history of German song and poetry (may heaven provide one soon). Other than those instrumental pieces about the Prince and Count Wilhelm of Thuringia, there are two more pieces in Spangenberg,[l] a song mourning the fallen Emperor Adolph, and a rather long song about the siege of Magdeburg, which Spangenberg set in the German of his day, and which has some very fine verses and, like most songs of the same type, described the exact conditions of the contents themselves. The first song is also in Glafey's *Sächsische Geschichte* [Saxon History],[m] whereas the second can be found in Pomarius's *Chronik*.[n] In the third part of the continuation of Spangenberg's *Hennebergische Chronik* [Henneberg Chronicle] there is a song about the feud between Reinhard von Haune with Wilhelm von Henneberg.[o] In Falkenstein's history of Erfurt one finds the origins of a song that children in Erfurt still today sing in a garbled form on the eve of Saint John's Day.[p] It is a song about the destruction of Dienstberg Castle in 1289, and the song has the incipit "Eichen ohne Garten" [Oaks without a yard]. In this same history there are fragments from songs that were sung by the flagellant sect in the fourteenth century, which also appear in Pomarius and in the *Limburger*

---

l. [JGH] Cyriacus Spangenberg, *Hennebergische Chronica* (Meiningen: Scheidemantel, 1755).

m. [JGH] Adam F. Glafey, *Kern der Geschichte des Chur- und Fürstlichen Hauses Sachsen-Altenburg* (Nuremberg: n.p., 1568).

n. [JGH] Johannes Pomarius [Johann Baumgart], *Chronik der Sachsen und Niedersachsen* (Magdeburg: Johann Francken, 1589), 482.

o. [JGH] Johannes Heim, *Hennebergische Chronik* (Meiningen: Hartmann, 1766).

p. [JGH] Johann Heinrich von Falkenstein, *Civitatis Erffurtensis Historia* (Erfurt: Johann Wilhelm Ritschel, 1739).

Chronik [Limburg Chronicle]^q from the third book, of which an extract was presumably taken. A song deriding the peasants and their failed uprising in 1525 appears in Falkenstein and Pfefferkorn. There is a description of the battle of Hempach in 1450, as well as the war between Nuremberg and the Markgrafs in Reinhard's publications.[r] Schöttgen and Kreisig's *Diplomatische Nachlese* [Diplomatic Record] contains a song about the annexation of the city of Hetstädt in 1439.[s] Other historical events are chronicled in published songs: concerning trade in Aachen (1429), about the 1448 siege of Grubenhagen, and a song with which I perhaps should have begun, which has as its subject the battle of Cremmerdamm.[t] If it had not been in Low German, I should have included it, for it would have quieted the nightingale recently made known by Lessing, and which may well already be in abundance in libraries.

Songs that found their way to print chronicled the religious unrest of the sixteenth century no less, especially those that in one way or another concerned princes and official occasions. In my hands at this very moment I am holding a volume of printed songs, most of which describe events in 1542–45 in Saxony and Brunswick, and between Saxony and the emperor in 1547. It seems as if the owner only collected songs that appeared in his own region, for most of them were printed in Leipzig and Erfurt, indeed quite a large number. We can presume that other regions produced collections with other songs about the same types of occasions. One can determine from the sheer number of songs, published twice in the course of two years, just how many of these Germany can actually claim for herself. For the most part, one can presume that they are relatively simple in character.... All of the songs are named according to their melodies, and these, moreover, reveal the names of very well-known folk songs: usually a new song is to be sung in the same "tone" as its predecessor, that is, to the same melody. Quite often this similarity characterizes the relation between sacred and secular songs, which seems rather remarkable when one finds a sacred song with a very secular melody, for example, "Es wohnet Lieb bei Liebe" [Kindness Resides in Love] and other

---

q. [JGH] Tilemann Elhen von Wolfhagen, *Die Limburger Chronik* (Marburg: N.G. Elwert'sche Verlagsbuchhandlung, 1875). [PVB] Cf. Hugo Moser and Joseph Müller-Blattau, *Deutsche Lieder des Mittelalters* (Stuttgart: Klett, 1968), 186–96.

r. [JGH] Johann Paul Reinhard, *Beyträge zur Historie Franckenlandes*, 3 vols. (Bayreuth: Lübeck, 1760–63).

s. [JGH] Christian Schöttgen and Georg Christian Kreisig, *Diplomatische und curieuse Nachlese der Historie von Obersachsen*, 12 vols. (Dresden: Hekel, 1733), vol. 5, p. 112.

t. [JGH] Johann B. Mencke, *Scriptores rerum Germanicarum praecipue Saxonicarum*, 3 vols. (Leipzig: Martini, 1728–30); Johann Letzner, *Dasselsche und Eimbeckische Chronica* (Erfurt: n.p., 1596); Samuel Buchholtz, *Versuch einer Geschichte der Churmarck Brandenburg* (Berlin: n.p., 1765).

similar songs. Often these seem as if they are crude parodies, which we find insulting, but at the time surely were not because they were quite common. This is the case, for example, with a new song in the collection I have just mentioned: the hunter in the well-known song "Es wollt ein Jäger jagen" [A Hunter Wanted to Hunt] becomes sacred because of the way he is meant to refer to the Angel Gabriel and to Mary.[u] Many versions and variants of older songs in the church trace their origins to just such melodies, and any history of church music would be insufficient if it did not take this into consideration. For the most part, the sacred and the secular flow together in folk songs such as these, and in old songbooks we witness attempts to bring this about. Luther, who created songs that fitted specific occasions, created a "new song" from two others, "Zwei Märterer Christi zu Brüssel" [Two Christian Martyrs in Brussels] and "Sophisten zu Löwen verbrannt" [The Burning of the Sophists of Leuven], both of which were published separately, often as contributions to the old songbooks. I have myself already introduced new verses into pre-existing songs when it has not seemed too inappropriate for a particular collection.[v] Luther's parody of the song "Nun treiben wir den Tod heraus" [Now We Drive Death Away][w] is known, and it too is found in old songbooks.[x] Because his "Cantio de aulis" [Song of the Court] is only found in the Altenburg edition of his works. His assistants and followers retained this practice only to the extent that they were able. Erasmus Alberus's parodies of the "Te Deum," "Aesop's Fables," and many other leaders are known.[y] Following the practice of versifying sacred legends (for example the story of Lazarus and the wealthy), stories and pieces were taken from the Bible and set as poems, something done in the art of the mastersingers by remaining true to the original, but more recently no longer true to the original.

"LIED VOM HOFE" / "SONG OF THE COURT"

PARODY BY MARTIN LUTHER OF "CANTIO DE AULIS"

Wer sich nimmt an,	Whoever tries,
Und 's Rädlein kan	And can take the wheel
Hübsch auf der Bahn	Charming in its track

u. [PVB] Both sacred and secular variants are included in *Des Knaben Wunderhorn* (cf. Arnim and Brentano 1806, 140, 292).

v. [PVB] Herder refers here to his addition of verses to the Luther song in *Von deutscher Art und Kunst* (Hamburg: Bode, 1773); cited here from the modern edition (Herder 1968), 55.

w. [PVB] Herder notes that he has encountered sources in which the beginning of this song is in Czech.

x. [PVB] Luther called the parody "So treiben wir den Papst hinaus" (Thus, We Drive the Pope Away).

y. [PVB] Alberus was a student of Luther, who lived ca. 1500–1553.

Lahn umher gahn,	Going around the court,
Und schmeichlen schön	And flatters so nicely
Findt jedermann	Finds everyone
Ein Feil und Wahn,	An arrow and crazy,
Ist jezt im Korb der beste Hahn.	The best cock is now in the basket.
(Oder der geht zu Hof jezt an.	(Or he goes to the courtyard up oben above.
Oder der ist zu Hof am besten dran.)	Or he is the best at court.)
Denn wer gedächt'	Who would have thought
Zu leben schlecht,	Life is so bad,
Fromm und gerecht	Faithful and just
Die Wahrheit brächt';	Would break the truth:
Der wird durchächt	He would not have considered
Und gar geschwächt	Much less weakened,
Gehönt, geschmät	worsened, wanted,
Und bleibt allzeit der andern Knecht.	And remained a servant to others forever.
Beim Schmeichelstab'	With such flattery
Gewinnt mancher Knab'	Many a youth gains
Groß Gut und Haab',	Great goods and possessions,
Geld, Gunst und Gab'	Money, favor, and gifts
Preiß, Ehr und Lob	Fame, honor, and praise
Stößt andre herab,	Taking away from others,
Daß Er hoch trab'	That he rises so high
So geht die Welt jezt auf und ab.	Thus, the world goes round.
Wer solchs nicht kann	Whoever cannot
Zu Hofe than;	Do such things at court;
Thue sich davon,	Acts in such ways,
Ihm wird zu Lohn	He will receive
Nur Spott und Hohn:	But insult and disdain:
Denn Heuchelmann	For the hypocrite
Und Spötterzahn	And the one who insults
Ist jezt zu Hof am besten dran.[z]	Are the best suited for courtly life.

At this point, I choose not to speak about these songs and their noble origins with the so-called minnesingers. They both were and were not folksingers in the ways that we consider them. To be a folksinger does not mean that they had to be one of the people, or that they sang for the people; so little were they attuned to the art of poetry that it never found its way into the mouths of the people. Being of the folk does not refer to the people on the street, who never sing or create poetry, but instead cry out and torture the language. It is

---

z. [JGH] Source: Martin Luther, *Der 5. Teil der deutschen Bücher und Schrifften des Doct. Martini. Lutheri* (Altenburg bei Meissen: Fürstl. Sächs. Officin, 1661), 504.

impossible to deny that poesy embraced a great deal in Swabian times.[aa] During this period poesy stretched from the emperor to the simple citizen, from the artisan to the prince. The "Minne" was not the only content of the songs, as I shall show elsewhere;[ab] the circle in which they were sung was neither one of scholars nor the simple confines of the home. The fragment I have included elsewhere in this work reveals just how widely and vividly these songs circulated at the time, perhaps even more extensively than in the readerships enjoyed by our own poets, with whose circles one is accustomed to make comparisons. At any rate, it is safe to say that such songs only rarely attracted large audiences. From any repertory of considerable size there can be no doubt that ten or fifteen songs were never sung again, but rather they simply died in the mouths of the singers. In the end, the entire noble art was no more than pedestrian mediocrity or a bunch of trash, to which passion and love nonetheless accrued, which in turn we can only presume and speculate about the early era in which they throve. . . .

This or that minnesinger and mastersinger [*Meistersänger*], as the case may be, does not belong to my concept of folk song, indeed, for the simple reason that their language possesses very little that for us can be considered lyrical. It was necessary for me, in the case of valuable and, to some degree, unpublished pieces I include here, to make certain changes in the structure of verses, fitting them to the melody and form, in order to make it possible for us to hear and understand them, which according to my approach meant that I mutilated them and they would have to wait for another occasion.

There is a so-called historical songbook by Johann Höfel, in which songs with biblical and non-biblical subjects, with saints and the events of history, are collected in three volumes.[ac] Because all of these utilize the tonality of church songs, most of them demonstrate a formal simplicity and are the product of very few writers. Accordingly I could not make much use of them. One example might be a song memorializing a famous man whose life is known well enough in history, but who is paid miserably for his services, at least as the sources report.[ad]

    aa. [PVB] The medieval period during which German literature employed Middle High German.
    ab. [PVB] See for example chapter 3, in which I translate from the minnesinger repertories in Herder's translation of the *Song of Songs*.
    ac. [JGH] Johann Höfel, *Historisches Gesangbuch* (Schleusingen: Göbel, 1681).
    ad. [JGH] The song is about Master Freundsberg, who wrote the song himself after the battle of Pavia. Adam Reusner later created a parody in praise of Freundsberg. That song is called "Mein Fleisch und Müh hab ich nie gespart" (I Gave Fully of My Courage and Strength). Using the same melody, it appears related to Luther's "Cantio de aulis," which had appeared two years before.

There is an abundance of romantic and love songs, which are spread all over the place, here and there, especially in anthologies printed in Nuremberg. The worthwhile character of the songs is very fleeting. There is relatively little poetry that has real substance and does not repeat itself, except at those gentle places or a particularly rich use of texture. One needs to refine the gold out of all the material that has been left behind, and there is relatively little that yields anything of real substance. The well-known song: love accompanies love; the love of someone who watches over one loyally. There is the song already in the Manesse collection,[ae] where however it possesses a different poetic form. There is the song of the daughter of the sultan, of lovers' quarrels, the song of the three roses, the seven requests, and others. One could perhaps point to other places and verses, or also demonstrate this with some songs, at least as far as they provide other models and songs that were well known at the time. Because, however, it had been pleasing to others to take a stance against folk songs in general because they were inappropriate and not customary, thus I do not want to be one who questions them because of some innocent sprouting tendrils and haystacks on their wise horns. Instead, I prefer to offer some little French songs that might provide their wreaths....[af]

Conclusion of the Introduction to Part 2 of the *Volkslieder*[ag]

In conclusion, I cannot avoid including a few remarks about what I believe is the essence of song. Unlike the ways we would understand what makes a painting charming, I do not believe that beauty and polish serve to give a song its singular and primary perfection. Such a limitation would apply exceptionally just to the first and only genre of songs, which I prefer to describe as pieces for the drawing room or parlor, the sonnet, the madrigal, and similar types of pieces. The essence of song is singing, not painting: its perfection lies in the melodic path of passion and sensibility, which one can only appropriately call melodic manner.[ah] If this is absent in a song, it

---

ae. [PVB] The Codex Manesse, completed between ca. 1304 and 1340, contains manuscript sources for the songs of the approximately 135 minnesingers active between the mid-twelfth and early fourteenth centuries. For a more extensive discussion of the Codex Manesse, see chapter 1.

af. [PVB] At this point, the translation of the first part of the introduction to part two of *Volkslieder* comes to an end (in the 1975 edition pp. 167–77).

ag. [PVB] *Volkslieder*, 1975 edition, 182–85.

ah. [PVB] Herder employs the term *Weise* to represent the critical confluence of melody, tune, text, and genre, which are variously representative of the German terms that fill this concluding section to "*Stimmen der Völker in Liedern*": *Lied, Gesang, Ton, Melodie, melodischer Gang, und lyrische Weise*. Critical to Herder's sense is the way the differences between these designations blur within the anthology and the ways in which he translates folk songs to shape that anthology. My translations of has no true sound, no poetic modulation, no sense of movement and progress. It may possess an image and pictures as much as it wishes, even with colors that fit together with beauty and charm, but it is no longer a song. Should something disrupt a melody, should someone foreign to the tradition attempt to improve it, here with a nod to picturesque composition, there with the charming color of an accompanying word, such that we lose the sound of the singer or the melody of the song for just a moment, we are left attempting to draw nourishment from the hard seed of color. The song is gone! The song is gone, and so too is the joy it brings!

If, in contrast, the melodic tune remains secure, if it sounds fully in a sustained lyrical melody such that the content remains supported, then the song remains intact, and it will be sung. In the long run, rather than weak content, better content will emerge, and it will provide the basis for improving the song. Only the soul of the song, its poetic mode, and melody remain. If a song with a bold melody still possesses a few weaknesses, the weaknesses will disappear, just as the verses that are inadequate will no longer be sung. The spirit of song, which alone touches the soul and inspires the fervor of the chorus, this spirit is eternal, and its impact never ceases. Song must be heard, not seen, heard with the ear of the soul, which does not count individual syllables by themselves, measuring and weighing them; rather it listens for the way sound moves forward and swims together in a common current. The smallest stone that would encumber that current, even a precious stone, only stands in the way of melody. The finest improvement there might be comes from a single singer, who might have no knowledge whatsoever of the hundreds of singers and thousands of variants upon which he might have modeled the song. As perfect as the improvement might be for all the masters and apprentices of artifice, and for all those who have acquired so much learning, the song remains for its singers and children:

... purer puter Schneiderscherz	... pure and plain tailor's joke
Und trägt der Scheere Spur	And bearing the marks of the shears
... nichts mehr vom grossen vollen Herz	... nothing left from the large, full heart
Der tönenden Natur.	Of sounding nature.[ai]

It is most difficult, moreover, to translate this sound, this sound of singing, to capture the sound of song from a foreign language, as we witness in

---

these terms, which reflect the contexts of their use in the conclusion, differ in ways that I hope capture the nuance and breadth of meaning in Herder's German.

ai. [JGH] Matthias Claudius, in *Voßscher Musenalmanach* (1778), 130.

the case of hundreds of failed attempts to draw songs and lyrical vessels to the shores of our own and other languages. It is often only possible to retain a song in the language in which it is sung in order to capture and hold the ways it moves us melodically within. The tension between the two languages and ways of singing of the composer and the translator, however, is insufferable. The ear perceives it immediately and hates the limping messenger, which knows how neither to speak nor to keep quiet.

The primary concern of the present anthology, thus, has been to capture the melody and sound of every song and the way it is sung, and to remain true to them. Whether it has succeeded in so doing remains an open question. Accordingly, this observation helps to justify how I approached the contents of many pieces: my goal was not one of reproducing the contents, but rather of capturing the melody and tune. If this was successful, if a song from another tradition sounds good and pure in our own language, it can capture the contents of that other song, even when no word remains the same. It is always better to offer new and improved songs than to present songs simply improved in old and mutilated form. With a new song we ourselves are the masters of its content if we are but able to capture the soul of the earlier melody. If we merely improve a song, we are usually unable to come closer to any previous tunes. For this reason, I have changed old songs very little or not at all. . . .

This is my opinion about the essence of song, other opinions notwithstanding, and every young person, with more knowledge about the melodic manner of a song than before, is free to offer opinions of her or his own. I wish neither to refute them nor to offer a theory, but rather to clarify just what it is the present anthology attempts to accomplish.

SECOND BOOK

Observations on Several Songs That Follow

1. On Estonian Songs As I traveled about during the harvest season and met workers in the field, I heard a rather wild song sung by many of them as a work song. I learned from a pastor that it was an old pagan song without rhyme, of which one could not disabuse the workers.[aj] In Kelch's *Liefländische Historia* [History of Līvõmõ] there is an example of a love song called "Jörru, Jörru" [George], a rather common name, which appears

---

aj. [JGH] See Friedrich Christian Weber, *Das veränderte Rußland*, vol. 1 (Frankfurt am Main and Leipzig: N. Förster, 1744).

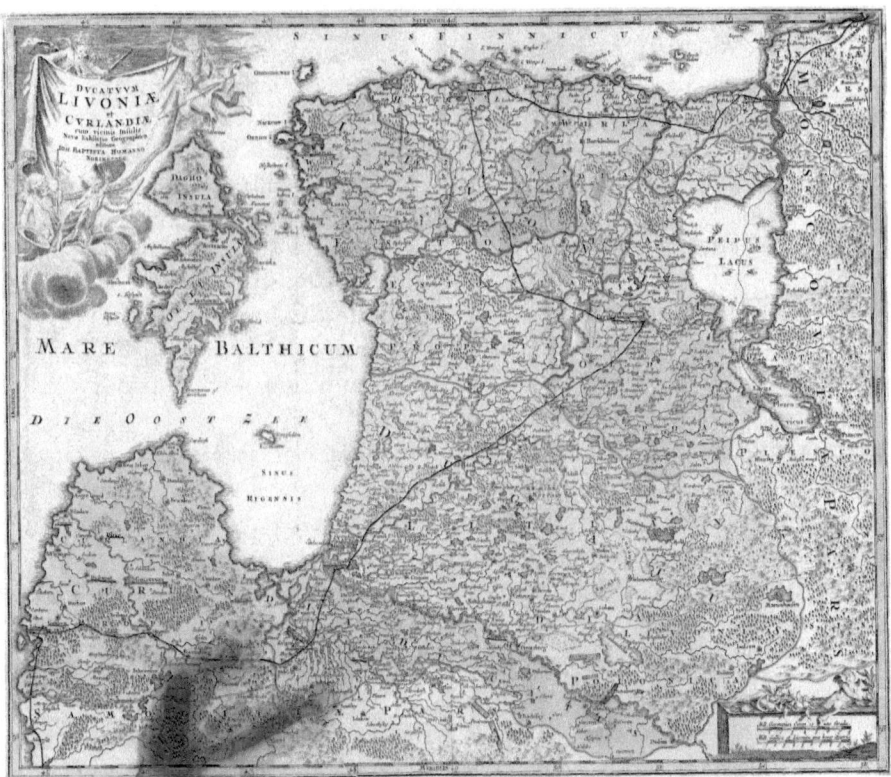

FIGURE 7. Estonia and Latvia, mid-eighteenth century. Courtesy the Map Collection, Regenstein Library, University of Chicago.

here as a title that leads some scholars to claim as proof that these people are descended from Jerusalem.[ak] The song goes something like this:

Jörru, Jörru, darf ich kommen?	George, George, may I come?
Nicht o Liebchen heute.	Not today, my love.
Wärest du doch gestern kommen,	If you had only come yesterday,
Nun sind um mich Leute.	Today, there are others with me.
Aber morgen, früh am Morgen,	But tomorrow, early in the morning,
Schlankes liebes Ästchen,	You slim, beautiful branch,

ak. [JGH] Christian Kelch, *Liefländische Historia, oder kurtze und eigentliche Beschreibung der Denckwürdigsten Friedens- und Krieges-Geschichte, So sich theils vor, theils nach der Liefländer Bekehrung zum Christenthum, biß auffs Jahr 1689 begeben* (Frankfurt am Main and Leipzig: Mener, 1695). [PVB] Heinz Rölleke suggests that "Jürri" would be the more correct spelling of the name.

Kannst du kommen ohne Sorgen,	You don't have to worry if you come,
Da bin ich alleine.	For then I'll be alone.
Wenn der Maienkäfer schwirret	When the June bug flitters about
Früh im kühlen Thaue!	In the cool morning thaw!
Hüpf ich, Liebe, dir entgegen	I'll hasten to you, my love,
Weißt, auf jener Aue.	On that you can depend.

The Estonian workers spend a substantial amount of their leisure time singing and making music. Song itself is actually the domain of women. There are women who specialize in singing at weddings. Men nonetheless join in with song once sufficient drink has spread the joy all around. When they are working in the fields, as well as at play, young women cry out with songs that spread joy shared by all. Some of them have good voices, and many demonstrate a natural disposition to song. This is more often the case with the Estonians than with the Latvians. Everything they sing is monophonic, but they do form two choruses, the first of which sings a melodic line, which the second group then repeats. They possess many different songs and melodies. In their wedding songs, they append a melodic tag to every line using the two words, *Kassike* and *Kanike*, which might have no meaning, but might also refer etymologically to a "cute kitten" [*schönes Kätzchen*] or to a "Maychen" (from "Maye," or young birch). The Latvians stretch out the last syllable a great deal, and sing in two parts when together, and thus some of them hum a sort of bass line against the others. The instrument that is the oldest and most typical of both Estonians and Latvians is the bagpipe, which they make themselves and play in two voices, with a great deal of volume and a strong sense of meter.[al]

They draw upon their customs and their way of life for their traditional sayings:[am]

> Gib die Sackpfeife in eines Narren Hände, er sprengt sie entzwei.
> Schätze den Hund nicht nach den Haaren, sondern nach den Zähnen.
> Ein nasses Land bedarf keines Wassers; d.i. betrübe die Betrübten nicht noch mehr.
> Niemand hält mich bei meinem Rockzipfel, d.i. ich bin keinem etwas schuldig.
> Wer bittet den Armen zur Hochzeit?
> Der Stumme (das Thier) muß wohl ziehen was der Unvernünftige auflegt.

---

al. [JGH] See August Wilhelm Hupel, *Topographische Nachrichten von Lief- und Esthland*, vol. 2 (Riga: Hartknoch, 1777), 133.

am. [JGH] There are many meaningful puzzles and sayings included in Gutsleff's *Estonian Grammar*. [PVB] Herder's reference is to Eberhard Gutsleff, *Kurzgefaßte Anweisung zur Esthnischen Sprache* (Halle: Orban, 1732).

Sey selbst ein Kerl, aber achte einen andern Kerl auch für einen Kerl.
Von des Reichen Krankheit und des Armen Bier hört man weit.
Die Noth treibt den Ochsen in den Brunn, u.a.m.
Put the bagpipe into the hands of a fool, and he'll break it in two.
Don't judge a dog on the basis of its hair, rather of its teeth.
Land with plenty of moisture needs no water; in other words, do not bring more sadness to those already sad.
No one holds me by the edge of my skirt; that means I am indebted to no one.
Who invites the poor to a wedding?
The dumb (the animal) must wear what those who are not clever leave out.
Be a good guy, but recognize when someone else is a good guy.
One hears everywhere about the rich and their illnesses, and about the poor and their beer.
Danger drives the ox into the well, etc.

Many Estonians have a predilection toward poetry, even in the ways they speak. When they create poetry, it immediately turns to song: this is folkloric proof that, among preliterate peoples, it is impossible to separate poetry and music. The improvisatory poet sings a verse aloud, and immediately everyone present repeats it. It is hardly surprising that many random words find their way into song in this way. They like to fill their songs with words of insult, and few Germans really know what this is about, all the more so because there are many names used by the Estonians to insult the Germans. Such songs cross from one area into another. Most of all they like to take advantage of words that make fun of the poor who spend very little for their weddings. It does not take much to bring shame and tears to the eyes of those they insult. Generally their songs do not make use of rhyme. The Estonians possess many different kinds of words for the ends of lines, which they attach to the end of every verse in many songs. At a feast they sing the praises of the generous tavern keeper and the like. A German rarely understands everything in the improvised songs, because many of the words are improperly used. It is possible to understand songs that one hears again and again.[an]

2. *On Latvian Songs* "Singe, dseesma"—"Sacred Song." Something sung, a song.[ao] I do not know if the latter word is even known to the older Latvians. One uses it now quite widely to designate a sacred church song.

---

an. [JGH] See August Wilhelm Hupel, *Topographische Nachrichten*, 157–58.

ao. [PVB] Herder's use of "Ein Gesang, Lied," signals his attempt to compare and contrast the meanings implicit in the two formulations. There is no comparable pair of contrastive terms in English.

"Singe," however, is the name with which the Latvians refer to their secular songs.[ap] The poetry and music of the Latvians is special, for it refers to nature, which was and still is song's instructor. Latvian poetry has rhyme, but only masculine. When one word occurs repetitively, one instance following another, it is for the Latvians already a rhyme. Thus we find it in one of their love songs:

Es, pa zellu raudadams	Weeping along the way,
gahju, tewi mekledams.	I am looking for you.

And that is considered a good rhyme. With the exception of their urban songs, which is to say those sung at certain festive occasions, they improvise most of their poesy. The urban songs possess all the satirical, sometimes also malicious, humor of English street songs. In contrast, their love songs possess all the tenderness that can be afforded to gentle melancholy; they know the intimate, thoughtful connections that are able at first to move the heart such that it touches their song in very basic ways. They lack feminine rhymes entirely, though their language is fully capable of producing them, as current sacred songs in translation reveal. Their music is crude and undeveloped. They choose one or two girls who sing the text, and the others sustain a single pitch, something like that of a bagpipe's drone. The girls who sing actually do not extend their range beyond a third, and this arrangement continues until the text comes to its end. The moment the basses sing the fundamental tone at the octave, the song is over.[aq]

"Miklah"—"A Riddle." The pleasurable display of knowledge to express these true jokes is very well known and customary among the Latvians, and it was probably even better known among their ancestors. We know that all earlier peoples loved to pass the time in this way, and that many earlier writers transmitted to us their attempts accurately to invent such riddles. Readers who are aware of the exact attention to the double nature of two things know how one can be hidden inside the other. What precision it takes not to overstep the *tertium comparationis*. And what care it requires to choose the expression that really fits a puzzle, so that the listener immediately grasps the perfect similarity between the reflection and the original. They will find it amazing that they are among an innocent, uneducated

---

ap. [PVB] Etymologically, "Singe" is a loan word from German.

aq. [JGH] See Johann Jakob Harder, *Untersuchung des Gottesdienstes, der Wissenschaften, Handwerke, Regierungsarten und Sitten der alten Letten, und ihrer Sprache (Gelehrte Beyträge zu den Rigischen Anzeigen)* (Riga: Hartknoch, 1764), ex. 12.

people capable of making such fine jokes that would be an honor for even the cleverest nations. They understand puzzles that possess all the true characteristics of this genre. Some puzzles reveal themselves to be of great age, and they were probably inherited from their ancestors. Take the following example.

"DER MOHNKOPF" / "THE HEAD OF A POPPY"

Ich keimte! als ich gekeimt hatte, wuchs ich,	I sprouted! When I had sprouted, I grew
Als ich gewachsen war, ward ich ein Mädchen,	When I had grown, I was a girl,
Als ich ein Mädchen geworden war, ward ich ein altes Weib,	When I had become a girl, I was a young woman,
Als ich eine junge Frau geworden war, Ward ich ein altes Weib,	When I had become a young woman, I was an old woman,
Als ich ein altes Weib geworden war, bekam ich erst Augen,	When I had become an old woman, I first received eyes,
Durch diese Augen kroch ich. selbst heraus	I crawled out through these eyes.[ar]

Latvians have an unconquerable predilection for poesy, and my mother does not deny that the Latvian language was already half poesy. Latvian sounds, she said, ring like a table bell, whereas German sounds like church bells. She could not deny that even the most uneducated Latvians spoke wisely and in verses when they are happy....[as]

There are many who believe that the Latvians still have traces of heroic songs. My father, however, does not support these claims:

> The genius of language, the genius of a nation lies in the genius of a shepherd. If they are crowned, it is with a sheaf of hay or at most with a wreath of grain, which is most appropriate for them. In my opinion, heroes are most at home in the North, where life is harder and where one must struggle against the climate almost every day. The Latvians might very well live under such conditions, but where is there any pull toward them? ... They would no doubt remain just as they are, should

---

ar. [PVB] The riddle relies on parallels between the growth of a poppy flower and that of a female from girlhood to maturity. The images rely on more general associations as well as those specific to Latvian folk culture, for example the common use of poppy flowers in wreaths worn by girls, which would be a familiar association in line 2.

as. [PVB] Herder's attribution of knowledge about Latvian songs to his mother provides one positive answer to ongoing debates about whether his mother was of Latvian heritage (see Jaremko-Porter 2009).

there be for them at the very least the soil of freedom and fame. In Kurland [Latvian, Kurzeme],[at] freedom and slavery are both at home....

My father, however, was hardly a great artist with the Latvian language. Someone who commands the full length and breadth of a language can speak with authority. Surely he was never able to gain a foothold in the heroic songs, but claimed there was evidence that the most distant ancestors had sung them. Where does one find a people, he asked, who do not sing them? He had, as he called it, collected a sheaf of tender songs, his translations of which I have in my possession, which I am able to share, and which reveal a departure from the very un-German Opitz of Pastor Johann Wischmann.[au] If I did not have this sheaf in my own hands, I should probably not accept the judgment about making this designation. My father was, after all, not a real Latvian from Kurzeme. Dominating these songs was a tender, peasant character, for the folk making them their own. The translation bears the earmarks of my father.[av]

3. *On Lithuanian Songs*   It will be annoying for many to read here that to this underdeveloped, crude language one must attribute delicacy. There is, however, something of the character of Greek loveliness in Lithuanian. The frequent use of diminutive forms and the combination of many vowels with the letters *l, r*, and *t* make it sweeter than the harsh sequence of three consonants that one finds in Polish. Especially evident from this is the Dainos or Oden created for the simple maiden, for just about any occasion.[aw]

4. *On the Laments from Greenland*   After the burial of the dead, those in attendance go into the house of the deceased, sit down quietly, place their arms on their knees, and lay their heads in their hands; the women, however, place their hands over their faces, while everyone sobs and weeps in the silence of the house. Then the father or the son, or whoever is the next of kin, gives a eulogy in a loud, mournful voice, in which all the positive

---

   at. [PVB] Kurland is the German name for the southern Baltic coastal areas of Latvia that were extensively settled by German speakers.
   au. [PVB] Herder's own footnote reads: Perhaps there are more, which I know and which the sheaf contains, than Herr Opitz wishes to see.
   av. [JGH] See Theodor Gottlieb von Hippel, *Lebensläufe nach aufsteigender Linie*, vol. 1 (Berlin: C. F. Voss, 1779), 72–74.
   aw. [JGH] See Philipp Ruhig, *Litauisch-Deutsches und Deutsch-Litauisches Lexicon: Nebst einer historischen Betrachtung der Litauischen Sprache* (Königsberg: Hartung, 1747), 74–75. [PVB] For a thorough study of Herder's own engagement with Latvian song and a critical assessment of Herder's publications in Latvian reception history, see Jaremko-Porter 2009.

characteristics of the deceased are listed, and which is punctuated at the end of every section by loud sobbing and crying. After this kind of lament, the women continue sobbing and crying, all of them in unison descending by half steps to the fifth below. At those moments during which they restrain themselves, the real singer inserts a few meaningful words into the song; the men, however, continue only to sob.

The style, or way, in which they speak possesses none of the exaggeration, emphatic tone, or bombast of the Oriental, which one experiences also among the native peoples of America, but rather is simple and natural. Instead they take advantage of the similarities, while not employing extensive contrasts in their speaking, even when they must repeat a subject right away for the sake of clarity. They often speak so laconically that, though they have no difficulties understanding themselves, foreigners can barely understand them, even with many years of experience.

They frequently possess a range of figurative ways of speaking and proverbs, and the *Angekoks*[ax] express themselves with metaphors and phrases often quite contrary to the expected sense, so that they sound learned when speaking and also so that they will be appropriately paid for interpreting the oracles. Accordingly they refer to a stone as "that which is big and hard," to the water as "that which is soft," and to a mother as "a sack."

In their poesy they use neither rhyme nor syllable length. Their sentences are short, but they are still sung according to a certain beat or cadence. Between each sentence a chorus will interject with multiple repetitions of the phrase "Amna ayah ayah hey!"[ay]

5. *On Sámi Song*   It is called "Mårse fauros." At this time the young suitor again visits his lover, and while he is on his way to her he entertains himself with a love song, thus avoiding boredom. For the most part they do not take care to sing such songs according to specific tunes; rather, each chooses the ones he feels are best. They sing them, moreover, quite differently, sometimes one way, at other times another way, depending on what is pleasing at a given moment.[az]

---

ax. [PVB] A type of medicine man.

ay. [PVB] Herder bases this passage on David Cranz, *Historie von Grönland* (Barby and Leipzig: H.D. Ebers, 1765), part 3, pp. 48 and 44. It was his Königsberg teacher, Johann Georg Hamann, who drew his attention to Cranz's history.

az. [PVB] The preceding section appears in the 1975 edition of *Volkslieder* on pp. 235–42. Herder writes this passage in Latin. His source is Johannes Scheffer, *Lapponia, id est Regionis Lapponum et gentis nova et verissima descriptio* (Frankfurt am Main: M. Hallervorden, 1673), 282.

CONCLUDING PROSE OF *VOLKSLIEDER* (1779)[ba]

And at this point we have enough folk songs, or perhaps even many too many. The preface has already clarified how the editor made his decisions, and what he intended to achieve. Despite all these different decisions and best intentions, it is not even half possible to gather all the pieces from all times, nor is it possible that the songs of all peoples are equally good, especially of the same quality according to the standards of a reader, much less a judge of art, who looks at the collection in a single sitting, seeking the qualities that justify a book. Every rational being will view each song according his or her own place and time, not according to what a piece in and of itself should be, that is, not by reading straight through the volumes as a dizzying representation of all peoples everywhere. What does not manage to please one reader is still there for others. I pass no judgment that some pieces are not to a certain degree remarkable. I could wax eloquently, should I wish to speak about the value that many of the decaying branches of our own poesy might acquire if nourished by the dew that falls from foreign clouds. Still, I leave this to the reader and the student who desire to use and apply my efforts, the happiness and endeavors of earlier, lonelier, and past years. I began early on to collect what would become a history of lyrical song, and I disdained nothing that would not serve this end. This goal, too, combined with the obstinacy of chance, led me to include much that otherwise might never have appeared in these volumes. Whoever speaks about folk songs also comes to understand her or his own time and all that is part of it, even after ceasing to speak about folk songs. In my case, I have now reached the final songs, for over the course of many years I myself have heard a sufficient number desecrated by the name folk song, so that I shall allow myself, if modestly, to claim that I have reached my initial goal, and thus with my own island lying before me, I might swim in the lap of blue Thetis.[bb] ... The muse of the Mantuan[bc] calls out to me:

... let us henceforth sing of matters transcendent,
no longer of the bushes and shrubs that lie low upon the ground.

And thus, farewell my own folk songs, bad as they may be, and those of the common person, better as they are!

---

ba. [PVB] The conclusion follows the final song, "Evening Song": no. 30 in that volume, no. 15 in the anthology that follows as the appendix to chapter 2 (in the 1975 edition, pp. 366–67).
bb. [PVB] A Greek sea nymph and goddess of the water.
bc. [PVB] The Latin poet Virgil (70–19 BCE).

APPENDIX A
Introduction to the Folk Song Texts

PHILIP V. BOHLMAN

In none of Johann Gottfried Herder's writings was his concept of folk song more comprehensive, complex, and contradictory than in the two editions of his *Volkslieder* (1778/79 and 1807), and it is the goal of the anthology that follows to capture as much of Herder's intent as possible, and to convey it further through English translations of twenty-four songs I believe key to Herder's folk song project. Several principles guided me as I chose a representative sample from the 194 that filled the second edition, entitled *Stimmen der Völker in Liedern* (Voices of the People in Song), edited by Johann von Müller, with the assistance of Herder's wife, Karoline, and published by Cotta in Tübingen. Above all I apply the principles here to give the reader a sense of what it was like to encounter this most comprehensive gathering of vocal works understood not only as the first collection of folk songs, but also as a representative anthology of world music, consciously locating and organizing the texts of individual songs in the historical and contemporary contexts from which they were drawn. We are not left to speculate about Herder's choices and organizational plan, for he annotated the songs himself, citing sources, explaining his decisions for inclusion, and clarifying the historical and scientific contribution of his folk song project.

First of all, the twenty-four folk songs in this anthology follow the order and organization in the first and second editions (1778/79 and 1807). This order reflects the serial appearance of the songs in the first edition especially, which the Leipzig publisher Weygand gathered in folios that would be gathered as six books in two parts. The order of folk songs that follows here reflects a dynamic that stretches over much of two years. The addition of songs to the second edition, especially the inclusion of an appendix, further enhances the dynamic of a Herder whose concept of folk song underwent considerable change and growth, especially an expansion beyond a

Europe bounded by literate and historical practices. The density of songs from Eastern European and Baltic sources increases as the individual books appear chronologically, as does the appearance of songs from non-European sources, notably Africa and South America, in the 1807 appendix.

Second, in the anthology that follows I attempt to include songs that illustrate the themes, subjects, and genres that were most important for Herder. Some of Herder's larger themes are easy to identify, whereas others are more difficult to specify. There is overlap between some, whereas others are more distinctive, emerging only later in Herder's life. Schematically the themes upon which I have drawn for this anthology are the following: 1) *historical folk songs*, especially those described by Herder as "old" or "ancient" in the 1774 *Alte Volkslieder* (see chapter 1 in the present volume); 2) *European balladry and narrative songs*, not only German ballads from historical sources, but Spanish and French *romances* and epic song from northern and southeastern Europe; 3) *German songs* in general, not only historical, but also lyrical songs in local and regional dialect, hence vernacular; 4) *Nordic songs* in general, as with the German songs, from both historical (e.g., epics from Greenland) and vernacular sources (e.g., the many songs by the *Skalden*, bards chronicling everyday life); 5) *songs from English-language sources*, not only Shakespeare, but earlier volumes of English folk song (e.g., those by Thomas Percy and Thomas d'Urfey); 6) *Scottish songs*, some narrative, but more important for Herder's conscious employment of translation theory, those from the Ossian debates (see also chapters 4 and 5 in the present volume); and 7) *songs from colonial and global sources*, those that express Herder's engagement with music beyond Europe.

Third, I also attempt to include the folk song genres that emerge during the course of the folk song project. Some of these genres are Herder's own, and they reflect the literary and musical culture of his day. Narrative genres, especially the ballad, appear frequently in the earliest stages of publication and illustrate the ways in which the folk songs were components in a more extensive counterpoint with contemporary literary practices (e.g., of Goethe and Matthias Claudius). Certain other genres are applicable retrospectively from the reception history of Herder's folk song project, especially those that take cultural context and ethnographic analysis into consideration. Although I make the case throughout this book that Herder's understanding of music was expanding globally, observations about his use of world music and related genres are specifically my own.

The final motivation for the choice of these twenty-four songs reflects the impact of the folk song project in its day and on subsequent histories of music and nationalism. Several songs are among the first instances of genres that will be influential during the nineteenth century (e.g., "Lament of the Noble Wife of Hassan Aga," a Dalmatian epic from the medieval Balkan tradition critically important for the emergence of epic as a genre of nationalism in the nineteenth century). The counterpoint between literary and vernacular songs—German ballads in *Hochdeutsch* and lyrical songs in regional dialect—breaks down social and national barriers while at times reimagining them as political and nationalist borders. Most critical of all, Herder's folk song project opened a cultural and historical space cohabited by difference, musical and national. To the degree that twenty-four folk songs from Herder's own anthology can evoke the most critical dimensions of that space, they too gather music to sound the growing encounter with the world on the eve of the era of nationalism.

APPENDIX B

From the Folk Song Texts

JOHANN GOTTFRIED HERDER,
TRANSLATED BY PHILIP V. BOHLMAN

Volkslieder (1778/79)

Part 1, Book 1

1. [1]A "DAS LIED VOM JUNGEN GRAFEN" / "THE SONG OF THE YOUNG COUNT"

German[b]

Ich steh auf einem hohen Berg	I stood high upon a mountain,
Seh 'nunter ins tiefe Thal,	Looking down into the deep valley,
Da sah ich ein Schifflein schweben,	There, I saw a little ship sailing,
Darinn drey Grafen sass'n.	Therein were sitting three counts.
Der allerjüngst, der drunter war,	The youngest among the three,
Die in dem Schifflein sass'n,	Who were sitting in the ship,
Der gebot seiner Lieben zu trinken	He ordered his beloved to take
Aus einem venedischen Glas.[c]	A drink from a Venetian glass.
"Was giebst mir lang zu trinken,	"What are you so slowly giving me to drink,
Was schenkst du mir lang ein?	What pour you so slowly into my glass?

---

a. [PVB] For the purposes of the anthology I designate the songs first with their order of appearance in the anthology and then with a bracketed number for their appearance in the respective book within a volume of Herder's 1807 edition. When the published anthology includes no bracketed number, there is also no bracketed number in the translation.

b. [JGH] From the voices of the people in Alsace. The melody is sad and touching. It is almost a hymn in its simplicity.

c. [JGH] According to tradition, a glass that poisoned the drink it contained.

Ich will jezt in ein Kloster gehn,	I wish now to enter a cloister,
Will Gottes Dienerin seyn."	I wish to be God's servant."
"Willst du jetzt in ein Kloster gehn,	"You wish now to enter a cloister,
Willst Gottes Dienerin seyn,	You wish to be God's servant.
So geh in Gottes Namen;	Then go in the name of God;
Deins gleichen giebts noch mehr!"	There is no longer one to compare with you!"
Und als es war um Mitternacht,	And as midnight approached,
Dem jung'n Graf träumts so schwer,	The young count had troubling dreams,
Als ob sein allerliebster Schaz	As if his dearest sweetheart
Ins Kloster gezogen wär.	Would be taken to the cloister.
"Auf Knecht, steh auf und tummle dich;	"Get up, my servant, and hasten;
Sattl' unser beide Pferd!	Saddle up both of our horses!
Wir wollen reiten, sey Tag oder Nacht;	We must ride, be it day or night;
Die Lieb ist reitens werth!"	My beloved is worth the journey!"
Und da sie vor jen's Kloster kamen,	And as they arrived at that cloister,
Wohl vor das hohe Thor,	At the foot of the high gate,
Fragt er nach jüngst der Nonnen,	He asked about the youngest of the nuns,
Die in dem Kloster war.	Who were in the cloister.
Das Nönnlein kam gegangen	The young nun approached
In einem schneeweissen Kleid;	In a snow-white dress;
Ihr Häärl war abgeschnitten,	Her hair was fully shorn,
Ihr rother Mund war bleich.	Her red mouth was pale.
Der Knab er sezt sich nieder,	The youth sat down,
Er saß auf einem Stein;	He sat upon a stone;
Er weint die hellen Thränen,	Bright tears flowed from his eyes,
Brach ihm sein Herz entzwey.	His heart was torn in two.

2. [8] "ZAID UND ZAIDA" / "ZAID AND ZAIDA"

Spanish[d]

Durch die Strasse seiner Dame	Through the streets on which his lady lived

d. [PVB] Herder's source for "Zaid and Zaida" is Ginez Péres de Hita, *Historia de los vandos de los Zegries, y Abencerrages, cavalleros moros de Granad, de las civiles guerras* (Barcelona: S. deCormellas, 1647). With two successive variants of "Zaid and Zaida" Herder illustrates his basic approach to Spanish *romances*, in this case also one with Arabic versions in its history from al-Andalus. The Arabic Zaid/Said is etymologically related to the Spanish Cid (see chapter 8).

Wandelt Zaid auf und nieder,	Paced Zaid back and forth,
Harrend, daß die Stunde komme,	Waiting for the hour to come,
Endlich komme, sie zu sprechen.	Finally to come, so that he might speak with her.
Und schon geht der Mohr verzweifelnd,	And, in doubt, the Moor was already thinking
Da es sich so lange zögert,	That it had been such a long delay,
Denket: nur von ihr ein Anblick	He thought: If I could but once glance upon her,
Wird all meine Flammen kühlen....	All my flames would be quelled....
Und da sieht er sie! Am Fenster	And then he saw her there!
Tritt hervor sie, wie die Sonne	She approached the window
Aufgeht in dem Ungewitter,	Like the run rising after the storm,
Wie der Mond im Dunkel aufgeht.	Like the moon rising in the night.
Leise tritt ihr Zaid näher:	Quietly Zaid drew closer to her:
Alla mit dir, schöne Mohrin!	Allah be with you, lovely Moor!
Ist es wahr, was meine Pagen,	Is it true, what my pages,
Deine Dienerinnen sagen?	What your servants say?
Sagen: Du willt mich verlassen,	They say you wish to leave me,
Wollest einem schnöden Mohren,	That you desire a despicable Moor,
Der von deines Vaters Gütern	Barely arrived from your father's
Kaum noch ankam, dich vermählen?	Estates, who wishes to marry you?
Ist es wahr, o schönste Zaida?	Is it true, oh lovely Zaida?
Sage mir es, täusche mich nicht,	Tell me, do not deceive me,
Wolle mir es nicht verhelen,	Do not keep in secret from me,
Was so laut ja alle wissen!	What all others so clearly know!
Tiefgebeugt erwiedert Zaida:	Humbly bowing, Zaida responds:
Ja, mein Guter, es ist Zeit nun,	Yes, good man, it is now the time,
Daß sich dein' und meine Freundschaft	To end the friendship between us,
Trenne, weil es alle wissen.	What all others so clearly know.
Um und an bin ich verlohren,	How miserably I'd be lost,
Wenn die Sache weiter fortgeht,	Should we thus continue,
Alla weiß, wie es mich schmerzet,	Allah knows how it pains me,
Wies mich drücket, dich zu lassen.	How it weighs upon me, to leave you.
Du weist wohl, wie ich dich liebte,	You well know how much I love you,
Troz des Widerspruchs der Meinen,	Despite opposition from my family,

Weist, was ich mit meiner Mutter	You know how my mother
Für Verdruß und Kummer hatte,	Would despair and sorrow,
Wenn ich dich zu Nacht erharrte,	Should I wait for you into the night,
Harrte, dich noch spät zu sehen;	Waiting much too late to see you;
Dies auf Einmal mir zu enden,	To end this for me once and for all,
Wollen sie jezt—mich vermählen.	She wants you now—to marry me.
Bald wird eine andre Dame	Soon there will be another woman
Schön und artig dein seyn, Zaid,	For you, Zaid, pretty and polite,
Die dich liebet, die du liebest,	Who will love you, and you will love her,
Weil du es verdienst, o Zaid.	Because you have earned it, oh Zaid.
Tiefgebeugt der Mohr erwiedert,	Humbly bowing, the Moor responds,
Hingedrückt von tausend Kummer:	Weighed down by a thousand sorrows:
"Nicht versteh' ichs, schöne Zaida,	"I don't understand, beautiful Zaida,
Wie du mit mir also handelst?	Why you are treating me thus?
Nicht versteh' ichs, wie du also	I don't understand how you can thus
Wechselst meine treue Liebe?	Exchange my true love?
Einem häßlich schlechten Mohren,	For an ugly, common Moor,
Der so grossen Guts nicht werth ist.	Whose huge estates have such little value.
Warst du's, die auf dieser Stelle	Was it not you, who on this very spot,
Zu mir sprach, noch jenen Abend?	Spoke to me on that very evening?
Dein bin ich, dein bin ich ewig!	I am yours, I am yours forever!
Dein, o du mein Leben, Zaid!"	Yours, oh, you, my life, Zaid!"

3. [21] "DIE DREY FRAGEN" / "THE THREE QUESTIONS"

A STREET SONG

English[e]

Es war ein Ritter, er reist durchs Land,	There was a knight, who traveled throughout the land,

---

e. [JGH] From the English collection of songs and ballads [by Thomas d'Urfey] called *Wit and Mirth: Or Pills to Purge Melancholy; Being a Collection of the Best Merry Ballads and Songs, Old and New*, vol. 2 (London: J. Tonson, 1712). The same song is included on page 129, with a melody called "a riddle wittily expounded." [PVB] "The Three Questions" is a variant of Child Ballad no. 1, "Riddles Wisely Expounded," best known in the modern setting as Simon and Garfunkel's "Scarborough Fair."

Er sucht ein Weib sich aus zur Hand.	In search of a wife he might make his own.
Er kam wohl vor ein'r Wittwe Thür,	He came to rest before a widow's door,
Drei schöne Töchter trat'n herfür.	Three daughters presented themselves.
Der Ritter, er sah, er sah sie lang;	The knight looked upon them, long and hard;
Zu wählen war ihm das Herz so bang.	His heart was too perplexed to allow a choice.
Wer antwort't mir der Fragen drei, Zu wissen, welch' die Meine sei?	Who will answer the three questions, Hence to know who will be mine?
"Leg vor, leg vor uns die Fragen drei,	"Pose for us, pose for us, the three questions,
Zu wissen, welch' die Deine Sey?"	Hence to know who will be yours?"
"O, was ist länger, als der Weg daher?	"Oh, what is longer than the journey here?
Oder was ist tiefer, als das tiefe Meer?	Or what is deeper than the deep sea?
Oder was ist lauter, als das laute Horn? Oder was ist schärfer, als der scharfe Dorn?	Or what is louder than the loud horn? Or what is sharper than the sharp thorn?
Oder was ist grüner, als grünes Gras? Oder was ist schlimmer, als ein Weibsbild was?"	Or what is greener than green grass? Or what is worse than a woman?"
Die erste, die Zweite sie sannen nach,	The first and the second thought a while,
Die Dritte, die jüngste, die Schönste sprach:	The third, the youngest and most beautiful, spoke:
"O lieb ist länger, als der Weg daher,	"Oh, love is longer than the journey here,
Und Höll ist tiefer, als das tiefe Meer.	And Hell is deeper than the deep sea.
Und Donner ist lauter, als das laute Horn, Und Hunger ist schärfer, als der scharfe Dorn.	And thunder is louder than the loud horn, And hunger is sharper than the sharp thorn.
Und Gift ist grüner als das grüne Gras,	And poison is greener than the green grass,

Und der Teufel ist ärger, als ein Weibsbild was."	And the devil is worse than a woman."
Kaum hatt sie die Fragen beantwort't so,	Scarcely had she the questions thus answered,
Der Ritter, er eilt und wählt sie froh.	Than the knight quickly made his happy choice.
Die Erste, die Zweite, die sannen nach,	The first and second thought a while,
Indeß ihn'n jezt ein Freier gebrach.	About what a suitor had brought to them.
Drum liebe Mädchen seyd auf der Hut,	Thus, dear maidens, be well prepared,
Frägt euch ein Freier, antwortet gut.	Should a suitor ask you, answer him well.

Part 1, Book 2

4. [6] "DIE JUDENTOCHTER" / "THE JEWISH DAUGHTER"

Scottish[f]

Der Regen, er rinnt durch Mirrilandstadt,	Rain was pouring down in Milan,
Rinnt ab und nieden der Po!	Flowing down into the Po!
So thun die Knaben in Mirrilandstadt,	In the same way, the boys play in Milan,
Zum Ballspiel rennen sie so.	When playing ball, they run the same.
Da 'naus und kam die Judentochter,	The Jewish daughter came outside,
Sprach: willt du nicht kommen hinein?	Saying: Won't you come inside?

---

    f. [PVB] Herder cites Percy's *Reliques of Ancient Poetry* (1765, part 1, 35) as his source for a European ballad from the widespread tradition of blood-libel narratives directed against Jews in Europe (for a critical treatment of the theme of blood libel against the Jews in music, see HaCohen 2011). He demonstrates his predilection for the Anglo-Scottish ballads rather than using German sources, which contain more songs with more sympathetic portrayals of Jews and Roms. Herder was familiar with the well-known ballad "Die Jüdin" (The Jewish Woman), which circulated in German and Yiddish also from the late Middle Ages to Herder's day and beyond to the twenty-first century. For historical and modern variants of the ballad from both Jewish and non-Jewish sources, see Bohlman and Holzapfel 2001, 15–23. In his note to the song Herder writes: [JGH] "A gruesome, dreadful fairy tale, which tells of a legend that has so often cost Jews both land and life. The sense of death and sorrow in the original is almost untranslatable."

"Ich will nicht kommen, ich kann nicht kommen Von allen Gespielen mein."	"I do not want to come, I cannot come away From all my playmates."
Sie schält einen Apfel, war roth und weiß, Zu locken den Knaben hinan. Sie schält einen Apfel, war weiß und roth, Das süsse Kind der gewann.	She peeled an apple, it was red and white, To draw the boy to her. She peeled an apple, it was white and red, It won over the sweet child.
Und aus und zog sie ein spizig Mess'r, Sie hatt's versteckt beiher; Sie stachs dem jungen Knaben ins Herz, Kein Wort sprach nimmer er mehr.	And she pulled out a pointed knife, She had it hidden with her; She stabbed the young boy in the heart, He never again uttered a word.
Und aus und kam das dick dick Blut,	And the thick, thick blood flowed forth,
Und aus und kam es so dünn, Und aus und kam 's Kinds Herzensblut; Da war kein Leben mehr in.	And out it flowed so thin, And out flowed blood from the child's heart; It no longer contained any life.
Sie legt' ihn auf ein Schlachtbrett hin,	She laid him out on a butcher's block,
Schlacht't ihn ein Christenschwein,	Butchering him like a Christian swine.
Sprach lachend: "geh und spiele nun da Mit allen Gespielen dein!"	Laughing aloud: "Go now and play With all your playmates!"
Sie rollt ihn in ein'n Kasten Blei; "Nun schlaf da!" lachend sie rief;	She stuffed him in a leaden chest; "Now sleep here!" she called out, laughing;
Sie warf ihn in ein'n tiefen Brunn, War funfzig Faden tief.	She tossed him into a deep well, It was fifty fathoms deep.
Als Betglock klang und die Nacht eindrang, Jede Mutter nun kam daheim; Jede Mutter hatt' ihren herzlieben Sohn, Nur Mutter Anne hatt kein'n.	As the prayer bells chimed and night drew nigh, Every mother now came home; Every mother had her dear, sweet son, Only mother Anne had none.
Sie rollt ihren Mantel um sich her, Fing an zu weinen sehr,	She wrapped herself in her coat, And began bitterly to weep,

Sie rann so schnell ins Juden Castell,	She ran quickly to the castle of the Jews,
Wo keiner, ach! wachte mehr:	Where no one, ah!, remained awake:
"Mein liebster Hönne, mein guter Hönne,	"My dearest Hugh,[g] my fine Hugh,
Wo bist du? antwort mir!"	Where are you? Answer me?"
"O Mutter, o rennt zum Ziehbrunn tief,	"Oh, mother, run to the well so deep,
Euren Sohn da findet ihr!"	You'll find your son there!"

Mutter Anne rann zum tiefen Brunn,	Mother Anne ran to the well so deep,
Sie fiel danieder aufs Knie!	She fell down upon her knees!
"Mein liebster Hönne, mein guter Hönne,	"My dearest Hugh, my fine Hugh,
O antwortet, bist du hier?"	Oh, answer, are you here?"

"Der Brunn ist wunder tief, o Mutter,	"The well is extremely deep, oh mother,
Der Bleikast wunder schwer;	The leaden chest extremely heavy;
Ein scharf, spiz Messer geht durch mein Herz;	A sharp, pointed knife pierces my heart;
Kein Wort sprech nimmer ich mehr.	I'll never again utter a word.

Geh heim, geh heim, mein' Mutter theur,	Go home, go home, my dear mother,
Mach' mir mein Leichenkleid,	Sew for me a shroud,
Daheim da hinter Mirrilandstadt	At home, there beyond Milan,
Komm' ich an eure Seit."	I'll be again at your side."

5. [17] "MORGENGESANG IM KRIEGE" / "MORNING SONG DURING WAR"

Skaldic[h]

Tag bricht an!	It's daybreak!
Es kräht der Hahn,	The cock crows,
Schwingt's Gefieder;	It brandishes its plumage;
Auf, ihr Brüder!	Rise up, brothers!
Ist Zeit zur Schlacht!	It is time for battle!
Erwacht, erwacht!	Awaken, awaken!

---

g. [PVB] "Hönne" is an endearing form of "Johannes" or "Hannes." Percy uses "Hew" for the boy's name, hence my translation using the more modern "Hugh."
h. [JGH] Source: Thomas Bartholin, *Antiquitatum Danicarum de causis contemptae a Danis adhuc gentilibus mortis libri tres* (Copenhagen: Literis Joh. Phil. Bockenhoffer, 1689), 178.

Unverdrossen	Indefatigable
Der Unsern Führer!	In service to our leader!
Des hohen Adils	Fellow soldiers
Kampfgenossen,	So very noble,
Erwacht, erwacht!	Awaken, awaken!
Har mit der Faust hart,	Prepare to strike hard with the fist,
Rolf, der Schütze,	Rolf, the defender,
Männer im Blize,	Men moving with lightning speed,
Die nimmer fliehn!	Who never flee!
Zum Weingelage,	I'm not waking you
Zum Weibsgekose	For an evening
Weck ich euch nicht;	Of wine and women;
Zu harter Schlacht	But for the hard battle ahead,
Erwacht, erwacht!	Awaken, awaken!

Part 1, Book 3

6. [11] "ANS RENNTHIER" / "TO THE REINDEER"
Sámi (Lappländisch)[i]

Kulnasaz,[j] Rennthierchen, lieb Rennthierchen,	Kulnasaz, reindeer, dear reindeer,
Laß uns flink seyn,	Let's hasten our pace.
Laß uns fliegen, bald an Stell' und Ort seyn!	Let's fly, and we'll soon reach our goal!
Sümpfe sind noch weit daher,	The marshes are a long way away,
Und haben fast kein Lied mehr.	And they have almost no song left.
Sieh da, dich mag ich leiden, Kaiga-See,	See there, I wish to reach you, Lake Kaiga,

---

i. [JGH] Source: Johannes Scheffer, *Lapponia, id est Regionis Lapponum et gentis nova et verissima descriptio* (Frankfurt am Main: M. Hallervorden, 1673), 282. [PVB] Herder's interest in the Sámi took several forms, first, because of the historical *longue durée* of Nordic Europe, and second, through the traditional practices of Indigenous peoples, in this case the Sámi. Though the practice of singing to animals, generally referred to as *yoiking*, is traditional among the Sámi, this song employs lexical words rather than vocables, perhaps to attribute meaning to it for the German reader. Herder also includes a different Sámi song, incorrectly attributed to Scheffer via its publication in German by Ewald Christian von Kleist, in "Extract from Correspondence about Ossian and the Songs of Ancient Peoples," the first part of *Von deutscher Art und Kunst* (JGHW2 1993, 460). The original German and my English translation appear in chapter 4 of the present volume (p. 153).

j. [PVB] A term of Sámi intimacy.

Leb wohl, du guter Kailva-See,	Farewell, you good Lake Kailva,
Viel schlägt mir's schon das Herze	My heart already beats
Auf'm lieben Kaiga-See.	In anticipation of dear Lake Kaiga.
Auf, Rennthierchen, liebes, auf,	Arise, dear little reindeer, arise,
Fliege, fliege deinen Lauf!	Fly, fly as you race!
Daß wir bald an Stell' und Ort seyn,	That we'll soon reach our goal,
Bald uns unsrer Arbeit freun.	Soon rejoice in our labors.
Bald ich meine Liebe seh –	Soon I'll see my beloved—
Auf, Rennthierchen, blick und sieh!	Arise, little reindeer, look all about you!
Kulnasazlein, siehst du sie	Dear Kulnasaz, don't you see
Nicht schon baden?	Her bathing already?

7. [24] "KLAGGESANG VON DER EDLEN FRAU DES ASAN-AGA" / "LAMENT OF THE NOBLE WIFE OF HASSAN AGA"[k]

Serbian[l]

Was ist weisses dort am grünen Walde?	What shines so brightly in the green forest?
Ist es Schnee wohl, oder sind es Schwäne?	Is it white snow, or is it the white of swans?

k. [PVB] "Lament of the Noble Wife of Hassan Aga" remains a part of twenty-first-century Balkan epic repertories. In 2003, Nada Petković and I recorded a performance by the Montenegrin American *guslar*, Boro Roganović, at the University of Chicago and published it in 2012 (Bohlman and Petković 2012, 331–34) together with a sound recording. The introductory section of this song from the fourteenth-century epic about the battle between the Serbs and the Ottoman army on the plains of Kosovo appears below in Montenegrin Serbian together with Nada Petković's translation of Boro Roganović's performance. The similarity to the Dalmatian version Herder has chosen, differing only slightly in the total number of stiches and in the narrative itself, is striking.

"Хасанагиница" / "The Wife of Hassan Aga"
(Under the Ottoman Empire)

Шта се б'јели у гори зеленој?	What shines so white there in the green forest?
Ал' је сниjег, ал' су лабудови?	Is it white snow or a flock of white swans?
Да је сниjег, већ би окопнио,	If it were snow, it would have melted now;
лабудови већ би полетјели.	if it were swans, they would have flown away.
Нит' је сниjег, нит' су лабудови,	It is not snow, nor is it the white swans;
него шатор аге Хасан-аге;	it is a tent of Hassan Aga.
он болује од љутијех рана.	He lies there ill with grievous battle wounds.
Облази га мати и сестрица,	Both his mother and his sister are there,
а љубовца од стида не могла.	but not his wife, for she is too ashamed.

l. [PVB] Herder calls the Dalmatian dialect of Serbian in which this epic from the *Kosovo Cycle* was published "Morlakisch."

Wär es Schnee da, wäre weggeschmolzen,	If it were snow, it would have already melted;
Wären's Schwäne, wären weggeflogen.	If it were swans, they would have flown away.
Ist kein Schnee nicht, es sind keine Schwäne.	It is neither snow, nor is it the white of swans.
'S ist der Glanz der Zelten Asan Aga;	It is the brightness of Hassan Aga's tent;
Niederliegt er drein an seiner Wunde.	He lies within it, suffering mortal wounds.
Ihn besucht die Mutter und die Schwester,	His mother and sister visit him there,
Schamhaft säumt sein Weib zu ihm zu kommen.	His wife is too ashamed to come.
Als nun seine Wunde linder wurde,	Once his wounds had begun to heal,
Ließ er seinem treuen Weibe sagen:	He sends word to his faithful wife:
"Harre mein nicht mehr an meinem Hofe,	"Don't wait any longer for me at my court,
Nicht am Hofe, und nicht bei den Meinen!"	Neither at my court, nor among my people!"
Als die Frau dies harte Wort vernommen,	While this lady receives these cruel words,
Stand die treue starr und voller Schmerzen,	She stands there, firm in faith and full of pain,
Hört der Pferde Stampfen vor der Thüre,	The hooves of horses are heard before the door,
Und es deucht ihr, Asan käm', ihr Gatte,	And it seems that Hassan, her husband, came,
Springt zum Thurme, sich herab zu stürzen.	She rushes to throw herself from the tower.
Ängstlich folgen ihr zwei liebe Töchter,	Her two dear daughters followed her,
Rufen nach ihr, weinend bittre Thränen:	Calling out to her, weeping with bitter tears:
"Sind nicht unsers Vaters Asans Rosse!	"It is not our father Hassan's steed!
Ist dein Bruder Pintorowich kommen."	His brother, Pintorović, has come to us."
Und es kehrt zurück die Gattin Asans,	And the wife of Hassan Aga returns,
Schlingt die Arme jammernd um den Bruder:	Tormented, she throws her arms around the brother:
"Sieh die Schmach, o Bruder, deiner Schwester!	"Oh brother, see the disgrace of your sister!

Mich verstossen! Mutter dieser Fünfte!"	Disown me! The mother of these five!"
Schweigt der Bruder und zieht aus der Tasche,	The brother is silent and pulls from his pocket,
Eingehüllet in hochrothe Seide,	Wrapped in dark red silk,
Ausgefertiget den Brief der Scheidung,	A writ of annulment, filled out,
Daß sie kehre zu der Mutter Wohnung,	That she can return to her mother's home,
Frei sich einem andern zu ergeben.	Free to offer herself to another.
Als die Frau den Trauer-Scheidbrief sahe,	When the lady saw the writ of annulment,
Küßte sie der beyden Knaben Stirne,	She kissed both boys on their foreheads,
Küßt die Wangen ihrer beiden Mädchen.	She kissed both girls on their cheeks.
Aber, ach! vom Säugling in der Wiege	But ah! From the baby lying in the cradle
Kann sie sich im bittern Schmerz nicht reissen;	She cannot tear herself in bitter pain;
Reißt sie los der ungestüme Bruder,	The unmoved brother tears her away,
Hebt sie auf das muntre Roß behende,	Lifts her up to the brave steed,
Und so eilt er mit der bangen Frauen	And he hastens away with the unhappy woman,
Grad nach seines Vaters hoher Wohnung.	Straight to the noble home of his father.
Kurze Zeit war's, noch nicht sieben Tage,	The time was short, not even seven days,
Kurze Zeit gnug, von viel grossen Herren	It was time enough for many suitors
Liebe Frau in ihrer Wittwen Trauer,	To come to the widow in her mourning,
Liebe Frau zum Weib begehret wurde.	Who wished to win her hand in marriage.
Und der gröste war Imoskis Cadi.	And the greatest of all was the Cadi of Imotski.
Und die Frau bat weinend Bruder:	And the lady pleads, weeping with her brother:
"Ach, bei deinem Leben! bitt ich, Bruder:	"Oh, by your life! I beg of you, brother:
Gib mich keinen andern mehr zur Frauen,	Do not offer me as a wife to any others,

Daß das Wiedersehen meiner lieben Armen Kinder mir das Herz nicht breche."	So that my heart will not break When I once again see my poor children."
Ihre Reden achtet nicht der Bruder, Fest Imoskis Cadi sie zu trauen.	The brother pays no heed to her pleas, But gives her hand in marriage to the Cadi of Imotski.
Doch die Frau, sie bittet ihn unendlich: "Schicke wenigstens ein Blat, o Bruder,	Still, the lady pleads to him without ceasing: "At the very least, oh brother, send a letter,
Mit den Worten zu Imoskis Cadi: Dich begrüßt die junge Wittib freundlich,	Written to the Cadi of Imotski: The young widow greets you in friendship,
Und last durch dies Blat dich höchlich bitten,	And she pleads kindly with this letter,
Daß, wenn dich die Suaten her begleiten,	That, when your wedding party comes with you,
Du mir einen langen Schleier bringest, Daß ich mich vor Asans Haus verhülle,	You bring me a long veil, So that I may cover myself before Hassan's house,
Meine lieben Waisen nicht zu sehen."	And not see my dear orphaned children."
Kaum ersah der Cadi dieses Schreiben, Als er seine Suaten alle sammelt, Und zum Wege nach der Braut sich rüstet,	Scarcely had the Cadi seen this letter, As he gathered his full wedding party, And they hurried off to the bride,
Mit dem Schleier, den sie heischte, tragend.	Bearing the veil she had requested.
Glücklich kamen sie zur Fürstin Hause,	Joyfully, they arrived at the princely house,
Glücklich sie mit ihr vom Hause wieder;	Joyfully, she departed with them from the house;
Aber als sie Asans Wohnung nahten,	But as they approached Hassan Aga's home,
Sahn die Kinder oben ab die Mutter,	The children saw their mother from above,
Riefen: "Komm zu deinen Kindern wieder,	They called: "Return again to your children,
Iß mit uns das Brod in deiner Halle!"	Break bread with us in your own hall!"
Traurig hört es die Gemahlin Asans,	With sadness, the wife of Hassan Aga heard,

Kehrete sich zu der Suaten Fürsten:	She returned to the prince's wedding party:
"Bruder, laß die Suaten und die Pferde	"Brother, let the wedding party and the horses
Halten wenig vor der lieben Thüre,	Pause a bit before the dear doorway,
Daß ich meine Kleinen noch beschenke."	That I may offer my children presents."
Und sie hielten vor der lieben Thüre.	And they stopped before the dear doorway.
Und den armen Kindern gab sie Gaben,	And to the poor children they presented gifts,
Gab den Knaben goldgestickte Stiefel,	To the boys she gave gilded boots,
Gab den Mädchen lange reiche Kleider,	To the girls she gave flowing dresses,
Und dem Säugling hülflos in der Wiegen	And to the baby lying helpless in the cradle
Gab sie für die Zukunft auch ein Röckchen.	She also gave a little dress for the future.
Das beiseit sah Vater Asan Aga,	All this saw the father, Hassan Aga,
Rief gar traurig seinen lieben Kindern:	He called in sadness to his dear children:
"Kehrt zu mir, ihr lieben armen Kleinen,	"Return to me, you poor, dear children,
Eurer Mutter Brust ist Eisen worden,	Your mother's breast has turned to iron,
Fest verschlossen, kann nicht Mitleid fühlen!"	Her back turned away, she can feel no pity!"
Wie das hörte die Gemahlin Asans,	When the wife of Hassan Aga heard this,
Stürzt' sie bleich, den Boden schütternd, nieder,	She fell, pale and shaking, to the ground,
Und die Seel' entfloh dem bangen Busen,	And her soul departed from her wretched bosom,
Als sie ihre Kinder vor sich fliehn sah.	As she saw her children departing from her.

8. "SHAKESPEAR" / "SHAKESPEARE"[m]

Wie süß das Mondlicht auf dem Hügel schläft!	How sweet the moonlight sleeps upon this bank!

---

m. [PVB] Herder concludes part one of the folk song project as he begins it, with Shakespeare. The epigraph on the title page is taken from *Hamlet*, the final song in

Hier woll'n wir sizen, und den süssen Schall	Here will we sit and let the sounds of music
Zum Ohre lassen schlüpfen. Sanfte Stille	Creep in our ears: soft stillness and the night
Und Nacht wird Taste süsser Harmonie.	Become the touches of sweet harmony.
Siz, Jessika, sieh, wie die Himmelsflur	Sit, Jessica. Look how the floor of heaven
Ist eingelegt mit Stücken reichen Goldes!	Is thick inlaid with patines of bright gold:
Da ist kein kleiner Kreis, den du da siehst,	There's not the smallest orb which thou behold'st
Der nicht in seinem Lauf wie'n Engel singt,	But in his motion like an angel sings,
Stimmt ein ins Chor der jungen Cherubim.	Still quiring to the young-eyed cherubins;
Die Harmonie ist in den ew'gen Tönen;	Such harmony is in immortal souls;
Nur wir, so lang dies Kothkleid Sterblichkeit	But whilst this muddy vesture of decay
Uns grob einhüllet, können sie nicht hören. –	Doth grossly close it in, we cannot hear it.

. . .

Der Mann, der nicht Musik hat in ihm selbst,	The man that hath no music in himself,
Gerührt nicht wird vom Einklang süsser Töne,	Nor is not moved with concord of sweet sounds,
Zu Ränken, Raub, Verrath ist der gemacht;	Is fit for treasons, stratagems, and spoils;
Die Triebe seines Geistes sind wie Nacht,	The motions of his spirit are dull as night
Sein Herz ist Schwarz, wie Erebus –	And his affections dark as Erebus:
Trau nicht dem Manne!	Let no such man be trusted. Mark the music.

Volkslieder, part one, from *The Merchant of Venice*, here Lorenzo speaking to Jessica (act 5, scene 1). The influence of Shakespeare in shaping Herder's concept of folk song—sound, substance, and subject—is evident in the many texts he takes from Shakespeare to provide songs for the three books of part one. In this instance, "Shakespeare" stands outside the enumerated songs in the anthology, without number and placed epigrammatically as an epilogue. The English remains that of Shakespeare, with the German providing an interesting insight into the sound of the song as Herder realized it in translation.

Part 2, Book 1

9. [1] "DAS LIED VOM FISCHER" / "THE FISHERMAN'S SONG"

German[n]

Das Wasser rauscht', das Wasser schwoll,	The waters roared, the waves swelled,
Ein Fischer saß daran;	A fisherman sat upon them;
Sah nach dem Angel ruhevoll,	He gazed calmly upon his catch,
Kühl bis an's Herz hinan;	At peace in his heart;
Und wie er sitzt und wie er lauscht,	And as he sat and as he listened,
Theilt sich die Fluth empor:	The rising waters parted:
Aus dem bewegten Wasser rauscht	From the parting sea rose
Ein feuchtes Weib hervor.	A woman washed by the waters.
Sie sang zu ihm und sprach zu ihm:	She sang to him and spoke to him:
Was lockst du meine Brut	What draws you, my pondering one,
Mit Menschenwitz und Menschenlist	With the humor and cunning of a man,
Hinauf in Todes Glut?	To the embers of death?
Ach, wüstest du, wie's Fischlein ist	Ah, if you but knew how pleasant it is
So wohlig auf dem Grund,	For the fish on the sea floor,
Du kämst herunter wie du bist	Then you would descend just as you are
Und würdest erst gesund.	And you would truly feel well.
Labt sich die liebe Sonne nicht	Is the dear sun not refreshing,
Der Mond sich nicht im Meer?	The moon the same over the sea?
Kehr wellenathmend ihr Gesicht	Is its face not twice as beautiful
Nicht doppelt schöner her?	When the waves wash upon it?
Lockt dich der tiefe Himmel nicht	Do not the deep skies attract you
Das feucht verklärte Blau?	With their wet transfigured blue?
Lockt nicht dein eigen Angesicht	Does your own reflection
Dich her in ewgen Thau?	Seduce you into eternal dew?
Das Wasser rauscht', das Wasser schwoll,	The waters roared, the waves swelled,
Netzt ihm den nackten Fuß;	Grasping him by his naked foot;

n. [JGH] Source: Ballads by Johann Wolfgang von Goethe, written 1778, published in Karl Friedrich Siegismund von Seckendorf, *Volks- und andere Lieder, mit Begleitung des Forte piano*, vol. 1 (Weimar: Hoffmann, 1779), 4. [PVB] The publication of Goethe's "The Fisherman's Song" to initiate part two of the folk song project illustrates the extent to which folk songs—collected, composed, set to piano accompaniment—were circulating widely within German Enlightenment circles already by the end of the 1770s, six years after Herder coined the term *Volkslied*.

Sein Herz wuchs ihm so sehnensvoll	His heart filled with longing,
Wie bey der Liebsten Gruß.	As with the most tender greeting.
Sie sprach zu ihm – sie sang zu ihm –	She spoke to him—she sang to him—
Da wars um ihn geschehn –	Then it happened all about him—
Halb zog sie ihn, halb sank er hin	She half pulled him, he half sank in,
Und ward nicht mehr gesehn.	And he was never seen again.

10. [14] "EIN ALTFRANZÖSISCHES SONNET" / "A SONNET IN OLD FRENCH"

From the thirteenth century°

Ach könnt' ich, könnt vergessen Sie!	Ah, if I could, if I could forget you!
Ihr schönes, liebes liebliches Wesen,	Your beautiful, dear, lovely being,
Den Blick, die freundliche Lippe, die!	Your face, your inviting lips!
Vielleicht ich möchte genesen!	Perhaps, then, I might become well again!
Doch ach! mein Herz, mein Herz kann es nie!	Alas, my heart, my heart is unwilling!
Und doch ists Wahnsinn, zu hoffen Sie!	And, thus, it is madness to place hope in you!
Und um Sie schweben	And to linger about you
Gibt Muth und Leben,	Brings courage and life,
Zu weichen nie! –	Never waning!—
Und dann, wie kann ich vergessen Sie,	And then, how can I forget you,
Ihr schönes, liebes liebliches Wesen,	Your beautiful, dear lovely being,
Den Blick, die freundliche Lippe die!	Your face, your inviting lips!
Viel lieber nimmer genesen!	I much prefer never to be well again!

---

o. [JGH] In an earlier sense, a song with instrumental accompaniment. [PVB] This song is attributed to Thibaut IV, Count of Champagne, King of Navarra (1201–1253). Both Carl Friedrich Zelter (1758–1832) and Johannes Brahms (1833–1897) composed songs using Herder's text. Brahms sets the Herder text strophically as a troubadour song among the *Lieder und Romanzen* (published 1861), calling it simply "Ein Sonett" (op. 14, no. 4).

11. [24] "KLOSTERLIED" / "CLOISTER SONG"

German[p]

Kein' schönre Freud auf Erden ist	There is no greater joy on earth
Als in das Kloster zu ziehn.	Than entering into a cloister.
Ich hab mich drein ergeben,	I dedicated myself to the cloister,
Zu führen ein geistlich Leben;	So that I might live a life of faith;
O Liebe, was hab ich gethan!	Oh love, what have I done!
O Liebe etc.	Oh love, etc.
Des Morgens, wenn ich in die Kirche geh	In the morning, when I enter the chapel
Muß singen die Mess alleine;	I must sing the mass alone;
Und wenn ich das Gloria patri sing',	And when I sing the Gloria Patri,
So liegt mir mein Liebchen immer in Sinn,	My thoughts turn always to my beloved,
O Liebe, was hab ich gethan!	Oh love, what have I done!
O Liebe etc.	Oh love, etc.
Da kömmt mein Vater und Mutter her,	Whence my father and mother come,
Sie beten für sich alleine;	They pray there alone for me;
Sie haben schöne Kleider an,	They wear beautiful clothes,
Ich aber muß in der Kutten stahn;	While I must clothe myself in a cowl;
O Liebe, was hab ich gethan!	Oh love, what have I done!
O Liebe etc.	Oh love, etc.
Des Abends, wenn ich schlafen geh,	In the evening, when I go to bed,
So find ich mein Bettchen alleine;	I lay myself in the bed alone;
So denk ich denn, das Gott erbarm!	At that moment I think about the merciful God!
Ach hätt' ich mein Liebchen in dem Arm,	Alas, had I but my beloved in my arms!
O Liebe, was hab ich gethan!	Oh love, what have I done!
O Liebe etc.	Oh love, etc.

p. [JGH] From oral tradition in Thuringia. In Swiss dialect the song is more complete and perhaps also better. In the version here it is easier to understand, and so I am using it. In the *Limpurger Chronik* [Wolfshagen 1875] there is also a song about a nun, which begins thus:

Gott geb ihm ein verdorben Jahr	God, give a cursed year to him
Der mich gemacht zur Nonne,	Who made me a nun,
Und mir den schwarzen Mantel gab.	And gave me the black robe,
Den weissen Rock darunter u.f.	With the white dress underneath, etc.

Part 2, Book 2

12. [16] "ERINNERUNG DES GESANGES DER VORZEIT" / "REMEMBERING THE SONG OF THE DAYS OF OLD"

From Ossian[q]

Rühr Saite, du Sohn Alpins des Gesangs,	Son of Alpin [Albion], strike the string.[r]
Wohnt Trost in deiner Harfe der Lüfte?	Is there aught of joy in the harp?
Geuß über Ossian, den Traurigen, sie,	Pour it, then, on the soul of Ossian:
Dem Nebel einhüllen die Seele.	It is folded in mist.
Ich hör dich Bard' in meiner Nacht,	I hear thee, O Bard, in my night,
Halt an die Saite, die zitternde	But cease the lightly-trembling found.
Der Wehmuth Freude gebührt Ossian,	The joy of grief belongs to Ossian,
In seinen braunen Jahren.	Amidst his dark-brown years.
Gründorn, auf dem Hügel der Geister,	Green thorn of the hill of ghosts,
Webend das Haupt in Stimmen der Nacht,	That shakest thy head to nightly winds!
Ich spüre ja deinen Laut nicht,	I hear no sound in thee;
Geistergewand nicht rauschend im Laube dir.	Is there no spirit's windy skirt now rustling in thy leaves?
Oft sind die Tritte der Todten,	Often are the steps of the dead,
Auf Lüftchen im kreisenden Sturm.	In the dark-eddying blasts;
Wenn schwimmt von Osten der Mond,	When the moon, a dun shield,
Ein blasser Schild, ziehend den Himmel hindurch.	From the east, is rolled along the sky.

---

q. [JGH] The last two pieces are an attempt to engage with original texts that James Macpherson included in his anthology *Temora* [1763]. Though the translation here is not by the editor, he has some interesting observations to make about the songs, but he does not include them here. [PVB] Herder includes three songs from Denis's Ossian translations in the second book of part two of *Volkslieder*, placing them in a part of the project that is dominated by songs from Northern Europe, from the Baltic regions to Greenland. His engagement with the problems of translating songs in Macpherson's Ossian publications appears in chapters 4 and 5 of the present volume. *Temora* is one of the Scottish epics attributed by Macpherson to the fictitious Ossian. "Remembering the Song of the Days of Old" is the final song of book 7 in *Temora* (Macpherson 1763, 132–33).

r. [PVB] The English here is the original of Macpherson's *Temora*, itself claimed to be a translation from the original Gaelic in oral tradition.

Ullin und Carril und Raono,	Ullin, Carril, and Ryno,
Vergangne Stimmen der Tage vor Alters,	Voices of the days of old,
Hört' ich Euch im Dunkel von Selma;	Let me hear you, while yet it is dark,
Es erhübe die Seele des Lieds.	To please and awake my soul.
Nicht hör' ich euch, Söhne des Gesangs,	I hear you not, ye sons of song;
In welcher Wohnung der Wolken ist eure Ruh?	In what hall of the clouds is your rest?
Rührt ihr die Harfe, die düstre,	Do you touch the shadowy harp,
Gehüllt in Morgengrau,	Robed with morning mist,
Wo aufsteigt tönend die Sonne,	Where the rustling sun comes forth
Von Wellen, die Häupter blau?	From his green-headed waves?

13. [23] "RÖSCHEN AUF DER HEIDE" / "HEIDENRÖSLEIN"[s]

German[t]

Es sah ein Knab ein Röslein stehn,	A youth saw a little rose,
Röslein auf der Haiden:	Little rose in the meadow:
Sah, es war so frisch und schön,	It looked so fresh and beautiful,
Und blieb stehn es anzusehn,	And it remained there for all to see,
Und stand in süssen Freuden:	And it stood in sweet peace:
Röslein, Röslein, Röslein roth,	Little rose, little rose, red rose,
Röslein auf der Haiden!	Little rose in the meadow!
Der Knabe sprach: ich breche dich,	The youth spoke: I'll pick you,
Röslein auf der Haiden!	Little rose in the meadow!
Röslein sprach ich steche dich,	The little rose said, I'll prick you,
Daß du ewig denkst an mich,	So that you think about me forever,
Daß ichs nicht will leiden.	So that I'll not have to suffer that.
Röslein, Röslein, Röslein roth,	Little rose, little rose, red rose,
Röslein auf der Haiden!	Little rose in the meadow!
Doch der wilde Knabe brach	Still, the wild youth did pick
Das Röslein auf der Haiden;	The little rose in the meadow;

    s. [PVB] The English translation of this song would be "Little Rose in the Meadow." Even in English, however, the song is best known in Franz Schubert's setting as "Heidenröslein" (D. 257). It circulates in oral tradition as a folk song in a setting by Friedrich Silcher (1789–1860), and both of these use Goethe's 1789 folklike setting of "Heidenröslein" from 1789. Herder includes the song as an oral version of Goethe in *Von deutscher Art und Kunst* (1773; see chapter 4 in the present book).

    t. [JGH] From oral tradition.

Röslein wehrte sich und stach,	The little rose protected itself and did prick,
Aber er vergaß darnach	But he forgot anyway,
Beim Genuß das Leiden.	Enjoying the suffering.
Röslein, Röslein, Röslein roth,	Little rose, little rose, red rose,
Röslein auf der Haiden!	Little rose in the meadow!

14. [27] "ERLKÖNIGS TOCHTER" / "THE ELF KING'S DAUGHTER"

Danish[u]

Herr Oluf reitet spät und weit,	Oluf rode far and wide,
Zu bieten auf seine Hochzeitleut';	To offer his hand in marriage;
Da tanzen die Elfen auf grünem Land',	The elves were dancing upon the green fields,
Erlkönigs Tochter reicht ihm die Hand.	The Elf King's daughter offered him her hand.
"Willkommen, Herr Oluf, was eilst von hier?	"Welcome, Oluf, why be in a hurry?
Tritt her in den Reihen und tanz' mit mir."	Join our circle and dance with me."
"Ich darf nicht tanzen, nicht tanzen ich mag,	"I dare not dance, I do not wish to dance,
Frühmorgen ist mein Hochzeittag."	For tomorrow morning is my wedding day."
"Hör an, Herr Oluf, tritt tanzen mit mir,	"Listen, Oluf, join me in dance,
Zwei güldne Sporne schenk ich dir.	I'll give you two golden spurs.
Ein Hemd von Seide so weiß und fein,	A shirt of silk so white and pure,

---

u. [PVB] Herder draws upon publications of Danish "battle songs" (*Kjæmpe viser*) that appeared in German during the eighteenth century, which similarly provided sources for tales of the Elf King for Wilhelm Grimm and the well-known 1782 ballad by Goethe, which Franz Schubert set as "Der Erlkönig" (D. 328). Herder's inclusion of "The Elf King's Daughter" in part two of the *Volkslieder* was a critical link in an extensive process of circulation among Nordic songs in oral and written tradition, and their transformation to German ballads as poetry and art song.

Meine Mutter bleichts mit Mondenschein."	My mother bleached it with moonlight."
"Ich darf nicht tanzen, nicht tanzen ich mag,	"I dare not dance, I do not wish to dance,
Frühmorgen ist mein Hochzeittag."	For tomorrow morning is my wedding day."
"Hör an, Herr Oluf, tritt tanzen mit mir,	"Listen, Oluf, join me in dance,
Einen Haufen Gold schenk ich dir."	I'll give you a pile of gold."
"Einen Haufen Goldes nähm ich wohl;	"I'd gladly accept a pile of gold;
Doch tanzen ich nicht darf noch soll."	But I dare not dance, nor should I."
"Und willt, Herr Oluf, nicht tanzen mit mir;	"And if, Oluf, you wish not to dance with me;
Soll Seuch und Krankheit folgen dir."	Then disease and illness will follow you."
Sie thät einen Schlag ihm auf sein Herz,	She struck him through unto his heart,
Noch immer fühlt er solchen Schmerz.	Never before had he felt such pain.
Sie hob ihn bleichend auf sein Pferd,	She lifted him, pale, upon his horse,
"Reit heim nun zu dein'm Fräulein werth."	"Ride home, now, to your wife so precious."
Und als er kam vor Hauses Thür,	And as he arrived at the door of his home,
Seine Mutter zitternd stand dafür.	His mother stood there, shaking.
"Hör an, mein Sohn, sag an mir gleich,	"Listen, my son, and tell me straightaway,
Wie ist dein' Farbe blaß und bleich?"	Why is your coloring so pale and white?"
"Und sollt sie nicht seyn blaß und bleich,	"And should it not be so pale and white,
Ich traf in Erlenkönigs Reich."	For I've been in the kingdom of the Elf King."
"Hör an, mein Sohn, so lieb und traut,	"Listen, my son, so dear and true,

Was soll ich nun sagen deiner Braut?"	What should I now tell your bride?"
"Sagt ihr, ich sey im Wald zur Stund,	"Tell her I've been in the forest for a while,
Zu proben da mein Pferd und Hund."	Training there my horse and dog."
Frühmorgen und als es Tag kaum war,	Early morning, as day had barely broken,
Da kam die Braut mit der Hochzeitschaar.	The bride arrived with the wedding party.
Sie schenkten Meet, sie schenkten Wein,	They poured the mead, they poured the wine,
"Wo ist Herr Oluf, der Bräutigam mein?"	"Where is Oluf, who is my groom?"
"Herr Oluf, er ritt' in Wald zur Stund,	"Oluf has been riding for a while in the forest,
Er probt allda sein Pferd und Hund."	He's been training there his horse and dog."
Die Braut hob auf den Scharlach roth,	Scarlet red, the bride departed,
Da lag Herr Oluf und er war todt.	There lay Oluf, and he was dead.

Part 2, Book 3

15. [30] "ABENDLIED" / "EVENING SONG"[v]

German[w]

Der Mond ist aufgegangen,	The moon has risen,
Die goldnen Sternlein prangen	The little golden stars shine
Am Himmel hell und klar;	In the skies, bright and clear;
Der Wald steht schwarz und schweiget,	The forest stands dark and silent,
Und aus den Wiesen steigt	And from the fields there rises
Der weiße Nebel wunderbar.	The white fog, so marvelous.

---

   v. [PVB] This version of Matthias Claudius's "Evening Song" is the final song in the first edition (1779) of the *Volkslieder*. Its moral lesson of simplicity and trust in God intentionally reflects Herder's sense of deeper meaning and humanity that he attributes to folk song, fittingly bringing the folk song project to a close.

   w. [JGH] By [Matthias] Claudius [1740–1815]. This song is not included to increase the number of songs in the anthology, but rather because its content demonstrates what is and will remain the best folk songs. The songbook is the Bible of the people, its comfort and most important means of uplifting.

Wie ist die Welt so stille,	How very silent the world becomes,
Und in der Dämmrung Hülle	And shrouded by the dusk
So traulich und so hold!	So familiar and so dear!
Als eine stille Kammer,	As a quiet chamber,
Wo ihr des Tages Jammer	Where you should put to rest and forget
Verschlafen und vergessen sollt.	The clamor of the day.
Seht ihr den Mond dort stehen?	Do you see the moon up above?
Er ist nur halb zu sehen,	Only half of it is visible,
Und ist doch rund und schön.	But it is still round and beautiful.
So sind wohl manche Sachen,	So, too, are so many things,
Die wir getrost belachen,	We sense, and that make us laugh,
Weil unsre Augen sie nicht sehn.	Though they remain invisible to us.
Wir stolze Menschenkinder	We, proud children of humankind,
Sind eitel arme Sünder,	Are but vain, poor sinners,
Und wissen gar nicht viel;	Who know so very little;
Wir spinnen Luftgespinnste,	We trace vast plans in the sky,
Und suchen viele Künste,	And seek much in artifice,
Und kommen weiter von dem Ziel.	Only to stray farther from our goal.
Gott, laß uns dein Heil schauen,	God, reveal to us your salvation,
Auf nichts Vergänglichs trauen,	Turn us away from things past,
Nicht Eitelkeit uns freun!	Prevent us from rejoicing in vanity!
Laß uns einfältig werden,	Let us live simply,
Und vor dir hier auf Erden	In reverence for you on this earth,
Wie Kinder fromm und frölich seyn.	As children with faith and happiness.

Appendix to the 1807 Edition

16. (FIRST SONG IN THE 1807 APPENDIX) "DER HAGESTOLZE" / "THE CONFIRMED BACHELOR"

An Estonian song

Liebchen, Brüderchen, du sagtest:	Dear little brother, you said:
Daß man ohne Weib ja leben,	That one can live without a wife,
Daß man ungefreiet sterben,	That one can die without marrying,
Daß man könn' alleine tanzen.	That one can dance alone.
Brüderchen, du lebtest also,	Dear brother, thus you lived,
Und du fandest dich gar einsam,	And you found yourself totally alone,

Und du unternahmst aus Holze	And you attempted to shape
Dir ein Weibchen selbst zu bilden,	A wife for yourself from wood,
Gar ein reines, gar ein weißes,	Totally a wife pure, fully lily-white,
Gar ein grades, gar ein schlankes,	Completely a wife tall and slender,
Gar ein dauerhaftes Weibchen.	Indeed a wife who would be lasting.
Liebchen, Brüderchen, drei Dinge	Dear little brother, three things
Sind zu einem Weibe nöthig,	Are necessary for a wife:
In ihr eine zarte Seele,	She should have a gentle soul,
Goldne Zung' in ihrem Munde,	Speak with a golden tongue,
Angenehm Witz im Haupte.	Have a head full of pleasant humor.
Und du unternahmst dem Bilde	And you tried to gild
Sein Gesichtchen zu vergülden,	The image with her face,
Seine Schultern zu versilbern	To cover her shoulders with silver,
Nahmst es nun in deine Arme	Then you took her in your arms,
Eine, zwei und drei der Nächste:	One, two, three, and then the next:
Fandest kalt des Goldes Seiten	You found the golden cheeks cold,
Fandest hart ihrs untern Armen	Beneath her arms it was hard,
Grauerlich die Spur des Silbers.	The traces of silver grayed.
Liebchen, Brüderlein, drei Dinge	Dear little brother, three things
Sind zu einem Weibe nöthig,	Are necessary for a wife,
Warme Lippen, schlanke Arme	Warm lips, slender arms,
Und ein liebevoller Busen.	And lovely breasts.
Wähl' ein Weib dir aus den Mädchen,	Choose a wife from the maidens,
Wähl' ein Weib aus unserm Lande,	Choose a wife from our own land,
Oder richte deine Füsse	Or direct your feet
Hin zum Rudern, hin zum Laufen.	To sail away, to run away,
Richt' dein Schifchen hin nach Deutschland,	Direct your boat toward Germany,
Deine Segel hin nach Rußland,	Your sail away toward Russia,
Hol' ein Weib dir aus der Ferne.	Take a wife for yourself from afar.

17. "AN DIE JUNGFRAU MARIA" / "TO THE VIRGIN MARY"
"Ein sicilianisches Schifferlied" / "A Sicilian Sea Shanty"[x]

Latin	German	English
O sanctissima!	O du Heilige,	Oh, most holy,
O piisima!	Hochbenedete,	Oh, most virtuous,

---

x. [JGH] As the most beautiful from Italian folk songs, I am including here a single example rather than many. The Sicilian sea shanty has a gentle melody in its original form, which allows it to be easily sung in translation.

FIGURE 8. "An die Jungfrau Maria" / "To the Virgin Mary," from Johann Gottfried Herder, "Stimmen der Völker in Liedern," 1807. Public domain.

Dulcis Virgo Maria!	Süße Mutter der Liebe.	Sweet mother of love.
Mater amata	Trösterin im Leiden,	Comfort in times of suffering,
Inte merata mora,	Quelle der Freuden,	Source of all joy,
Ora pro nobis.	Hilf uns, Maria!	Help us, Maria!

"On the Songs of Madagascar"

(from the French of Évariste Desiré de Forges, Vicomte de Parny [1753–1814])

Preface by Count Parny   The island of Madagascar is crisscrossed by an infinite number of tiny regions, each one with its own prince. These princes incessantly raise arms against each other, with the only real goal of their wars being that of taking prisoners, whom they will then sell to the Europeans. Without us, therefore, these people would live peacefully and happily.

The people of Madagascar possess skill and understanding; they are talkative and hospitable. For good reasons, those who live along the coasts do not trust foreigners, and they make their treaties with great caution, reflecting wisdom, indeed even a fine quality of spirit. By nature the people of Madagascar are happy. The women work while the men lead idle lives. They are passionate in their love for music and dance. I have collected and translated some songs that can give us some idea of their customs and cultural practices. They do not have poetry per se, but rather their poesy is little more than enhanced prose. Their music is simple, gentle, and always melancholy.

18. "DER KÖNIG" / "THE KING"[y]

What is the name of the king of this land? ... Ampanani ... Where is he? In the dwelling of the king. ... Lead me to him. ... Are you coming with an open hand? ... Yes, I come as a friend. ... You may enter.

Long live Prince Ampanani! ... May you also live long, white man; I am preparing a favorable reception for you. Slaves, prepare a mat on the floor, and cover it with the broad leaves of the banana tree.

Bear forth rice, milk, and ripe fruits. Go, Nehale; the most beautiful of my maidens should serve this foreigner, and her youngest sister should delight him at dinner with her dances and songs.

19. "DER KÖNIG IM KRIEG" / "THE KING AT WAR"

What foolhardiness dares to drive Ampanani into struggle? He clasps his spear, which is armed with a pointed bone, and he proceeds with great strides across the plain. His son goes forth with him at his side, proudly erect like a young palm tree on the mountain.

Stormy winds, spare the palm tree on the mountain.

His enemies are legion. ... Ampanani seeks only one of them and finds him. Brave enemy, your fame is great: the first parry of your spear has already spilled Ampanani's blood. His blood, however, does not flow without vengeance! You fall! And your fall unleashes the horror of your soldiers. They flee back to their dwellings; and here, too, they are pursued by death. Blazing with the fires of misfortune, the entire village already lies in ashes.

---

y. [PVB] Herder presents the songs from Madagascar either as prose passages or as dialogues, rather than translating them into discrete song texts. There is, therefore, nothing to be gained by placing the original song next to my parallel translation, and I therefore include only the translation in the anthology to chapter 2.

The victors joyfully return, forcing before them the anguished troops, the prisoners bound together, and the crying women.... Innocent children, you smile, and you are slaves.

20. "TODTENKLAGE, UM DES KÖNIGS SOHN" / "LAMENT FOR THE KING'S SON"

AMPANANI: My son has fallen in battle! Oh, my friends, weep over the son of your leader. Take his body to the place in which the dead live. A high wall will protect him, for there will be the heads of bulls on that wall, which will be armed with threatening horns. Respect the place in which the dead live. Their sadness is terrible, and their revenge is gruesome. Weep over my son.

THE MEN: Never again will the blood of the enemies turn his arm red.

THE WOMEN: Never again will his lips kiss those of another.

THE MEN: Never again will fruit ripen for him.

THE WOMEN: Never again will his head rest on a tender bosom.

THE MEN: Never again will he sing, resting under a tree thick with leaves.

THE WOMEN: Never again will he whisper new enticements to his beloved.

AMPANANI: Cease, now, with your weeping over my son! Happiness should follow the mourning! Tomorrow, perhaps, we too will follow to the place he has gone.

21. "TRAUET DEN WEISSEN NICHT" / "HAVE NO PITY FOR THE WHITE PEOPLE"

Have no pity for the white people, you who live along the coasts! The white people landed on our island in the time of our fathers. One said to them: here is the land your wives want to build; be just, be good, and be our brothers.

The white people made their promise and then turned nonetheless with their tails in the air. A threatening fortress appeared; the thunder was trapped in perpetual abyss; their priests wanted to give us a god we did not know; they spoke incessantly about obedience and servitude.

Death would be preferable! ... The massacre was long and dreadful; but despite the thunder they unleashed to crush entire armies, they were not all destroyed. Have no pity for the white people.

We have seen new, stronger, and more numerous tyrants plant their flags on our shores. The skies fought on our behalf. Downpours, thunderstorms, and poisoned winds were sent to sweep over them, so that they were no more. But we live and live in freedom.

Have no pity for the white people, you who live along the coasts.

22. "ZANHAR UND NIANG" / "ZANHAR AND NIANG"

Zanhar and Niang have created the world. Oh, Zanhar! We do not turn toward you with entreaties; why should one ask anything of the good god? It is because of Niang's anger that we must be quiet.

Niang, angry, powerful god, do not let the thunder roar over our heads; do not command the seas to rise above the coasts; spare the fruit as it grows; do not dry up the rice before it is fully grown; do not open the wombs of our women on inauspicious days, and force no mother to bury the hope of her age in the sea.

Oh, Niang! Do not destroy all of Zanhar's good deeds. You reign over the evil; their number is sufficient; do not torture the good.

23. "AMPANANI" / "AMPANANI"

AMPANANI: Young prisoner, what is your name?
VAINA: I am called Vaina.
AMPANANI: Vaina, you are beautiful, like the first rays of the day. But why are you crying?
VAINA: Oh king, I had a lover.
AMPANANI: Where is he?
VAINA: Perhaps he is still in battle; perhaps he saved himself by fleeing.
AMPANANI: Whether he is dead, whether he has fled, I shall be your lover.
VAINA: Oh king, have pity on my tears that fall upon your feet.
AMPANANI: What is it that you wish?
VAINA: That unfortunate soul has kissed my eyes, has kissed my mouth. He has slumbered on my breast, he is in my heart, and there is nothing I can do to tear him from me....
AMPANANI: Take your veil, hide your arousal. Leave this place.
VAINA: Let me seek him among the dead or among the living.
AMPANANI: Go, beautiful Vaina. The monster must die who has stolen the kisses that were mixed with tears.[z]

---

z. [JGH] Source: Parny, p. 544.

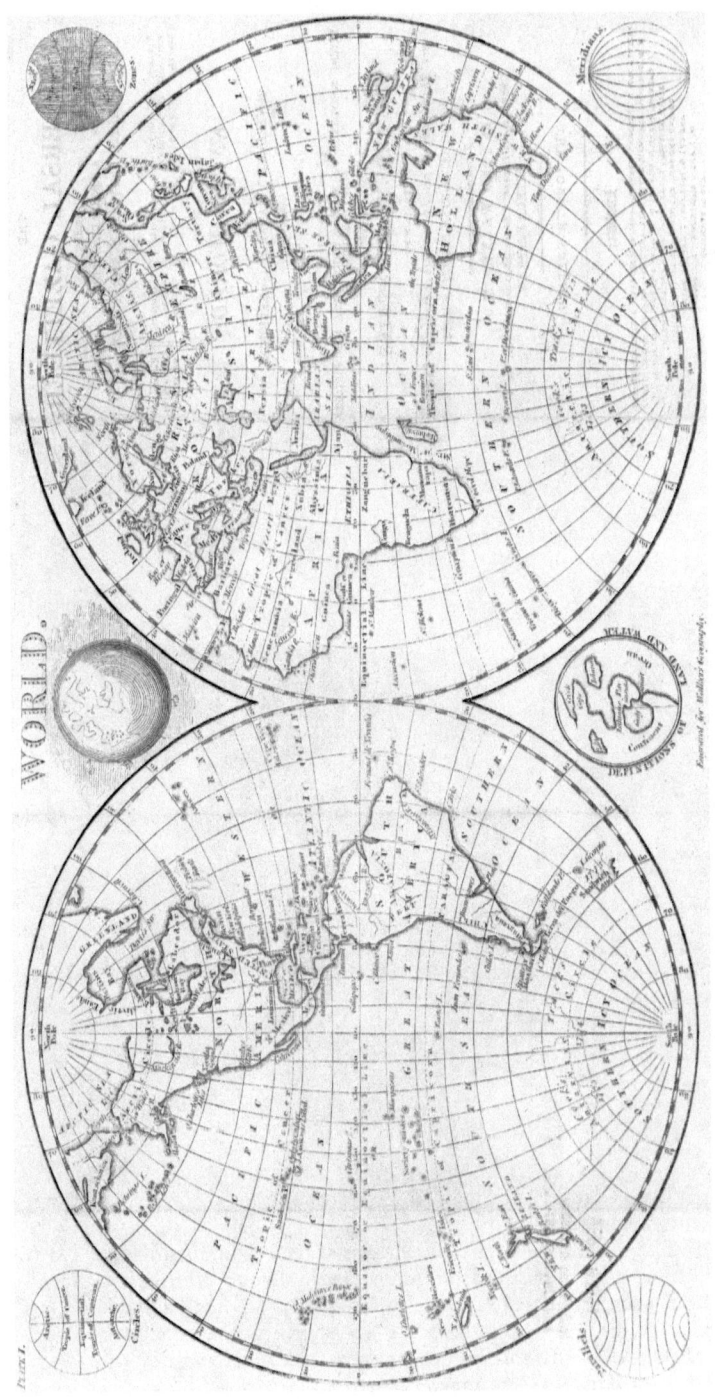

FIGURE 9. Map of the world, circa 1807. Courtesy the Map Collection, Regenstein Library, University of Chicago.

Chapter 2 Appendix

(Final song in the appendix to the 1807 edition)[aa]

24. "AN SEIN MÄDCHEN" / "TO HIS CHILD"

Peruvian[ab]

Schlummre, schlummr', o Mädchen,	Slumber, slumber, oh my child,
Sanft in meine Lieder,	Gently in my songs,
Mitternachts, o Mädchen,	It's midnight, oh my child,
Weck' ich dich schon wieder!	I'll wake you once again!

---

aa. [PVB] With this Peruvian lullaby Herder concludes his efforts to gather and publish anthologies of folk song.

ab. [PVB] "An sein Mädchen" also appears at the beginning of Herder's writings about folk song, in fact as the third song reproduced in "Extract from the Correspondence about Ossian and the Songs of Ancient Peoples" (*Von deutscher Art und Kunst* [1773]); see chapter 4 in the present volume, p. 151. The source for that citation is Garcilaso de la Vega, *Histoire des Yncas rois du Peru etc. Traduite de l'Espagnol de l'Ynca Garcilasso de la Vega, par J. Baudoin* (Amsterdam: Gerard Kuyper, 1704).

3. Singing the Sacred Body

Essay on *Lieder der Liebe* (1778)

Philip V. Bohlman

> O Solomon don't leave me here
> Cotton balls to choke me
> O Solomon don't leave me here
> Buckra's arms to yoke me
>
> Solomon done fly, Solomon done gone
> Solomon cut across the sky, Solomon gone home.
> —TONI MORRISON, *Song of Solomon*

Religion lives in remarkably diverse forms in the books whose biographies reveal the soteriological possibilities of returning generation after generation, age after age. The narratives of sacred forebears are told again, the allegories of the past translated to give new form for belief in the future. Music, especially song, often provides the essential accompaniment necessary to translate past lives into meaningful afterlives. Song situates the sacred text between written and oral traditions, unleashing variants from previously authentic texts and breathing new life into the vernacular. Generation upon generation seeks a "new song" (Psalm 96) that sounds the stories of the past as their own.

Johann Gottfried Herder, as we witness throughout this volume, was an active translator of religious texts, especially those that invested Christianity with modern, enlightened meaning. For Herder, translation was an everyday engagement with the past, not only because translation served his professional life as a pastor and church administrator, but also because it opened a path toward religious understanding beyond the liturgical canons of Protestantism. In chapter 8, for example, we witness Herder through the eyes of his wife, Karoline, who wrote in her diaries that it was his everyday practice during the 1770s to translate one or two cantos of *El Cid*. In the 1790s it would be Herder who championed the translation of the epic of Krishna and Arjuna in the Hindu *Bhagavad Gita*, publishing several parts himself, and laying the groundwork for the wave of translations that would follow the turn of the nineteenth century (see Davis 2015, 84–87). Both the

Cid and the *Bhagavad Gita* translations—*gita* is glossed as "song" in Sanskrit—led Herder to weave music into the paths along which his epic heroes passed. The Cid and Krishna sang throughout, and song echoed through the translational choices that Herder made. In making such choices, Herder found himself returning again and again, through translation, to biblical texts—large and small, individual verses and complete books—which together constituted one of the most enduring leitmotifs in his published work. In perhaps no other place does he sound the leitmotif of song and the sacred more resonantly than in his translation of *Shir ha-shirim*, the *Song of Songs*, which he published with the name *Lieder der Liebe*.

At the heart of his translation of the biblical *Song of Songs* lies a concerted attempt to interpret and represent difference.[1] *Lieder der Liebe* (1778) recognizes difference and then examines the intricacies of its many meanings from multiple perspectives, which together allow the project to set in motion a transition from the Enlightenment to a new era of engagement with the religions, cultures, and music of the East. Following German practice of his day in *Lieder der Liebe*, Herder refers to the East as the *Morgenland* (land of the morning). This equivalent of "Orient," of course, clearly reveals the orientalism that provided the historical and theological framework for his translation and interpretation. The musical practices and song repertories that Herder describes exegetically reflect orientalist imagery, for example when he observes that the eyes are the initial point of reference in song across Asia (see footnote e). In his *Lieder der Liebe* and elsewhere, nonetheless, it is the possibility of drawing East and West closer together (see my discussion of *Annäherung* in the prologue to the present volume) that motivates his turn toward the singing of the sacred body in the *Song of Songs*.

The intimacy of the love songs themselves expresses what John Baildam calls "paradisal love," the religious allegory of the sacred realized in the intimacy of the human body (Baildam 1999). Remarkably, the biography of *Shir ha-shirim* itself, as a book in the Bible, enhances rather than loses this intimacy in the course of centuries of translation. Herder fully recognized the very possibility of enhancing the intimacy of the songs through translation, turning not only to the standard, quite free translation by Martin Luther, but also to those of his own contemporaries, among them Johann Wolfgang von Goethe, his Königsberg teacher Johann Georg Hamann, and Johann Gottlieb Lessing (see footnote h in the present chapter). Together, these translations provided a new collective biography in the life of *Shir ha-shirim*.

The *Song of Songs* project appeared in the same year as the first edition of *Volkslieder* (1778/79; see chapter 2 in the present volume), and it expresses much of the same engagement with the expressive power of song, and by extension the arts, to embody the diversity of human experience. It is indeed crucial to the *Song of Songs* project that difference assumes so many forms. At the core of the project are distinctions between West and East, Occident and Orient, which in turn are enriched by metaphors of self and other. Herder both draws upon Enlightenment concepts of orientalism and extends them. We witness this in a tension between Herder's treatment of the Orient as a site of myth and mystery, and his clear goal of seeing the aesthetic power of the songs as transcending the usual repertory of expressive techniques available in the West. The other sites of difference in the songs and interpretive texts are notable for the ways in which they presage future aesthetic domains for Herder. We witness his ambitious move in the ways in which he establishes difference only to blur the boundaries between its categories. Gender distinctions, especially between lovers, are often blurry, which in turn leads to a mixing of voices in the songs: Which lover is praising his or her beloved at a given moment? What does Herder mean to signify when equating love to the attraction between brother and sister? The difference between art and artifice, nature and the political realization of Israel at the time of King Solomon, also assumes different forms. The role of Lebanon in the songs that follow, for example, varies from song to song, context to context, at one moment being the geographical site from which nature flows (out of the heights of the north, Mount Hermon), at another moment being a place with which Solomon must reckon to retain power. The difference between sacred and secular, love as moral lesson and love as sensual experience, could not be more evident in the songs.

Herder's German enhances the sensual, even sexually erotic, quality of the language. He does nothing to hide the sensuality of the songs, and he translates that quality into a new language for exegesis, punctuating his remarks on the songs with exclamation marks, ellipses, and an interpretive voice that does not hide its passion and the excitement conveyed by the narrative itself. These translation conventions are common throughout Herder's writings, especially those in which he himself engages translation as exegesis. In his translations of song texts, lyrical and narrative, such conventions mark the space of transition and ellipsis between oral and written tradition. Herder uses such conventions, moreover, to draw himself and his readers closer to the physicality and the intimacy of the oral, for example, in his evocation of fragments in texts from the 1770s (see, e.g., chapters 1, 2, and 8 in the present volume). In the following translation of parts from *Lieder der Liebe*, I render all such spaces of in-betweenness with the usual punctuation conventions for ellipsis, thereby realizing them as Herder's approach to translation itself.

Lieder der Liebe is of interest for understanding Herder's larger projects because of the ways translation becomes a means of more directly engaging with difference. Not only does Herder translate the *Shir ha-shirim* (Song of Songs) of the Bible, but the three chapters of the book themselves are texts about translation, its mechanics and its history. Anyone looking for a systematic presentation of *Shir ha-shirim* will be disappointed. The first chapter, from which I draw the songs and the commentary surrounding them that I translate below, unfolds as a dialogue between the song itself, in part or in whole, and Herder's interpretation of it, also specifically directed or connected to the larger interpretive undertaking of the first chapter. Herder had originally intended to translate Martin Luther's standard translation of *Shir ha-shirim* into German, which itself had provided the song texts for an extraordinary number of musical settings from the Renaissance to the Enlightenment (see, e.g., *Lied der Liebe* 2013 and its accompanying CD). As he began work on his translation from Luther, however, Herder decided against a simple compilation of new versions, opting instead to paraphrase Luther, often quite freely, in order to evoke a new sense of the songs themselves. It is this *Nachdichtung*—the reimagination of poetic intent—that expands Luther's translation in dramatically new form.

Herder's chapter 2, "On the Content, Form, and Goal of This Book in the Bible," contains the interpretation of a theologian, which in turn transforms the way in which one reads the first chapter, that is, as not only aesthetic but also exegetic. In the course of the second chapter, however, Herder's lifelong examination of the relation of parts to wholes assumes the foreground (see chapter 2 in the present volume), and as it does so, it heightens the potential of translation itself to create unity from fragments. Finally, with chapter 3, "On Translations of the Book, Especially One from the Early Minnesongs," Herder draws the history of translation into the present and future. Briefly surveying the rich possibilities available in German and in the Enlightenment for translating biblical texts, the chapter immediately moves to the only body of songs presented in the book, medieval translations of texts from the *Song of Songs*, which were treated in Herder's age as a corpus of love poetry. This body of songs has an important narrative function for Herder, for it serves as a German connection between the past and the present, and it is this connection that he extends to his collections and exegesis of folk song.

In the translation from chapter 1 of *Lieder der Liebe* that follows, I seek to reflect many of the approaches that Herder employed during his own *Nachdichtung*, not only the 1778 publication, but also the revisions for a 1781 edition. Neither of these bore Herder's name on the title page (fig. 10),

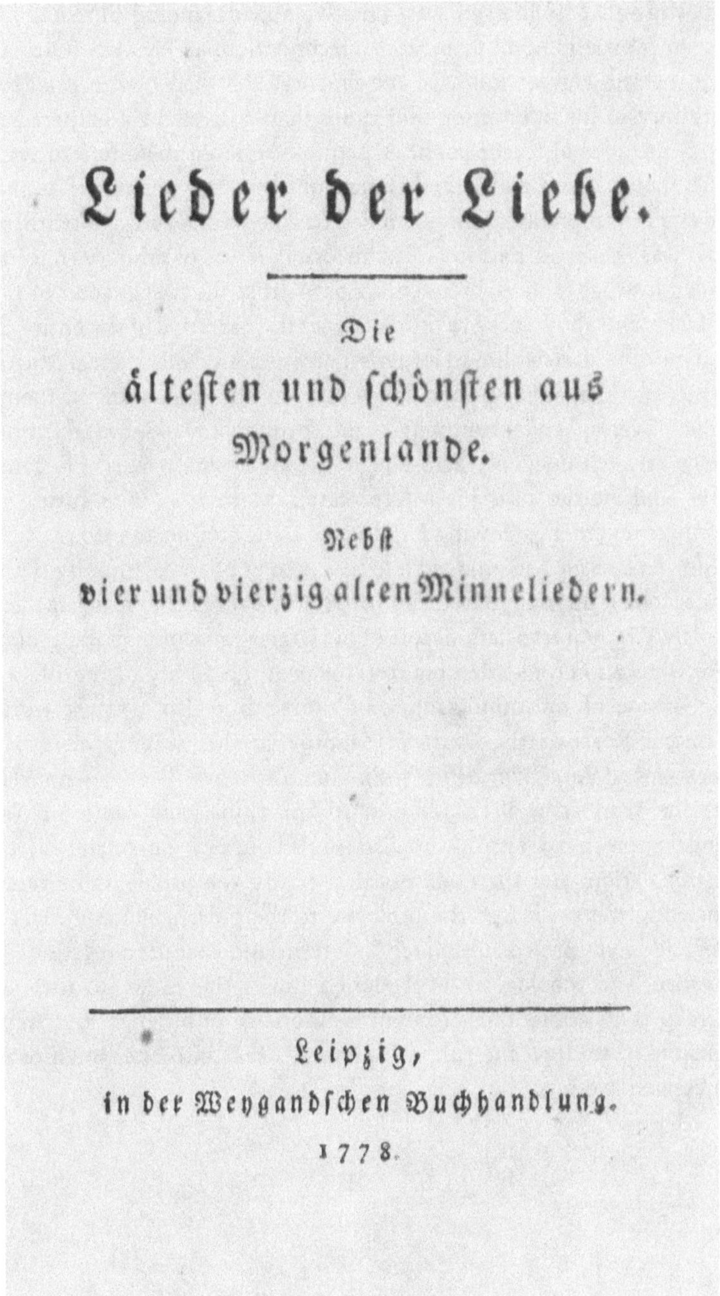

Lieder der Liebe.

Die
ältesten und schönsten aus
Morgenlande.

Nebst
vier und vierzig alten Minneliedern.

Leipzig,
in der Weygandschen Buchhandlung.
1778.

FIGURE 10. Title page of Johann Gottfried Herder, *Lieder der Liebe*, 1778 edition. Courtesy Special Collections, Regenstein Library, University of Chicago.

suggesting that he himself was tentative about claiming *Shir ha-shirim*, even in translation and exegetical interpretation, as his own (Otto 1992, 169). Instead, Herder followed the practices that had been crucial to the continuity in his publications for more than a decade. He gathered fragments, included different poetic structures, explored the different ways in which they cohered, and compiled them, interspersing them with commentary and interpretation. The assembled fragments and songs notwithstanding, it was the larger narrative and history that was of primary concern for Herder. In what follows, I too extract parts from the first chapter of *Lieder der Liebe*, and allow these to unfold across the narrative of the entire chapter. The nine parts follow Herder's narrative arc, and I am particularly attentive to the ways specific songs and the commentaries on them are paired. Overlap and asymmetry run throughout *Shir ha-shirim*—six "songs" stretch unevenly across eight verses in this remarkably compact book—and Herder uses his interpretation to find ways to suture their meanings together. Following Herder as a translator, so, too, do I.

Shir ha-shirim had enjoyed a long tradition of translation by the time Herder took it up in 1778 (see Timm 1982). Martin Luther had provided the standard German translation, part of his larger translation of the Bible, and there were numerous attempts to transform the poetry of the Bible into song—those of the minnesinger, of course, but also a major work by Salamone Rossi at the court of Mantua in the waning years of the Renaissance (*Ha-shirim asher li-Shlomo*, ca. 1620). Herder's translation must be seen as well in relation to the translation work of Moses Mendelssohn (1729–1786), who also singled out *Shir ha-shirim* for a special translation, and then addressed critically the problems he faced in translating the work (see the prologue to the present volume). Herder's *Lieder der Liebe* project, ultimately, is a translation about translation. At an exegetical and theological level Herder draws the reader to the means whereby translations must recognize difference in order to find ways to overcome it, to draw the other of another's text into one's own orbit of expressive meaning.

From *Lieder der Liebe: Die ältesten und schönsten aus Morgenlande* / *Songs of Love: The Oldest and Most Beautiful from the Orient*

JOHANN GOTTFRIED HERDER,
TRANSLATED BY PHILIP V. BOHLMAN

CHAPTER I: THE SONG OF SOLOMON
Part 1

> He kisses me
> With the kisses of his mouth:
> For your love is sweeter than wine.
> Like the fragrance of your sweet ointment,
> So too is your name
> A soothing balm:
> Thus, the maidens give you their love.

> Draw me unto you! . . .
> We hasten; me . . .
> The king leads me into his chamber.
> We rejoice, we share your pleasure!
> Remember your love,
> More than wine . . .
> We love you from our heart.

This sigh may have accompanied a languishing flower, with a sweet-smelling morning rose, so that a young woman, longingly, would smell it.

The absent kiss is for her so sweet, the very fragrance of his ointment! If only she knew his name, the fragrance filling her body would be that of a balm.

She is not the only one to love him in this way: he is loved thus by all. The fragrance of his name alters her playfulness, endowing it with sensuality: "Oh, if he would but wave to me!" ... And then take note, she is preferred above all others. *"Draw me nigh! ... The king takes me into his chamber."* She rejoices, she takes pleasure in him, ecstatic with incomparable joy.

And it is the same within the circle of her friends. All love in the way in which she loves, all rejoice, all speak of his embrace, rather than of wine and pleasures. Her entire heart and soul are with him.

Could you imagine an oriental monarch who is more lovingly flattered in his garden of love? Instead of envy and jealousy, quarreling and betrayal, all voices join as a single voice; all thoughts, every heart, are a single heart.[a] A shy dove delivers the letter, enveloped lovingly, but only as a message from her sisters. Unintentionally she releases her sigh, and thus she enjoys him always. *You* and *he*, *I* and *we* are interchangeable: at a distance he also draws nearer, she may speak with him if she so desires.

> Her voice falls silent; thus, it is heard in an entirely different way:
> I am black and yet so gentle,
> You daughters of Jerusalem!
> Just as the tents of cedar
> Provide shelter for Solomon.
>
> Look not upon me, so that I appear as if black:
> The sun burns me.
> My mother's sons are angry with me:
> They place me in the protection of the vineyard,
> And mine, my own vineyard,
> Does not provide me with dwelling.
>
> Oh, tell me
> Whom my soul loves:
> Where are you at pasture?
> Where are you encamped

---

a. [JGH] The situation of women in the East is well known through more than a few critical travelers' accounts: see D. Friedrich Hasselquist, *Reise nach Palästina in den Jahren von 1749 bis 1752* (Rostock: J.C. Koppe, 1762), 126; and Jean de Thévenot, *Voyages de Mr de Thévenot tant en Europe, Asie et Afrique, divisez en trois parties* (Paris: Angot, 1689). In his *Lettres persannes*, Charles Louis de Secondat Montesquieu (Amsterdam: Chez les Librairies associés, 1764) sought to incorporate Uzbeki women into his letters. Here, however, everything is entirely different.

At midday? . . .
That I do not go, as one sheltered,
To the flocks playing about you.

"And do you not know,
Most beautiful of all women;
Follow the footprints of the flock,
And pasture your goats
Near the tents of the goatherd."

Everything is different here! In the first song there is fragrance and ointment, wine and pleasure, girlfriends and the chambers of the king; in the second there is a shepherdess with unencumbered passage, a dark-skinned maiden from the countryside, envied by all of Jerusalem's daughters. A child of the sun from her very youth, and now, languishing as if in the midday sun. Her lover is himself a shepherd, who pastures his flocks among others that she seeks, with whose dwellings she compares herself, answering with just that tone one would expect from a shy girl from the countryside. The entire song breathes of the open fields, the time of rest at midday, shepherds, and the unity of the countryside.

Part 2

It is well known that the female palm tree is pollinated from a bush of male flowers. Alternatively, one takes the male flower buds before they open and encloses them in the small branches of the female flower. Under such conditions, the palm blossoms are said to be *kopher*, which is to say, enclosed. They become fertile while still unopened, their fullness awaiting the delicate, aromatic thaw, which then transfers delicacy and spiciness to the first freshness of the dates. While *enclosed* in the female flower, he breathes fragrance and life into her. Could one find any more beautiful image than this: "Without you my blossoms are without life. Your breath . . . a tender, young, fresh thaw of heaven . . . bestows everything that lives within me with new strength and feeling, and with new creation."

And this is what we witnessed in the previous pictures of *nardus*[b] and *myrrh*, and it is what the *palm buds* say more beautifully than anything else. What is a youth, whose most intimate image may be that of the protected, sweet blossoming of youth? How tender is the love that he thus observes, thus loves, and feels as a blossoming palm tree! Everything in the Orient

---

b. [PVB] A species of fragrant grass.

derives from nature, the beloved can possess a language no more beautiful, so that they send each other flowers, in order to give answers to the questions.[c] Each one finds an intimate personal meaning in this dictionary of love. You are myrrh that spends the night,[d] and you are an enclosed palm blossom. How you offer gold and jewels as contemplation of the beloved!

> "Oh, you are so beautiful, my love,
> Oh, so beautiful you are!
> Your eyes are little doves. . . ."

> "Oh, you are so handsome, my love,
> You are also so lovely,
> And our bed becomes sweet.

> The balconies of our house are of cedar,
> The walls of cypress;
> And I am the rose of the field,
> The lily of the valley."

> "Like the lily among the thorns,
> Such is my lover among the daughters."

> "Like the apple tree among the trees of the forest,
> Such is my lover among the sons.
> In a shadow
> I quicken my step,
> And I sit upon the earth,
> And his fruit
> Is sweet in my mouth.

> He led me
> Into a tavern!
> And his bread crumbs,
> Sprinkled upon me,
> Are love itself.

> Oh, give me strength with the wine!
> Oh, refresh me with the apples!
> For I am sick with love.

> With his left hand
> He lifts up my head:

---

c. [JGH] See the flower, *Muscherumi*, in D. Friedrich Hasselquist, *Reise nach Palästina*, 37.

d. [JGH] At night, myrrh assumes the form of bushes and not individual flowers. What would be the meaning for us of such a detail? In a love poem?

With his right hand
He draws me to him. ...

I beseech you, daughters of Jerusalem,
By the doe and the deer in flight.
If you awaken her!
If you excite her! ...
Until it pleases her."

What sweet dreams of love! In the transports of intoxication that follow, may I succeed in fleshing her out, Shulamit, who is so often misunderstood. What a scene of paradise! ...

The praise from the beloved for his love begins. He will picture her beauty, and the first verse itself—the first verse of the first description in the entire book—is of humility and innocence. *Her eyes are little doves, timid little doves.*[e]

Part 3

Voice of my love!
Look, he is coming!
Leaping across the mountains,
Springing over the hills.
My love is like a deer,
Like a stag in flight.

Look, he already stands
Behind the wall,
Gazing through the banister,
Looking through the railing,
My lover speaks,
He speaks to me:
Arise, my love,
Arise, my beauty,
Come! ...

For see that the winter has passed,
The rain is no more, has passed!
Already one sees flowers on the ground,
The time for song has arrived.
One hears the voice

---

e. [JGH] For those who live in the East, the praise of beauty always begins with the eyes. Without the gazelle and the eyes, there is no love poem. See Laurent d'Arvieux, *Voyage dans la Palestine*, vol. 3 (Paris: A. Cailleau, 1717), 249.

> Of the turtle dove
> In our hallways.
>
> The fig tree has spiced
> Its figs with sweetness.
> The young fruits of the vineyard
> Are already redolent.
> Arise, my love,
> Arise, my beauty,
> Come!
>
> My little dove in the cracks in the rocks,
> In the deep fissures of the heights,
> Let me see your shape,
> Let me hear your voice,
> For your voice is sweet,
> For your shape is beautiful.

Everyone recognizes that this song differs from the previous. In that song the young woman awakens from her sleep under the apple tree, dreaming of her lover, who had sung her to sleep with a lullaby. In this song her lover is at a distance, and has long been away. She has spent the winter as a dove ensnared in the cracks in the rocks; now she is awakened, not by spring or by the lark, rather by *the voice of her lover,* who comes from afar, bringing her spring and joy.

She *knows* his voice from afar, and *he is it. He leaps, he springs over the low mountains, a leaping deer. There he is, standing behind the green wall, peering through the banister,* like a newly blossoming flower, *through the railings,* first he *speaks,* then he *sings,* listen! Everything that spring and love, garden and dawn, can offer lies within his love; the caressing sound of the original, however, cannot be translated.

Part 4

> Who is there,
> Who rises up from the desert?
> As pillars of smoke,
> As the odor of myrrh and incense,
> And the precious fragrance of spices.

We shall see the beginning of this fragment again and again; without doubt it is a common song incipit and the entry to a new scene in the Orient, like that of every nation and language. It is here that something rises up from the desert, narrow and luminous like a pillar of smoke, redolent of myrrh and precious incense; to the people of the East it is common to compare the appearance of the young woman with night and dusk. The gentle expanse of her limbs becomes pillars of smoke; it must smell of ointment and incense in their beauty and love.

> See the bed, Solomon's bed!
> Sixty of the mightiest of all
> The mighty in Israel stand about it.
> All have sword in hand,
> All of them learned in war,
> Each with a sword at his waist,
> For the horror of the night.
>
> King Solomon has made himself a noble bed
> From the cedars of Lebanon.
> He made the bedposts from silver,
> The canvas they bear from gold,
> The bedspread of crimson,
> Pillows of love at the center,
> For the daughters of Jerusalem.
>
> Go forth and gaze upon him,
> You daughters of Zion, upon King Solomon;
> In the crown with which he crowned his mother,
> On the day of his engagement,
> On the day with joy in his heart.

The preceding scenes of the *night* present occasions followed now by the proud song, which also begins with *night* and *fear*, albeit in a special connection!

The song has three verses, whereby the opening two obviously fit together as they unfold. The first bed is so terrible *"because of the horror of the night,"* the second noble *"because of the daughters of Jerusalem,"* the third fulfills the king's pride and the joy in his heart.

Was ever a wedding sung with such high estimation? The song rises from the bed of the hero to the bed of love, and from there to the wedding crown and the joy in his heart. At first the king is merely terrifying, but then envied and noble, and finally beloved and holy. The first decorates the hero, the second the paramours, the third the mother and eternal friend. For the king the bridal garland of his mother transcends heroic fame and the king's crown. . . .

Part 5

The lover is no less modest, paying homage with an equal fullness to her shame. The reasons she does not turn away from his praise are immediately forthcoming:

> You are so totally beautiful, oh love,
> You are without reproach.
> Oh bride, from Lebanon with me,
> You will come from Lebanon with me,
> You will have a view from the heights of Amana,
> From Senir, from Mount Hermon far into the distance,
> From the dwellings of the lions,
> From the mountains of the leopards. . . .
>
> You hearten me, oh my sister bride!
> You hearten me with the focus of your gaze,
> With pearls about your neck.
>
> How sweet is your love,
> You, my sister bride!
> How much sweeter your love is than wine!
> The smell of your ointments
> Than all other fragrances!
>
> Honey drips from your lips, oh bride!
> Milk and honey lies beneath your tongue,
> The smell of your clothes
> Like the fragrance of Lebanon.
>
> You are a holy garden, my sister bride,
> A holy spring, a sealed well,
> Your orchard a paradise of apples
> With the most precious fruit of all.
>
> Floral and crocus,
> Cinnamon and lily,
> Every kind of incense.
> Aloe and myrrh,
> With a complement of spices.
>
> A fountain in the garden,
> A spring of flowing water,
> Which runs from Lebanon. . . .
>
> Lift yourself up, north!
> And south wind, come,
> Waft through my garden,
> So that its spices are released. . . .

His modest beloved interrupts him, bringing his spirited praise to an end as if she did not understand it:

> So enter, my love,
> Into his garden
> And eat his precious fruit.

And he, yielding thus also to her:

> I entered into my garden,
> Oh my sister bride!
> And broke off my myrrh
> And my spices,
> And ate from my honey
> And the flowing honey,
> And drank from my wine
> And from my milk.
> Now eat, my beloveds,
> And drink, and become drunk, you loved ones. . . .

Thus comes this incomparable embroidery of desire, simplicity, love, and beauty to its conclusion; had I but succeeded in rendering only the main threads from it in the spirit of the East!

Picturing the image of his beloved is accomplished entirely with scenes of vivid nature, so different from that with which we are familiar. Most of the comparisons of this kind thus seem to us unnatural, Eastern, and exaggerated; in the Orient, however, they provide an *exact* language, and therefore they appear repeatedly in this song when the part of human beauty they represent is mentioned. The eyes, thus, are more than once *simple doves*, which *peer out from behind the full*, beautiful *curls; the hair* more than once *a chamois cloth*, the *teeth* more than once the *flock of lambs*; nature and truth reside in these pictures! . . . Can soft hair, also in the flow of its waves, in the way its curls fall, be pictured in any more beautiful ways than in the scene of a shining flock, here and there in a pasture, and as in the gentle turns and twists that flow from the beautiful Gilead? The fullness, the wisdom, the unbroken order, the health and fullness of the teeth,[f] can they acquire a better scene in *vital* nature than in a flock of newly

---

f. [JGH] Because the people of the East have such strong feelings about the cleanliness of the mouth and the health of breathing, there could be no better image for the teeth than a *newly washed, newly shorn flock*. I do not understand how a translation in a new version wishes to state that the sheep come from the spring and are prohibited from drinking. One does not need to ask if there is such a thing as a flock of similar sheep, all of them bearing twins, or something like that? There is such a thing . . . here, in the mouth of the beloved.

shorn, newly washed lambs, in which each mother carries twins with her, and nothing is absent, nothing is wanting? Who can recall for me a more beautiful image of soft *lips* than the *thread of crimson* that whispers *sweet words* like love songs? And a sweeter image of *soft* blushing cheeks as the nectar of milk and blood from a peeled *fruit of the Orient*? The throat, compared with *David's Tower*, is often the subject of laughter; I cannot imagine what could be a more appropriate comparison in this respect? Firm and round and beautiful and adorned, he towers over the breast of the king's bride; just as on the proud vest of David, so too hang the *spoils of war* around his neck, once borne by a *hero*, now openly displayed anew as shining necklaces. In this way, the imagery continues, reaching the *two does, also twins, that are pastured beneath the lilies*;[g] as long as nature is nature, one will find no more charming and vivid images than those from the world and countryside of the shepherd.

Part 6

If I could but free some of the dewdrops from my lover's skin so that they could become drops of forgetfulness for my readers, and so they could feel that passage fully and isolated and untrammeled by previous shadings and impressions!

> I sleep and my heart awakens!

> Voice of my beloved!
> He proclaims!

> "Offer yourself to me, my sister, my friend,
> My turtle dove, my doe,
> Offer yourself to me."

> "My clothing is removed;
> How? Should I dress myself?
> My feet are washed;
> Should I soil them again?" . . .

> My lover stretched
> His hand through the lattice,
> My innermost being quivered.

---

g. [JGH] For those in the East, the gazelle is the image of all that is soft, shy, and lovely. For fitting images of pastures likewise shy, gentle, and peaceful, see D. Friedrich Hasselquist, *Reise nach Palästina*, 564; Laurent d'Arvieux, *Voyage dans la Palestine*, inter alia.

Quickly I arose,
To offer myself to him, my beloved.

My hands touched myrrh,
My fingers touched myrrh,
Which encompassed the door's lock.

I offered myself to my beloved;
My lover had escaped,
Disappeared....

I abandoned my very soul,
That he would speak to me ...
I searched for him, but found him not.
I called for him, but he
Answered me not.

The watchmen found me,
Who surrounded the city.
They struck me,
They wounded me,
They stole my veil from me,
The watchmen of the walls.

I swear to you, daughters of Jerusalem!
If you find him,
My beloved,
What should you say to him? ...
That I am sick with love for him.

"What kind of lover is your beloved,
You most beautiful of all women!
What kind of lover is your beloved,
That you must swear thus to us?"

My beloved is white and red,
He is one among ten thousand.

His skin is of the finest gold,
His hair wavy,
And black, like a raven.

His eyes are like those of a dove in the wild,
Bathed in milk,
Afloat in their fullness.

His cheeks are like the flowers of the field,
Like a locket filled with spices.

His lips like roses,
They are redolent of the fragrance of myrrh.

His hands like golden vessels,
Full of turquoise.

His belly is like pure ivory,
Covered with sapphires.

His hips are like marble pillars,
Resting upon golden foundations.

His face is like Lebanon,
Transcendent like a cedar tree.

His mouth is sweet,
And his entire being is made of delicacies.

He is my beloved, he is my friend,
You daughters of Jerusalem.

"Where, then, has your beloved gone?
You most beautiful of all women!
In what direction did he turn, your beloved?
We wish to join you in your quest."

My beloved entered his garden,
In search of the flowers of the field,
In order to graze in the gardens,
So that he could gather roses.

My beloved, I am his,
My beloved, he is mine,
He who grazes among the roses. . . .

And so ends this song, and undoubtedly there are even *more* songs that the collector gathered together because of the opportunity and the ways they fitted well together. The wandering maiden of the night invoked the daughters of Jerusalem, and because they responded and asked about the characteristics of her beloved, so it was an auspicious moment for one frightened by lovesickness to describe the shape of her beloved with a brilliance and longing that almost illuminated the night. Because the daughters of Jerusalem press on with their questions, and she wishes to confide nothing to them, the song returns once again to the songs of shepherds and roses, in which she repeats the images of the roses as previous recognition of love, just as the nightingale echoes its song toward the same end. . . . I, too, must once again note how different this scene appears when compared to the previous one, in which a *royal wedding*, the Mount of Gilead and Mount Hermon, the Valley of Elah and all of Lebanon, awaited command. All the images possessed this fullness and were thus suspended—the hero could turn his gaze toward her: the golden chain about her neck drew the beloved to her. We see her as a *maiden from the countryside,* who sleeps alone in her dwelling, in her garden. Her beloved arrives at a door in disrepair, where he can grasp the handle like the shepherd who applies an *ointment* to the door of his beloved.[h] He has no place to stay and is chilled to the bone, and he wishes to enter—she slumbers, and between sleep and waking she speaks like a maiden from the countryside. Thus she arises, searches, calls out, encounters those watching over her, confides to the daughters of Jerusalem as one unknown to them, and thus they answer her; briefly, the measure of humility and the connection to the soil form the soul of this superb song. A queen takes her place in the golden hall, and all else disappears. . . .

Part 7

Who is it that radiates like the dawn?
Is as lovely as the moon,
As pure as the sun,
As terrifying as a commander in war?

"I went to the grove of the nut trees,
In search of the fruits of the valley;
In search of the vineyard, if already ripened,
If the apple trees had already blossomed?

And I knew not that my soul
Drew me to the battle chariot
Of my noble people."

Turn around, turn around, oh Shulamit!
Turn around, turn around,
We want to see you!

"What do you wish to see when gazing upon Shulamit?"

---

h. [JGH] The original version makes it clear that the ointment is on the handle of the door, and not on her fingers. Some translations, moreover, have included this interpretation when appearing in print. The ointments and wreaths on the beloved's door are an old custom in the region. The tradition was also common among the Greeks, and, I can imagine, it still is. See also Johann Gottlieb Lessing, *Eclogae Regis Salomonis* (Leipzig: Dyk, 1777), 90. [PVB] Cf. Baildam 1999, 160.

The dance of God's army.

How beautiful are the dance steps you take,
You daughter of nobility!
The movement of your hips
Is like that of chains in the master's hands.

Your navel is a round chalice,
That never overflows.

Your belly is like a mound of hay,
Planted all about with roses.

Your two breasts are like two does,
As if one is the mother of twins.

Your neck is a pillar of ivory.
Your eyes ponds of Heshbon,
Before the door of the prince's daughters.

Your nose is like the palace of Lebanon,
Which is turned toward Damascus.

Your skin is like Mount Carmel.
The hair on your head is like satin,
Braided about a captive king.

How beautiful you are,
And how lovely you are,
Oh love, in your desire!

Your stature
Is like that of the palm tree,
And your breasts are like grapes.

I spoke: "I climb upon the palm tree!
I hold tight its branches.
Your breasts should be my grapes,
And your breath
Has the fragrance of apples,
And your mouth has the taste
Of fine wine...."

"The wine flows sweetly
Into my love,
And caresses his lips,
Whispering.

Yes, I belong to my love,
And his desire belongs to me;
Come, my beloved,

We want to go to the countryside.
Do we wish to live in villages,
There to arise early,
To go to the vineyards,
To see if the vines have already blossomed?
If the grapes are already ripening?
If the apple trees are in bloom?

I wish to give you
All my love!

The flowers of love are already fragrant,
And above your door
Is beauty of every kind,
New and old,
My beloved, I retain everything for you.

Who gives you to me
As a brother to me?
Who has nursed
At the breasts of my mother?

Were I to find you in public
And to kiss you,
And no one would have judged me ill.

I wish that you would lead me,
I wish that you would bring me
Into the house of my mother.

You should teach me,
I would drink you
With the drink I had prepared,
With cider from my tree.

Your left arm
Would rest under my head,
And your right
Would hold me tight."

"I beseech you, daughters of Jerusalem,
When you awaken her!
When you stir, love!
Until it pleases her!"

Let me begin by examining the structure and form of the entire song, for it is therein that most of its charms lie.

Very clearly, the familiar opening "who is it who awakens?" announces the shift to *a new scene*. In this instance, however, she does not unfold as dusk, with its sweet incense, but rather as if she were *beautiful, like the sun, moon, aurora*. The glow of the dawn spreads . . . it will become the moon, it will become the sun, it will become the fearsome, fiery army.

She appears thus in the full *splendor of love*; but how? why? . . . From her first appearance singing. She sings the shepherd's song, "I entered the grove of nut trees," reminding us of her pastoral simplicity, her quiet, peaceful life, as she cares for the nature about her, nurtured, loved, and without further thought. At this moment she is unaware that *her soul, indeed, her courage and cleverness, have bestowed the dignity upon her* in which she now appears. She advances *as if in battle* and she is greeted with song comparing her with a fearsome *army*. Thus she refers to her dignity as warlike, the *defending chariot* of a *noble people*, and we come to understand this comparison because we are familiar with the story of Solomon and the Hebrew language. *The chariot and steed of Israel* . . . the most common way of describing military might and the bastions heroically holding their positions.[i] It was Elijah who was called to heaven by God;[j] and so she now employs an expression that it is possible only to rule a *free and noble people*. The story of Solomon tells us that he would never allow the people of Israel to become servants, rather that they were to be *"warriors, and as princes and counts and knights with command over servants and chariots."*[k] Would a loving king, who had created such distinctions among his people, also not possess such differences for his love? It is said of him:[l] "He commanded all about him with peace so that all in Israel could live in security in their vineyards and amid their date orchards," and thus *"he mobilized chariots and cavalry riders so that he possessed fourteen hundred chariots and twelve thousand cavalry, which he brought to encampments and to Jerusalem,"* forming a fearsome army! Would it even be possible that there would be no such traces remaining in the sound of his songs? Must his queen and lover not also find her way, mixed into such magnificence? How very natural it is that she should reflect on her previous peace and pastoral simplicity! Briefly, let us consider something similar in a magnificent and prophetic psalm:[m]

---

i. [JGH] Psalm 20:8; Isaiah 31:1.
j. [JGH] 2 Kings 2:11–12.
k. [JGH] 1 Kings 9:22; 2 Chronicles 8:9.
l. [JGH] 1 Kings 10:26.
m. [JGH] Psalm 110:3.

Your people, so noble, join with you
On the day of victory
In festive clothing,
As the shining dew . . .
Born of the dawn.

She appears as a prophetess in *regal military magnificence*.

The passage undergoes transition, shifting to *dance*, dance like *the dance of angels, the heavenly army*: I know of no other song in which dance is so ennobled and idealized. The chorus calls out to her that *she turn herself*, again and again, letting all *look upon her*. "*What is it that you wish to see when gazing upon Shulamit?*" she answers artfully. "*The Dance of Mahanaim!*" sings the chorus in return, and a song of joy sounds, with each phrase in command of this picture of love and movement, without which the song would come to a standstill.

Clearly we enter another world at this moment. We think about dance in different ways, and we seek to distinguish between the just and the unjust; it suffices to say that, from the earliest days, those in the Orient thought about innocence in completely different ways. They regarded the angels and the stars as a *vibrant victorious army*[n] dancing about the throne of the Almighty. Choir and antiphony . . . the two encampments of *mahanaim*[o] . . . celebrate him in eternal song. Like song, dance too was *sacred* among the people. The song of victory at the Red Sea rose from the chorus of women, with tympani and dance, like the victory song of the prophetess.[p] It is because this dance is not gentle and voluptuous that it is revealed here to be magnificent and warlike.

Part 8

And she continues thus: "Yes, my beloved, my love is his, and his passion is mine; but let us go forth. There is no ear here capable of enduring your words. There in the simple dwellings, where nature is pure and unencumbered, it is there that we now discover the springtime of love. It is there that the blossoms of the tree and the first buds of the vineyard blossom together with us. Early in the morning, when all else is sleeping, only the flowers of love surround us with their fragrance:

It is there, beloved, that I wish
To be yours with all my love.

n. [JGH] Psalm 68:18; Job 38:7.
o. [PVB] Two army encampments in biblical usage.
p. [PVB] The reference here is to Exodus 15, a "Song of Moses."

And already its fragrance surrounds us, the mandrake."q She decorates and crowns the door of her dwelling with fruits and flowers from the countryside.r There is nothing wanting in her dwelling, and there is nothing wanting for her beloved, for she has saved the beauty of the fruits from the previous year. In short, she is entirely at home in the simplicity and sweetness of pastoral life....

Still, it is not sufficient. She wishes to make her love even more innocent, transforming love fully to the *love between brother and sister*.

> Oh, that you were not my brother!
> And you had kissed our mother's breast with me.
> Oh, that where I should find you,
> I could kiss you
> Such that no one would mock me,
> And imagine it was sin.
>
> I desire to embrace you and hold you tight,
> And to lead you
> Into the house of my mother.
>
> You wave to me,
> I should bring you
> The drink I have prepared,
> The nectar from my tree.
>
> With his left hand
> He lifts up my head:
> With his right hand
> He draws me to him....

Who is the judge of tradition who would be able to imagine a more chaste and heavenly marriage? Who has a heart that does not sing of the lovely dove three times with the song of the slumbering love:

> I beseech you, daughters of Jerusalem,
> Do not waken her!

---

q. [JGH] To all that is said about the mandrake, one must also join with Luther in saying: "Go there yourself and inquire about what a mandrake is." I might say that one should follow the legend and not be frightened because Rubin found mandrake in the wheat harvest. Indeed, he found it only as something strange, late in coming. If it had been the season for its blossoming, Rachel could have found it herself. Even in the text with which we are now concerned, it is its early appearance and strong fragrance that receives attention. [PVB] In biblical texts, mandrake was associated with restoring fertility to women unable to conceive children.

r. [JGH] See Friedrich Hasselquist, *Reise nach Palästina*, 125.

Do not arouse her!
Until she herself awakens.

And at this place of innocence let us look once again at the *palm tree* from before and at the *mandrake of love*. For those living in the East, the palm was the most beautiful image of marital love, in its growth and blossoms, in its fertility and the sweetness of its berries, its nectar, and its fruits. Even in the present day, the most beautiful offering served at the wedding feast is the palm's honey,[s] from the sweet wine, given so gently to the lover so that he might slip into a drunken sleep. The nectar, drawn from the palm's growth, its branches, its berries, and the sweet breath of the growing fruit, is what finally fills him and brings his restless slumber to a close, is treated with such gentleness, so that I feel almost the shame of one ill formed, who might find such things offensive or irregular. Assume just the opposite of everything, and regard it as if it were the true human nature! Let the swift flight of the king's step through the lover sink to the heavy step of the beggar. Take notice that the bracelet of the greatest artist is transformed, the deer flees from its peak, and dims the pool of Heshbon. Lebanon's palace lies in the mud, and the once-joyful Mount Carmel stands naked and swaying: the round goblet is wanting for drink, and the thin palm tree is a thornbush. . . . You Pharisees, you who judge like Cato, is humanity any better, happier, or nobler? Is not the nectar of paradise created so that it may be enjoyed spiced with innocence and as the love between brother and sister? Oh, nature, nature, you holy and consecrated temple of God! You are the most consecrated where you are most boldly sheltered and most beautifully cared for, where one celebrates in the chambers of innocence and cultivation of the blossoms of the tree and the innocent buds of the vineyard. . . .

Part 10 (Close of Chapter 1, Lieder der Liebe)

It is as good as complete, for what follows appears to me as but an additional echo, so that nothing of this kind will be lost. It is the ingenious and proud *conversation between a sister and her brothers.*

THE FIRST ONE SPEAKS:

Our sister is still small,
Her breasts are still buds;
What shall we do with our sister
When a suitor comes to court her?

---

s. [JGH] Thomas Shaw, *Reisen, oder, Anmerkungen verschiedene Theile der Barbarey und der Levante betreffend* (Leipzig: B. C. Breitkopf und Sohn, 1765), 128.

THE SECOND:

Were she a wall,
We would wish to build upon her
A silver palace.
Were she a gate to a city,
We would seek to protect her
With cedar timbers.

THE SISTER:

I am indeed a wall,
And my breasts are towers.
Thus I was in his eyes
Like one who had found peace.

Deliberately I retain the oriental, puzzling dusk in this translation so that the rays of enlightenment will be even more pleasing. Clearly we witness here the advice of older, wiser brothers seeking to protect the honor of their sister when she becomes a young woman. The advice comes rather too early, and the piece of advice itself is rather clumsy. One brother answers, *"Were she a wall,"* in other words, she should be protected in the appropriate ways. *Silver weapons* and jewels should adorn her. *Were she, however, a gate to the city* (which is not a wall), then we must keep her closed (*they secure it with cedar timbers*) ... the customary way in the Orient to secure loyalty and chastity.... Unwilling to accept such conditions, the sister interrupts: *"I am indeed a wall* and no gate. Moreover, I have no desire for your towers and bastions, for *my breasts are towers* that give me security and protection. Indeed, this is no protection against attack, but rather victory and peace at first glance. The enemy appears in front of the wall, and in the moment it views the weapons confronting it the enemy withdraws, leaving the city in peace. My very presence will fill him with awe, and I shall remain in peace.... I have no need for your advice and your protection." There can be no doubt that this is the meaning, as the following brief story illustrates, when the young woman mocks her brothers:

Solomon had a vineyard
On the slopes of Baal-Hamon.
He built small dwellings on the slopes of the vineyard,
So that each would bring him
A thousand silver pieces for his harvest.

The slopes of the vineyard
Stand before my eyes:

A thousand go to Solomon,
And those who watch over the harvest
Receive two hundred more.

Obviously this story *makes fun* of what comes from *caring for and watching over the vineyards*. The king receives what he claims for himself, and everyone else takes what is appropriate for the privilege of working in the vineyards. The young woman herself, as she says, *protects her own vineyard*, and so she will not be betrayed and have to pay additionally for the privilege of laboring in it.

We might ask if this lovely fairy tale has been understood in this way until the present. I do not know, and at the very least I have not found anything that suggests that it has. I do not, however, wish to argue whether it is possible that "an elderly rabbi may once have made the claim." ... For me, at any rate, the sense of the story is clear and beautiful, and it captures the ingenuity of the Orient. One knows that those in the East love such puzzling wordplay in pictures, likenesses, and images of all kinds. I am willing to go so far as to say that this is one of the most beautiful tales of its kind to come to us from the antiquity of the Jewish people. For this reason and because Solomon's name and vineyard are contained in the tale, we presume a connection to the *Song of Songs*.[t] It could also be a small part of the treasury of the great king, which was used for the household, among these presumably also to serve the purposes of a relationship with a lover. ... The moral of the story is the following. "Whoever truly protects the harvest, beauty, and honor does so herself. She does not need secure locks, bastions, dwellings, and towers, for these offer her assistance almost not at all." This moral, moreover, is clothed with femininity and youthfulness....

Here is yet another *fragment from a conversation*:

You, who dwell in gardens,
Your playmates harken to your voice,
Let me hear it....

"Dash, my beloved, quickly to the deer,
To the young stag on the fragrant heights." ...

---

t. [JGH] Undoubtedly Baal-Hamon was one of the most distant regions in which Solomon built vineyards, clearly also a favored place. [PVB] Whereas Herder suggests that Baal-Hamon is geographically associated with Baalbek, now in the Bekaa Valley of Lebanon, where it remains the most important area for wine in Lebanon, the exact location of the biblical Baal-Hamon remains open to question.

And with that, the story comes to an end. Either the collector did not want to omit anything, so he just inserted a little *duet*, or there was much more to reveal, as we would like to explore ourselves. Obviously this is the voice of a young lover who wishes to hear the voice of a nightingale. She motions to him to flee, like a stag to the fragrant mountains . . . and thus comes the book to its close. . . .

PART II

The History Project

4. The Nation and Its Fragments
Essay on "Briefwechsel über Ossian und die Lieder alter Völker" (1773)
Philip V. Bohlman

> Song! It will again be what it once was! Sensitive to the entire being of life! Speaking from the human heart ... with God, with itself, with all of nature!
>
> —JOHANN GOTTFRIED HERDER,
> *Über Ossian und die Lieder alter Völker*

The epistolary fragments that fill Johann Gottfried Herder's 1773 "Correspondence about Ossian and the Songs of Ancient Peoples" unfold across a narrative fabric of in-betweenness. The language of the letters lies between prose and poetry, forming a paean to poesy. "What a genre poesy really becomes, a genre truly between painting and music!" Herder writes in lieu of a conclusion that might enclose the spaces that he passionately and performatively opens in the pages that precede his final thoughts. At a moment of transition in his own life, professionally and personally, Herder turns to poesy as he passes from the earliest aesthetic writing, which occupied him during the Riga years of the late 1760s, to the full engagement with folk song that would consume much of his literary and philosophical activity through the remainder of the 1770s. It is at the moment of transition in the early 1770s that Herder begins to establish himself in German lands, moving through the positions that would lead him from Strasbourg to Weimar.

It was during the transitions of the early 1770s, moreover, that Herder's publications entered the aesthetic and philosophical in-betweenness of *Sturm und Drang* (Storm and Stress), which itself opened the space of the arts and music in the waning decades of the Enlightenment to presage the Romanticism of the nineteenth century. Filling the space of *Sturm und Drang* was a search for the fragments of a national past—in literature, in painting, in music—that could cohere as a new whole, that of the nation. It was his work on *Von deutscher Art und Kunst*, for which the fragments from the Ossian correspondence would provide the lead essay, that charted the path toward a music that filled the historical conditions of a German national style and narrative for the arts ("deutsche Art und Kunst").

FIGURE 11. Title page of Johann Gottfried Herder, *Von deutscher Art und Kunst*, 1773. Reproduced in a modern edition.

The project that led to the publication of *Von deutscher Art und Kunst* in 1773 began with Herder's work on the Ossian correspondence and his essay on Shakespeare. Both of the earlier essays enabled Herder to turn toward subject matter and rhetorical approaches that would shape the work of the 1770s, and to some degree his entire career. His essay on the translatability of Shakespeare would appear as a chapter in the 1774 *Alte Volkslieder* (see chapter 1 in the present book), and he would return to Ossian when seeking to understand the historical durability of epic, for example in the 1794 essay on "Homer and Ossian" (see chapter 5 in the present volume). Herder's new publisher in Hamburg, Bode, foresaw the potential of combining the Ossian and Shakespeare essays with additional essays—*einige fliegende Blätter*, or "several broadsides"—which together would intensify the aesthetic search for German-ness in architecture and history: Johann Wolfgang von Goethe (1749–1832), "Von deutscher Baukunst" (On German Architecture); Paolo Frisi (1728–1784), "Versuch über die Gotische

Baukunst" (Essay on Gothic Architecture); and Justus Möser (1720–1794), "Deutsche Geschichte" (German History). *Von deutscher Art und Kunst* itself came to represent an attempt to suture together a larger whole from fragments, gathered from diverse sources, but with the potential to build a common edifice. In Herder's Ossian correspondence, the in-between space of poesy provided the landscape upon which the German edifice of poesy, and its exemplary form, folk song, should rise.

The seeds of what would be Herder's formulation of a concept for folk song lie in this essay, which employs the context of a critique of Michael Denis's translations of James Macpherson's publication of songs and epics attributed to Ossian. With Ossian and the Scottish songs as a point of departure, Herder draws upon a number of the most important debates during the Enlightenment. Already in the title of the essay, he situates himself on the ancient side of discussions about the ancient and the modern in music and the arts. Classical literature and poetry provide a foundation for discussions about form and structure, notably the ability effectively to use hexameter for the German translations of the Ossian songs. Similarly, Herder shows his acute awareness of the philological attention of his contemporaries to the Nordic languages, particularly the epic poetry of the *Edda*, the Old Norse literary cousins of the German *Nibelungen*. No less evident at this early stage of his theoretical growth is Herder's attention to the literature growing from encounters with peoples beyond Europe, whose "wildness" offers a basis for comparison globally, as well as more specifically with the Scottish singers who would have conveyed the songs of Ossian. As he begins to refer specifically to folk songs in the course of the essay, it is already from the broadly comparative perspectives of encounter with music throughout the world. If the chapter is but a single essay, the lead chapter in *Von deutscher Art und Kunst*, it nonetheless has very ambitious—indeed, global—goals. The discussion of song in the chapter, therefore, has both historical and ethnographic contexts.

The essay itself drew upon earlier publications, with the first version appearing in 1771, and then another 1772 version as a single publication, at which time it had the same form and substance it would have when appearing in 1773 in *Von deutscher Art und Kunst*. Songs and poems appear throughout the essay, several of them providing the foundations for what would become the imagination of folk song in the remaining publications by Herder, which in turn proliferated to form the path to folk and art song throughout the nineteenth century (Gelbart 2007). Herder's German translation of the Scottish "Edward" ballad, for example, appears in this essay for the first time, and it would pass from here into the *Volkslieder* later in the

1770s, and then beyond to provide the textual model for Franz Schubert, Johannes Brahms, and other composers, even before it entered the canon of the English and Scottish Child ballads later in the nineteenth century (see for example figure 13).

Herder's concern for cultural context, too, is clearly present in the essay. He reflects upon the genesis and transmission of folk song within cultures such as the early Scots, whom Ossian's songs presumably chronicled. From the Old Norse epics to the songs of Sámi of circumpolar Europe in his own day and beyond to the Indigenous peoples in traveler's accounts, Herder moves the discussion of song in nature to include new dimensions, not least among them the role of auditory culture in processes of perception and mediation. In 1773 this essay was groundbreaking, and for Herder it would set in motion the engagement with song, culture, and nation that would occupy him for the remaining three decades of his life.

The fragmentary form of the parts in the essay is essential for understanding it. These letters, fragments, and personal observations are addressed specifically to the reader "Sie," a personal "you" with which we, as readers, are meant to identify. By placing each reader in the position of that "Sie," Herder rhetorically evokes and captures a sort of immediacy. Such fragmentary forms are a literary genre of the age, although they clearly stand at the border between the late Enlightenment and early Romanticism, and then extend beyond to our own day (see especially Constantine and Porter 2003).

The extract from "Correspondence about Ossian and the Songs of Ancient Peoples" performs its own fragmentary structures, which in turn reflect those of the songs that appear throughout the essay. Not only does the essay unfold in fragments—segments and sections—but there are different syntactic and grammatical fragments at work. Questions are asked, and locative voice is used, just as they are in several of the songs themselves. Sentences are long, run-on, sometimes without necessary syntax or even complete verbal structures. Herder moves between vernacular speech and conversational rhetoric, giving the reader the feeling that the essay really is the substance of correspondence. In the translation that follows I retain as many of Herder's conventions as possible—the abundant dashes as ellipses, the excessive punctuation, and the intentional breaks in the conversational flow, which mark the points at which one letter breaks off and another begins, often as if it were already following another line of thought. The fragmentary form also provides a simulacrum and metaphor for the problems of translation and the limitations of language versus feeling; it is the latter of these, feeling, with the evident passion and immediacy of *Sturm und Drang*, that dominates Herder's epistolary prose.

The core argument in Herder's Ossian essay concerns the problems of translation and of transforming the songs that express one culture's customs and notions of beauty and sensitivity into another language. The point of departure is Herder's criticism of Michael Denis's translation of Macpherson's translations, which will also enter into chapter 5, the other chapter in the present book in which Ossian appears in literary dialogue with Homer. Herder argues that the meaning, aesthetic beauty, and emotional core disappear when Denis renders the Ossian songs in appropriately poetic German, with its bow to classical literary procedures. The essay in many ways is about translations all the way down: Herder positions himself in the role of a cultural translator, concerned about the meanings that are translated into German after Macpherson has translated Ossian from Gaelic into English. By extension, language is the crucial but problematic link to the music of other peoples and cultures.

Questions of encounter and ethnography grow from the critique of translating folk song. Herder makes distinctions, though often subtle ones, between *Übersetzung* and *Übertragung*. This distinction will be critical to the different paths he follows later in the 1770s, with the *Song of Songs* project growing from the former, the *Folk Song* volumes and the *Cid* translation exemplifying the latter (see chapters 2, 3, and 8 in the present volume). Herder powerfully makes an argument for his own transformation through ethnographic encounter, particularly during his 1769 ship journey from Riga to France and Germany (see the epilogue in the present volume). By experiencing the places where Scandinavian songs arose and the historical sites where specific events took place, he assumes a power to observe from his senses. Indeed, he speaks about the ways in which his reading of Macpherson/Ossian undergoes a transformation because he is on the storm-tossed North Sea. Ethnographic encounter for Herder, thus, is not necessarily fieldwork with the people of another culture. Encounter occurs when experience opens the senses to a closer feeling for the culture of other peoples and a deeper sense for the wildness and *Sinnlichkeit* (attunement to the senses) of the Ossian songs and epics.

From "Briefwechsel über Ossian und die Lieder alter Völker" / "Correspondence about Ossian and the Songs of Ancient Peoples"

JOHANN GOTTFRIED HERDER,
TRANSLATED BY PHILIP V. BOHLMAN

...[a] Just like you, I too am charmed by the translation of Ossian for our own people and in our own language; I am no less charmed than were it an original epic. A poet so full of sublimity, innocence, simplicity, capability, and bliss for human life must, if only in a moment of deprivation, not entirely doubt the value of great books that have an impact and touch the heart. This is so even as the poet wishes to live in a meager cabin in Scotland, where such festivities take place.... Michael Denis's translation, moreover, reveals so much hard work and good taste, in part through the joyful force of the images, but also because of the strength of the German language, that I immediately placed it among the favorite books in my library, and I hoped that Germany might have the fortune of claiming such a bard, awakened for the Scottish by their bard.... You, however, who had previously been so obstinate in doubting the validity and authenticity of the Scottish bard, listen now to me, the defender, rather than obstinately doubting that, despite all the hard work and feeling and force and power in the German translation, our Ossian is surely no longer the true Ossian of Scotland. I do not have enough space to prove that just

---

a. Herder largely uses hyphens and dashes to mark the ellipses between the fragments of the letters in the Ossian correspondence. I use the standard practices of three and four periods to mark these ellipses throughout the translated text (see also the "Note on Translation and Commentary" at the beginning of this book).

now: I must now only defend my observation as a Turkish Mufti would his *fatwā*, his legal opinion, and here the name of that Mufti is....

... The grounds for my stance against the German Ossian are not simple, as you so kindly mention, obstinacy against German hexameter *above all*: For why should you trust in my sensitivity, for tone and harmony of the soul, if I should not, for instance, feel the hexameter of Kleist or Klopstock? Indeed, you yourself once recognized the hexameter of Klopstock in Ossian? Indeed, hence the shedding of tears! Had Denis only considered the real feeling for Ossian as we perceive him in our inner ear! ... Ossian so immediate, powerful, masculine, broken into images and feelings, ... Klopstock's manner so complete, so striking, sensitivity flowing without restraint. How the waves crash, retreat, and then return again, the words unleashed like the flow of speech ... what a difference! And how does Ossian stand up against Klopstock's hexameter? Against Klopstock's realization? I do not know two beings who could be less like each other, even if we really consider Ossian as an *Epopöist*, an epic singer.

That is, however, not what he is, and that is exactly what I wanted to say to you, for there was already talk, I believe, about a critical edition, which is none of my business. For you, instead, I wanted to recall that Ossian's poems, *Songs, Songs of the Folk, Songs*, are those of an uneducated but sensitive people, who are able to sing them over the course of the historical *longue durée* in the tongue of their fathers' tradition.... Did these supply evidence for our own beautiful epic form? Could they have done so? ... My friend, when I first voiced my stance against your doubts that reduced the originality of Ossian's songs to nothing, to the inner witness, to the spirit of the work itself, who was it that acquiesced and claimed: "It would have been impossible for James Macpherson to write such a thing! No one could write such poetry during our own century!" With that same sense of inner witness I now say just as forcefully: "No one could really have sung that! No uncivilized mountain people would truly have been able to sing and maintain such a music! It could not have been Ossian who sang these, indeed, who could have sung them over the course of so many years!" What do you say about my evidence from the songs themselves? ... Now, perhaps, I shall present you with more pages filled with evidence!

... I should never have imagined you to be so stubborn about our German Ossian! To want to convince through analysis and individual comparison "that he is just as good as the English!" What is there to compare when it comes to matters of simple, immediate sensation? What can one not prove through thoughtful analysis; ... surely it will not be any kind of immediate sensation. Have you also not taken into consideration what you so very, very often—indeed, every day—sense: "What might it mean to

FIGURE 12. Nicolai Abraham Abildgaard, *Ossian's Swan Song*, ca. 1782. Statens Museum for Kunst, Copenhagen. Public domain.

leave out one word, to add another, or to rework and repeat yet another word; what might produce another accent, viewpoint, or voice yielding an entirely different sound?" I can always leave the meaning aside; but the sound? the color? the most immediate feeling for the distinctiveness of the place, of the singer's goal? . . . And let alone the beauty of a poem, all the spirit and power of speech? . . . I grant you that our Ossian, as a poetic work, is just as good, even better, than the English Ossian . . . indeed because Ossian becomes such beautiful poetic work for us, he is no longer the old Scottish bard, Ossian. This is for me the bottom line.

Just take one of the old songs that appear in Shakespeare or in a similar English collection, and strip it of the lyricism of melodious sound, of rhyme, of the resonance of the words, and of the dark path of the melody. Leave the meaning just as it is, but transpose it in some way into another language.

Does it not mean anything if you rework the notes in a melody by Pergolesi or the letters on a sheet of paper? What remains of meaning on that sheet? What remains of Pergolesi? I just had that song from Shakespeare's *Twelfth Night* before me, in which the lovestruck count wishes to take his leave: . . .

> that old and antik song
> Me thought it did relieve my passion much . . .
> *More than light airs and recollected terms*
> *Of these most brisk and giddy-paced times.*
> . . . it is old and plain
> The Spinsters and the Knitters in the Sun
> And the free Maids that weave their Thread with Bones
> Do use to chant it: it is silly sooth
> And dallies with the innocence of Love
> Like the old Age . . .

With such a song, does your desire not become as passionate as that of the knight himself? Of course! Now quickly translate this into the hexameter used by Denis:

SONG

> Come away, come away, death!
> And in sad cypress let me be laid!
> Fly away, fly away, breath!
> I am slain by a fair cruel Maid!
> My Shroud of white stuck all with yew
> Oh prepare it!
> My part of death, no one so true
> Did share it!
>
> Not a Flow'r, not a Flow'r sweet
> On my black Coffin let there be strown
> Not a Friend, not a Friend greet
> My poor Corpse, where my Bones
> shall be thrown.
> A thousand thousand Sighs to save
> Lay me o where
> True Lover never find my Grave
> To weep there.

Anyone who is not moved by this song, so simple and affectless, when it is sung with such a feeling for life, should not be my friend! However, if it is translated (*Wieland*,[b] just like most of the other translators, failed to

---

b. Christoph Martin Wieland, *Prosaübersetzung von 22 Dramen Shakespeares*, in *Shakespeares theatralische Werke*, 8 vols. (Zurich: Orell, Geßner and Comp., 1762–66).

translate it), if the only ones, to whom I entrust such suppleness, the skaldic singer of the old Norse songs[c] and Aspasia's grave inscription, and the "Schnitterliedchen" and the sweet "Nänie auf den Tod einer Wachtel" and the "Schnittermädchen des Himmels" and "Auf die Herzensangst jenes guten Pfarrers" ... if a poet[d] who translated so very much, so much that is truly splendid, had translated it. It might have conveyed inner feeling, impressing it upon the external, the meaningful, in form, sound, tone, melody, all that is dark and nameless, which flows with the song like a stream into our soul. Page through the Dodsley edition of Percy's *Reliques of Ancient Poetry*[e] from one end to the other; translate something, making it as beautiful as you wish, ignoring the sense of tone in the song, and just see then what you have left!

You know, of course, the lovely, sweet ballad [*Romanze*] that I find so marvelous, which however is not found in the Dodsley edition, "Henry and Catherine":

> In ancient times in Britain Isle
> Lord Henry was well knowne ...

An English schoolmaster by the name of Samuel Bishop celebrated a certain *Ferias poeticas*, which is to say he wrote a *Carmina Anglicana elegiaci plerumque argumenti latine reddita* (I am writing out the full title so that you can find a copy of the book).[f] In this *Carminibus Anglicanis latine redditis* one of our romances is also *Elegiaci argumenti*, and thus also *Elegiaco versu*, which allows one to scan it and divide its phrases in the following manner:

---

c. *Skaldengesang*. The *Skalden* were court poets and singers who sang the epics of Norway and Iceland, known generally as the *Edda*.

d. Herder refers here to the contemporary poet Heinrich Wilhelm Gerstenberg, and his poems that were later published as "Gedicht eines Skalden" (Gerstenberg's *Vermischte Schriften* [1815], vol. 2:87 [Frankfurt am Main: Athenäum, 1971]); "Aspasia" (ibid., 128); "Schnitterliedchen" (ibid., 221); and "Auf die Herzensangst jenes guten Pfarrers," which refers to "An die Nacht" (ibid., 261). "Nänie auf den Tod einer Wachtel" is not by Gerstenberg, but rather by Karl Wilhelm Ramler, who again makes an appearance in the postscript to Herder's chapter.

e. Herder refers here to the Dodsley edition of Thomas Percy's *Reliques of Ancient Poetry, Consisting of Old Heroic Ballads, Songs, and Other Pieces of Our Earlier Poets; Together with Some Few of Later Date*, 3 vols. (London: J. Dodsley, 1765). Herder possessed his own copies of Percy's *Reliques*, the most important source for English folk song and one of the most comprehensive early anthologies of ballads.

f. Herder provides the entire title for this work, which first appeared in 1766. See Samuel Bishop, *Ferias poeticas: Carmina Anglicana elegiaci plerumque argumenti latine reddita* (London: D. Leach, 1766).

Angliacos inter proceres innotuit olim
Henricus priscae nobilitatis honos!

And where is the ballad here? . . . We see that it is no different with Ossian when we take a look even once at the beautiful Macpherson translation of *Temora*.[g] Was the author himself a Scot? Did he himself hear Ossian sing? Did he even have a feeling for who Ossian might be? Just see now what the nimble Latinist was able to make out of the moving moment in the text in which Oscar falls and the poet suddenly breaks off, turning toward his beloved. It is possible to compare all three translations, by Macpherson, MacFarlane, and Denis, side by side in the same publication.[h] Just take a look for yourself! . . .

. . . The objections to the authenticity of Ossian are of a particular sort. You grant me my position when it comes to the old Gothic songs, as one might refer to them, in their rhymed poems, ballads, sonnets, and similarly artistic or artificial stanzas. When it concerns the ancient, artistic songs of wild, uncivilized peoples . . . wild, uncivilized peoples . . . when is it a different story? I am barely able to comprehend how they live. Do your Ossian and his great and noble Fingal conveniently live among a wild and uncivilized people? And if he treats them idealistically, how does he manage this, and for whom were they idealized? The same images, the same history, the dreams at night and the outlook during the day, all serve to restore character and the greatest passion. Was that an uncivilized people? If one's favorite opinions could only be so steadfast.

You must realize that the wilder a people is, which is to say, the more life and freedom a people possesses—and we cannot understand anything else from the meaning of *wild*, in other words, the more life and freedom they possess . . . the more sensual and lyrical they are in their actions. They are all the more so when they possess songs, indeed, songs that are their own! The more removed that people is from artificial, rational ways of thinking, speaking, and writing, the less they lend themselves to being represented on paper, where they would simply become the dead letters of poetic verse. The true being of song depends on its lyricism and how it conveys a feeling for life and dance. Song depends on the ways its images project the life of

g. Robert MacFarlane, *Temorae liber primus versibus latinis expressus* (London: T. Becket and P.A. De Hondt, 1769). James Macpherson (1736–1796) was also the translator and falsifier of the Ossian songs. For a more detailed discussion of the Ossian controversy and Herder's participation in it, see chapter 5 in the present book.

h. Christian Felix Weiße, *Neue Bibliothek der schönen Wissenschaften und der freien Künste*, vol. 9 (Leipzig: J.G. Dyck, 1769), 344.

the moment, and the ways in which meaning coheres while still possessing immediacy. The sensations, the symmetry of the words ... in many cases, even of the letters ... the flow of the melody, and a hundred other things that belong to the living world, to the sayings and songs of the nation, and also disappear with them: all this gives song its ultimate meaning. It is what gives song its marvelous power, its charm, and its driving force, which in turn make it song that embodies the heritage and joy of a people! Such are the arrows of wild Apollo, with which he targets the heart, and with which he captures the soul and memory! The longer a song survives, the more powerfully and sensually it must awaken the soul. In this way it can overcome the impact of time and the change wrought by centuries. And where do such realizations lead us?

Unquestionably the Scandinavians, even as they also appear throughout Ossian's songs, are a wilder and coarser people than the gently idealized Scots. I do not know one poem of the Scandinavians from which gentle sensitivity flows. When they walk, it is always on stone and ice, and on the frozen earth, and understandably, being aware of such struggle and culture, I know of no piece by them that compares in any way with those in Ossian. If one, nonetheless, looks at the poems in Worm, Bartholin, Peringskiöld, and Verel, what a collection of poetry one discovers![i] How immediately the ear gains a feel for the meter! It senses the ways in which the open syllables in the middle of the verses form symmetrical patterns, and the metric accent always unfolds in the same pattern, reflecting the very movement of the army. The opening assonance and sounds no less effectively accompany the attack, the ringing sound of the bard's song striking the shields! The couplets and verses achieve the same end! So do the vowels! The syllables possess such a consonance, which is truly embedded in the rhythm of the verses ... with such craft, swiftness, and accuracy ... that it is very difficult for those of us who received our education from books to discern them only with the eye. We must not imagine, however, that it was equally difficult for those living peoples who heard them rather than reading them, who from their youth listened to them and sang along, and whose entire aural

---

i. Olaus Wormius [Olaf Worm], *Danica litteratura antiquissima, vulgo gothica dicta* (Copenhagen: Georg Holst, 1636); Olaus Wormius [Olaf Worm], *Runica, seu danica litteratura antiquissima* (Copenhagen: Martzan and Holst, 1651); Thomas Bartholin, *Antiquitatum danicorum de causis contemptæ a danis adhuc gentilibus mortis libri tres* (Copenhagen: J. P. Bockenhoffer, 1689); Johan Peringer de Peringskiöld, *Monumenta Sveo-Gothica* (Stockholm: Olavus Enaeus, 1710–19); Olof Verelius, ed., *Hervarar-Saga på gammal götska med Olai Vereli vttolkning och notis* (Uppsala: Henricus Curio, 1672).

perception evolved together with the songs. Nothing is more powerful and long-lasting, swifter and more refined, than the habits of the ear! Once deeply internalized, the ear retains song forever! Once the ear captures the sound of language during youth, it forever retains its essence, and because language is so bound to all that appears in the real world, it returns again and again, rich and powerful. Were I myself a psychologist, I should be able to elucidate for you an incredible range of unique phenomena in music, song, and speech.

Do not think that I am exaggerating. Among the 136 types of rhythmic figures in the Old Norse songs I have examined, only one has singable character when experienced more closely. As far as I can determine, the second part of the *Edda* epic has yet to appear, and it is there that one finds real prosody! What can you imagine if not even two distiches in this rhythmic figure of eight rows really are metric, but rather three beginning letters, three words and sounds, and these only in the places they are found, thus simultaneously giving the entire strophe the texture of a rune. It all comes from the sounds of a living song, which awakens time and memory, so that everything pulsates and sounds together! Try it yourself and take a look at "Regner Lodbrog's Song of Death" in the runes that appear in Worm's collection, where you can read the excellent and detailed translation.[j] The version we have in German uses an entirely different syllable pattern, which gives it another sound altogether, the distorted print made from a beautiful portrait! Someone could now come along and transform "Dysen's Battle Song," Odin's enchanted words at the gates of hell, or the most recent judgment pronounced by the *Edda*'s gods into a heroic poem in hexameter or pretty Greek syllable patterns, which is precisely what Denis did with "The Speech of the Gauls," "Morni," "Fingal," and "Rosengranen."[k] From "Evind Skaldaspiller's Song of Mourning" on Hako comes an elegy that sounds like Klopstock's ode on Rothschild's grave. What would Father Odin and Old Skaldaspiller say? From George Hickes and others you know that such skaldic rhythms were not specific to Iceland and Scandinavia.[l] Most recently we witness an attempt to transform the Anglo-Saxon accord-

---

j. Page 57. Herder had already cited the "Song of Death" for the Danish king of the eighth century in volume one of the *Kritische Wälder* (1769; JGHW2, 63–245).

k. All these songs appear later in Herder's *Volkslieder* (1778/79; see chapter 2 in the present volume).

l. George Hickes, *Linguarum veterum septemtrionalium thesaurus grammatico-criticus et archaeologicus* (Oxford: Sheldonian Theatre, 1705).

ingly in the Dodsley edition of Percy's *Reliques* in the prolegomenon to the *complaint of conscience*.

But there's still more. Just go through Ossian's poems. In every case of the bardic songs they resemble those of another people who are still singing and going about their lives today. Without predilection or prejudice I can sense in their narratives the history of Ossian and his ancestors, which has more than once been given life. Here I refer to the Five Nations of North America:[m] songs of death and songs of war; songs of battle and songs for the grave; historical songs about the ancestors and addressed to the ancestors.... I find all these common to Ossian's bard and to the Indigenous peoples of North America. The more recent martyr and revenge songs serve as an exception, for the gentle people of Caledonia color their songs with the gentle blood of love. Now take a look at what all the travel reports by Charlevoix, Lafitau, Rogers, and Cadwallader Colden say about the sound, the rhythm, and the power of the songs and their effect on the ear.[n] Take a look again at how all the observations in these reports are captivated by lively movement, melody, symbolic language, and pantomime. In those instances in which the travelers were also familiar with the Scots and then had lived with the Americans, an observer such as Captain Timberlake found himself able to recognize the obvious similarities among the songs of both nations.[o] This makes the case even more convincingly. With Denis we find ourselves anchored firmly to the earth: we sense that we are hearing a truly poetic language, but in comparison with the native peoples there is no feeling for sound or singing, no real sense of fresh air from the hills of Caledonia, which in turns elevates us and sets us in motion, and which allows us really to hear the sound of life in their songs. We sit there and read the songs, but we remain glued firmly to the ground.

When a trip to England still livened my soul ... oh friend, you have no idea what the Scots meant to me at that time! One glance at the open spirit and I felt myself as if I were on the stage, indeed at the entirely vital theater

---

m. The Five Nations included the largest groups of Native Americans who occupied the northeastern United States and eastern Canada. They had extensive political organization and distinctive cultures (see, e.g., Diamond 2008).

n. Pierre François Xavier de Charlevoix, *Histoire et déscription générale de la Nouvelle France* (Paris: P.F. Giffart, 1744); Joseph François Lafitau, *Mœurs des sauvages amériquains comparées aux mœurs des premiers temps*, 2 vols. (Paris: Saugrain et Hocherau, 1724); Robert Rogers, *A Concise Account of North America* (London: J. Millan, 1765); Cadwallader Colden, *The History of the Five Indian Nations Depending on the Province of New-York in America* (New York: William Bradford, 1727).

o. Henry Timberlake, *The Memoirs of Lieutenant H.T., Who Accompanied the Three Indians to England in the Year 1762* (London: [Henry Timberlake], 1765).

of the English people. Thus, I might enlighten myself with the breadth of ideas that enter the head of a foreigner viewing the history, philosophy, politics, and all the special traits of this marvelous nation, which form images so dark and distinctive that they lead one astray. Suddenly, however, there is a change of scene on the stage, which in turn opens upon the Scots! On Macpherson! There I want to see for myself the songs of a truly vital people, to witness everything they produce and do, to see the very places themselves that come to life throughout the songs, to study the rest of the customs in this ancient world! I want to be a Caledonian for a while ... and then I should return to England in order to learn more about their literary monuments, the works of art they have gathered, and the details of their character.... How I look forward to embarking on this plan! As a translator I should surely have wanted to follow a different path, that is, to do what Denis did not do! For him, Macpherson's attempt to realize the original language in print was entirely in vain.p

... You laugh about my enthusiasm for Indigenous peoples, just like Voltaire laughed at Rousseau, as if walking about on all fours would make him really happy: do not believe for a minute that it is for this reason that I despise our own cultural predilections and the customs in which they lie. Human beings are distinguished by progress through scenes upon the stage of history, education, and culture: woe to the person who takes no pleasure from encountering these conditions! Woe also to one who philosophizes about humanity and its customs, for whom this scene is the only one, and who regards the customs of Indigenous peoples as if they were of the lowest order! If everything were simply a component in the entire scene of progress unfolding on a stage, then a new, unfamiliar side of humanity would be exposed in everyone. You might also recognize that I do not now intend to plague you with a "psychology from the poems of Ossian." At the very least, such ideas occupy a deep and vital level in my soul, wherein you would discover much that is quite remarkable!

At this point, do you know why I have such feelings about the songs of native peoples, especially for Ossian? First of all, I read Ossian under circumstances that did not place him simply in entertaining and occasional literature, affording exotic pleasure to an occasionally distracted reader. You know about the adventure of my journey on a ship.q But you cannot

p. See James Macpherson's "Dissertation Concerning the Poems of Ossian," in Macpherson, *The Works of Ossian* (London: T. Becket and P.A. Dehondt, 1765).

q. Johann Gottfried Herder, *Journal meiner Reise im Jahr 1769* (JGHW9/2, 5–126). Herder's travel account of his journey from Riga to France appeared posthumously, some forty years after his death (see the epilogue in the present book).

imagine just what an impact such a lengthy journey by sea has on one, how it affects one's feelings. Removed suddenly from the business, the tumult, and the distractions of the civilized world, pulled away from the easy chair of a scholar and from the gentle wisdom of the social world, without distractions, libraries, learned and not-so-learned newspapers, standing instead on a ship's deck and gazing across the wide, expansive sea, in a small world with other humans, who have more stringent laws than the republic of Lycurgus, in the middle of a completely different play, in a vital and swaying nature, floating between heaven and the abyss, surrounded daily by the same expanse of elements, and then only once in a while encountering an unknown, distant coastline, a new cloud, an idyllic region of the world ... now, with the songs and deeds of the ancient singers of the Old Norse poems in hand, opening the soul entirely to the places in which the songs and deeds took place ... here passing by the cliffs of Olaf,[r] from which so many marvelous stories have emanated ... there across from Eiland, where Zauberase plows with the four powerful steers with stars marking their heads, "the sea pounded, as if throwing itself in the air in a downpour, and where the steers turned, pulling their heavy plow, with eight stars glowing before their heads,"[s] from there toward Jutland, where the Old Norse singers and the Vikings previously navigated the seas with sword and song upon their horses on ships upon the sea, hugging the shores of the sea, passing closely along the coast, where Fingal's deeds took place and Ossian wistfully sang his songs, suspended in the movement of the wind, the world, the stillness ... believe me, in the midst of such experiences the Old Norse singers and the bards emerge from your reading entirely unlike anything you might experience in a professor's classroom. For me at least, such experiences possess a deep sensibility with an undeniable impact: [Robert] Wood with his Homer in the ruins of Troy,[t] and the Argonauts, Odysseans, and *Os Lusíadas*,[u] under the billowing sails and at the rattling helm; the stories of *Uthal* and *Ninathoma* within sight of the island where they took place.[v]

---

r. Cliffs along the straits between the Danish island of Seeland and the Swedish coast, from which the Norwegian King Olaf Tryggvason threw himself into the sea in 1000 CE after a crusade to Christianize Pomerania, the coastal border region shared today by Germany and Poland.

s. Herder takes this passage from his own notes about the *Edda*.

t. Robert Wood, *An Essay on the Original Genius of Homer* (London: n.p., 1769).

u. Written in Homeric style after extensive travels during Portuguese voyages of colonial expansion in the sixteenth century by Luís Vaz de Camões (1524–1580), *Os Lusíadas* (1572) is regarded by many as the Portuguese national epic.

v. Both from Macpherson's Ossian volumes.

And I still remember the feeling of the night, when I was upon a foundering ship, which neither storm nor flood could move any farther, washed over by the sea and swept by the midnight winds ... at that moment, I read *Fingal* and hoped for the dawn. . . . Forgive me this earlier conceit, which causes me to stumble upon impressions of this sort as if upon an old and dear friend. . . .

That too, however, is not really the genesis of the enthusiasm of which you have accused me, for in such a case it would have been no more than an individual mirage, a sea sprite, that had appeared to me. Know therefore that I myself had the opportunity to see the living descendants of these ancient, wild songs, rhythms, and dances, performed by living human beings who had not entirely assimilated our culture into language, songs, and customs, with the concomitant mutilation or degeneration thereof. Know therefore that when I heard such an ancient song, sung with a wild tempo, I was almost always reminded of what the French dance master Marcell exclaimed: *Que de choses dans un menuet!*[w] Even more to the point, what would such cultures have gained by exchanging their songs for a degenerated minuet or a little rhyme that was like the minuet? . . .

You know of the little Latvian songs that Lessing took from Ruhig's *Litteraturbriefe*,[x] and you know how much more sensual the rhythm of the language expresses their essence. Let me turn to a few Peruvian songs from Garcilaso de la Vega,[y] which I translate here with as much care for the text, sound, and rhythm as possible. You yourself will immediately see just to what extent they readily allow themselves to be translated.

The first is the serenade of a lover at dusk:

Schlummre, schlumm', o Mädchen,	Slumber, slumber, oh my child,
Sanft in meine Lieder,	Gently in my songs,
Mitternachts, o Mädchen,	It's midnight, oh my child,
Weck' ich dich schon wieder!	I'll wake you once again![z]

What could one say more eloquently and sweetly to one's lover? . . . The other song is simply an image, a fiction of their mythological portrayal of thunder and lightning. A nymph in the clouds holds a water pitcher in her

---

w. "What things there are in a minuet!"

x. Philipp Ruhig, *Betrachtung der litauischen Sprache in ihrem Ursprung, Wesen und Eigenschaften*, in *Litthauisch-deutsches und deutsch-litthauisches Lexikon* (Königsberg: J. H. Hartung, 1748), 75.

y. Garcilaso de la Vega, *Histoire des Yncas rois du Peru etc. Traduite de l'Espagnol de l'Ynca Garcilasso de la Vega, par J. Baudoin* (Amsterdam: Gerard Kuyper, 1704).

z. Under the title "An sein Mädchen," this appears as a Peruvian song as the final song in the 1778/79 *Volkslieder* project; in the present volume, see chapter 2, pp. 104.

hands, and at the appropriate moments she pours from it to provide rain for the earth. If she neglects her duty, she lets the soil languish in drought, so that her brother comes along and smashes the pitcher, which produces thunder and lightning, which then releases the rain. If such poetry about storms during drought, accompanied by rain, pleases you, if you feel its sensibilities, then listen to the song or prayer as you yourself would wish:

Schöne Göttin,	Lovely goddess,
Himmelstochter!	Daughter of the skies!
Mit dem vollen	With the full
Waßerkruge,	Water pitcher,
Den dein Bruder	Which your brother
Jetzt zerschmettert	Now smashes
Daß es wettert	So the weather
Ungewitter,	Will storm
Blitz and Donner!	With thunder and lightning!
Schöne Göttin,	Lovely goddess,
Königstochter!	Daughter of the king!
Und nun träufelst	And now you drizzle
Du uns Regen,	Us with rain,
Milden Regen!	Gentle rain!
Doch oft streuest	But you often spread
Du auch Flocken	Snowflakes too
Und auch Schlossen!	And also hailstones!
Denn so hat dir	For in this way
Er der Weltgeist!	He who is spirit of the world!
Er der Weltgott!	He who is god of the world!
Virakocha!	Virakocha!
Macht gegeben	He gave you power
Amt gegeben!	He placed you in your position!

I did not introduce the song here because of its wisdom, for are you aware of how the intelligence of the Peruvians is generally regarded? I am speaking instead about the symmetry of the rhythm and of the singability. In this sense my attempt to re-create something of the original can only be regarded as feeble and weak.

You know the Kleist song about a Sámi man,[aa] and the hand of this fine man could not be anything else for us but to create beauty. If, however, I

---

aa. Ewald Christian von Kleist, *Neue Gedichte* (Berlin: Christian Friedrich Voss, 1758), 16. Cf. Herder's *Volkslieder*, XXV, pp. 93 and 405. Herder employs the customary name for Sámi, Lappländer.

were to give you the coarse Sámi version? It will have to be a thirdhand source, for I do not have my copy of Scheffer with me:[ab]

> O Sonne, dein hellester Schimmer beglänze den Orra-See!
> Ich würde den Fichtengipfel ersteigen, könnt' ich schauen den Orra-See!
> Ich würd' ihn ersteigen, den Gipfel, meine Blumenfreundin zu sehn!
> Ich würd' ihn bescheren, ihm alle Zweige, seine grünen Zweige stümmeln –
> Hätt' ich Flügel, zu dir zu fliegen, Flügel der Krähen
> Dem Laufe der Wolken folgt' ich, ziehend zum Orra-See!
> Aber mir mangeln die Flügel! Enteflügel! Füsse der Ente!
> Rudernde Füsse der Gänse, die mich zu dir bringen!
> O du hast lange gewartet, so viel Tage! schöne Tage,
> Du mit erquickenden Augen, mit deinem freundlichen Herzen! –
> Was ist stärker, als Flechte Sehnen! als eiserne, mächtige Ketten?
> So fesselt uns die Liebe, die Umschafferin Sinns und Willens:
> Denn der Wille des liebenden Jünglings ist Windesgang
> Die Gedanken des Liebenden lange Gedanken!
> Folgt' ich ihnen allen, ich irrte vom rechten Weg' ab.
> Drum bleibt mir Ein Entschluß, die sichre Bahn zu gehn!

> Oh sun, your brightest shimmer reflects off the Orra Sea!
> I would climb to the top of the fir trees, if I could but see the Orra Sea!
> I'd climb to the top, if only to see my girlfriend amid the flowers!
> I'd trim it of all its branches, cutting its green branches to their stumps—
> If I had wings with which I could fly to you, wings of the crows
> I'd follow the path of the clouds, pulling me to the Orra Sea!
> But I do not have any wings! Wings of ducks! Feet of ducks!
> Paddling feet of geese that will bring me to you!
> Oh, you have waited so long, so many days! Beautiful days,
> You with refreshing eyes, with your loving heart!—
> What is stronger than braided tendons! Than powerful iron chains?
> Thus, love binds us, love that undoes the sense and will:
> For the will of the youthful lover is the blowing of the wind
> The thoughts of the lover are lengthy thoughts!
> Were I to pursue all of them, I'd surely go astray.
> Thus, I stand by my decision to follow the safe path!

---

ab. Johannes Scheffer, *Lapponia, id est, Regionis Lapponum et gentis nova et verissima descriptio* (Frankfurt am Main: Christian Wolff, 1673). Herder notes only that he does not use Scheffer, and fails to identify the "thirdhand" source.

This Sámi song comes to us, as I mentioned, from thirdhand, but it is nonetheless striking just how it retains its naturalness and conveys the sensibilities of the young Sámi singer, for whom the way to the woman for whom he longs must be too long, because it is encumbered by all he sees separating him from the Orra Sea: the sun, the treetops, the clouds, the crows, and the webbed feet! How natural everything is that creates the speed and slowed pace of his way, the haste of his soul, the flight of his thoughts, his passion, his search for the right path! How much longing in the return! *Que de choses dans un menuet!* And I have provided you with only the stammering, surviving traces.

I wanted to share with you another Sámi love song, this one to his reindeer, but I have misplaced it, and who has time to search for the notes one has misplaced? Instead, I include here an old, truly terrifying Scottish song,[ac] which is even more representative because I have taken it directly from the original language. It is a dialogue between mother and son, and in Scottish it is accompanied by a very moving country melody, which provides considerable space for the text.

"EDWARD, EDWARD"

Dein Schwert, wie ists von Blut so rot?
   Edward, Edward!
Dein Schwert, wie ists von Blut so rot
   Und gehst so traurig da! – O!
Ich hab geschlagen meinen Geyer tot!
   Mutter, Mutter!
Ich hab geschlagen meinen Geyer tot,
   Und das, das geht mir nah! – O!
Dein's Geyers Blut ist nicht so rot!
   Edward, Edward!
Dein's Geyers Blut ist nicht so rot,
   Mein Sohn, bekenn mir frei! – O!

---

ac. "Edward" (Child Ballad 13) from Percy's *Reliques* and included as song 5 in the third book of the second part of Herder's 1779 *Volkslieder* (JGHW3, 365–67). Herder does not present the ballad with strophic divisions here, though strophic form would become essential for understanding the narrative form and structure of ballads in the nineteenth century. "Edward" was set as a ballad with and without text by several composers in the nineteenth century, including Franz Schubert (D. 923a, 923b, and 923c) and Johannes Brahms ("Ballade" in d minor, op. 10, no. 1; see fig. 13). For a discussion of the nineteenth-century translations based on Herder's publication of "Edward," see Bohlman 2010b and 2011c.

Ich hab geschlagen mein Rotroß tot!
  Mutter, Mutter!
Ich hab geschlagen mein Rotroß tot!
  Und 's war so stolz und treu! O!
Dein Roß war alt und hasts nicht not!
  Edward, Edward,
Dein Roß war alt und hasts nicht not,
  Dich drückt ein ander Schmerz! O!
Ich hab geschlagen meinen Vater tot,
  Mutter, Mutter!
Ich hab geschlagen meinen Vater tot,
  Und das, das quält mein Herz! O!
Und was wirst du nun an dir tun?
  Edward, Edward!
Und was wirst du nun an dir tun?
  Mein Sohn, bekenn mir mehr! O!
Auf Erden soll mein Fuß nicht ruhn!
  Mutter, Mutter,
Auf Erden soll mein Fuß nicht ruhn!
  Will wandern über Meer! O!
Und was soll werden dein Hof und Hall,
  Edward, Edward,
Und was soll werden dein Hof und Hall,
  So herrlich sonst und schön! O!
Ach! immer stehs und sink' und fall,
  Mutter, Mutter,
Ach immer stehs und sink' und fall,
  Ich werd' es nimmer sehn! O!
Und was soll werden dein Weib und Kind,
  Edward, Edward?
Und was soll werden dein Weib und Kind,
  Wann du gehst über Meer – O!
Die Welt ist groß! laß sie betteln drinn,
  Mutter, Mutter!
Die Welt ist groß! laß sie betteln drinn,
  Ich seh sie nimmermehr!—O!
Und was soll deine Mutter tun?
  Edward, Edward!
Und was soll deine Mutter tun!
  Mein Sohn, das sage mir! O!
Der Fluch der Hölle soll auf Euch ruhn,
  Mutter, Mutter!
Der Fluch der Hölle soll auf Euch ruhn,
  Denn Ihr, Ihr rietets mir! O.

"EDWARD, EDWARD"
                        THOMAS PERCY's *Reliques*[ad]

Why dois your brand sae drap wi' bluid,
    Edward, Edward?
Why dois your brand sae drap wi' bluid?
    And why sae sad gang ye, O?
O, I hae killed my hauke sae guid,
    Mither, mither,
O, I hae killed my hauke sae guid,
    And I had nae mair bot hee, O.

Your haukis bluid was nevir sae reid,
    Edward, Edward,
Your haukis bluid was nevir sae reid,
    My deir son I tell thee, O.
O, I hae killed my reid-roan steid,
    Mither, mither,
O, I hae killed my reid-roan steid,
    That erst was sae fair and frie, O.

Your steid was auld, and ye hae gat mair,
    Edward, Edward,
Your steid was auld, and ye hae gat mair,
    Sum other dule ye drie, O.
O, I hae killed my fadir deir,
    Mither, mither,
O, I hae killed my fadir deir,
    Alas, and wae is mee, O.

And whatten penance wul ye drie for that,
    Edward, Edward?
And whatten penance will ye drie for that?
    My deir son, now tell me, O.
Ile set my feit in yonder boat,
    Mither, mither,
Il set my feit in yonder boat,
    And Ile fare ovir the sea, O.

And what wul ye doe wi' your towirs and your ha',
    Edward, Edward?
And what wul ye doe wi' your towirs and your ha',
    That were sae fair to see, O?

---

ad. The original version of "Edward" in Percy's *Reliques* is used in lieu of a more literal translation from Herder's German.

Ile let thame stand tul they doun fa',
    Mither, mither,
Ile let thame stand tul they doun fa',
    For here nevir mair maun I bee, O.

And what wul ye leive to your bairns and your wife,
    Edward, Edward?
And what wul ye leive to your bairns and your wife,
    Whan ye gang ovir the sea, O?
The warldis room, late them beg thrae life,
    Mither, mither,
The warldis room, let them beg thrae life,
    For thame nevir mair wul I see, O.

And what wul ye leive to your ain mither deir,
    Edward, Edward?
And what wul ye leive to your ain mither deir?
    My deir son, now tell mee, O.
The curse of hell frae me sall ye beir,
    Mither, mither,
The curse of hell frae me sall ye beir,
    Sic counseils ye gave to me, O.

Could Cain's fratricide appear through more horrific lines in a popular song? And what kind of impact does the song possess in the vitality of its rhythm? And so it is with so many songs of the folk [*Lieder des Volks*]!^{ae} No book, etc., nevertheless, will ever emerge from my letters.... Finally you will take note of this and insist upon even more folk songs [*Volkslieder*] like this. The only thing I offer in return is obstinacy, for in the letter before your last one you struck again straight at my heart: "Mr. Denis also has so many lyrical pieces, and they would be so beautiful!"

He does indeed include lyrical pieces, and they are also beautiful, but just how many lyrical pieces are there, and why are they beautiful? What is different in the original that for him is not beautiful? The soil for the poem, upon which his odes merely turn into flowers, is hexameter? And if so, how? With Latin, Roman, and Greek syllable patterns, and the beautiful order they provide, I have to insist that these beautiful bardic songs are no longer those of Ossian! Whatever allows Macpherson in every piece to draw the feeling of wildness, gentleness, celebration, or war from

---

ae. In this passage, Herder uses a more or less literal version of "folk songs"—*Lieder des Volks*—for the first time. Two sentences later he employs the form *Volkslieder*.

FIGURE 13. Johannes Brahms, "Ballade," op. 10, no. 1 (opening). Based on Herder's translation of "Edward, Edward."

their rhythm, melody, syllable pattern, and soul of the song—all that, I'm afraid I must admit, has nothing to do with Latin and Greek syllable patterns, either consciously or subconsciously. In fact, whenever I am able to sense the deeper tone in songs of Indigenous peoples, it has nothing whatsoever to do, even in a single case, with the presence of Latin and Greek syllable patterns. I have no desire to compete with Denis. He commands considerable poetic style and speech. I should like to see, however, one of his pieces that is just as good in another syllable pattern, that reveals itself equally as affect. Many song translations, to be perfectly frank, are just plain bad.

To witness this, simply take a look through the third volume. There we find that someone—I cannot imagine which expert in the arts—had given

Denis the advice that he should stress syllables from the Old Norse epics, and just see how the translator has failed. The marvelous, multi-stringed golden harp that could have been in the hands of the Danish epic singers, resonant with tones of magic and power, minstrel and miracle, and in contrast the tones of love, friendship, and charm, is transformed by the hands of the translator into a march-like wooden drum.... It is only a shame that the beautiful songs of *Selma* and of the sweet *Carric-thura* are thereby disfigured. In the first volume the translator invented a cantata with rhymes that adhere to all the rules, and because only two of these rhymes succeeded for him, the entire piece fails to pass critical muster.

How completely different were the ways in which Klopstock worked with the language in the same case! How fleeting, for a poet who is otherwise so fluid and flowing! How strong and articulated! How "old German" he strove to express himself in his "Hermanns-Schlacht"! What prose could approximate his hexameter! What lyrical syllable patterns could equal his otherwise flowing Greek syllable patterns! If there is little drama in his bardic style, at least there is lyricism, and in the lyricism the word structure is so dramatic, so German! ... Just read this noble, simple piece, for instance:

> Auf Moos', am luftigen Bach etc.
> On the moss along the breeze-swept stream....[af]

and so many, indeed almost all others, and then show me something with the sound of a bard in Denis. Klopstock was capable of suppressing so much of himself that he must transform so many other things ... is not this the lesson we "must" really learn? Recently you wrote to me that you praised Denis's syllable patterns as they appeared in his *Fingal und Roskrane*, just as Klopstock did in *Hermann und Thusnelde*.[ag] This is even worse, because Klopstock's new bardic style is not like that in *Hermann und Thusnelde*. I am surely not the only one sensitive to this altered, hard bardic style in the new Klopstock. For better or worse, as far as I am concerned, I have followed the poet's development over time and according to nature. I take pride in encountering the feeling for a German bardic style in his

> Was that dir Thor, dein Vaterland
> What does Thor give you, your fatherland[ah]

---

af. Friedrich Gottlieb Klopstock, *Hermanns Schlacht*, scene 11.
ag. In *Neue Beiträge zum Vergnügen des Verstandes und des Witzes*, ed. Karl Christian Gärtner (Bremen: N. Saurmann, 1744–57).
ah. From Friedrich Gottlieb Klopstock's ode "Wir und Sie," opening line.

and in all the recent pieces, in which one senses a dramatic dialogue and interplay of thought that are so much tighter. . . .

. . . The thread of our correspondence has stretched in so many directions that I hardly know where I should pick it up and continue. . . . The best place would be, I suppose, just where I happen to hold it in my hands.

The remark you make "about the *dramatic in ancient songs*" of this kind is so much akin to the sense that I have always had about the character pieces of the ancient peoples, in other words, the only thing we today find in the more recent pieces is a momentary portrait of a living, ongoing scene that, however, no longer exists. They become our odes, these lyrical pieces from the ancients, especially those of the uncivilized cultures. Every saying and every poem from the ancients sets the stage. Read, for example, the sayings on war and peace of the Eskimos that you find in Charlevoix: nothing is absent from the picture, from its verses, from the scene itself! What action there is in "Odins Höllenfahrt," in the "Webegesange der Valkyriur," and in the "Beschwörungslied der Hervor."[ai] In Ossian this is the case in every song! Just so you do not again accuse me of arguing without sufficient evidence, I shall try to begin allaying my guilt in the brief time remaining to me by illustrating below what I mean with some of the pieces to which I have been referring. I should have been able to present them anew for you, idealized, for they do not survive as they once were. They possess for you and me only the patina of a statue, with only the dark and singular magical sound of the North in the poems:

"ODINS HÖLLENFAHRT" / "ODIN'S JOURNEY INTO HELL"

Es erhub sich Odin	Odin rose up
Der Menschen höchster	The tallest of the men
Und nahm sein Roß	And took his steed
Und schwang sich aufs Roß	And mounted the steed
Und ritt hinunter	And rode down
Zu der Höllen Thor.	To the gates of Hell.
Da kam ihm entgegen	There he was approached
Der Höllenhund!	By the hound of Hell!
Blutbesprizt	Covered with blood
War seine Brust!	Was his breast!
Mit offnem Rachen,	With open jaws,

---

ai. Herder employs these poems from the Scandinavian *Edda* myths elsewhere, particularly in the *Volkslieder*. I include here only the first of the three songs, "Odins Höllenfahrt" (Odin's Journey into Hell), which concludes the main body of the portion of the Ossian correspondence I include in the present chapter.

Und scharfem Gebiß	And sharp teeth
Und Wut und Schaum.	And foaming with anger.
Und riß den Rachen	And tore the jaws
Und bellt' entgegen	And howled against
Dem Zaubervater	The magical father,
Und bellte lang!	And howled long!
Und fort ritt Odin	And Odin rode forth
Und die Erd' erbebte.	And the earth shook.
Da kam er zum hohen	There, he came
Höllenschloß,	To the high castle of Hell,
Und ritt gen Aufgang	And rode to the entrance
Zum Höllentor,	To the gates of Hell,
Wo die Seherin	Where the prophetess
Im Grabe lag.	Lay in the grave.
Und sang der Weisen	And sang the songs
Totenerweckenden	That awakened the dead
Gräbergesang:	Songs of the graves:
Und sah gen Norden	And looked to the North
Und legte Runen	And laid runes
Und beschwur und fragt',	And made an oath and questioned,
Und foderte Rede	And uttered his challenge
Bis sie zürnend endlich	Until finally they in anger
Sich erhub und begann	Rose up and began
Todtenstimme:	In the voice of the dead:
"Wer ist der Mann?	"Who is this man?
Ich kenn' ihn nicht!	I do not know him!
Der meine Ruhe	Who begins
Zu stören beginnt!	To disturb my peace!
Ich lag mit Schnee	I lay covered
Und Eis bedeckt,	With snow and ice,
Und Regen beflossen	It has rained upon me
Und Thau benetzt,	And dew has covered me,
Und lag so lang!"	So long have I here lain!"
Ein Wandrer bin ich,	I am a traveler,
Kriegerssohn.	The son of a warrior.
Du sollst mir Kunde	You should tell me
Vom Höllenreich geben.	About the kingdom of Hell.
Ich will sie dir geben	I wish to come to you
Aus meiner Welt!	From my own realm!
Jener goldne Sitz	For whom is that golden
Wem ist er bereitet?	Throne prepared?

Jenes goldne Bette Für wen stehts da?	For whom does that golden Bed stand there?
"Für *Balder'n* steht, Sieh her! der Trank, Der Honigtrank Und der Schild liegt drauf! Bald werden um ihn Die Götter trauren! Unwillig red' ich Nun laß mich ruhn!"	"It awaits *Balder*, Look! The potion, The potion with honey And the shield lies upon it! Soon, the gods Will mourn him! Regrettably I say, Now leave me in peace!"
Noch ruhe nicht, Jungfrau! Ich forsche weiter Und lasse nicht ab, Bis ich Alles weiß! Sprich, wer wird *Baldern* Den Tod bereiten? Und Leben berauben Odins Sohn?	Not yet in peace, maiden! I shall search further And do not give up, Until I know everything! Tell me, who will prepare *Balder* for death? And steal Odin's son From life?
"*Hoder* ists, Der wird dem Bruder Den Tod bereiten Und Leben berauben Odins Sohn! Unwillig red' ich Nun lass mich ruhn!"	"It is *Hoder* Who will prepare the brother For death And steal Odin's son From life! Regrettably I must say, Now leave me in peace!"
Noch ruhe nicht, Jungfrau! Ich forsche weiter, Bis ich Alles weiß! Sprich, wer wird *Hodern* Den Haß vergelten Und *Balders* Mörder Zum Grabe senden?	Do not yet rest, maiden! I shall search further, Until I know everything! Tell me, who will retaliate With hatred against *Hoder* And send *Balder*'s murderer To the grave?
"In Westen wird Rinda Dem Odin zu Nacht Einen Sohn gebären, Der kaum geboren Wird Waffen tragen, Seine Hand nicht waschen, Sein Haar nicht kämmen, Bis er Balders Mörder Zu Grabe gebracht.	"In the west Rinda Will give birth to a son In the night, Barely a child He will bear arms, His hands not wash, His hair not comb, Until he brings Balder's murderer to the grave.

Unwillig red' ichs	Regrettably I must say,
Nun laß mich ruhn!"	Now leave me in peace!"
Noch ruhe nicht, Jungfrau!	Do not yet rest, maiden!
Ich forsche weiter	I shall search further
Und lasse nicht ab,	And not give up,
Bis ich Alles weiß!	Until I know everything!
Wer sind die Jungfraun,	Who are the maidens,
Die stumm dort weinen	Who silently weep there
Und Himmel an werfen	And cast their veil
Im Schmerz den Schlei'r	Toward heaven in pain
Noch das sprich mir	You must also tell me that
Eher sollt du nich ruhn!	Before you can find peace!
"O du kein Wandrer,	"Oh, you're no traveler,
Wie ich erst gewähnt!	As I first imagined!
Du bist Odin selbst	You are Odin himself,
Der Menschen Höchster."	The greatest of all men."
Und du keine Weise	And you're no sage
Propheten Jungfrau;	Prophesying young maiden;
Keine Seherin!	No prophetess!
Drei-Riesen-Mutter	Mother of the three giants,
Vielmehr bist du!	You are much more!
"Weg, Odin! Wandre	"Away, Odin! Travel
Nachheim! hinweg!	Homeward! Away!
Und rühme daheim,	And boast at home
Daß Niemand der Menschen	That no human being
Wie du's vermocht,	like you will be capable
Forschen wird,	Of searching,
Bis einst der Arge	Until once the wicked
Die Ketten bricht	Breaks the chains
Und die Götter fallen	And the gods fall,
Und die Welt zerfällt	And the world disintegrates,
Und Nacht beginnt!"	And night begins!"

. . .

POSTSCRIPT[aj]

Postscript, indeed! Where nothing is written, where total nonsense alas surrounds that half-extinct and disfigured staging of human nature, Ossian;

>   aj. The first part of the translation ends at the halfway point in the Ossian correspondence, and it begins again with the postscript (*Nachschrift*) that serves as a conclusion to the first chapter of *Von deutscher Art und Kunst*.

or it is at best a perpetual preface to what might come or should come, yet never will come. Do we, dear reader, leave things as they once were for those readers who are more clever . . . or more stupid . . . at the very least who circulate silent rumors about how invalid it is to seek Ossian clothed in correspondence, in the promised psychology . . . when it is worthwhile to take note of the printing error . . . to leave without any remark the imaginary trip to his islands! How unfaithful would a Scandinavian translation be, in which the author translated only literally and word by word, and beyond that only from hearsay, other than what perhaps was said here and there, and could and would provide less evidence than what *was rumored to be said* around the world? Above all, the lyrical nature appeared at that time, to which Ossian, too, contributed broken phrases. He naturally must have fallen into the countenance of the listener, who believes he heard something where others perhaps heard nothing, or perhaps no more than a moment's murmur.

It is fortunate that he sees all his critical imagination and suspicions now overcome by something palpable, to which he wanted to toss his garland with the fervor of Pindar, if indeed the garland had not withered. No critical vessel of creation, and all the urns of the Danaides provide water where there is no spring . . . and it is and will forever alone remain that miraculous hoof-fall of the flying stallion of genius that taps and unleashes the sevenfold spring.[ak]

Sevenfold spring! If the German ear were only more capable of sounding such words and syllables! If no fairy tale from April 1 had not remained so that the goddess of harmony

. . . child of the Greek heavens . . .

would again visit with the Astraea[al] or Urania Venus of the far Cimmerian lands.[am] Above all, however, the youthful era of the world could and should be revived again in its full blossom, so that the rigid rules, without Horace, Pindar, or Pupillus, do not replace the odes and table prayers, the sacred songs and love songs, flowing from our own hearts. The gods might appear once again with the garlands of human grace and genius,

---

ak. The Danaides were the fifty daughters of Danaus, forty-nine of whom, according to Greek mythology, were forced to carry water to fill a bottomless bath after killing their husbands on their wedding nights.

al. The "star maiden" in Greek and Roman mythology, symbolizing purity and innocence.

am. Herder seeks to contrast the origins of German poetic sensitivities with the earliest poetics of Greek antiquity, drawing attention to the virtual impossibility of overcoming the historical gap.

which could again be retrieved and called forth and made visible before our eyes

... profane and sacred!

Surely our own lesson books have long been filled with the "lyrical staff" of odes, hymns, psalms, elegies ... indeed, what else? ... in order to portray images without subject, merely artificial and with perspectives devoid of compositional spirit, color, and all other fine details! All this is done in order to appropriate the authority of a foreign model, which cloaks all that is familiar with hundreds of borrowed conventions. These, in turn, fail to allow the possibility of study from the German mind, labor, fortune, and honesty, all of which are sacrificed. Finally, even the resonance of the meter, syllable, and verse, organized according to the prosody articulated through declamation—all this is done to raise the art,

... as if the flute
sounds, or ...
as if rising above the flute.[an]

Out of all this there must come a *Rembrandt*, and as if *Rembrandt* was a great master....

Arise, my friends, to our ... how should I say it? ... *Guido d'Arezzo, Correggio,* or *Raphael*! But he painted the faces of angels in the forms of human beings! Gaze upon that image! What truth, life, and depth of soul! How the figures lift themselves from the canvas and speak ... not with us, for they do not see us because they are painted by us! ... rather among themselves, as they act and speak, and in so doing reveal for us visage and soul. We call out in lament: "and so it was once sung," but it is quietly felt "as formerly had it possessed such sensitivity, or" ...

Song! It will again be what it once was! Sensitive to the entire being of life! Speaking from the human heart ... with God, with itself, with all of nature!

Harmony! It will be what it once was. No artificial exercise of measured harmony, rather movement, melody of the heart, and dance! Its flaws and individuality will remain, just as genius everywhere instructs us!

We know so well, my friend, that we have already heard compositions on the "Ever-present, the celebration of spring," such songs and others like them. We once heard such songs, but no more. Allow me now to depart from my dismal praise and close with one or two wishes.

an. Friedrich Gottlieb Klopstock, "Teone," verse 5.

Let me turn to the structure of our musical poetics today, with all its gothic form! How do the meters unfold? Where do they flow together? Where do we find transition? Sustaining the chaos, until it is camouflaged by beautiful madness? Where, finally, does the center assume its form, mastered and served by neither of the sisters, when the Pierides challenged the Muses?

Our own church music has an even more pitiful form. The earliest and most famous of all, Karl Wilhelm Ramler's *Der Tod Jesu*[ao] [1755], is a work of genius, of the soul, of the heart, also of the understanding of human nature. . . . What a piece of music! Who is speaking? Who sings? Speaks of anything in the recitatives . . . so very cold? It is so scholastic, surely as no Simon of Cana[ap] would have done, for he came from the fields, and accordingly expressed joy. And, moreover, within the arias, in the chorales and choruses . . . who is speaking? who sings? All at once there appears a valuable lesson drawn from the biblical story, commonplace in the truest sense, and in this sense like every person and all poetry in life! It jumps from one lesson to the next in the most curious fashion, so that there is no single point of view throughout the entire work, no thread that consistently unifies the sensibility, the story, the goal! . . . Ramler's *Der Tod Jesu* is an edifying, useful work, which I have thus admired a thousand times over! Each aria is virtually complete in itself! Many recitatives are the same . . . because of the great music . . . the poetic work of genius! Ramler has a much too sensitive feeling to notice this even himself.

His *Shepherds at the Manger*![aq] What poesy for the music? What a concept for the narrative? How does it fit the whole? From beginning to end, and it almost always creates the same impression! The impression of idyll, with which mere images of shepherds and words from beginning to end reveal not the slightest breath from the soul of a shepherd! Merely a mask of Isaiah, Virgil, and Pope in shepherd's clothing! . . . And finally, poesy for music . . . throughout the entire piece, images, but without any feeling! Pictures for the canvas—the ways in which the spear remains rooted in the earth, striving to rise above it, as if becoming a palm tree, etc. . . . throughout the entire work seemingly without the feeling of a

---

ao. *The Death of Jesus*, the most frequently performed German oratorio in the late eighteenth century. The libretto was written by Carl Heinrich Graun.

ap. Simon the Zealot, or Saint Simon, one of the twelve apostles in the New Testament of the Bible.

aq. *Hirten bei der Krippe zu Bethlehem*, by Johann Friedrich Agricola, with a libretto by Karl Wilhelm Ramler.

musician! And so it continues, to say nothing at all about how Christ would *rise again*!

And now, how do our musicians create all this, *accomplishing all that is once accomplished*? Because the very origins of this creation, the circumstances under which it came into existence, from which each individual, and surely we Germans, must call out: "Do not imitate anything, or you will always lag behind! It will be an eternal disgrace to measure a *Münter*[ar] against a *Metastasio*!" What a genre poesy really becomes, a genre truly lying between painting and music! And what a genre music becomes, when it does not attempt to become the master of poesy!

---

ar. Balthasar Münter (1735–1793), German pastor and composer of Lutheran sacred music.

5. Songs of the Enlightenment Bard
Essay on "Homer und Ossian" (1794)
Philip V. Bohlman

Johann Gottfried Herder's interests in the narrative of history grew from different types of comparisons between the past and the present, particularly in the similarity of literary engagement with both. The Greek poet Homer and the Gaelic poet Ossian were especially important to his comparison of epic in past and present, above all because they symbolized the attributes of bardic nationalists in the Enlightenment (on bardic nationalism, see Trumpener 1997). Herder returned at various points to both Homer and Ossian in the course of his literary works. Homer served Herder as the narrator and critic of the classical world, establishing the convergence of history and art in his great epics. The history that Ossian would have consolidated was more problematic for Herder, on one hand, because Ossian was a fictitious figure from a much more recent past, invented by James Macpherson for a series of song anthologies in translation (see, e.g., fig. 14, the title page of Macpherson 1765a), and on the other, because Herder could not entirely disentangle himself from contemporary controversies about the authenticity of the history that the Ossian songs might realize as an eighteenth-century epic—controversies that had occupied him already in his earliest writings on folk song in 1773 (see also chapter 4).

The Ossian controversy arose after it was discovered that Ossian, whom Macpherson identified as an ancient Scottish bard who had chronicled the myths of the early Scots with epic and song, which appeared in a series of published translations in the mid-eighteenth century (e.g., Macpherson 1760, 1762, 1763, and 1765a), was a complete invention. The Ossian songs appeared in quick succession in further translations into several languages (in German in Macpherson 1764a, 1764b), which subsequently influenced the painting, poetry, and music of Romanticism (e.g., Felix Mendelssohn's "Fingal's Cave," the overture to *The Hebrides*, op. 26 [1829]). Questions of

Ossian's authorship arose immediately but were complicated by the role that Macpherson claimed to play as a translator. Herder, as the present chapter reveals, entered the controversy largely because of his criticism of the German translation of Macpherson's English translation (for a classic study of the ways in which the Ossian controversy became an emblem of the invention of Highland tradition in Scotland, see Trevor-Roper 1983). Though he acknowledged the charges that Ossian did not really exist, Herder remained on the wrong side of the controversy (as this chapter will show).

The problem of convergence lies at the heart of the following essay from late in Herder's life. Homer and Ossian needed to be both the same and different for Herder. It is as mediators and authors of song and epic that they were the same. Through this similarity, moreover, they raised questions about the representation of the premodern nation. Herder fully admits to the controversy over the possible fabrication of Ossian by Macpherson, but for him the question of authorial role is closer to the case of Homer, whose own identity—as a historical individual, or simply a figure assigned responsibility for transforming Greek epic from oral to written tradition—was open to question in a different way. Running through "Homer and Ossian," then, are Herder's references to how the Ossian songs represent the heroic figures of Scottish history in ways that lend themselves to documentation. Contrasting Ossian with Homer is essential to Herder's claims that epics grow from a particular people at certain moments in their history, and that song represents their language and natural conditions, which in turn become cultural and national contexts. We hear in Ossian's songs, according to Herder, the very reality that they could never have been sung by the Greeks.

The contrast between Homer and Ossian also leads Herder to formulate a larger theoretical framework for situating song in cultural and linguistic contexts, which in turn resonate for understanding nationalism. The authorial roles of Homer and Ossian are critical for such resonance. Herder writes in part 1 (JGHW8, 72–74) that "Fingal, Ossian, and Oscar are children of the legends, creations of an era that uplifts them through continuous songs." We might well take this statement as a theory for the cultural specificity of epic. In part 3 (ibid., 77–81), Herder strengthens his claim for the ways in which each author and the songs he or she conveys could only be the products of different worlds. The rich metaphor with which Herder represents these differences derives from both language and nature, but he increasingly situates these as cultural landscapes that separate north from south, which in the course of history provide the political landscapes of song for the nation (part 4; ibid., 81–84).

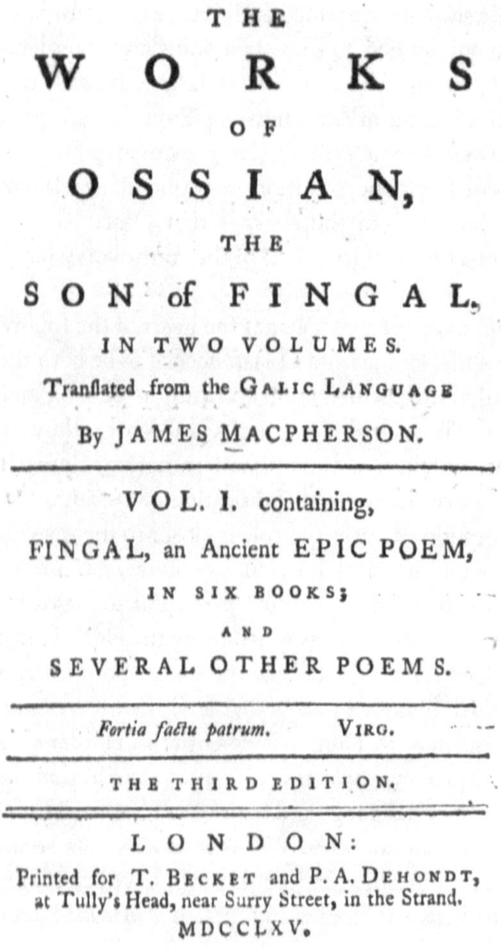

THE
WORKS
OF
OSSIAN,
THE
SON of FINGAL,

IN TWO VOLUMES.

Tranſlated from the GALIC LANGUAGE

By JAMES MACPHERSON.

VOL. I. containing,

FINGAL, an Ancient EPIC POEM,

IN SIX BOOKS;

AND

SEVERAL OTHER POEMS.

Fortia factu patrum. VIRG.

THE THIRD EDITION.

LONDON:

Printed for T. BECKET and P. A. DEHONDT, at Tully's Head, near Surry Street, in the Strand.
MDCCLXV.

FIGURE 14. Title page of James Macpherson, *Fingal, an Ancient Epic Poem*, 1765. Courtesy Special Collections, Regenstein Library, University of Chicago.

Ultimately the essay concerns itself more with Ossian than with Homer. Homer's position for Greek epic and literature was far more unassailable than Ossian's. In part 2 of the essay, Herder may not really mount a full criticism of James Macpherson, but he poses questions about authorial practice that clearly undermine the latter's project (cf. chapter 4 in the present volume). Why was Macpherson not more transparent about his sources? The criticism of Ossian in part 4 is more subtle and substantive, and it suggests an ethnographic move toward the anthropological, for it grows from Herder's assertion that the Ossian songs fail to respond to the moment of decline experienced by the peoples of the Hebrides at the moment of their encounter with modernity. Here we learn more about Herder than about Ossian or Macpherson, for the crucial point is that song does, even must, capture the spirit of the age in which it is created and transmitted. The seeming dearth of laments in the Ossian corpus, therefore, again raises the question of credibility.

The essay closes with a move to ethnographic criticism in the present. Part 5 (ibid., 84–87) consists almost entirely of a contemporary Scottish writer, John Buchanan, whose lengthy quotes in the section are meant to illustrate that the people of the western Hebrides at the end of the eighteenth century are very much like those of the mythical world described in the Ossian songs (see Buchanan 1793, 1795). We also witness in this essay, published at the beginning of the final decade of Herder's life, that he does not restrain himself from identifying the impact of cultural and colonial contact, especially its potential for destroying the culture of subjugated people. Herder is drawing myth and history together with this rhetorical gesture, and it is striking that song and other musical practices provide him with the means to sound similarities. Music becomes evidence for the continuity between myth and history. Epic—in this case, the body of Ossian songs—and its authors survive because they remain vital in the ongoing historical retelling of the past.

"Homer und Ossian" / "Homer and Ossian"

JOHANN GOTTFRIED HERDER,
TRANSLATED BY PHILIP V. BOHLMAN

The magnificent goal entrusted to those seeking to understand history, to bring humankind's works of art to light, to breathe life into the birth of the spirit, to endow art with a depth and fullness that leads to the harvest of fruit—this goal unfolds as a *golden chain of human spirit*. Wherever a name from the past emerges to reach a point of perfection, sooner or later the names of those who carry his work forward will accrue to that name. These names, perhaps, disappear, but the work, the name of those bearing it further, remains; everything they accomplish sheds ever greater light on it. He *who possesses value, to him will more be given*; all those who follow, thus, labor in the workshop of the great master.

In the Orient the names of Salomon, Lockmann, and others are well known.[a] All those things later attributed to the wisdom of nature, sayings, and myth were accumulated by each name in the temple of the everlasting, where it is understood as the wisdom of Lockmann or Salomon. Similarly, the final psalms came to be referred to as the Psalms of David; in the course of Western civilization Alexander the Great is famous as the destroyer and Suleiman the Magnificent as the builder of all that is great and noble; they serve as perpetual monarchs in the kingdom of the ages. . . . It is not any different with the Greeks. Everything that can accrue to Homer, Hesiod, Aesop, Anacreon, Sappho, Theognis of Megara, etc. has accrued to them. Later foot soldiers may have anonymously joined the ranks of these venerable gener-

---

[a]. Herder refers here to the biblical King Solomon and to Luqman, an Arabic poet and pre-Islamic commentator of the twelfth century BCE.

als; later scholarship may attempt in vain to ascribe a specific historical time and place to the struggles and accomplishments of these subsequent toilers. New life was breathed into the philosophical traditions of Pythagoras and Plato during the Christian era; new commentary accumulated to them accordingly, and their significance increased over the course of history.

Should it be any different with Ossian? We do not want to speculate idly, but rather acknowledge his contributions, as with Homer, in the course of time as they are revealed to us.

1

Many readers will remember just how enchanting it was when Ossian's poetry emerged during the years 1761 to 1765. First there were the short songs that appeared as *fragments*, and perhaps it is because many of those who love Ossian became acquainted with him through the first songs that they continue to love these the most.[b] We encountered Ossian through the brief Romantic tales of Schilrick and Vinvela, of Connal and Crimora, of Ronnan and Rivina, of Fingal, Ossian, Oscar, and Minona; we listened to the songs of Selma; Comala appeared, then Carthon, the death of Cuchullin, Berrathon, Karricthura.[c] Throughout these anthologies of song we witnessed scenes of innocence, of friendship, of a father's love, of the love of children, brothers, and sisters for one another, and we experienced melancholy in the most moving tones as it separated lovers and spouses. Obviously the torn image of these tales, their intense naïveté, and, if I may say so, the limited horizons of their common sky, contributed to the impression that they were the product of youthful souls. One heard sweet voices as if from a distance, from a cave, from across the sea, from a valley, or from the mountains on a neighboring island, and as if in a dream we saw the tiny cottages, wrapped in mists, of the nobles and loved ones.

Fingal appeared; soon thereafter also *Temora*, along with other poems. They were called epics as if they would vie with the epics of Homer, possibly even superseding them. James Macpherson himself, Ossian's immortal editor, pointed toward this goal in his own remarks; so too did Hugh Blair in his critical response,[d] and even more so Melchiore Cesarotti in the Italian translation of the poems.[e] Subsequently Michael Denis sang these for the

  b. See Macpherson 1760.
  c. For the early translations to which Herder refers see Macpherson 1764a, 1764b.
  d. Blair 1763.
  e. Cesarotti 1763.

Germans, in beautifully ringing Homeric hexameter mixed with lyrical syllabication, and accordingly gave them the appearance of a unified, continuous whole. More prose translations followed. At the same time, however, there appeared objection and doubt of very different kinds.

The Irish doubt is of the least concern for me. Ireland, which is to say Erin, tried to claim Fingal and Ossian as its own countrymen; it reclaimed the singer no less than the hero. Fingal became Fion or Fin, a king of Leinster; Ossian became Oisin, the son of Fion. It seems to me that one can respond to all of these rather briefly: "Just prove that this is the case. Produce Irish songs, songs more beautiful than the Scots have produced. Then we'll believe you." Fingal does not appear randomly in history; in Ossian's poems he is no longer Fion or Fin in Leinster, rather Fingal, the king of all humans, the commander of heroes. Song removed him from his everyday existence and raised him to epic heights so that he transcended death. Would Achilles, Ajax, Ulysses, Penelope, and Agamemnon recognize themselves in Homer's portrayal of them? I hardly think so; not any more than King Artus, Charlemagne, Gottfried of Jerusalem, or Ariostes's heroes would recognize themselves in the songs about them. Only after they were transformed did they become epic heroes. In legends they were transmitted from mouth to mouth; only in the sagas did they come to occupy a realm between heaven and earth. The bard chronicled them and immortalized them; as everyday, common individuals they would not have inspired his creativity. Fingal, Ossian, and Oscar are children of legend, creations of an era that uplifts them through unbroken song.

How then can geographical, historical, or chronological rivalries alter such things? Ossian's poems belong to the entire Gaelic people [*Völkerstamm*],[f] to precisely those who understand their own origins and know how to value Ossian. He lives on this side of the Irish Sea, as well as beyond the sea. Even the Greeks quarrel among themselves about just to whom Homer belongs: indeed, more than seven city-states and lands are at odds concerning his origins. They do not do this intentionally, as some means of minimizing Homer's poems in the ways they have been transmitted. Perhaps all sang a single Homeric epic, albeit with slight modifications. Similarly the Scots and the

---

f. The most direct translations of *Völkerstamm* require the translator to use a vocabulary with historical contingencies that would be misleading at the end of the eighteenth century. *Stamm* has a common use in German anthropology as "tribe." Herder's sense of *Völkerstamm*, moreover, borders on "race," which would not be entirely inaccurate as a projection of Enlightenment meaning, but it differs from more modern meanings of race. With "people" I aim to capture a more neutral, less racialized meaning.

Irish want to read a single Ossian and believe in a single Fingal, as long as Ireland, using its own means, can call forth a gentler Ossian and a nobler Fingal than James Macpherson portrays in his publications of Ossian. Accordingly we should want to thank the romantic sage for distinguishing between two dialects, each of which is appropriate in its own way. Until now we know of no characteristics of Irish poetry that are equivalent to the Scottish.

2

Considerably more important were the questions raised about the authenticity of Macpherson's Ossian. One must wonder, all the impudence with which the English attack Ossian notwithstanding, just why there has yet to be a satisfactory resolution to these questions. Macpherson himself would be in the best position to settle this concern once and for all, if he would only identify specifically and credibly just "where he found each and every poem, song, and piece of evidence. In what form did he gather them? And to what extent did he contribute additional evidence?" The original version of these songs in fragments, accompanied by poetic feet and the song forms, whose charming simplicity and variation have been extolled by many who honor Ossian, would be, even without critical commentary, irrefutable proof of truthfulness for today and tomorrow, against which no one from Britain, no Samuel Johnson, would be able to raise his voice in criticism. To my knowledge Macpherson has not answered his critics in these ways, and the fact that he has not done so has only exacerbated the doubt. Are you so impoverished, you Scots, that you cannot come up with the melodies and lyrics that you could apply to the songs of your own Homer, whom the Greeks praise so highly, in the ways they continue to sing his epics, and in this way you would rescue him from the abyss of being forgotten, to which Ossian is now so close? You would thereby ensure his immortality, indeed, the most noble, classical immortality there is. Or are you awaiting something more beautiful than Ossian? Or do you believe that these songs will be transmitted orally forever? Or have you convinced yourselves that simply by claiming that the beauty of the poems in their original language is inexpressible and that the melodic charm characterizing the songs needs no effort on your part, you will state your case most convincingly? Insistence and blind acceptance awaken the same faint praise. Only by exerting real effort will you make your case.[g]

---

g. The bracketed paragraph that immediately follows appears as a long footnote in Herder's text. Because of its substance and the doubt with which Herder now confronts the critical reception of Macpherson, I integrate it into the body of

[Until now, I have not had the fortune to find any authentic melodies for Ossian. I am also unaware of any authentic edition of Ossian in the Erse (Gaelic) language; the specimen in the seventh volume of *Temora* is indecisive. Where did Macpherson get it? Does everything appear just as he found it? Did it come from oral tradition or from manuscripts? Do the manuscripts agree with one another? Do the lyrical forms coordinate with the live performance of the songs? From what period does the diction of the songs and in the manuscripts come? Investigation and clarification of these questions would do more than all the praise currently heaped on Ossian. The *Gaelic Antiquities*[h] were indeed edited with the Erse title *Sean Dana*.[i] That these poems, quite unlike Macpherson's Ossian, appeared without any criticism, at least that I can find, does not really help us understand the veracity of Ossian in this instance. In 1784 the Irish scholar Arthur Young collected a volume of Gaelic poetry in northern Scotland that contains references to the story of Fian,[j] but I have myself yet to see these. One appropriate reference that I have found is part 138 of the *Allgemeine Literaturzeitung* of 1795.[k] If there are similar references elsewhere, especially by Gaelic speakers, we might finally reach a convincing solution. At this point, the evidence we need has simply not appeared. Some sources, moreover, among them the *Works of the Caledonian Bards*, appear even to be at odds with the mythology in Macpherson's Ossian. Perhaps it is the case that no other manner of singing appears so simple as that of Ossian, hence confirming its origins among the Gaelic peoples.]

Surely it would be critical to apply more scrutiny to the sources from which Ossian's songs come, for that is the only rational way to proceed. Whatever results such scrutiny might produce, be that as it may, they cannot harm Macpherson's fame. Should they take away from the tradition everything he chronicled, Macpherson at least collected and established the tradition. He was the Solon and the Hipparch who rescued the songs of this Homer from being lost forever, and this was agreeable to the entire learned world, in whose understanding ear and sensitive heart the songs truly resonated. His name remains unforgettable. On the contrary, if he simply took raw material and formed what he presented with his creative hand, his fame is all the more justified, and all the more instructive for us. If he

---

the translated text. I do this with other such substantive footnote texts in the present chapter, each time employing square brackets.
  h. Smith 1781.
  i. Smith 1787.
  j. Cited as Young 1784 in JGHW8: 76fn.
  k. By F.D. Gräter.

neglected one small thing or another, or if he introduced some nuance from the Jewish, Greek, or modern traditions to fill out the complete picture, to give the noblest and gentlest elevation to the whole ... his Fingal, his Ossian, his Bragela ... then all the better. He did what a clever man must do. He felt himself entirely in a position to treat his own songs in this way, for it was the spirit of his fatherland and his ancestors, the spirit of his own language and the songs sung in that language, that possessed him. He invested many of the songs, also those gathered from other periods, with a value and the beauty of a sensitivity from his own heart. We cannot excuse him for doing this under the mask of Ossian, but we must recognize also that he was perhaps acting from the duty of thankfulness and necessity. Ossian's songs had awakened his innermost spirit. He ascended, borne by their wings. A sacred deceit of this order was almost necessary to overcome the effusively modal poesy of the English, for what would be the equivalent of the pride of this nation of merchants, of their "Gimaces, Faces, and Graces," their "fashionable Poëtry," of the "pleasure's, measure's, and treasure's" in their rhymed verse?[1] What is more contrary to the English than the simple, unpretentious Ossian? At that time and place, it was entirely appropriate for Macpherson to lay his manuscripts at the feet of merchants in their London shops. He was well aware that they could not do anything with them.

What Macpherson did not do, however, has now been overtaken by his friends, even though many of them have intimate knowledge of exactly what the issues are. No single Englishman or Irishman is about to be allowed to parade around as the spokesperson for literary tradition. Rather, by honoring Ossian and Macpherson, we discover the true state of affairs, critically, clearly, and honestly. There is now more accurate examination and understanding of the origin, transmission, stability, and change of the legends, of the consideration of the moral, spiritual, and political concepts of their history. Accordingly the full extent of their aesthetic value will reach far beyond the individual songs themselves. I entrust to the test of time that such evaluation, too, will find its rightful moment.

3

What does the parallel between Homer and Ossian really have to say to us? That Homer was no Ossian, and that Ossian was no Homer? Who would have thought otherwise?

---

1. The phrases in quotation marks retain the English of Herder's original text.

Our earth has many different climates; our human condition allows for many different peoples. Ionia is not Scotland, and the Gaelic are not Greeks. We find here no Troy, no Helena, no palace in which Circe lives. Why would we unnecessarily compare such things? The region, world, language, the entire way of seeing and thinking, all this is different in the two nations. The different ages in which Homer and Ossian lived fail to justify comparison. Would one want to unify as a single form all that has been separated by thousands of years and vast distances?

Homer and Ossian are fully differentiated one from the other because the one, if I may thus formulate it, writes purely objective poetry, while the other creates purely subjective poetry. Homer is primarily a storyteller; his hexameter assumes singular and multiple forms, without any influence from the ways content is presented. Homer's entire artistry affixes itself to his consistent use of a hexameter that can bear all passions, that reveals all the conditions and events in heaven no less than on earth than in Orcus's underworld. Poetically, Homer's use of hexameter renders gods, heroes, and humans all the same. From Homer's unified hexameter and from the pure wisdom that enlivens him arose the style of Greece that witnesses the clarity of Greek thought. Herodotus took that style and used it to attribute different periods through his historical writing. From that style was derived a system of understanding the gods, art, and wisdom.

With Ossian everything stems from the harp of sentiment, from the feelings of the singer. He gathers his listeners about him, and he pours out his soul. He withdraws into this world, and he spreads this magical world around him. Thus he begins his songs with introductions, with which he can bring the souls of his listeners into accord. He expands his palette of conditions—the place, and day and year in which songs take place. For the most part he paints with tones perceived by the ear, for these express feelings more than images for the eye. He elevates all: every legend is illustrated with its own individual sentiment, as with the touch of love. As quickly as possible it assumes its individual voice, the lament of loss, the song of the harp. Even in the larger poems, *Fingal* and *Temora*, everything departs from the tones of a lonely harp, only to return. All the feelings from the heart linger on the harp's strings, among them the spent fate of those who came before. Song responds to each emotion. The Scots cannot praise highly enough the peacefulness of each unexpected shift in the soft or sad, wild or clever, syllabic meter. Homer knew nothing of such emotion in song. Tirelessly he would linger on the same sweet string, and with that he became the model for the harmoniousness of any situation or condition. Ossian is a *purely epic*, one might say a *lyric epic*, poet.

Such distinctive types of song differentiate the total genius of both poets. In the case of Homer, all shapes and forms emerge as if under a vast, clear sky; they appear there, or rather they stride boldly forward, as if truly alive. Similarly all his parables and images of nature are fully visual and clear; slowly they rotate in order continually to reveal and present all sides of their naturalness. There is no place projected in greater light than the field of Troy; under a continually illuminated Asian sky one heroic figure after another moves forward. There is not one element of their movement, I might say, not one limb of their bodies, with which they measure their accomplishments, that possesses any ambiguity. Homer also took pains to present the specific traits of the groups so that even in the chaos of the wildest battles the gaze of the beholder would remain without fog or confusion. As far as the individual strands of poetry are concerned, each one is unraveled from the fabric of history in a way so unbroken and peaceful that it is as if the hand of Parze, the goddess of destiny, drew it forth.

With Ossian it is completely different. His forms are nebulous figures, and they should be. They are shaped from the light breath of feeling, and they slide by as if made of breezes. Thus it is not merely spirits who inhabit the clouds, through which the stars shine. Ossian implies far more about the figures he lovingly shapes than he actually presents and portrays. We hear their footfall or their voice. We see the glow of their arms or their faces, as if a ray of light flashes across them. Their hair waves gently in the wind. In a moment they whisk by and are gone. He paints his heroes in similar fashion, not as they are, rather as they approach us, first appearing and then disappearing. With Ossian it is a world of spirits, in contrast to the world of living bodies that animates Homer. In Homer we see what really happens, whereas in Ossian we are left with the impressions, signs, and impacts that allow us only to intimate what happens. As far as the exposition of the poems is ultimately concerned, Macpherson and Blair should have remained true to the original materials, if we are to compare both poets. With Homer everything just narrates itself; one thing follows effortlessly upon another. In comparison, *Fingal* and *Temora* are poems strung together darkly, with entire episodes whose sense is difficult to disentangle. There is no truly sweet figure in any of the poems, which one can interpret at once as heroic romances or as peaceful idylls, some of which, for example *Comala*, even approach drama. In such poems we witness his spiritual portrayal, his heart full of wistfulness, love, and innocence. The narrative arc of an epic, perhaps as Macpherson realized only in the larger pieces, is here entirely foreign.

It becomes evident just how different the impact and results of both poets had to be. Whoever wants to encounter gods and heroes needs to turn to Homer, not to Ossian. For him, one figure is just like another, none of them really portrayed for the artist. The painter Ossian must do the creating himself; only from his own sense of poetry can he draw the color of feelings and adapt the darkness of the situation. In contrast, there is a source of feeling in Ossian full of the gentlest cultural intimacy. Homer would never invest his heroes with such intimacy. The two poets are distinct, just as one side of the Alps is different from the other. In the north, human nature closes more in upon itself. Those in the north have a tougher bark, which requires more effort from the outside to bore into their breasts in order to tap the deep sources of cultural intimacy embedded in stone. In the warmer southern regions, nature is expansive. People interact with each other more loosely, and they share among themselves more easily and vividly. In contrast, there are feelings that continue to slumber that could only awaken under the northern skies, such as the feeling of loneliness and the sense of impending danger. For Ossian, song possesses an intensive strength, evident only for an intimate circle. For Homer, song communicates expansively, across the broadest possible range, and this is to his great advantage.

Out of Homer has arisen what time has prevented Ossian from developing. Homer blossomed together with a nation of people still young; his garland adorned each new call to fame claimed by that people. With song he chronicled the first wars undertaken by Greece. When Greece later went to war on an even grander scale against the Persians, Aeschylus, Sophocles, and others were able to serve their fellow citizens according to new tastes in the meal they had shared with Homer. The honor of the entire Greek nation sprouted from his songs. They bore luscious blossoms and fruits of every kind with each new endeavor they undertook as a people, for above them stretched a bright sky, and around them blew Ionian, Greek, and Italian breezes.

4

And Ossian? It would be unfair to expect fruits from a tree that was incapable of bearing them. Ossian was no less anchored to his own place than Homer; he was simply standing somewhere entirely different. He was the last of a line of heroes among his ancestors, witness to the deeds of the famed Fingal and those serving him; in his era he was the last voice of a heroic time, now speaking to a weaker world that followed. This is where a singer stands, who at the same time must bear with him the entire character of Homer's style of poetry. His is the voice of an earlier era; it is no less a tragic voice, unaccompanied by an awakening call for the era that follows.

In every country, folk song responds to the internal and external conditions of the nation. It fixes itself quietly to a specific condition, from which it takes its character. For the Greeks this moment of character was the Trojan War, and Homer was the singer who established it. For the Gaelic peoples it was the departure of the heroic clans, and Ossian was the sad chronicler. Whence in the entire world did this lamentable moment of time come to the Gaelic peoples, and indeed with it for all subsequent time a diminishing, yet also defeated, tone in the old legends? How did it bring about such a foreign subjugation? Or the intruding religion of the Culdees, of the English clerics and Christian monks? The poems play upon both themes, but why do they always do so darkly? Have the collectors until now merely silenced the passages and sounds that possessed a cruel ring as a courtesy, with which the voice of the Gaelic peoples chronicled the decline of the old heroism? Or was that voice so gentle that it patiently remained silent, or perhaps must have been silent? The chronicles should have portrayed it as it was, for it seems impossible that any people would lament without complaint, without specifying the reason for their decline and without calling upon and celebrating the spirit of their ancestors, if only tentatively and halfheartedly.

In the songs of Ossian we find almost no trace of lamenting the decline of the Gaelic peoples. The heights spanned by the clouds, the stormy sojourn of the ancestors—these provide their sole comfort. In their earthly realms they bear witness only to saddening deserts, the spread of extinction across the places they once occupied; they hear sounds that dissipate and become evermore silent. One sees that the songs of a tolerant, subjugated people continue to be sung in order to revive themselves by celebrating the fame and happiness of their ancestors.

[The Irish Academy chronicles a conversation between Ossian and a Christian priest, which in turn has been translated into German. It contains a number of difficult passages, of which some, so it appears, had to be suppressed. Obviously this conversation must come from a later date, for it has none of the noble character distinguishing the other poems of Ossian.]^m

Just as nature contains different seasons, so too do they exist in human history. Peoples, too, have their spring, summer, autumn, and winter. Ossian's poems reveal the autumn of a people. The leaves become colored and brittle, and they yellow and fall. The breeze that blows them about possesses none of the refreshing quality of spring; its play with the falling leaves is therefore bittersweet.

---

m. The bracketed paragraph appears as a footnote in Herder's original text (JGHW8, 82).

Lament, too, is not without charm. The elegies of Mimnermu and Solon, the laments from the Jewish imprisonment in *Jeremiah* and the *Psalms*, move us. We are moved even more powerfully by Job's cry of anguish. In whose heart does one of Ossian's laments sound in vain, from the son or father left behind, or from the abandoned bride, from the lonely husband, or from the vanishing heroic clan? The lament is so entirely suited to this muse that it is drawn to the very roots of the language, to its very derivation and etymology. In every sense, the sound itself and the manner of singing the songs possess the same form of expression.

I admit that Ossian can be misused, not only if one sings his melodies without his sensitivity, but also if one abandons oneself too easily to his feelings of lament and gives way wistfully and subconsciously to the images that refresh the sweet, comforting mists. Meanwhile he possesses such a pure overview of humankind in its most intimate connections and situations that, if I may say so, I desire these to be entirely composed of purely human passages and emotions, as if fashioned from pearls. [We can only hope that such a collection of passages from Ossian, determined for composition, might appear soon.][n] In itself the song would here be a gentle recitative, there a wistful expression of emotion, here a passionate declamation, there antiphony between voice and chorus that one can block out of one's ear and hear only with difficulty. Who for instance did not hear Sigmund Seckendorff's burial song for Darthula without calling out?

> Awaken Darthula!
> Spring is here, the breezes stir,
> On a green slope, charming girls
> Weave flowers! Sprouting foliage covers the meadow.

And who would not be moved by the sad farewell?

> Never, nevermore will the sun again rise,
> Awakening on your place of rest: Wake up!
> You sleep a long sleep in the grave,
> Your dawn is far away.

> Forever, forever give way, then, sun,
> To the maiden of Kola, she sleeps!
> She will never arise again in her beauty,
> You will never again see her sweetness![o]

---

n. The bracketed sentence appears as a footnote in Herder's original text (JGHW8, 83).

o. Herder reprints this from Seckendorff 1779.

When I heard this song and the sighing Vinvela, also in Seckendorff's song,ᵖ it seemed to me as if his spirit hovered among the lovely tones and heard them together with me.

Ossian has withstood his trials among all nations, even among the Italians. Not only are we Germans indebted to him for the gentle tones in Gerstenberg's "Minona," in Klopstock's "Odes," in Kosegarten's and Denis's poetry, etc., but also anyone who wishes to give voice to the fate of their time to many different nations of Europe. Could that person sing with a vision different from that of Ossian?

5.

Whoever would like to know how things stand today with this ancient singing heroic nation, the descendants of Ossian, should read Buchanan's *Journeys in the Western Hebrides, from 1782 to 1790*.ᑫ With thoroughness Buchanan challenges each reader to prove the smallest inaccuracy in his descriptions. To what end are the noble clans diminished in any way! To what conditions have they descended! "One overlooks," Buchanan says, "what we have done to the western Hebrides in general, which is revealed most often in the picture of sadness and suppression, yet emerges everywhere. Above all these islands are the melancholy domains of lament and of suffering of all kinds, for those living there were used as beasts of burden, or even worse. If the neglect and wailing cannot entirely harden the slave against his dependency, against the abuse and humiliation that are heaped upon him, then the tears, the anguish, and the entreaties of a people suppressed in so many ways, but by no means a people stripped of its sense of self and spirit, cry out to the state's administrator for sympathy and rescue."ʳ

After centuries of suppression Ossian's Gaelic people are still recognizable here. Buchanan writes:ˢ

As a whole the residents of the western Hebrides possess good natural dispositions, understand more quickly, and penetrate perhaps more deeply into a subject than the residents of the inner regions of a

p. Ibid.
q. German translation, Berlin, 1795 (see Buchanan 1795).
r. Buchanan 1795, 174–75. Herder draws the reader's attention to passages in Buchanan that call for a type of political engagement for the Hebrideans, what he calls their rescue (*Rettung*). Herder further wonders if this sort of engagement might draw the reader closer to a way of rescuing Ossian from his detractors.
s. Buchanan 1795, 71–75, 125.

country are capable. This must surely be the case because they have so much contact with people of such entirely different personalities, with whom they meet daily through sea travel, and accordingly they must be cautious, deliberate, and careful. They are also regularly in danger of the elements to which they must relentlessly react, which places them in the unnatural necessity of having to keep eye and senses awake for anything that might happen. Such continuous exercise becomes for them regular custom, with which each one of them makes evident in leading life itself.

They have a fortunate predisposition to poetry, as well as to singing and instrumental music, especially on both of the Uist Islands of the Outer Hebrides, where one need not simply study, but rather hears the sudden outpouring of a very sharp and bitter satire, which allows itself to cut through bone and marrow, and sit where it cuts.

A gentle, light sound that is deeply touching flows through even these songs, which enlivens the soul to heartfelt sensation and love. One also hears painful laments and tones of anguish about lost lovers and friends, and one finds those who sing these not only among the highest classes, but also among the lowest. In this way they surpass all the ancient English and Scottish songs known until the present day, regardless of how much acclaim these have found among those truly knowledgeable about song. Were the Gaelic language sufficiently well known, the masterpieces of Gaelic music would reach every stage on which taste and charm ruled with honor and amazement.

Their *luinneags*[t] and the unity of all the voices joining it are unspeakably pleasant for the ear. The eye, too, will be engaged when one sees them standing in a circle, waving hands and scarves. Singing and instrumental music are their means of social interaction. Their skill at dancing probably surpasses that of all other peoples.

The common people arrive at concepts and skills remarkably quickly. Women are just as good at weaving as men. They learn this art in only a few months. In so doing they heartily sing their *jorrams*[u] and *luinneags*. One person sings the melodic voice, the others the chorus, which after each statement of the song is repeated two or three times. The sweet sound of their songs usually attracts many listeners, who join in the chorus.

Buchanan writes about Saint Kilda:

Men and women love song and have beautiful voices. Their connection and predilection for poetry is no less than that of others born in the Hebrides. They love the descriptions in their songs and display an uncanny fantasy. The objects of the descriptions are the charms of their

---

t. A Gaelic poetic form, from the Irish Luimneach, the region around Limerick.
u. A Gaelic poetic form.

loved ones, as well as the heroic deeds of the hunters and fishermen, and the tragic death that overcomes them between the cliffs. As on Harris,[v] the men sing while at the helm of their boats, and while working they move themselves through competitive and choral singing, thereby keeping the tempo of their labors.

. . . If a second Fingal could return again for these poor Gaelic people, his son Ossian would also appear again. He would no longer sing in order to realize *whence each tone came and would need to continue singing, alas, of the sad times*: the fall of the heroes, oppression, lament, and anguish. . . .

---

v. The southern part of the Hebridean island of Lewis.

6. Redemption through Sacred Song

Essay on Letter 46, *Theologische Schriften* (1780/81)

Philip V. Bohlman

The sacred and the secular are seldom separate in the writings of Johann Gottfried Herder. As a pastor, theologian, and teacher he engaged with religion and religious education every day, and it is thus hardly surprising that the everyday assumed such a powerful and unifying presence in all his projects, sacred and secular alike. For Herder religion was an experience shared by the many and the masses, and so, too, was music. Religion and music were most fully efficacious when made available for those to whom he referred in his theological writing as "common" (*gemein*),[1] and in his anthropological writings as *Volk*. Whether writing on sacred or secular music, he believed that it was singing that transformed the common culture of the *Volk* into the universal expression of the sacred, thereby elevating the secular to the sublime.

Their confluence notwithstanding, the sacred and the secular were not the same for Herder. As the forty-sixth letter from his *Theological Writings*[2] makes abundantly clear, there were many occasions, arguably more often than not with other areas of his thought and writing, in which he devoted himself to religion. Music was a frequent topic in his theological writings—to a larger extent, even a leitmotif. In order to understand the context and meaning of his writings on religion, it is essential to evaluate the presence of music and to do so exegetically. The forty-sixth letter points us toward some of the biographical reasons why this is so. When Herder writes critically about collections of sacred song in the eighteenth century, he does so with reference to several hymnbooks that he himself had compiled and edited (e.g., Spalding 1780; Zollikofer 1766). When he turns to George Frideric Handel's *Messiah* as the ultimate confluence of the sacred and secular, he chooses not only a sacred genre, the oratorio, that gathers all of humankind on the secular stage, but also a work whose biblical lyrics he had himself translated for recent performances. Both interventions with sacred song, moreover, arose from the local practice of a pastor and theologian, for the new songbooks and the *Messiah* performance were prepared for Weimar, where Herder served as a pastor at the church of Saint Peter and Saint Paul.[3]

The publication of epistolary writings was standard literary practice in the eighteenth century, and we therefore recognize that Herder's use of the letter as a form for religious and moralistic pedagogy was by no means unusual. Letters provided the form for the novel, especially during the eighteenth century, when the novel was coalescing as a form and genre (e.g., Samuel Richardson's 1748 *Clarissa* and Johann Wolfgang von Goethe's 1774 *The Sorrows of Young Werther*). The epistolary essay was critical to moral philosophy as well as to theology before the eighteenth century and long thereafter—indeed, even until the present day.[4] Herder published epistolary essays throughout his career, not only for his theological writings, but also within the context of his writings on moral philosophy (see, e.g., the *Letters for the Advancement of Humankind*[5] [1793–97] from the final years of his life [JGHW7]). It was through correspondence, furthermore, that he presented some of the central debates and arguments surrounding his most significant contributions to aesthetics and music (e.g., the Ossian correspondence that he published as fragments in 1773, much of which appears in translation in chapter 4 in the present volume). The forty-sixth letter, dedicated to sacred song, is personal, even intimate, in tone, addressed at various times to "my friend." Herder's friend, however, is the everyperson, indeed, the "common person" who constitutes the eventual collective for which sacred song has the most redemptive meaning. In this way, Herder's case for a sacred music of the present and future is also addressed to us when we read it in the twenty-first century.

As with most of the writings that fill the chapters of the present volume, the forty-sixth letter sketches a history of texts and contexts. The tension that frames the history forms around the relation of song texts to the music—melody, vocal and choral practice, and to a lesser degree instrumental traditions of the church—and can be resolved only when sacred music is accessible as extensively as possible for those who sing it, not only because it expresses what is in their hearts, but also because it is ultimately the music that truly leads toward the exaltation to the sublime. Past and present are inseparable in the letter, though never because of an atavistic aesthetic. The past is usable and renewable to create a better present and future, and it is for this reason that Herder advances his call for drawing upon the best sacred songs as a force of renewal. In order to be efficacious and beautiful, sacred music must be returned to the congregation, where it gathers the voices of the many. The history that unfolds in the letter thus signals the possibility of redeeming sacred music from the past that has fallen into decay.

In the course of the forty-sixth letter Herder increasingly establishes the conditions whereby sacred music becomes the music of the people. The theologians who identify songs for worship recontextualize them as hymns and liturgy, and place them in anthologies so that they are accessible, in both oral and written forms, to as many people as possible. Accordingly they are creating a repertory of sacred songs whose functions are like those of *Volkslieder*. Herder disdains sacred music that is abstract and elaborated in ways that complicate its accessibility. The songbook is crucial to the process of gathering the right songs for the most widespread use, for such songbooks draw upon the provincial variants, even in dialect, as much as do the canons of Luther. Critical to the function of the songbooks are the ways in which they afford change, expunging the superfluous while opening worship spaces for new songs. Additionally critical for the agenda in the forty-sixth letter is the argument Herder makes for genre and its role in generating dimensions for folk song. By claiming Handel's *Messiah* as a Christian epic for the modern worshiper, he opens connections to genre in several ways. On a more general, textual level, he makes allusions to his own interpretation of epic as the narrative genre connecting the past to the present (e.g., Homer and Ossian in chapter 5 of the present volume, and the *Cid* in chapter 8). On a more practical level, the *Messiah* opens modern possibilities for the performance of the common people, for whom the oratorio and the genres of its movements are well suited, as allegory and as song itself. The singing by many redeems music for the sacred and the sublime.

In the single letter that follows we witness the ways in which Herder as a polymath comes full circle. We recognize, even in the modest confines of a relatively brief letter, that Herder's theological and musical thought always coalesces around common and related ideas. Its seemingly modest claims notwithstanding, the forty-sixth letter contains many, if not most, of the fragments and wholes, allusions and unifying theses, that we encounter in the other chapters of the present volume—and that we similarly find as unifying themes throughout Herder's creative output. Questions and theories of translation punctuate the letter; he develops theories about the ways anthologies of song become the most effective vehicles for the "voices of the people in song"; aesthetic judgment and moral imperative accompany discussions of song and singing; music that issues from the heart finds its fullest expression amid the common people, who are the true force behind its exaltation to the sublime. Once again the transformation of song as an object to singing as a subject provides Herder with a way of understanding the redemption that lies at the heart of sacred song.

Letter 46, *Theologische Schriften* / *Theological Writings*

JOHANN GOTTFRIED HERDER,
TRANSLATED BY PHILIP V. BOHLMAN

From time to time I have sent you poetic pieces, among them those in aesthetic genres from hymns, songs, parables, fables, etc., and with a few thoughts to accompany them. I do not believe, however, that such things offer atonement for what has otherwise been neglected, for I do not entirely understand what, in correspondence of this kind, might really atone for neglect. The letter writer ceases to write when he wishes, and the reader ceases to read when she comes to the end of the letter. Given the sheer abundance of reading material about which we speak, moreover, it is only likely that we skip over several lines here and there. You will have long known from your good sense and intelligence that poesy is *the force that shapes delivery, the treasury of all great thought, and the active description*, finally, *the artistic design* that speech and, above all, prose must acquire. We have thus frequently observed that prose emerges from poetry, which simultaneously gives shape to poetry, both in the texts of the songs and music of the prophets inspired by God and throughout the history of all peoples. Criticism and oratory, too, began with poetry, as demonstrated in the teachings of Plato, Aristotle, Cicero, and Quintilian, as well as in the recent writings of Johann Heinrich Voss (1751–1856), Charles Rollin (1661–1741), and others.[a] Poesy is the lifeblood of the human soul, as well as the shaping inspiration for the youthful years of our all-too-fleeting life.

    a. Herder repeatedly expresses indebtedness to Johann Heinrich Voss, especially for his translations of Homer. Herder is referring here to Charles Rollin, *De manière et d'étudier les belles-lettres*, 4 vols. (Paris: J. Estienne, 1726–28).

In order to clarify the theological borders requisite for the present undertaking, you should obviously note that we are not concerned here with the poetry that a young person *himself* must strive to create. You are well aware that I have often and long ago warned against stealing foreign flowers of poetry and prose, as well as opulent decoration in speech. If poesy were so unusable that one covered one's nakedness with colorful, shiny rags from the rubbish, or, in contrast, modestly dressed himself in simple, honest clothing, then would not a humble person try to distance herself as far as possible from the rubbish bin? How unfortunate this situation is when it comes to poesy! Poesy is, as already noted, the *most perfect expression*, and the most artistic *form* of speech, which draws the *strictest laws* and *most precise rules* from an apparent freedom, and in the most appropriate way possible *combines thoughts and words*. Because poesy is capable of awakening the *noblest* thoughts and combining these with the *finest* words, one is able to create something of greater *content* and *form* in ways otherwise unavailable. One employs *rules* and *regulations*, both in the most natural and pleasant ways possible. Just as I have hinted at the ways young theologians might use fable, dialogue, and parable, I should now like to speak about other types of poetry, above all the *biblical epic, song, and pedagogical poetry*.

Pedagogical poetry, as its name and function suggest, is surely the simplest of the three. No person, whether a member of society in general or an occupant of the rarefied offices of hexameter, speaks in such ways after coming to understand such poetic practices. Similarly, he will not show off with single verses—he would need very special circumstances to do so—whether in everyday or common speech. Such poetry, nonetheless, contains the most powerful and truest thoughts in the most straightforward language, and these shine as precious stones in the midst of gold. To such ends he has the most sublime pedagogical poems in the Bible at his disposal, such as the book of *Job*, the *Proverbs* and *Ecclesiastes*, and the *Prophets*. The poets who created the most sublime pedagogical songs were inspired by *Moses, David*, and *Isaiah*. The true *ode*, indeed the *hymn* itself, is nothing more than a *higher* form of pedagogical poetry with a specific purpose, which then ascends to a higher level of inspiration. If you do not believe me, then read *Ulrich Zwingli's* (1484–1531) foreword and afterword to his writings on Pindar, and you will see the degree to which a theologian draws lessons from such a mythological poet. You will thus come to honor our own poets writing pedagogical poetry and odes, just as you will those of other nations, and from them you will learn to express true and noble thoughts in the most sublime, beautiful, and economical language.

As far as *sacred song* is concerned, as I have elsewhere already observed, its use is even more valuable to the popular, practical theologian as is the most sublime ode. The songbook is the *veritable Bible* for the common Christian. The songbook is his comfort, her teacher, his retreat, and her inspiration in the home. In public assembly the songs and the melodies that accompany them should unite and exalt the souls of those assembled as the ether and air on high. What music here is able to do, especially the highest form of all music, *holy* music, cannot be described with words, only felt with sensation. It moves through its simplicity, it can exalt because of its dignity. "In music," writes one author, "we have progressed farther than in poesy, especially after God invented that astoundingly noble instrument, the organ. The organ speaks every language. It breathes the love of God into the listening ear of the worshiper with the seductive language of a lover. It shouts with the fear of God into the ear of the tyrant. With the counterpoint of brass instruments it ennobles the praise of God, it sounds his miracles and their majesty, making them eternal."[b] If this is the case, how should we use church music? And with what celebration and dignity! ... Surely not that of Saint Cecilia, but rather that of heavenly *worship* itself, which draws us through our holy congregation up to the heavenly throne on high! ... Allow me, my friend, to share some more complete thoughts about songs and music for the church (for a theologian, always important matters), according to the situation of our own day. I am sure that you will gladly take the following, not-unnecessary step with me.

Just as all peoples sought to hold worship services as an offering of *dignity* and *celebration* for the past, so too should we not entirely throw away the traces of the past that might still survive. Those who wish to make the language of the worship service and religion opulent and feminine, whether in the music or in the liturgy, in song or in the sermon, should instead be reprimanded in the same manner as the Greek[c] who sought to make certain melodic modes softer ...

... banned, that is, not from the world, but rather from official functions. What is music when a large percentage of the people are unable to sing it, when they do not understand it? What about music that no one is able to sing because it is uneven and broken apart by so-called embellishments—enjambments ... in the ascending and descending scales? Sacred song

---

b. Herder attributes this passage to Christian Gottlieb Berger (1764–1829) in correspondence with his Königsberg teacher, Johann Georg Hamann (see JGHW9/1, 1994, 1086).

c. Herder refers here to Terpander (ca. seventh century BCE), recognized as one of the first Greeks to systematize music and poetry.

moves *slowly* and *ceremoniously*; why does it need to skip about? Sacred song is *for the masses*—for their needs, for the ways they think and see, for the conditions and language of their lives. They should pray to God with sacred song, using the noble language of the heart. One *model* should be song, upon which they draw because of the ways it functions for them, because it provides them with intimate feeling above all, even if it is wanting for eloquence. What should they do with the fancy language of books, or with poetic and abstract trifles? Would we take that away from the people and silence *their own* songs and music, which have accompanied them from their childhood throughout their life, whose authorship was familiar to them, which had served them in time of great need, and whose true poet was the language of the heart? Would we, instead, subject them to poetic banality, superfluous rhyme, and youthful exercises, which had no real application or meaning, no real connection to human need and function, but rather were created in order to provide the printer with style primarily of value only for fame and fashion? Would this be even a cheap exchange for people who actually *hear the songbook*, even while there are others who are wealthy, learned, and self-important, who possess no taste for sacred song?

You can trust me that I am here not speaking with the least bit of jealousy. I also believe that you do not understand me to be one of the barbarians who have no respect or sympathy for our songbooks. Many of them have simply lost their distinctiveness.... How should I describe it, as sea or swamp? How can we find the best among the worst, the pearls in all the rubbish? One can sweep much of the rubbish away! No rational person could be opposed to removing the ox and pigeon manure from the temple in order to make the holy place clean. Similarly there can be no doubt that the best songs by the finest composers often contain passages, styles, and verses that we no longer can sing. We could remove these, or improve them, though we should do so *silently* and *gently.* Silently and gently so that, when attempting to straighten one limb, one does not destroy all the other limbs and joints just to embellish the language. Similarly one does not move around the parts of the body in such a manner that the nose takes the place of the ear, the toes the place of the thumbs, in the way that Hanon did with the servants of David in the Bible.[d] How modest were the initial attempts by *Johann Joachim Spalding, Georg Joachim Zollikofer,* and others to create a collection for *refined* people, indeed, a *refined* songbook

---

[d] 2 Samuel 10, 1–5.

especially intended for *private use*!ᵉ And how these were then distributed everywhere! Have I ever known of a songbook in which the founding principle was: "*No* song should be left untouched, accept *nothing* that is unchanged or that would not lend itself to change." Is it a valid question any longer: To alter or *not* to alter? Or is there any *reason* to make a change? Does one ask if people who have never dreamed of poesy in their entire lives, not to mention have never sought to improve one of Luther's songs, can or even may undertake the relatively difficult task of *serving* the spirit of another and *gently assisting* it? None of this really comes into question: one makes and introduces change from the most merciful commission.... Now, true Christian and poetic spirit requires no commission. This situation can have no other consequences than those it already has, namely that Germany will become a Babylon, overrun with dialects and authorities, as well as with songbooks ... and thus with God ... and very soon with *newly translated Bibles*.

My friend, do not let yourself be dismayed by all the songs now being born so that you no longer study and continue to love the old songs with their dignity and simplicity. The old songs afford us a richness of language and religious sensitivity that we have inherited from almost all the church fathers. What I should wish to instill in our language from many of their *hymns* would not be the words, but rather the spirit. Even the Latin of the medieval monks employed some of the sound of worship, celebration, and humility that has no equivalent in the language of the present day, from which I here note only expressions of need: *stabat mater dolorosa*; of horror: *dies irae, dies illa*, and many other well-known chants I need not mention. Some of our songs that Luther and others have translated stem from very old Latin, and if its expression is outdated here and there, one should, in my opinion, offer some assistance, but without weakening its power and removing the entire body of the form of age, at least to the extent that this is possible. Who would destroy a Strasbourg Cathedral or a Notre Dame in Paris in order to plant a light opera house or theater for entertainment in its place?... There is often a simplicity and reverence, a feeling of intimacy and brotherhood, in the songs of the Bohemian Brothers that we must leave

---

e. Herder refers here to Spalding's *Neues Gesangbuch zum gottesdienstlichen Gebrauch in den königlichen preußischen Landen* (Berlin: Voss, 1780), and to Zollikofer's *Neues Gesangbuch oder Sammlung der besten geistlichen Lieder bey dem öffentlichen Gottesdienst* (Leipzig: Weidmanns Erben und Reich, 1766), for both of which he himself provided new editions for the synod of Weimar and Saxony in 1778.

as it is, for we no longer possess it ourselves.ᶠ It is a pity that we do not seek at least the gold from these mines and adapt it for our own common needs. Still, it is perhaps better that the songs are protected for a *few* of those who love them.

Some of the songs by Luther—even though others, I am sorry to say, are too personal and antiquated—are very precious songs from the previous century and from the beginning of the present century, and they are filled with melody and the language of the heart. One feels, nonetheless, that there are contrasts with sacred song from time to time. Song becomes more refined, and it loses its power; it becomes sweeter, and it almost ceases to be choral song. I should go so far as to say that a well-known pious school in Germany has recently removed all the power from sacred song, leaving it to decay.ᵍ Pietism has reduced sacred song to chamber song with sweet, feminine melodies, filled with tender sensitivity and rubbish, thus stripping it of all the majesty that commands the heart, and making it a weakling at play. I write these lines, nonetheless, with great respect for the leading figures of such pietism, who are much deserving because of their work with sacred music. All in all, however, rubbish of this sort could only lead to nothing more than philosophical indifference and poetic dissection.

It is too bad that, among the large number of bad songs found in our old songbooks, the *good ones* are never gathered in a single source, but rather are scattered about amid the mess filling provincial collections. And many songs of this sort even have national melodies, without which they would be half dead. A bee seeking to create an anthology of Christian song would first need to collect the best songs, both old and new, with their melodies, from all the provinces, without regard to the differences among the Protestant religions, and this would be the *foundation* for a good songbook for Germany. Regardless of the name and stature of their composers, the bad songs must be discarded. The bad verses, moreover, should be removed from the good songs, for many of them are much too long. And it is better to remove the bad songs than to alter them. Even in the songs of *P. Gerhard, Spener, Franke, Scriver, Freilinghausen,* and others there are some for which this is necessary; this is even more the case with *Angelu, Rist,*

---

f. The Bohemian Brothers were one of the earliest Protestant sects, initially following the teachings of Jan Hus (ca. 1369–1415). Already in the sixteenth century, the Bohemian Brothers gathered and published collections of hymns in German that widely influenced the songs of German Protestantism.

g. Herder refers here to German branches of pietism, who reduced their hymns and songbooks in melody and harmony in ways akin to their North American pietist cousins, the Amish and the Mennonites.

Heermann, Hermann, and others.[h] From the new songs, only those should be included that are singable and understandable for the common person, and not those songs that are simply rhymed abstractions or poetic tirades. All changes must be directed in such a way that *anything shocking* is eliminated, but that the color employed by a composer is not removed, and even more so that the song does not simply melt into *our* way of thinking. Some of those making improvements appear to have adhered strictly to these principles. Is it the case, however, that the results are positive in all instances? That is a different question altogether. In sum, for the practical theologian it is necessary to know the best of the old songs and the best . . . or at least the best from among the improved . . . of the new songs. The ability to distinguish both is critical for the study of the language and the type of sensitivity to the sacred conditions and the impression made by the materials used for the sermon.

As far as church music is concerned, we undoubtedly have many more songs whose quality lies in their melodies rather than in their words, for the texts in the common church cantatas are usually ordinary or dreadful. In this regard, there is much that we should wish for worship before *Klopstock's Golden Dream* would be fulfilled.[i] Read Luther's commentaries on his songbook and all that he says about music elsewhere, and observe how he praises music as a *second theology*. How this would make the music of the worship service a different thing altogether! Recently I have felt this myself and applied it to *Handel's Messiah*.[j] Oh, friend, what a magnificent work the *Messiah* is, truly a Christian epic in music! You become aware of this in the gentle *comforting voice* right from the beginning and hear the arrival of the Messiah in the *mountains and valleys* stretching across the natural world, until he *is gone up on high, and the Lord gave the word,* and the *sound is gone out into all lands*. You feel it in the magnificent aria, *but who may abide the day of his coming?* Who does not feel *why the nations so furiously rage* in their entire bodies? And then the joyful, clear message appears with his song of the lark, *rejoice greatly, o daughter of Zion?* And the people who follow the way of the cross, *the people that walked in darkness,* and then daybreak, *arise, shine, o thou that tellest good tidings to Zion?* When there is a chorus alone of this kind, *for unto us a child is born,* all the names of newborns spill like silver drops from heaven? And sud-

---

h. Lutheran hymn writers.

i. Herder refers here to Friedrich Gottlieb Klopstock, *Oden* (Hamburg: Bode, 1771).

j. Herder refers to his translation into German of the *Messiah* for a 1780 performance in Weimar.

denly everything is silent, and the most gentle pastoral music spreads sleep across the night?[k]

You well know, my friend, that words are incapable of expressing any of this. Listen to the aria "He Shall Feed His Flock Like a Shepherd, Come unto Him, All Ye That Labor"; listen to the chorus, "Behold the Lamb of God," and then the heartrending solo that immediately follows, "He Was Despised"; listen to everything, everything that follows, leading to eternity itself in the "Hallelujah" chorus; then, after a brief intermission, experience the gentle certainty of "I Know That My Redeemer Liveth," and then feel the universal "Since by Man Came Death" and "Behold, I Tell You a Mystery," followed by "The Trumpet Shall Sound and the Dead Shall Be Rais'd"; listen to the conversation from beyond the grave, "O Death, Where Is Thy Sting?"; and once again we hear about everything, everything until the end of the world, for "Worthy Is the Lamb That Was Slain," which lays *thanks* and *sovereignty* at his feet *forever and ever*! Listen to all this, and have just some feeling for *religion* and *music*! How, then, will you think about many of our church musicians? And still, everything is so simple! With words from the Bible, God be praised, merely words from the Bible; it is not a cantata filled with beautiful rhymes. Farewell.

---

k. Herder discursively weaves the texts from his own *Messiah* translation into this passage, thereby posing questions about the sublime nature of sacred song to his epistolary companion. The style of my translation deliberately follows Herder's rhetorical style, mixing texts and titles from the different sections of the *Messiah*. In the concluding section that follows, Herder refers specifically to arias and choruses by their titles, and I again follow his style.

PART III

The Nation Project

7. The Shores of Modernity
Essay on "Wirkung der Dichtkunst auf die Sitten neuerer Zeiten" (1777)[1]
Philip V. Bohlman

With the final chapter of his history of poetry and its influences on culture, Johann Gottfried Herder reaches a point of both arrival and departure. This *Wirkungsgeschichte*, an intellectual history that charts the influence of historical objects and subjects across time, chronicles the ways in which the literature, art, and music—poetry and poesy in their fullest sense—from one age and culture exert an impact on the eras that follow. Herder begins this intellectual history of three large sections, each with several chapters, by establishing the nature of poesy (JGHW4, 151–58), and then proceeds in successive chapters to move from one generation to the next, from Greek antiquity to the late Enlightenment of his own day, arriving finally at Germany and the problem of its modernity and nationalism. The chapters also unfold cross-culturally, with a counterpoint between more traditional Western civilization and the epochs and regions of other peoples and literary practices (e.g., section I, chapter 2, on the "Influence of the Poetry of the Jews" [JGHW4, 158–69] or section II, chapter 4, on the "Influence of the Poetry of the Nordic Peoples" [JGHW4, 184–88]). Beginning with antiquity, Herder's intellectual history follows the principles he had established at the beginning of the 1770s, searching for an understanding of poesy and, by extension, folk song in its classical precedents. With chapters of the third section, however, he reaches the present, and with that arrival at the shores of modernity, his aesthetic and ethical journey shifts from past to present, from history to anthropology.

In 1777 Herder is ready to turn his full attention to folk song. In the final chapter, which I translate in the pages that follow, that turn is realized with the critical shift in vocabulary and voice that accompanies his work in the mid-1770s, the point of transition between the "folk songs of early times" (see chapter 1 in the present volume) and the "voices of the people in songs" (chapter 2 in the present volume). In this 1777 intellectual history, the critical terms in Herder's vocabulary both proliferate and acquire more specificity and nuance. The terms with which he refers to peoples and cultures, for example, range from *land* to *nation* (*Land* and *Nation*), and they reflect distinctions between the collective and the individual (*Volk* and *Völker*). Poetic and musical expression, too, contain rhetorical distinctions traditional and innovative (*Dichtkunst* and *Poesie*), genre-specific and universal (*Dichtung* and *Musik*). Most critical, however, is the confluence of the cultural and the aesthetic, and the concomitant emergence of a language that is broadly ethnographic and political.

Nations have their own distinctive poetic and musical practices, and not just because they speak different languages. Literature and the arts are not only the results of cultural distinctiveness; they also shape and transform societies to make them modern. Most important, the "influence of poetry" that is now important for modernity moves from external conditions to the internal forces that afford human beings agency through the arts: the influence of poetry and the arts takes place in the heart and soul. Such influence creates agency, which in turn has the power to change culture. With this realization, expressed for the first time in the chapter here, Herder embarks upon the new journey that will take him to the folk song anthologies in the following years, the *Volkslieder* of 1778/79.

In this chapter, Herder struggles to find a modern vocabulary to describe the connection between agency and culture, employing the terms *Wirkung* and *Sitten* throughout. He is trying to capture the sense of transition from an early era to the present and the future, the moment of modernity at which he has arrived. To capture his struggle with that transition, I generally use the more literal, eighteenth-century terms "influence" and "customs" rather than the more modern "agency" and "culture."

This chapter is also a literary history, in which Herder makes connections between specific writers, the works they produce, and the ways in which these exert an influence on their own age and subsequent literary cultures. Throughout he therefore charts the historical transition to orality from literary sources and the ways in which imitation of the past takes place. In the course of the historical *longue durée* traced through the chapter, therefore, we witness a gradual shift from text to context, from the literary objects of antiquity to the reading subjects of the contemporary age. In the earlier stages of the literary history, the focus falls primarily on texts themselves and what kinds of models they become for later writers. When he reaches his discussion of more recent traditions, for which his sources are almost entirely from the seventeenth and eighteenth centuries, he increasingly introduces the role of the reader, both generally and specifically. Again, he noticeably struggles to find an appropriate vocabulary. His modern readers are, for example, male and female, and he employs the gender inclusivity of both the masculine *Leser* and the feminine *Leserinnen*. These various transitions to a society of "living readers" who feel the influences of poesy within them signals a wide-ranging ontological shift in Herder's work, which is crucial for the political turn that he has fully set in motion by 1777.

Literary history thus becomes political history, and the one that Herder sketches here ends with Germany at the end of the eighteenth century. Nationalism is having an ever greater impact on national styles, and Germany's national problem—that it is not one nation but many provinces, each content with its own customs and culture—once again occupies Herder. He does not, however, leave the problem unresolved, as he did in the unpublished chapters of the 1774 *Alte Volkslieder* (chapter 1 in the present volume); rather he seeks a political solution, which in turn he finds in poesy and music. The chapter's modernity further results from the changing ways in which poesy and music reflect the influence of religion on contemporary societies. In the broadest historical terms, Herder makes a distinction between mythology and religion, the former representing the external objects of the classical world, the latter influencing the inner subjectivities of the heart and soul. Not surprisingly Herder favors literary cultures in which religion exerts its influence on the inner workings of the sentient reader, and he makes this clear in the very opening of the first chapter of *Wirkung der Dichtkunst*, assessing poetry in Hebrew. Religion returns again in the final chapter, above all as a critical assessment, albeit restrained, of the most important influences of German writers. Those who capture the spirit of religion affect the connection between external and internal influences most effectively.

Singing, increasingly so in the final sections of the chapter and centrally so in the discussion of national bards in the final pages, affords the critical link between the nation and its people. The identity of the folk is growing more evident and more important as customs become modern. By the end of the chapter Herder has inverted his account of the impact of diversity on poetry. The imitation of the ancients, which had led to literary enervation in the Renaissance, especially in Italy, gives way to the diversification of influences, when writers and artists recognize the cultures that lie beyond their national borders. Such diversity was evident in the legacy from the Nordic peoples, and it offered promise to Germany as it sought to consolidate a national culture. Herder concludes the chapter and the book with a sort of hopefulness about the ways difference and diversity bring new life to poetry and song. Originality, distinctiveness, even a more global mix become the keywords for the poetry of the modern nation.

We witness here an unfinished project, with many ideas left as fragments. The logical development from ancient Israel through the Greeks and the Romans, across the Arabic and Nordic worlds, with the return to the Renaissance and early modern Europe, is not entirely credible. Herder's politicization of culture and the arts does not always benefit from convincing evidence. His own biases, for example, about the role of publishers and booksellers in his own day, do little to strengthen his arguments. The political and the ontological remain inchoate, but their interrelations are beginning to take fuller shape. If Herder's modernity project remains incomplete (see Habermas 1990), he will endeavor to change that situation, to suture the fragments so they might cohere as a modern political and aesthetic project. This is the task he sets for himself with the *Volkslieder* project, and that he pursues throughout the final quarter century of his life.

From "Wirkung der Dichtkunst auf die Sitten neuerer Zeiten" / "The Influence of Poetry on the Customs of Modernity"

JOHANN GOTTFRIED HERDER,
TRANSLATED BY PHILIP V. BOHLMAN

At the time when the sciences and scholarship flourished in Italy, new languages for *poetry* began to emerge, first of all *modern Latin* and, where possible, *modern Greek*. One was so enamored of everything newly discovered from the ancient world that one imitated it to the extent possible, even evoking the ancient gods and goddesses with beautiful language. In so doing, one was convinced that one was writing correctly in the *classical manner*. Needless to say, it was not possible overnight to transform oneself into a Greek or a Roman, nor was it possible to turn the surrounding world into one that was Greek or Roman. Still, that did not really matter, for it was such a beautiful *language*, and it provided such a beautiful *paragon* for imitation that one wrote verses and poetry that were *Roman*.

Disadvantages must have arisen for many from the use of classical languages for poetry, as these became a setback for the *greater purpose of poetry*. Common people could not understand this language, and poetry therefore could have no influence on them. The most significant *goal* and *touchstone* of poetry, thus, were lost. The learned wrote for the learned, and pedants wrote for pedants, most of whom, if we judge by the ways they handled ancient materials, were incapable of investing poetry with any kind of *influence* whatsoever.... If you write for the likes of these, you really do not need to possess *talent* or *skill*, or even *intend* to have any influence. The model we see among the earlier writers is that one need but write, as they did, with beautifully structured lines, usually following miserably inappropriate *external* rules. The *spirit* of the ancient style would mean that one *writer* applauded another, saying, "You are classical! I am too.... The *people* are barbarians. The masses enslaved to the *dear madam mother tongue* be damned!" Accordingly, miserable, paralyzed, and weak shadows came to be revered. They were the dream of a dream, and from that they became a *model*....

And thus poetry became that tepid thing that no one wanted to have or to enjoy. Poetry was foreign to the nature and senses of the common people, to their hearts and to the hearts of the poets themselves. And thus it should work miracles! Just how long did Italy torture itself with such imitation, and just how long did other nations, of even a lesser status, turn to Greek theater from the very start! *Apostolo Zeno* (1669–1750) bequeathed a library to the Dominicans in Venice, which contained four thousand items in the style of the so-called *classical comedies*, all of which were written during a single century and then forgotten again in the same century.[a] It was the same story with the *tragedies*, and still Italy had nothing of its own. Zeno adapted everything in order to make *opera* Greek, from *pastoral* to *arcadian rubbish*, which should have been in the ancient style, thus overflowing into Italy. How could these works have influenced Italy, for at the time and place they were far too foreign, and to a degree unnatural? The art of poetry at the time comprised *entertainment, pretty art, games*.

There were influences from every corner of the globe that converged at this time *to change the customs of Europe*, but with these the imprint on poetry was in large part different, that is, *without influence*. The Moors were driven out of Spain; their Carthage was thus destroyed; *their gallantry diminished gradually*; their country embarked on a path toward a gentle death, that is to say, its political *order*. It is the same with gallantry in all lands; after the Moors had been humiliated, next came the vassals so that provinces could be unified. The state monarchy raised its head. The more *freedom, nature, and the individuality of customs* at all levels of society diminished, the more individual *strengths* weakened in order to prostrate themselves at the feet of a single power. The more an overall *mechanical order* took the place of courage and replaced the influence of individual souls, the more poetry from *vital sources* and *vital influences* disappeared. The gallantry of earlier times entirely fell victim to *scorn*. The new customs ... which had no more to do with poetry than they depended on poetry ... developed from rules and regulations, which reflected completely different

---

a. [PVB] In addition to his contributions to literary life in Venice, the center of Italian publishing in the eighteenth century, Zeno served the Habsburg court in Vienna as the "Kayserlicher Poet und Historicus" (Imperial Poet and Historian) beginning in 1718.

circumstances in the world. The *goal* of poetry became the flattery of the ruling class and the singing of unilateral military action, political legal maneuvering, and Machiavellian negotiations.

The situation for *religion* was no different from that for gallantry. Its influence became the target of jest; it was greeted in poems with *grimace* and called *mythology*, given authentically Latin, classical, and mythological names. This is how religion appeared in poetry. I do not wish to name specific well-known poems or poets who sought to shed *a new light* according to the tastes of a new era on their poetry. The *religion* of a people lives together with their *poetry* in their heart and soul. For a people who have no religion, or for whom it is used as burlesque, *poetry that influences* life is also impossible.

More often than not, we refer to this situation as the growth of *philosophy*, and that it is. Still, this is a philosophy that possesses little that serves poetry and the human heart. If you remove all that is wonderful, sacred, and magnificent in the world and simply replace it with *names* only, then this can never be a creation of God for the world, as the learned wordsmiths would wish. Poetry can never come into being and exert its influence just because one feels a sort of *power* that one can appropriate and plant elsewhere. *Bayle*'s aesthetic republic probably contained no poets, or only those who were miserable as philosophers.[b] Poets are neither *allowed* into the republic, nor can it *produce* them, nor can they *offer their art* to a more informal, conversational public.

In ancient times, all great *revolutions* flowed together like a sea, upon which poetry could swim in no other way than *playfully*. *Two contrasting parts of the globe* were *invented*, at least so one might imagine at first glance. There should be new, richer material for poetry! Such success showed, however, that this material had little meaning, especially in comparison to the total loss of *influence* on poetry. Gold and silver, spices and luxuries, might bring about much good, but they have no impact on poetry. A cup of coffee is no drink for *Odin*, and the delight of foreign spices on the tongue and in our blood is no golden arrow from *Apollo*.

The *publication of books* has created much that is good, but it has also *stolen* much of the vital influence from poetry. Formerly poems were found in *living* circles, playing the harp, enlivened by the voice, courage, and heart

---

b. [PVB] Herder refers here to Pierre Bayle (1647–1706), who wrote extensively on the republic of letters during the French Enlightenment. The bibliographical reference is to Bayle's widely influential literary journal *Nouvelles de la république des lettres*.

of the singer or the poet. Now they are merely black on white, beautifully printed on paper by *scoundrels*. It would be as if, *in the same moment*, a piece of paper came to a reader, and then was read fleetingly and carelessly, and tossed aside. It is true that a vital *present, awakening, and mood* in the soul does the most for the reception of poetry. There is a considerable difference between *hearing* and *reading* something. There is also a difference between hearing it *oneself* and hearing it from the poet or the one performing it, and hearing the godly rhapsodists and thinking it through as syllabic patterns in one's head. All in all, this means that when one considers the *new custom* in its fullest, one must realize how much poetry has gained *in artistry*, but has *lost in influence*!

Nowadays the poet *writes*, while previously he *sang*. He writes slowly in order to be read, while previously he gathered *accents* so they would vividly sound the heart. Today he must write to be *understood* well. Commas and periods, rhymes and metric patterns, should carefully replace, determine, and fulfill what the *living voice* itself enunciated, indeed, a thousand times more simply, better, and more powerfully. Finally, the poet now writes primarily for the lovely *classical work* and *being* as well as for the pages of eternity, while the singer and rhapsodist of the past sang for the *immediate moment*, in which he created something so that the heart and memory would replace the library *for centuries* to come.

Music became its *own art form* and distinguished itself from poetry. Just as it is certain that both were able to gain something as *art forms*, so too did they lose a certain part of their influence. Music must express *darkly* the feelings that it alone is able to express. If one does not embrace without noticing the *artistic sensibility*, much of what music contains is like a book with unknown letters, and surely we would not tolerate such indefiniteness for long. Poetry without sound and song must quickly become a bunch of letters, natural science, philosophy, folklore, dry wisdom, and pedantry.

Diverse lands found common ground so that the culture of the sciences, the *community* of different social statuses, provinces, kingdoms, and parts of the world, expanded. As they did so, like the rest of literature, poetry exerted an influence on *space and surface*, while losing even more its ability to *penetrate with depth and certainty*. Poetry had blossomed and exerted its greatest influence in smaller states with smaller populations and more commonplace customs, for which even the smallest and singular member was shown interest, and who could be judge and jury of their own deeds. The flame now melts, and its glow now sinks into the earth. Who could overlook what a prince desired, and what rights he could demand? And if one could, who wished to do so, who could do so? Neither the people nor the poets. The voices of the medieval satirists were completely muted; no poetic deeds flamed from the mouths of cannons. Neither heroes nor common citizens in antiquity were drawn to distant wars, for which they had little interest and about which they had little knowledge. Only the poor soldiers were forced to fight such wars, and most of them cared very little about the mechanical gods[c] to whom they were enslaved and whom they were supposed to serve. The trumpets of war and peace gladly abandoned all nine muses and at best lamented the shedding of blood, hunger, disease, and the violation of human rights, *regardless of which side* they were on.

Finally and above all, when the *customs* and *hearts* of all the so-called *learned* peoples gradually become *well-worn* coins, such that poetry is only a matter of *display*, how should it be anything different from all such things ... fine in appearance, convenient and beautiful, but almost always without the *content* and *value* of the older, more intimate *national poetry*? For the most part, such poetry would be like stamped coins in which the copper is exposed. We leave the really noble part unused so that it does not tear our pockets, or we change it quickly into that for which we have greater need, as the *customs of the old, authentic poetry*. We are motivated by laws, societies, fashions, social status, and concerns about feeding ourselves; our muses are those of pleasure, and the Apollo thereof is sweet necessity. ... Poesy is *literature*, a paradise full of beautiful flowers and joyous fruits. Alas, the beautiful color reveals none of this, even less its sweet flavor.

Italian poesy was the first to take shape. Its beautiful language, the land, the character of the nation, and its composition, assisted by the other arts, made its contribution in such ways that it quickly appeared as a blossoming shape, a lovely flower on the tombs of the Romans, but still only a flower. In the great works of *Dante* all his passions continue with their struggle. His poetry is the entire breadth of his heart, his soul, his scholarship, and especially the openness of his life. He is still a limb from the ancient forest of freedom and the influences of the monks.... In *Petrarch* his Laura is alive to the degree that the sonnets and the song of the Provençal permit it. Everything upon which he draws owes much more to *mythology* or to the *boisterous customs* of his age.

In the century of the *Medicis* everything was *classical*: one wrote in Latin, or beautiful sonnets and lovely stanzas in the style of Petrarch. *Ludovico Ariosto* (1474–1533) first appeared, and the godlike Ariosto wrote

---

c. [PVB] Herder employs the phrase "Deus ex machina" here, but does so in the more literally dramatic sense of theatrical machinery, hence my more literal translation.

a novel for *pleasure*, and his master and friend was left wondering about how he could find everything that he put in the novel.[d] He and *Torquato Tasso* (1544–1595) lived from the *legacies* of the *Middle Ages* because there was little left of poetry in their own age from which they could draw influence; it was even more so for their successors. The poetry of the Italians is like their soul, a quiet sea, filled with deep passion and strength. Deep beneath the surface storms might rage, but on the surface itself the waves remain gentle. *Poetry*, perhaps, had itself *contributed* much to these *customs*, whose image it bore. It sustained everything so gently and peacefully, and amused so sweetly. The gondolier on the sea and the pilgrim on land sing and play, and are everywhere happy. When facing pressure they can still enjoy, when in poverty they also remain happy. . . . How much, however, does not reveal itself through the flurry of sparks, and what kind of flame slumbers within them, under other circumstances merely awaiting the storm unleashed by heaven?

When it comes to the *poesy of France*, I speak with all the humility of an amateur who dares pass judgment according to his feelings. . . . It is even more difficult so say anything specific about the *influence on customs*. Just as this people perhaps has less poesy and poetic language than the Italians, so, too, according to such measurement, must their lesser poesy exert a *lesser* influence *on their customs*. *Propriety* serves as their great judge, and *polite society* is the stage for their poesy; indeed, theater provides the very setting for their society. On the upper level, a party of lords and ladies is acting, who possess an authorial voice, while underneath there are the miserable who must obey only what the Oracle of Delphi has already determined! Often one marvels at the *statements, tirades,* and *declamation* of the upper levels of society, and everyone begins *speaking as society* does! The theatrical and military *Pierre Corneille*[e] (1606–1684), the poet of tragic idylls *Jean Racine* (1639–1699), and the painter and philosopher *Voltaire* (1698–1778) are the masters of the measures by which society is judged; in other words, they choose how society finds light amusement. This is especially the case with *Voltaire*, he, the philosopher of poesy and the poet of prose, he, the great *teacher of our age* in popular *philosophy* and

---

d. [PVB] Herder refers here to *Orlando furioso*, which was an epic poem rather than a novel (*Roman*). The epic appeared in print between 1516 and 1532, commissioned by and dedicated to Cardinal Ippolito d'Este (1509–1572), to whom Herder refers as Ariosto's "master and friend" in this passage.

e. [PVB] Herder's criticism of the great French writers of the seventeenth and eighteenth centuries notwithstanding, it was Corneille who compiled the first modern version of *Le Cid*.

skepticism, the great author of fugitive pieces, godlike and untouched.... What *deficiencies*, what *necessities* of the century—of other countries even more than for his own peoples—he fails to meet! What pure, firm *standards* he fails to establish! As if today a poet need not write in order to establish standards? If not, why does he write at all? He seeks fame, he follows his mood, he offers himself to the idols of the century, he contents himself with amusement. Good or bad, whichever happens ... what *is* good or bad to the poet?

My intent is not to pass judgment on art, but rather to clarify what I think about these matters. At the time of Louis XIV, French poesy appeared as a sort of *entertaining society lady*, and we ask ourselves if she does not remain so. The epic works of *François Fénelon* (1651–1715) have been forgotten, or at best one speaks about them as *flowers*. We still know the tender sentiments in *Philippe Quinault* (1635–1688), and we remember *Nicolas Boileau-Despréaux's* (1636–1711) writings on morality and inequality, as well as *Jean de la Fontaine's* (1621–1695) lovely fables. *Molière* wrote as a great poet for whom, however, everything was the same, whether it made one laugh, and now ... I do not really know what constitutes poetry. One repeats words, one warbles in a thousand ways like an Italian, one begs. *Gessner* and *Young*, *Haller* and *Ossian*, *Shakespeare* and the *antipodes*, all of them exerted the same influence—none whatsoever!

This means, as the great Voltaire has claimed, that the light is so widely dispersed that it is no longer possible to have a flame. The *customs* of the *nation* are so *learned* that no learning is anymore possible ... and, indeed, the poetry of Paris should somehow become the culture of a *nation*! Why not for the entire universe? And what are the morals? And what are the impact and effects that would follow from the French? And, finally, what does it mean for poesy to have influence? Something like a drinking song or a novel about love?

We cross the channel and suddenly we find ourselves in a formerly uncivilized land that now has become very *cultured*: it is that proud nation, *England*. Even in the great era of chivalry it had poets, great poets ... *Chaucer, Spenser, Shakespeare*! Especially *Shakespeare*, a man who embraces a world filled with strength of character, passions, customs, and skills ... a world whose influence continues to have its impact on us. What a treasure it is for a nation to have a *Shakespeare* whose works contain the customs and moments of humanity with such influence! He has no real system, of course, because his soul is as expansive as the world; he has built a stage upon which customs of every kind and all peoples can appear. A similar soul encompasses Shakespeare, and he adapts and applies it as he wishes! And because one prefers to have everything in a fleeting moment, and lacks the ability to measure because of wanting taste, so too do *Zaire* and the French *Hamlet* pale in comparison with Shakespeare's *Desdemona* and *Hamlet*.^f Some might say that for *our* customs, Shakespeare is too powerful, too coarse, too erratic, too *tasteless*.

Since good taste replaced genius, and England banned her last genius, *Jonathan Swift (1667–1745),* to Ireland, poesy has become *more correct, moral, classical, and refined.* Does this not also mean that at the same time it has *lost its impact,* becoming *less poetic and colder*? Who was able to sound morals more beautifully with rhyme than *Alexander Pope (1688–1744)*? Who sketched a more intimate feeling for the place of domestic life than *Joseph Addison (1672–1719)*? We do not have to ask about the origin, purpose, and *impact* of every word. We know with certainty that, if moralistic essays and weekly journals alike can generate *learned influences,* so, too, have *Pope, Addison, and Richard Steele (1672–1729)* created *learning* for their nation, especially, in the case of the latter two, in the English coffeehouses. Their writings will be the first of their kind to have lasting impact, and *Addison* especially is the Socrates of his people.

Meanwhile it has become increasingly true that the spirit of the century, which *provides comfort,* however clothed, for even the noblest writers, wishes to find an audience for each *poem,* whether read in a *periodical* or in a *weekly review.* How often does the *beauty* of such clothing, even its *artistry* and its *finery,* destroy its influence! Rhyme is a beautiful thing when it is not forced. *It lends support,* as a German poet says, and *heightens fantasy . . .* and glues speech to memory. Meanwhile it has become just as certain that when no other soul and no more exalted spirit is awakened, rhyme *lulls* one to sleep, and it becomes gently silent with its *sweet sounds.* When temperament is *buried* under the so-called seeds of virtue and at the same time is too thickly *sowed,* then nothing can grow, particularly because *everything* is like everything else, and nothing finds its *correct place.* If someone sees in himself that he is a *poet* and that he writes as the nightingale sings and as a versifier or as an artsy *moralistic* writer, then one also reads him *as such,* listening to the nightingale as a nightingale, extending gratitude, and going home. With all moralistic poetry of this kind, does it not depend on how we *read* it, whether it is comic or serious? Whether it is mine! Why must this be the main trait for the strength of all of our customs? Why must that strength remain *so indistinct*? Why must the poet

---

f. [PVB] All these characters appear in Herder's *Volkslieder,* either in his essays or individual songs, for example, about Zaire (see chapter 2 in the present volume).

convince us with his artistry, providing eternal *comfort* for our *delight*, such that it is *only* about this or that word of praise? If he erases with one hand what the other writes, how does this uplift our spirit? What should we believe? And with how many poets, writers of rhyme, fashion tailors, and novelists especially is this the case!

The English have two genres of novel. The first is idealistic, the other faithful in nature. *Samuel Richardson* (1689–1761) and *Henry Fielding* (1707–1754) are their leading figures. Both genres have their advantages and disadvantages, depending, above all, on how they are *used*. To fall in love with the idealistic character can be uplifting, but also very dangerous. One finds a beautiful dream everywhere, or, where there is no dream, one sees all sorts of angels in Clarissa and Grandison flying about, all of them disturbingly deceptive.⁸ The angel in *Clarissa* merely takes one small false step, and everyone *forgives* him, and it has the consequences of remaining silent for every healthy peasant who is no angel. In both cases *exaggeration* and *idealization* help through accident, and it is overall such a fine feast, with such a sweet odor, that it brings about powerful movement and sweet juices, even when these do no harm. It is well known that *for those best served by these odors*, they achieve very little movement whatsoever, and they offer very little for the better understanding of the real human relations in life. It is hardly a wonder that, once they have fallen ill in such a way and then become addicted to such opium, they are no longer able to free themselves from it. This is what we call the *refinement of customs* and *of the sentiments* through *pleasant* and *entertaining reading*. The refinement, however, is actually often *corruption*. Usually such refinement changes all healthy foods to more thorough nourishment for the spirit and the heart, making them unfit for real joy and real value for life. When the romantic angels fall to earth from the lunar paradise and look from the distance of the holy veil face to face with the amateurs, the novel comes to a single conclusion. Truth that has been *displaced* through beautiful poetry then comes afterward and, like the Greek goddess Atë, takes its powerful revenge.

The genre of novel associated with *Henry Fielding* is not subject to *this* deceit; rather, it opens the eye to uncommon *truth*. And if, because of that truth, it opens the heart for *goodness* and employs it toward *specific* goals, we can call it the most beautiful *gallery of human life*. How does it happen, then, that writings *containing the weaknesses of the time* most often

---

g. [PVB] Herder refers here to Samuel Richardson's epistolary novels *Clarissa* (1748) and *The History of Sir Charles Grandison* (1753).

succumb to this genre, rather than *overcoming* it? How does it happen that *individual* characters are usually portrayed in such light that they so gladly possess a *dear heart*? Were the authors afflicted by the *disease* of these sympathies, were they thus touched by fear, because their hand flattered the *wounds* of our hearts? Poet, are you therefore a man? Are you truly a friend of humankind? Are you a servant of health, happiness, and truth? What would you take from a physician who offered opium or a sweet poison only so that a beautiful one stricken with illness would grasp his hand? Should the poet be a slave to the *lowly* conditions and the *evil* customs of his century? Or should he seek to improve them?

What if *Cervantes* had not created an appropriate novel to strike at the customs that led to the suffering of the nation by employing a laughable knight able to act with such virtue, even if these were not the principal aim of the poet? What if Samuel Richardson and Henry Fielding had not created the real-life characters of *Clarissa* and *Tom Jones*, whose actions were truly human: If they are human beings, why not we? If such cases are *true*, what poet would not himself shudder with *pure* praise and feelings of *warmth*, affording the sense of honesty and decency? Would not let himself be shaken! Generally, however, writings of this sort are unfortunately too often gentle kisses to a feeling of comfort that they can provide no higher *moral* influence on anything other than themselves, surely not on *poetry* and the *novel*. I may be saying this about the English, but it also applies to other nations.

Finally, the English *rage* for freedom comes to be master of a genre of poetry that was truly national and would influence its customs, namely *political criticism and satire*. *Butler* with his epic of Sir Hudibras is the most notable of these,[h] with *Swift* in the middle and *Churchill* following closely behind.[i] What they write comes *right to the point*, and it is not wanting for passion and forcefulness. Whether there is *moral* purpose in what they write, I cannot yet decide. For the most part it is so *biased, grim,* and terribly *exaggerated* that anyone who is not English is offended by the most severe passages. *Butler* aims to insult in this way and to cause damage. *Swift* uses tiger claws to tear at the flesh of humanity in such a way that one feels more pity for *him* than for humanity. *Churchill* flogs away so extremely ... that these are really bloody outgrowths, terrible but running ulcers of the highly

---

h. [PVB] Samuel Butler's (1613–1680) *Hudibras*, parts 1 and 2 (London: John Martyn and Henry Herringman, 1674–78).

i. [PVB] Winston Churchill (1620–1688), who wrote a history of the English monarchy.

praised English freedom, and that we need not be jealous of it. Usually they become weakened because of themselves. The opponents engage in *diplomacy*, letting them *speak* and become angry. After a few years everything has either been forgotten, or the sharpest arrows of genius, having been hardened in the embers of hell, are no longer sharp. . . . Generally when something is *exaggerated* (and who exaggerates more, and more happily, than the English?), it loses its effectiveness. Whereas *Milton* builds devils' bridges, he does not really affect them, and whereas *Edward Young* (1683–1765) descends deeper into the graves of transcendent madness, he does nothing to bring about improvement.[j] While *James Thomson* (1700–1748) and company reveal too much, they bore some and tire others. Whereas the eagles overload and stuff *Pindar's Odes* with commentary, they surely never will reach the sun. Perhaps the poesy of this country is like a bloated body that has been consigned to the pile of corpses because of the abundance of epithets! . . . And because everything English has to be so *nationalist*, the more the country's *culture* declines, the more its complaisance and self-satisfaction command heroic stupidity and corruption, so too must its poetry go into decline and lose its color. Their most recent, so godlike genius, *Laurence Sterne* (1713–1768) . . . if you read his *gentle* writings and thereafter the *letters* of his *life*, edited by his own daughter, you will know what I mean.

I should now speak about *my own* nation, although I can be brief because I must only repeat what I have already observed about other nations. Since the beginnings poesy had even *less* influence on us than on those nations. Our bards have disappeared, and the minnesingers lie peacefully in the libraries of Paris.[k] Throughout the Middle Ages Germany either abandoned what was truly German, or it was overrun by other peoples. Germany had no time to collect from itself and to find a voice for its own poetry. . . . Germany is, moreover, a divided country, a small sea full of little islands, each with its own monarchy. One province scarcely understands the next. Customs, religion, interests, level of education, and government are entirely different, thus preventing the best possibilities for mutual influence. *Martin Opitz* (1597–1639) sang on behalf of many German provinces for many years, just as he had sung in Transylvania.[l] The *Swiss* and the *Saxons* have

---

j. [PVB] Herder refers here to Milton's *Paradise Lost* and Young's *The Complaint, or Night-Thoughts on Life, Death, and Immortality* (London: R. Dodsley, 1743).

k. [PVB] Herder refers here to the Codex Manesse. For further discussion by Herder of this collection of medieval song, see chapter 1 in the present volume.

l. [PVB] Transylvania has a long history of multiculturalism, with a significant and culturally influential German presence. Martin Opitz spent the years 1621–22 there.

long wanted recognition as more than merely provincial, but *North* and *South Germany* still do not seek such recognition in many respects....

In our case, furthermore, when it comes to *customs* and *influence* from poetry, the *folk* come into consideration not at all. Poetry does not exist for them, at least in a *spiritual* sense. What remains for us as a *reading public* from any sort of poetic customs? *The learned?* These, however, already have their customs, and they are often incapable of exerting any influence on poetry. They read to pass the time, to provide a bit of stimulation for a dull mind. What about *art critics?* These, however, though they are generally *not* intellectuals, have a similar, in part even more aggravating, fate, which they read as critics from books borrowed from booksellers, probably not even meant for them, and thus often remain blind in body and soul. Does the shopkeeper enjoy the smell of his spices? And does it not provide some comfort for those cleaning up dark customs that his sense of smell no longer bothers him?...

Does one, then, write poetry for the *young?* These, too, according to the latest tastes, are also poets, and they are served by the almanac of German muses, and in this way the influence is broken and aped. Or does one write poetry according to the *tastes of young women,* surrounded by the comforts of the parlor? Or for those *noble readers,* men and *women,* who have absorbed what they have heard of the latest fashions of the French? Do they realize that Germany, *too,* has poets, and that one actually *can read* these?... What is left, even for these alone, to offer as poetry and as improvement of their *customs?* Is it really *reading poetry,* when after reading ten books in French to pick up one in German, and then to page through it, daydreaming and taking a bite of this or that in order to get a taste for the latest fashions? What good does that do? Who really wants to write poetry for such readers? Who wishes to lie in the arms of a shriveled lady of the court and provide her with art? For the *publisher,* then, there remains no other option than to turn to those writing for the average young person. What this chosen bunch (the *Jupiters, Apollos,* and *literary giants* among the German muses!) create, and what they assemble as poetic goods and call *customs,* only they themselves can know!

What good is it for the *influence* of a work of art if it is discussed and compromised again and again? What can a temple for poetry offer for *culture* when it is in the business of money changers and pigeon shops, critics and cattle traders?[m] If the poets of an earlier age appeared, *Ossian* and

---

m. [PVB] Herder adapts the biblical story of Christ driving the money changers from the Temple in Jerusalem, and he also includes a footnote of his own: [JGH] Friedrich Nicolai, *Das Leben und die Meinungen des herrn magister Sebaldus Nothanker,* 3 vols. (Berlin and Stettin: F. Nicolai, 1775–76).

Orpheus, would you recognize your fellow poets? Would you *sing for the press* and now become poets in Germany who were *published, reviewed,* and insufferably *imitated*? One will excuse me for clinging to these *external* questions, but the *internal questions* depend on them. The bookseller buys and sells, makes deals with writers and critics, determines the value of what he has to sell, and, according to what everyone has to say, he takes the next step. In Germany everything acquires the same value if it *is praised in the newspapers*. *Siegwart* and *Agathon*, the *Messiah* and *Nothanker*, *Werther's Sorrows* and *Werther's Pleasures* are read all in the same way.[n] And that bundle of things from outside Germany, wherever its origins may be and whatever its influences may be, is privileged for its cheapness. . . .

We do not really need to complain about this scanty situation of *literature* when it comes to the poets and customs that really *wish* to have an impact. *Opitz* and *Brockes, Gellert* and *Hagedorn, Kleist* and *Gessner, Haller* and *Witthof* are impeccable in this respect.[o] The upright and religious character of the Germans is also evident. They would rather be *lesser* poets than uncultured and unwise poets. The first poet to exert a notable influence on the nation was surely the religious *Gellert*.

The first garland to which the German muse aspired could do no harm to the nation's culture: *biblical poetry*. Had this exerted an influence on the nation and could it have served the faith of the people, it would have earned its just desserts! Then, however, there could not have been a *Milton* prior to *Klopstock*, the *Messiah* would not have achieved its position as the epitome of a mountain of poetry and writings that would eternally be uplifting for all belief! . . . As it is, however, Germany's poetry does not serve to offer praise to the angels; rather it provides a garland for innocent beings, devoted youth, and gentle children. No one would be able to speak against the muse of a cold, pedantically moral *Johann Jakob Bodmer* (1698–1783) when everything he produced was not heavenly gold.

Perhaps it was this excessive *morality* of the Germans that, as in so many patriarchal societies, accounts for the guilt expressed by the *bardic singers* in the most recent troubled times. The virtue of *Thusnelde* inspired as incomparably as the bravery of *Hermann*. It was the joy of one to

---

n. [PVB] Herder is citing works of literature and art that he finds of enduring and lesser importance. Goethe's *Sorrows of Young Werther* and Handel's *Messiah* belong to the former, while the latter includes Johann Martin Miller's (1750–1814) *Siegwart: Eine Klostergeschichte* (Leipzig: Weygandsche Buchhandlung, 1777).

o. [PVB] Martin Opitz (1597–1639), Barthold Heinrich Brockes (1680–1747), Christian Fürchtegott Gellert (1750–1769), Friedrich von Hagedorn (1708–1754), Heinrich von Kleist (1777–1811), Salamon Gessner (1730–1788), Albrecht von Haller (1708–1777), and Johann Philipp Lorenz Witthof (1725–1789).

encounter the other, and when *Ossian* entered the picture, bardic song was born. Should it not be the same way with the *influence* of these songs and *fables* on our *customs*? *A single* motto always remains upon the altar we have erected: Piety! "A noble monument, holy to *virtue* and to the *customs of our ancestors.*"

Because the German muse is such an honorable guardian and priestess of truth and virtue, why should we not also overlook the little things that here and there hold on to what is older and foreign? Is *Johann Wilhelm Ludwig Gleim* (1719–1803) only *Anacreon*, or is he not also the upright *singer* of *heroism* and *virtue*?[p] And has he not with each joke exceeded the boundaries of cultivation? Did *Christoph Martin Wieland* (1733–1813) not befriend himself too closely with the muse of *Claude Prosper Jolyot de Crébillon* (1707–1777) at certain points? How much else might he have written with different taste! In fact, there is a *great deal* that we demand from the muses of the Holy Roman Empire, and extremely *little* that we believe a *reading* public might offer us. I do not mean rewards and gifts here. Give us other *times*, other *customs*, other readers, *men* and *women*, and other *writings* that uplift the men and women who read, so that poetry does not work against them.

Indeed, it is also noble here *to proceed* knowing that a poet given by God will never be wanting for a circle of open ears and hearts. A poet is the *creator* of the people in whose midst he writes: he gives them a world *to see* and has their souls in his hand in order to *guide* them into that world. That is how it should be; that is how it was earlier. There is and always was, however, only one God who could give such poets. What humans create also issues from human customs. It comes from this world and speaks a worldly language. The singer who descends from Olympus is superior to all, and thus the measure of his *influence* is a credit to his profession. Like a magnet he can turn hearts toward him, and like electrical sparks he exerts a power to transform everything to the almighty. His lightning, thus, will strike the soul wherever he wishes. He is neither weak nor silly, nor will he destroy customs with rules borrowed from elsewhere, because instead he possesses a *nobler fire for a higher calling.*

We, who are merely minor gods when it comes to creating anything that *alters customs* or locating them in their time, still want to recognize their value and hold on to their *earthly* being. As long as our poetry is of measurable value and provides a song to celebrate the birthdays of the great, so

---

p. [PVB] The Greek poet Anacreon (ca. 582–ca. 485 BCE) was of considerable influence in the eighteenth century.

too will every *Chiron* engage with the arts, and the lyre will be taught to a young *Achilles*. No *Tyrtaios* will have to travel to America to join mercenaries in war, and no *Homer* will have to sing about this sad battle. If *religion, folk,* and *fatherland* are repressed and foggy terms, then every noble harp will sound *heavy* and *muffled*. Indeed, finally—and the cause of everything!—as long as we sing in lifeless timidity, without resolve, and seeking luxury in money and fame, there will never be a lyre that sounds, that *creates customs*, and that *uplifts culture*.

> The brave father has a brave people as offspring,
> The noble father, noble sons: Thus, the father's
> Strength when mounted on a steed: No eagle
> Thus riding has mere swallows as offspring.
> Only cultivation and learning nurture the natural strength
> Of a brave people: Practice steels the hero's breast!
> If human customs are allowed to decay,
> All that was nobly engendered will sink into shame.[q]

There can be no good poet who was not previously a good person.[r]

Poetry is a holy and godly thing. Whoever finds the way into the entry hall of poetry without the madness of the muses is able through art alone to become a poet. Such a person is immaculate, as is his understanding. Poetry is darkened by the mad.[s]

CONCLUSION

The main points of my essay are thus the following:

1. Poetry is most effective when it presents true customs, which are of a lively nature. When the customs are good and achieve the goals of a lively nature, then the customs can also have the appropriate influence and last for a long time.

2. Prior to the destruction of the temples in Jerusalem, God directed what the goals of poetry were and on which customs they must exert their influence. The folk were the primary purpose of God, who provided them with eternal inspiration. At the time of Greek antiquity, poetry came to influence customs from auspicious origins, but with incredible exceptions from mythology, the concoctions, the fine arts, and fairy tales that ruined their customs.

q. [PVB] Herder's text is the Latin from Horace.
r. [PVB] Herder's text is the Greek from Strabo.
s. [PVB] Herder's text is the Greek of Plato, from *Phaedrus*.

3. In Rome, poetry was independent of the state. It was good, but unfinished, as long as the customs were good. It became useless, superfluous, and worse when the customs fell amid the masses. In the Nordic lands, and amid the Arabs and all other vibrant peoples, poetry aspired to the character of the nation, whether good or bad.

4. As Europe received new customs and a new constitution from the Nordic people, its poetry also underwent change. Because these peoples migrated and mixed with each other, so too did their poetry acquire an *uncertain, hybrid folklike character.* Even in the most primitive times, the simple poetry of Christianity was of considerable usefulness, and this remains the case today.

5. When it began to imitate that which was recovered from earlier times and to adapt it to changing conditions in the world, poetry became more regulated, but it also became *less effective*, and cut off from the influences of living customs. It had become endlessly more refined, and it exhausted all manners of presentation and morals. It exerted, however, little influence, and it can and should have little influence. Poetry is meant for pleasure alone.

6. There are attempts now in certain genres to embrace more than a single people. This is a silent sign that poetry may acquire extended life and have greater impact.

8. The Epic as Nation
Essay on Herder's *Der Cid*
Philip V. Bohlman

The age of epic nationalism began with Johann Gottfried Herder's translation of the Iberian *El Cid*. From its inception, Herder's *Cid* project metaphorically and synecdochically unfolded as a narrative and historical process that formed the nation as European, Christian, and, ultimately, modern. In Herder's hands the epic, as form and performance, would itself pass from the oral transmission of late antiquity, flowing across the borders of al-Andalus, to the literary and musical genres that increasingly parsed the forms of modern narrative. The intimacy of the medieval epic singer's world would give way to the national ownership that Herder's *Cid* bequeathed to a post-Enlightenment Europe. Herder gathered and then translated the unwieldy fragments of the past and asked of them that they sing with the promise of a common future.

In the search for the epic of modern Europe, three issues guiding Herder became especially compelling for the age of nationalism. First of all, in a nine-century history of transmitting the Cid epic, Herder's translation marked a sea change. Its appearance was crucial to the establishment of a canonical version, which in turn, that is, reflexively, came to signify the canon of epic for modern nationalism. When nineteenth- and twentieth-century European linguists and historians set out in search of national epics, Herder's *Cid* was their inspiration and their model (Bohlman 2012).

Second, the search for Herder's *Cid* passes through a process of reception history, which seemingly claimed *El Cid* for and by Herder. In full and abridged versions, in editions for home, school, and mass consumption (see, e.g., figure 15), Herder was assigned authorship to a work published either as *Herders Cid* or *Der Cid von Herder*. Myth passed to history just as authenticity gave way to authority.

FIGURE 15. Ximena and the Cid, woodcut from the 1869 edition of Herder's *Der Cid*.

Third, just as Herder's publications of and on folk song established a modern genre of world music (see chapters 1 and 2 in the present volume), so too did his work on epic. Herder located epic in history, as well as in modernity. In so doing he rendered epic modern, translating allegory into the potential for ownership claimed by modern nationalism (see Bohlman 2011b; for the impact of the *Cid* on national literatures in Latin America see Altschul 2012).

With so many different versions of *El Cid* filling works of poetry and narrative, fiction and history, Herder had many Cids at his disposal.

Historically the Cid was an extraordinary epic figure, appearing in numerous chronicles that both agree and disagree in their details. Though we know little about the real-life circumstances of many other epic heroes, we know that Rodrigo Díaz was born in the village of Vivar near Burgos in ca. 1043 and that he died in Valencia in 1099. He was born in obscurity, and he died a powerful military leader who had entered the genealogy of the Spanish aristocracy. His life is a rags-to-riches story, ideally suited to the nationalist narratives that led many to identify with it.

Exactly how Rodrigo Díaz entered epic song in an emerging vernacular, Latin, Hebrew, and Arabic chronicles (by Abū l'Ḥasan ʿAlī ibn Bassām aš-Šantarīnī and others), and the narrative and lyrical traditions of troubadours, *juglares*, and *jongleurs*, is far more difficult to pin down. For purposes of understanding the biographical background of Herder's *Cid*, a few broad brushstrokes allow us to see the critical moments in the Cid's life. Upon being drawn into the court of Ferdinand I and into a closer family alliance with one of Ferdinand's sons, Sancho, to whom the Kingdom of Castile had fallen, Rodrigo Díaz ascended to the leadership of the Castilian armies against the other dominions in Iberia. He managed to anger the more powerful members of the Spanish aristocracy, whom he had defeated in battle, and hence was forced into exile, where he offered services to both Christian and Muslim leaders. By about the year 1090 Cid was again empowered by Castile for the task of consolidating Iberian power, and in 1094 he led the siege of Valencia, which was being held by Muslim forces from North Africa and Iberia.

The Cid of history and the Cid of myth constantly negotiate and blur the borders of medieval Iberia and al-Andalus. The Cid's role as a military leader was to eliminate borders, specifically by bringing more and more dominions under the control of Castile. These borders are of quite different kinds, but through myth they have come discursively to reflect each other and thus to overlap. We therefore keep in mind the borders between an Iberian center and the peripheries, between Christianity and Islam, and between Europe and its others. Narrative borders are also critical here. In particular, the Cid is moving across the borders between oral and literate traditions. In musical and literary genres, there is the constant negotiation of myth and history as well.

As the Cid's story entered epic, he became both Rodrigo Díaz and El Cid. Rodrigo Díaz was a historical figure quickly entering various literary traditions, but he did so always with various mythological epithets, Cid/Said from Arabic sources, Campeador from Spanish and Latin sources. The questions about authenticity slip across the narrative and historical borders, shifting thereby to questions about authority and authorship. Inside and outside of history, Rodrigo Díaz, Ruy, Count of Bivar, Said and Cid, Campeador and epic singer, the Cid of myth insistently and persistently becomes modern, in Herder's age no less than in eleventh-century al-Andalus.

It is into this tradition of translation that Herder stepped with his *Der Cid*. In certain fundamental ways, his translation succeeded because it was so thoroughly traditional. He seemingly sought a compromise between short and long forms. He recognized the narrative integrity of the strophic *romances*, but he wove these into what would be called a *Romanzenkranz*, an unending garland of ballads. Having created a long work out of seventy small narrative poems, Herder then sought a way of evoking the qualities of the epic, which he was able to do brilliantly because he knew Homer so very well (see chapter 5 in the present volume) and because he had labored over the problem of improvisation in contemporary narrative form. Herder used his translation to find the smallest divisible units for the German translation, hemistiches, and to suture these, stich by stich, into the whole, in a bold gesture that made it a new kind of epic. We experience this as Herder sings—"besingt," as he expresses in German the process of translation—the call to battle in Valencia at the end of the sixty-eighth *romance*:

> Auf nun, auf! / Trommeten, Trommeln,
> Pfeifen, Klar / inetten tönet,
> Übertönet / Klag' und Seufzen;
> Denn der *Cid* / befahl es da.
> Ihr gelei / tet auf die Seele
> Eines Hel / den, der entschlief.

> Arise now! / Trumpets, also drums,
> Flutes with clar / inets intoning,
> Sounding the / baleful sigh loudly;
> For the Cid / orders it thus.
> You are led / deeply from the soul
> Of a he / ro, who rises up.

The reception history of Herder's *Cid* is coeval with that of the rise of modern folk song itself. The Cid epic is strikingly present at the formation and formulation of the modern discourse of folk song in the late Enlightenment, at the historical moment of the 1770s, when Herder coined the term *Volkslied* (see chapter 1). Herder had acquainted himself with epic traditions from elsewhere in Europe and European history. Epic, as form and genre of national expression, linked Herder's studies of Homer and Ossian (see chapter 5). He was also acquainted with Balkan epic repertories though translations from Serbian and Croatian versions into other European languages (e.g., in the eighth song in the second book of the *Volkslieder* project [1778], "Ein Gesang von Milos Cobilich und Vuko Brankovich," [Herder 1975, 67–72]), which afforded him the opportunity to translate with hemistiches in German.

It was in the winter of 1777, months before his folk song volumes (see chapter 2) began to appear in print, that the polyglot Herder determined to learn Spanish. We know from his literary estate that one of the ways in which he taught himself the language was to write out Spanish ballads, *romances*, from a 1568 Antwerp *Cancionero* (*Cancionero de romances* 1568). In these first autodidactic lessons are the texts of thirty-eight *romances*, of which a total of eleven contain narratives about the Cid. In addition to making copies Herder also tried his hand at translating certain lines and fragments from the *Cid romances*. In her memoir, Herder's wife, Karoline, writes of this period in Herder's life: "Almost every day, when his official duties permitted, my husband translated a ballad [*Romanze*] from *Cid*, from his old manuscripts; in fact, at the time he was editing his folk songs, he was writing out *romances* from the *Cid*" (cited in Gaier 1990, 1287–88; memoir dated May 23, 1803).

The next time the *Cid* enters Herder's biography is five years later, when, in conjunction with the planning of a second edition of the folk song volumes, Herder sought complete editions of the Spanish *Cancionero*, which quickly led him to realize the full extent of the problem of the epic's wholeness. He was not, however, the only Enlightenment thinker to regard the problem of a complete epic in the full "heroic and poetic" style of the "Romantic era of the Spaniards" as being of critical importance. Long critical and polemical articles about *Cid* sources and historiography appeared in the leading literary journals of the time.

What Herder did, in a word, was provide a response to these debates, hence solving one of the vexing problems of the late Enlightenment, for which the *Cantar de Mio Cid* was emblematic: Herder determined that the only way to translate the *Cid* and give its epic fullness was to use both Spanish and French sources. He took as his Spanish source the text believed to be the first attempt to create a composite *Cid*, the volume of *romances* collected by Juan de Escobar and published in Lisbon in 1605. Chief among his French sources were *romances* from the *Bibliothèque universelle des romans*, though he turned to numerous French sources. Of the seventy *romances* translated by Herder, over three quarters—the first fifty-two—come from French translations.

Like his folk song works, Herder's *Cid* translation was ongoing, and he pursued it throughout his life. Folk song and epic both reflect a process of creation called by Herder, but also by others, *Übertragung*, literally the recuperation of a musical and poetic text, of poesy, from one source and representing it in the contemporary context of another. This process of recuperation and representation would become crucial to the collection of song in the name of the nation through the nineteenth and twentieth centuries, indeed, until the present, not because it allowed collectors to claim complete texts and authentic sources, but rather because it allowed them to fill in the gaps.

The representational gap, moreover, can be understood as the space between oral and written tradition. For Herder and the generations that followed, that space, too, was of extraordinary importance, for it was a space of movement, from transmission to reception, reflexively back to variation and transmission and reception of altered form. It was the space of agency, and in epic it was the space in which a nation's past was performed as the present (Bohlman 2011b).

Several different principles guided me as I chose the cantos for the present chapter. In the selective translation that follows I try to give a sense of the entire epic, choosing cantos that occur at structural moments—the beginning and ending of the entire epic, the beginning of part 2, points of narrative transition—and that, whenever possible, capture critical narrative moments, especially those of families and battles. The overriding principle, nonetheless, remains that of representing the two larger topoi of the Herder project documented in this book: music and nationalism. Music is present in several ways, some obvious, others less so. Clearly the epic's substance itself was sung, and it coheres around form and structure that, also in the German, reflect its existence as song. The cantos were originally ballads in form and narrative, that is, *romances*. The poetic structure relies on the syllable structure of individual lines; for the most part, Herder builds his translation around stichic structure, using this to give a rhythmic and metric sense also to the German. I have given some preference as well to cantos in which music itself—music making during ritual celebration or in preparation for battle—appears in the text.

Nationalism also assumes many different forms in Herder's *Cid*, and I have tried to reflect as many of these forms as possible in my choice of cantos to include in the translation. The story of the Cid is that of nation building. The Cid unifies the different kingdoms of the Iberian Peninsula, bringing them together as Castile in canto 46, "New Castile." Historically it was this Castile that would accelerate and expand as the Reconquista, also critical to the nationalist narrative in Herder's *Cid*, and that would embark upon the imperialism and colonialism that ushered in the Age of Discovery from the Middle Ages. The nationalism of *Der Cid* not only has local and regional political implications, but it also extends to the shaping of early modern Europe and the formation of a globalism driven by European colonial expansion (see, e.g., Altschul 2012). Unquestionably the Cid's national undertaking excludes as much as it includes, for it depends on uniting the Spanish kingdoms, but at the cost of driving Muslim North Africans from southwestern Europe. The cleft between self and other could not be clearer in Herder's epic. Herder's Muslim and Jewish others bear witness to some stereotypes, but they also project sympathetic language in which the understanding of cultural and religious difference is possible. In canto 52, for example, there are passages that respond to the multiple wives allowed by Islam, contrasted with the Cid's own monogamy (lines 20–21: "Eine nur ist meine Gattin / Eine, meine echte Frau"), and to practices of Jewish money lending (lines 30–45).

My goal as a translator has been to render the text in English while retaining the feel of the German as much as possible. I also attempt to heighten the feeling of the text as poetry, which was an important criterion also for Herder in his *Übertragung* from Spanish and French into German. In the course of translating *El Cid*, it becomes ever clearer that Herder drew upon different sources. The *romances* are structurally distinctive, and I endeavor to convey this distinctiveness as I allow my own translation to reflect the aesthetic framework within Herder's epic project.[1]

For Herder, epic was so critically important because it re-voiced the long debate between the ancients and the moderns. The *Cid* in Herder's re-voicing had the potential of being both ancient and modern. As Herder himself stated on the title page, the *romances* in the *Cid* were at once "historical" (*historisch*), or narrative, and romantic (*romantisch*), and he is therefore explicit in giving Romanticism a literal meaning arising from Cid's medieval world and translated through the late Enlightenment. Herder's *Cid* entered a space—a narrative border region—between the epic of Homer and that of the modern nation.

From *Der Cid* / *The Cid*

The Story of Don Ruy Diaz, Count of Bivar, According to Spanish *Romances*[a]

JOHANN GOTTFRIED HERDER,
TRANSLATED BY PHILIP V. BOHLMAN

THE STORY OF DON RUY DIAZ, COUNT OF
BIVAR, DURING THE REIGN OF KING
FERDINAND THE GREAT

1

Don *Diego* sat in deep sadness,
Never had one been so mournful;
Full of grief, he pondered day and night
The disgrace that had befallen his house.

The disgrace of the ancient, noble
Heroism of the house *of Lainez*,
Which had exceeded that of the *Iñigos*,
The fame of the *Abarkos*.

Deeply stricken, weakened by age,
He felt himself approaching the grave,

---

a. [JGH] Ruy means Rodrigo. No singer of *romances* is therefore obliged to tell this tale *historically* from the outset, for the person listening to the *romance* itself should experience it *romantically*. The listener should hear. Whoever does not love poesy may prefer the following *romances* as little tales, to be read instead as prose. They are also narrative and historical.

For meanwhile his enemy *Don Gormaz*
Triumphed without opposition.

Neither sleep nor food
Allowed him to close his eyes,
Crossing the threshold to his chambers,
He spoke not to his friends.

He heard not his friends' entreaties
When they came to comfort him;
For he believed the breath of one disgraced
Would bring shame to such friends.

Finally he shook himself free of the burden
Of the horrible and unspoken grief,
And he gathered his sons,
Though unable to speak to them;

They joined their hands together,
Strong and determined, with strong bonds;
All had tears in their eyes,
Entreating for mercy.

He had almost abandoned all hope,
When the youngest of his sons,
Don Rodrigo, restored
His strength, joy, and hope.

With the enflamed eyes of a tiger
He retreated from his father,
"Father," he said, "you have forgotten
Who you are and who I am.

Had I not received from your hands
My *weapons for defense*,
I'd take a dagger to lay waste
To the disgrace now offered me." . . .

Tears of joy streamed down
The cheeks of the father;
"You," he said while embracing his son,
"You, Rodrigo, you're my son.

Your anger again gives me peace;
Your displeasure heals my pain!
Not against me, your father,
Rather against the enemy of our house,

You will raise your arm!" ... "Where is he?"
Rodrigo cried, "Who disgraces
Our house?" He barely allowed time
For his father to explain.

8

The kings of the Moors
Had invaded Castile,
Five of them. Devastation, din, and fire,
Murder and death, drove them forward.

Already beyond Burgos,
Montesdoça, Belforado,
San Domingo, and Naxara,
All these lands had been ravished.

The flocks had been driven away,
So too the sheep, Christians, and children of Christians,
Men, women, boys, and girls;
They wept, and they asked:
"Mother, where shall we go?"

Gloriously, all the Moors had already mustered,
To return with the plunder they had gathered,
For no one stood in opposition,
No one, not even the king.

Rodrigo heard of this threat
While in his castle at *Bivar*;
He was not yet twenty years of age,
Still, he possessed the courage of a man.

As if ascending on high, he climbed on his steed,
Whose name was *Babieça*,
Like God in his chariot of thunder,
And charged throughout the land.

He urged the vassals of his father
Into action; they all
Arrived at *Montesdoça*
And awaited their enemy.

By the grace of heaven! Not one of the Moors
Dared to advance any farther ...
But the herds that had been seized,
The men, women, and children of Christians,
All were freed, joyfully
To proceed on their way. The five captured
Kings of the Moors ... *Don Rodrigo*
Presented them to *King Don Fernando*.
The prisoners were a gift.

16

The wedding party marched nobly
From the altar and from the church.
The king walked stately at the side
Of *Ximena*, the guardian
Of his wife; at *Rodrigo*'s side
Walked the pious, good bishop,
Followed by a long procession of nobles.

Turning back to display the honor,
The procession made its way to the palace.
Extending from all the windows
Were banners woven with gold,
And the ground was covered with greenery,
Fresh herbs, rosemary.

On the streets, along the pathways,
Stretching out toward the palace,
Choruses sounded antiphonally,
With the playing of strings and cymbals,
Well wishes, joy, and songs of happiness.

Alvar Fannez (among all
Cid's friends, always his closest),

Now accompanied generously by servants,
And adorned with beautiful horns,
Displayed himself grandly like a bull.

Antolin upon an ass,
Romping about like a stallion;
Martin Pelaëz with bags
Full of peas, which he tossed
To all the people with loud cheers.

The king laughed heartily,
Gave to the page, and to the ladies,
To the fright of a devil played,
A handful of maravedis,
To distribute among the folk.

Thus the king went forward
At the right hand of *Ximena*;
And the queen received them,
With the lords of the court behind her;
The procession was full of joy and honor.

Grain was thrown from the windows,
So that it covered the crown of the king himself,
And lay thick and full
On the flowers adorning Ximena's breast.
The king gazed at seed upon seed
Upon Ximena's adornment,
In full view of the queen.

Alvar Fannez, who saw this all,
Called as if a bull: "I should like well
To possess his hand,
Instead of the head of the king."
"Give him a basket full of grain,"
Said the king, "and *Ximena*,
Having arrived in the palace,
You embrace him for a joke."

But in Ximena's soul
The giddy laughter was
Far away; she was too happy
Openly to display her joy.

The silence that touched her deeply
Expressed more than the loudest happiness.

29

On the same day he returned
From Zamora, the Cid
Was deeply absorbed by his thoughts;
Straightaway he gave an account
Of his mission to King *Sancho*,
Who addressed him with these words:

"Such is the destiny of kings,
When they offer too much honor
Too foolishly to one
Who is but a proud subordinate.
You, Count of *Bivar*, I know well,
You proceeded to the impudent
Zamoraner, so reluctant
And disobedient to be ruled.

I know well the terms of your wisdom,
In no way are they my own;
And in this moment your head
Would lie at my feet;
Had I not with my father,
Had I with all my brothers
Not sworn on his head
That I must honor you! Then onward!
Onward to Castile! Forge ahead
All so dear to me!"
"Will all I have
Conquered for you also go forth?
Or only from those so close,
Whom I gathered for you, oh King?"

"Onward for all!"
Don Rodrigo,
Who stood there deep in thought,
Smiling, he looked around him,
And—he mounted his steed Babieça;
The silence of death filled the camp:
Then the Cid was off!

38

Before the altar of *Gadea*,
Kneeling, his hand placed
Upon the Gospels;
Frozen as by an iron lock
And immovable; with his head
Bared, thus awaited Don *Alfonso*
That the *Cid* would swear his oath.

Swearing this oath was horrific,
A horror to listen to him,
Awful for him who offered it:

"Cowardly must I be murdered
By the lowest of human beings,
By Don *Sancho of Bellido*;
My memory is dishonored.
My heart will be ripped
From the left side of my chest,
And I must swallow it;
If I do not tell the truth,
That I did not play even the smallest role,
Through knowing, willing, or counseling,
In the death of my brother."
"Say *amen*," the *Cid* called out.

Steadfast, with eyes aflame,
Inflamed by the fire of anger,
Stared Alfonso at the *Cid*,
As he took the oath.

46

Priests and soldiers alike, in full voice,
Sang mass for the Cid,
And trumpets loudly heralded
The holy secret;
Cymbals rang, kettle drums roared,
So that the holy archways
Shook; a renewed courage of heroes

Filled the hearts of all the soldiers,
The three hundred so intrepid,
To enter into struggle against the Moors,
The Moors in Valencia.

Once the flag was dedicated,
The Cid took it in his hand.
He spoke thus: "Poor flag
Of a poor and exiled
Castilian, after the blessing
That heaven placed upon you,
Muster now the attention of all Spain to you;
And this I now grant to you."

With that he unfurled the flag,
Lifting it and waving it above:
"Victory and fame will accompany you,
Flag, until perhaps you fly
Alongside the banner of kings.
Don Alfonso, Don Alfonso,
You slumber beneath the sirens'
Songs; Misfortune threatens you,
When you, when you awaken."

"Soldiers," spoke he, "is it not so?
We've awakened. We were
Dishonored, which had its value,
There, where no one had value.
Honor and service, through your
Endeavors you have the highest worth.

Consecrated by the sirens,
The brave king was sleeping there;
We'll use the deep slumber
To frighten those who are evil,
Not in the court, rather far away.
Nothing is worse than
The evil as those they hate,
Sweet fame won from afar.
A thousand noble hearts sigh
Secretly, persecuted by the evil;

Happy, when they reveal themselves
In full view of the entire world,
As the occasion commands us.

Noble flag, wave proudly
In the heavens, the shelter for all,
Who are victims of the vice."

Then he lowered the flag:
"Brave warriors, my friends,
The revenge of the vassal
Against the one born as his master,
Also just, it always appears
Only as uproar and treason.
The insult that causes pain
Is the trait of higher souls,
If it already feels it deeply.
Be worthy of revenge, my enemies
Flee not from me; I'll follow
Them to the ends of the earth.

Here, oh warriors, in the dwelling
Of freedom and of love,
Here, I cast to the winds
The memory of my disgrace.
With the breath of my body
I quicken each feeling of revenge.
Alone I bear my weapons,
Which I myself took up,
Alone I bear them for *Castile*
And for Christendom.
If I am strong enough, then
I'll plant my flag in *Toledo*,
And what I there establish,
Will be called *New Castile*.

Beyond this for now, dear friends,
Because there is for us no refuge,
It is critical for us to conquer
A small fortress forthwith.
Anyone who delays more than honor,
He should not follow my banner."

IV.
Der Cid zu Valencia und im Tod.

49.

Handelt ungerecht der König,
Will der Cid nicht also handeln.
Er verließ sein Weib in Thränen
Und in Thränen seine Töchter,
Alle von ihm hochgeliebet;
**Brach in Länder ein der Mauren,
Ueberwand sie in Gefechten,**

FIGURE 16. Canto 49, "The Cid in Valencia and in Death," woodcut from the 1869 edition of Herder's *Der Cid.*

Thus, he raised the flag:
"Noble flag, wave, wave
Unfurled in the skies.
Clarinets and trumpets
Sound! You snares and kettle drums,
Your fanfare frightens

Only the weak and the evil
And the false band of hypocrites."

THE STORY OF THE CID DURING HIS VALENCIA CAMPAIGN

49

The king negotiates unjustly,
The Cid refuses to negotiate in the same way;
He left his wife in tears,
His daughters no less in tears,
For they all loved him so very dearly;
The Moors[b] invaded the lands,
Overcoming them with battle,
The Moors also conquered their castles,
Placing taxes and obligations upon them;
When he conquered *Alcocer*,
He surrounded the Moors.
So numerous were the Moorish armies
That no one stood against them.

Alvar Fannez came to him,
Who called himself *Minaya*:
"Does it do justice to your troubles,"
Spoke he to the king's comrades,
"That we abandoned our land
To comb our beards here;
The bread from which we here idly live
Is not the warrior's bread of honor.
Forward! Forward against the Moors!"
"Alvar Fannez from Minaya,"
Spoke the Cid, "you speak with courage,
You speak as a man of honor,
Take the flag!"
"And by the name of God
I swear to you," he answered,

---

b. [PVB] Herder uses the singular, *der Maure* ("the Moor"), to refer to the Muslim forces of al-Andalus.

"Where you yourself would perhaps not
Bear it, with great concern
I bear it." The deception succeeded;
Alvar Fannez from Minaya
Pressed forth into the Moorish lands.
Indeed the Moors complained
Against the injustice, because they enjoyed
King Alfonso's protection.
But what conquered people
Does not protest against injustice?

52

"Because the Queen of Heaven,
The Virgin Mother of God
Had stood graciously beside us
So we could conquer *Valencia*:
Pedro, thus going to the Moors,
Brought recovery to the suffering
And a grave to the army's dead.

Say to all the vanquished,
Say to men and women alike,
That the proudest in battle,
We are the gentlest in peace,
We are humane and magnanimous.

Urge them to come to me,
That I myself may speak with them,
That for their treasures and their wives
They need have no fear.
For I have no chests
For their treasures, and I have
No harem for their wives.
I have but a single wife,
Only one, my true wife.

Alvar Fannez, go forth! To my
Poor, suffering *Ximena*,
And bring her here, and my children, too;
That they purchase only the most essential

And properly come here
To see this beautiful city
And Rodrigo, their friend.

Take also thirty coins of gold
With you to the holy *Pedro*
And place it upon the altar.
Also offer two thousand pieces
Of silver to the honorable Jews,
Israel and Benjamin,
Asking their forgiveness
For my one and only lie
That I've made throughout my life.

The two mortgaged chests,
Which they accept even though closed,
They believed were full of real gold,
But they were really full of sand.
It was, however, no deception:
For my word was in those chests,
And my word is as good as gold.

Antonlinez, you accompany
Alvar Fannez. His tongue
Is a little lazy; and your tongue,
It is for them so pleasing.
Go forth! Tell Ximena
Everything about our adventure,
Help her thus in song:
For she loves to while away
Happy hours with guitar and song.

Go to the court of the king,
Then when both were together:
The gifts were given to him,
With the respectful request,
That he let my blessed
Wife and children come with you.

Whatever you have to say
In your soldier's language, forget,

Alvar Fannez, not one word of this.
Well, that in the school of his apprentices
For a hero in the court,
You also abandon yourself to mirth.
Others would take my plans,
Thus mastering and jeering
With your words. Make it so,
That nothing of the envy remains
As poison in his breast.

Go, then, my friends, go!
When you return here again,
You will find the victor
Over other Moors, my enemies,
Or—you will find me no more."

54

Having arrived in Valencia,
Excited after long separation
In the beautiful city, captivated
By the bravery of the *Cid*,
There lived now *Donna Ximena*,
She, the mother and her daughters,
With the *Cid*, who loved her truly,
In honor, joy, and happiness;

As quickly as the message arrived:
"*Miramamollin*, the Great,
approaches with a powerful army;
Fifty thousand men on horses,
Countless numbers of infantry;
He approaches the Cid,
To take Valencia from him."

Experienced in armed battle,
He prepared the fortifications
With provisions and with men;
He then inspired his cavalry
Joyfully, as he always did,
Then led *Donna Ximena*,

Her and both his daughters,
To the highest tower of the castle.

From there they looked
Out upon the sea, the Moors approaching,
They saw them striking their tents
With great speed and care,
With battle cries and drums,
Battle cries and ringing timpani.

Mother and daughters alike
Were seized by fear: for they
Had never seen such forces
On the battlefield in a single place.
"Don't be afraid, my loved ones all,"
spoke the *Cid*, "as long as I live,
No worry or fear will draw near you.
Tomorrow; and you will see all
These Moors conquered;
Daughters, and from their goods
Will grow for you your dowry.
The more of them, the better,
The richer grow the spoils,
For the church in Valencia,
Which the people will enter
Tomorrow with great joy."

Now realizing that the Moors
Were approaching the gates,
With special order, amid assembled masses,
He spoke: "*Alvar Salvadores*!
Put on your armor,
Take with you two hundred riders,
Skilled in the riding of their steeds,
And go in search of the pagans,
So that Ximena and the girls
Might enjoy the hunt."

Barely had he spoken, then it happened:
The Moors fled to their tents,
Tumbling and clattering,
Whoever could not flee, remained;

Here, however, they all turned,
And because Alvar Salvadores
Had dared to advance too far,
He fell into the hands of the Moors,
Until many days later the Cid,
To great fame, could free him.

70

Sancho, King of Navarra,
So named because he possessed a hero's courage,
He, the great grandson of *Cid*,
Whom all of Spain still honors;
With *Alfonso* of *Castile*
He led victorious wars,
Pushing forward until *Burgos* was taken,
Taking spoils wherever he went,
Until he advanced, laden with riches,
So crazed by anger,
That no one could stand against him.

Thus came he in his retreat
To the Cloister of *Cardeña*,
In which *El Cid* was entombed,
Highly revered: since his days,
no one had been his equal in courage and strength
Or in honesty and goodness.

The spiritual father of this cloister
Was an abbot, a man of great age,
Who once as a knight in armor
Had earned honor and fame.
He was a man with whom to reckon,
With heart and soul; it was deeply painful for him
That the King of *Navarra*
In his quarrel with *Castile*
Had seized so many spoils.

As the king approached the altar,
Awed by its banners,
The likes of which he had seen
Nowhere in all of Spain,

The abbot tore them from the altar
And raised the flag . . . of the *Cid*.

"Know," he spoke, "great king,
Know, in this holy cloister,
Which has been entrusted to me,
There lies a hero, with whose flag,
Under which I take stock of myself,
Great king, especially with you.
For here is the tomb
Of the *Cid*, called *Campeador*.

To request favor from you,
Sir, I seize his flag
Boldly and present my request
To you in deepest humility.
Stop the plundering, oh king,
That you inflict upon our land;
You will achieve far greater fame,
If you dedicate yourself
To the hero's flag and to the tomb of the *Cid*."

For a moment, deeply moved and deep
In thought about the courage of this Abbot,
The king stood there;
Then he spoke: "For many reasons,
Father, I shall do what you request,
And I shall leave the spoils behind.

First, because I am myself born
Of the very blood of the Campeador,
I am the great grandson of the *Cid*.
His daughter, *Donna Elvira*,
The wife of *Don Garzia*,
Whom I honor, she is my grandmother.

Second, with honor to the hero's flag
And to the fame buried here,
Entrusted to your care,
I shall gladly leave
The spoils of war behind;

Justifiably said, I may not also
Seize something I should not have taken,
Were the *Cid* still alive;
Never should I have traveled so far,
Were I not so summoned,
Never should I have let them out of my sight,
The spoils seized from his land,
If brave Cid were still alive.
I thus leave them to the dead,
For you and sacred purpose."

He gave his order, and all the spoils
Remained in the cloister of *Cardeña*;
They became a pious bequest,
Charity for the poor,
Protection for those left behind,
That too bespoke the *Cid*, even in the grave.

9. Music Transcendent and Sublime

Herder's "Von Musik" (1800)

Philip V. Bohlman

Johann Gottfried Herder drew his literary career to a close much as he set it in motion, through critical engagement with Immanuel Kant (1724–1804), one of the most eminent philosophers writing in German in the second half of the eighteenth century. Herder encountered Kant initially in 1762 at the University of Königsberg, where the notes he took as Kant's student provided the point of departure for his first writings, among them the work usually identified as his first publication in 1764, *Versuch über das Sein* (Essay on Being; JGHW1, 9–21; see the prologue to the present volume).

Herder's initial engagement with Kant was that of a loyal student who paid homage to a revered teacher directly and indirectly in his philosophical and theological work. As he embarked upon his own career after leaving Königsberg and Riga, and then established himself in Weimar in the mid-1770s, however, Herder began to turn a critical eye toward Kant, especially as the latter sharpened his focus on philosophies of reason and ethics, first in the *Kritik der reinen Vernunft* (Critique of Pure Reason), published in 1781 by Herder's own first publisher in Riga, Johann Friedrich Hartknoch (Kant 1781), who would also publish *Kalligone*, and then in Kant's major aesthetic work in the first part of *Kritik der Urteilskraft* (usually glossed as Critique of Aesthetic Judgment; Kant 1790). With two volumes of his own, *Metakritik zur Kritik der reinen Vernunft* (1799) and *Kalligone* (1800), Herder sharpened and systematized his personal positions on the project that had dominated the late decades of Kant's life. It was in *Kalligone* (Greek, usually glossed as the origins of beauty) that Herder's aesthetic work reached its culmination and most fully contributed to the aesthetic and philosophical debates on the sublime and transcendence that led from the Enlightenment to the Romanticism of the nineteenth century (see Irmscher 1998).

The chapter on "Music" in *Kalligone* (JGHW8, 810–22) is one of the most sweeping and unified treatments of music in Herder's entire oeuvre. The chapter itself does not appear as an isolated study of music aesthetics, but rather is one of numerous chapters dedicated to the many different conditions of the arts, above all the ways in which those conditions distinguish the attributes of beauty. Several chapters, nonetheless, do stand out because of the ways in which Herder pays special attention to the attributes that lead toward the transcendence of beauty itself and its capacity to yield the sublime (*das Erhabene*), the concept dominating much philosophical thought fundamental to the late Enlightenment. Herder's chapter on music, however, does far more than locate his position on music in these debates. For Herder, music's capacity to realize the sublime reroutes the philosophical path of transcendence, and in this way serves as a corrective to the limitations even of Kant's aesthetic turn in *The Critique of Aesthetic Judgment*. The importance of *Kalligone* in a more recent reception history, too, is testimony to its role in a much larger history of ideas, for it was one of the few books by Herder to appear as a single volume intended for a broader readership after World War II (Herder 1955).

To understand properly the context of Herder's chapter on music in *Kalligone* one should read it as a criticism of Kant, particularly of the Kantian shift to a concentration on reason as the primary form of human interaction with the world. Herder, as the chapters of the present book reveal, rejected this shift in the late Enlightenment, developing instead a philosophy and anthropology formed of human experience. The arts, too, were central to Herder's anthropological project. When questions of identity and nationalism arose, the arts articulated these. Their power to do that, moreover, lay in the ways they created the aesthetic *and* cultural transformation crucial to Herder's understanding of the sublime. In *Kalligone* Herder works his way systematically through all the arts, examining how they enable human experience in ways that are excluded by reason alone, that is, in Kant's pure reason (Kant 1781). Quite remarkable in the chapter on music translated below are the complex levels on which music sets experience in motion. Again we witness Herder presaging many ideas that would develop in the nineteenth century, and in some cases much later. He openly describes the ways in which music is embodied, for example, affirming ideas that he developed a quarter century earlier in *Plastik* (1778) and expanded in his major works on human history, the four parts of *Ideen zur Philosophie der Geschichte der Menschheit* (published in 1784, 1787, and 1791, and collected in JGHW8, 1989), but reflecting on music and the body in ways that allow for a much more expansive musical anthropology. It is their human qualities that determine what music and the arts afford to humanity and humanism, thus truly endowing them with the sublime.

The chapter on music in *Kalligone* is, therefore, critically important as a summation of Herder's understanding of a much larger epistemology of music and the human, in which folk music and art music are not fundamentally separable. The translation of Herder's late "Von Musik" below asks that we reread his earlier writings on music, not so much in a new light, but as if from a transformed humanity. We recognize a unity that connects the culturally specific folk songs in the anthologies of 1774 and 1778/79 (see chapters 1 and 2) through the theological writings (see chapters 3 and 6) to the humanly grounded aesthetics of his late writings (the present chapter). The collectivity of which Herder speaks in *Kalligone*—of choral singing and communal dance—expands considerably upon his earlier and more comfortable reliance on speech and the philosophy of language (see Forster 2010). The focus on music's ontologies becomes more focused and more human, while at the same time the range of music's metaphysics becomes more expansive and more universal. Ultimately, in comparison with all the other arts, it is with music that Herder, appealing to shared sensibilities, raises all humans to what he calls in the final paragraph of the chapter the very "culture of humanity."

By 1800 it is clear that Herder applies the same aesthetic ideas to all kinds of music making, notably with a vocabulary drawn from the late eighteenth century. Concepts such as the sublime are not reserved only for music of the most refined nature; rather they arise from ontological conditions, for example the repeatability and temporality that distinguish music from the other arts. In the chapter on music in *Kalligone* Herder charts multiple routes to achieving and expressing the sublime, powerfully among them the role of devotion. This late passage on music, accordingly, also reflects a return and reformulation in his 1770s writings on nature, language, and song: Herder's anthropology has fully become a musical anthropology that embraces all musical phenomena. As his last major work published during his lifetime, *Kalligone* brings his aesthetic and philosophical thought—and ethnomusicological thought—full circle, investing it with the sense of wholeness critical for the foundational moment in the intellectual history of music it has become.

"Von Musik" / "On Music"

From *Kalligone* (1800), Part 2: "Von Kunst und Kunstrichterei" / "On Art and Artistic Judgment"

JOHANN GOTTFRIED HERDER,
TRANSLATED BY PHILIP V. BOHLMAN

CHAPTER 4: "VON MUSIK" / "ON MUSIC"[a]

In this way, we might speak about the "critique of independent aesthetic judgment,"[b] about poesy and eloquence, about sculpture and architecture, about painting, landscape architecture, interior decoration, and fashion. Alas, it is music alone among the fine arts that was left without commentary, and we are left wondering, Why music? Music is "a beautiful play of sensations,"[c] which are externally engendered, and which, nonetheless, at

---

a. Herder's original German bristles with short phrases and clauses that are only partly prepared and connected. The syntax is brisk, with a rhythm that is meant to convey immediacy and a spirit of conversational familiarity with the reader. I attempt to retain this feeling in my translation. See also the "Note on Translation and Commentary" at the beginning of this book.

b. The reference here, as it is throughout *Kalligone*, is to Immanuel Kant unless otherwise noted by Herder. Herder launches his chapter on music by taking Kant's critical assessment of rationalism, *Kritik der reinen Vernunft* (Kant 1781), as a point of departure. The quoted references in this chapter are both specific and general to Kant and ideas associated with his later critical philosophy of rationalism.

c. The concept of *Empfindung* runs like a leitmotif through this chapter, providing Herder with a rhetorical focus for his response to Kant's notions of reason and rationalism, above all to *Vernunft*. In the late eighteenth century, *Empfindung* was understood in many ways, and its uses and contexts would lead us to translate it variously as "feeling," "sensibility," "sensitivity," "sensation," "perception," et cetera. These meanings acquire more importance and nuance in a constellation of related concepts and terms, for example *empfindsam* and *Empfindsamkeit*. Variant translations are specifically necessary even throughout this chapter in *Kalligone*, for example to distinguish between Herder's use of the single or plural forms of *Empfindung*. My translations attempt to account for as much nuance as possible, but they will appear henceforth without additional commentary.

the same time must communicate in a common way. Music, for example, is the fine art capable of being nothing more than the proportions of different measures of the tuning (the measurement) of the senses, to which perception belongs, in other words, which can be represented by a tone in itself. In this wide-ranging meaning of the word, moreover, music can be the artificial play among tones that yields the sensation of hearing and feeling, in such ways that they are divided into music and painting." Each sensation, not only those with sound, must possess a certain measurement, and, beyond that, such measurements must be perceived by our organs, because every measurement displays proportions and because measurement is itself generated by proportions. All sensations, furthermore, exist within us as a *sensorium commune* [Latin, ca. common organ of sensation], which in turn reflects a common cultural meaning. We are endowed with an ability to reckon with the sensations in our many different organs of perception in the same way. All these considerations notwithstanding, we hear nothing about music.[d] Painting and music, and music and painting, are completely thrown together, as if colors without drawing might serve as an artistic medium that could generate sound. Finally we pause again to consider the claim that music is "a beautiful play of sensations, which are externally engendered, and which must communicate in a common way." Because everyone knows that sensations of such indisputably common meaning are least capable of being generated by sound, what more could we say about it? Let's get on with it!

Music, an Art of Humanity

We perceive that

1. All entities possessing elasticity found anywhere in nature are recognizable through the push and pull of their *inner essence*,[e] in other words the forces that excite them and lead to their reproduction, which we hear more clearly or less clearly. This is what we call noise, and when it is more subtle, we call it sound. Sound results when the same types of object are set in similar motion, and it creates an analogue to sensation in sounding entities. We found

2. That *the human being*[f] *participates widely* in these matters, realizing them on a universal level, so that the human becomes sensitive to every

---

d. Herder is critical here of the neglect of music in the aesthetic writing of the late eighteenth century.

e. I retain Herder's use of italics for emphasis throughout the translation.

f. I translate *Mensch* (literally, man, in the generalized sense) as "human being," here as throughout the present volume.

entity that is set in motion and whose voice succeeds in being sounded. Certain observations reach even those organs of hearing that are the most deeply embedded within the body, and this capability is so considerable that experience reveals that we hear virtually with our entire body. We remembered

3. *That every tone has its own manner of movement, its own meaningful power.* Not only does every object that can be sounded and every instrument existing within nature possess its individual way of producing tones, but through its movement it generates its own modulations and through these its own melodic character, which in turn has a particular impact on our sensations. We found

4. That our ear recognizes a *scale of individual tones* whose scale degrees unfold in a certain way, inseparable from one another, but whose distinctive order, to which our understanding of the scale permits many permutations, is transformed through the manipulation of artistry into a tool that produces abundant feelings. We realize that these modulations and permutations return again and again through the same creative forces in their own distinctive ways, and through this very repetition, in the same and different ways, these tonal transformations afford our inner elasticity its energy and productivity, its push and pull—in a word, its impact. Tonal transformations function more quickly and forcefully, and in greater variety, than in any other way. The force that creates sensation feels itself to be mobile, in other words, no longer at rest and through its own inner forces caused to reproduce itself. Because of such relations the force feels itself moved in ways that are pleasant and energetic, and through such relations it can do nothing else but come to rest again. This is music and nothing else.

5. *Everything in nature that sounds is music.* Nature contains all music's elements within it and requires only a hand that draws them out, an ear that hears, and a common feeling that is sensitive to it. No artist created a tone or invested it with power that was not first contained in nature and in his instrument. The composer discerns the ways of tones and forces them upon us with gentle strength.[g] "The sensation of music is not generated from the outside," but rather lies within us, within us. It is only the full movement of the sweet sound itself that comes to us from the outside,

---

g. Greek text.

    A profound, a richly bowed work,
    Is music; steadily it strives toward the new,
    Out of which it draws understanding.
              —Eupolis of Athenaeus

which arouses us in the forms of harmony and melody, and which furthermore has the power to rule through harmony and melody.

6. Similarly we know *that the voice of everything constituted in the same way communicates itself superbly to all constituted in that way.* This principle follows from the very genetic concept of what music truly is. In instruments that are similar to one another, ringing tones possess the strongest and purest consonance. It is the same with living beings. The voice of a particular species conveys itself most effectively to that species when it lives sympathetically in the social group, when it lives collectively in herds, as countless examples from the natural world reveal. The cry of fear provides cause for those in a social group to gather together, permitting them no peace as long as the cry continues; filled with fear, they noisily respond and hurry to lend assistance. The sounds of joy and of desire, they too ring forth no less powerfully. The original power of tones does not rest alone in the "proportions in the different degrees to which hearing is calibrated," as if sensation was a property of the ear, and as if the ear itself, isolated from creation, generated tones. This is merely a condition of dreaming or illness, which strives toward waking or health. The power of sound and the call of passion belong to the entire species, and they function sympathetically with its physical and emotional being. It is the voice of nature, the energy of that which moves within, rallying an entire species to the same feelings. It is *harmonious movement*.

7. From this comes *dance*, for the tones of music move with the *same sense of meter*, which they stimulate, just as sensation measures it, raising and lowering the body. The rhythm of music's expression expresses itself through the body's rhythms. Accordingly we recognize the ways in which *gesture* is bound up in music. When powerfully responding to sensation through movement, the human living in nature[h] can barely contain himself. The human expresses what she hears, through the lines on her face, the ways she moves her hands, by positioning and bending with her body. The dances of people living close to nature, above all those in warm climates, whose activity generates considerable movement, are all based on pantomime. For the Greeks it was no different; they speak of music as the guide for dance and of a dance for every movement of the soul.[i]

---

h. Herder uses *Naturvölker*, which in early anthropology and comparative musicology was glossed as "primitive people." With my translation I hope to convey political correctness only secondarily, emphasizing instead the human connection between music and nature that is truly at issue for Herder in this and other passages.

i. Greek terms. The most basic words in Greek used to describe music can express the same notions of both sound and dance.

8. If, therefore, *music, dance, and gesture* are bound internally through their common bond with nature as types that produce a social energy, how could they fail to give voice through their *common voicing* of sensibilities? We join in when we hear voices raised in song; the power of choruses, especially at moments when they join together and then join again together, is indescribable. It is indescribable how lovely voices are when they *accompany* one another. They are both one, but they are not one; they move apart, search for, pursue, contradict, struggle with, strengthen, and destroy one another, and they awaken, give life to, console, flatter, and embrace one another again and again, until finally they fade into a single tone. There is no more beautiful image of searching and finding, of friendly quarrels and reconciliation, of loss and longing, of doubting and then complete recognition again, and finally of the full, sweet union and melting together, as these two- or three-voiced musical passages and musical struggles, whether or not accompanied by words. In the final analysis, words do not function as the lazy expression of that which has meaning in a charming labyrinth, but rather they effectively struggle together toward common cause.

9. It was the nature of the thing that *music should have initially and long adhered to dances and songs,* not actually for the reason that many presume, that is, to afford meaning, in order that dance and song are expressive without feeling through the meaning of tones and melodies. Such unified expression does not bring understanding to something lacking feeling. Whoever lacks feeling for music is not able to clarify at all why one fiddles to such words or dances to such tones. "What fantastic hopping and jumping about! And how you tire yourself without any goal, without any critical and aesthetic reason! And why do you sing? Say what you will, but it is unnatural to sing with an affected voice. Rather one should simply say what needs to be said." One speaks so frequently about opera and refers to it as *criticism.* It is no different when it comes to nonvocal music. "Que me veux tu, Sonate?" The adagio "sounds so sweet and gentle; why doesn't one set words to it?" And with what abandon and fantasy the tones chase about each other—behind, through, "above, below, and next to one another." That senseless thing is called "Presto!" Obviously there are no words that could be set to such a presto, for what nightingale could whistle or follow all the voices at the same time?

10. For quite different reasons than the ways the above bring clarification and understanding to music, music has long adhered closely to dance and song: these are, indeed, the archetype of their own type, in other words, *they provide the truly natural expression of their own energy,* which gives them their feel of dancelike *movement* and their *rhythm.* Just as one does not

dance without music, so too no people would dance without any true feeling of passion. They would hop about, merely gesticulating with arms and legs. While reading the newspaper, no one is thinking about music. If one reads a passage that possesses a total and inner language of sensitivity, however, then one must read aloud, with sound and gesture. Sound and gesture call music to themselves in the same way that one seeks words for a sweet melody, but also music creates poetry within itself without speech, for it does so through its sensations. All people recognize or sense this natural bond between sound, gesture, dance, and text, and thus they abandon their complete expression of sensation to it. No person wishes to divide that which nature has bound together, indeed what in the most diverse ways remains unified. Accordingly, Greek music survived for so long in dance, in the movements, in the choruses, in the dramatic performances, which together remained true to this. Bound together fraternally as a single civilization, these forms of expression loved one another and achieved perfection, through both performance and transmission. Because of the distinctive excellence that the Greeks achieved in their dramatic and lyrical poetry, indeed through the elevation of their language through song and declamation, we cannot place their music in high enough regard among the appropriate arts, above all when we witness the ways music commands and leads dance, song, gestures, and words.

11. No one can doubt that the arts have a *remarkable impact* when combined together in such natural ways, for palpable evidence reveals itself both from the past and in the present, with examples among those peoples who so passionately abandon themselves to dance and pleasure. The very nature of this matter makes the strongest case for it. For whom do musical tones not resonate, for whom do the passionate gestures of a voice not join together tone, gesture, and word in such a heartfelt manner, for whom does music not lie each day inextinguishable in the soul? Gesture and tone, voice and sensation, together form such an intimate bond that in the very moment of perception, when the singer abandons herself completely to everything that lies at the core of her own heart, we believe in what she so magically and naturally communicates to us. At this moment, let us say, it is *her* words, *her* tones; the artist merely creates an occasion, in which she breathes life into *her* most intimate self. Noverre's *Letters* may well provide us with informative evidence about the capacities of music and dance [Jean Georges Noverre, *Lettres sur la danse et sur les ballets*; Noverre 1769]. Who is unaware of the power of poetry, which also is not accompanied by action, but rather only with musical tones? With the exception of the Italians in the past and the present, whose soul is not moved by the magical sounds of Handel, Gluck, or Mozart?

12. There are *three domains* specifically, in which word and tone, tone and gesture, are intimately bound up with one another and thus exert the most powerful influence: the domain of *devotion*, of *love*, and of the *impact of power*. All feelings are available through *devotion*, from weakened faintness to the most encompassing strength and power, from the most gripping sadness to loud rejoicing. Devotion endows the most basic words, tones, and gestures with the greatest significance and impact. The domain of *love* also contains its maximum potential for giving and receiving, in struggle and victory, in sadness and in joy. Gentleness is its chief characteristic. *Power*, finally, transforms nature. Its creative act results from courage, from decision, and from action. Action and change are its slogans. In all three domains we possess the most superb masterworks, against which there would be thankless transgressions and signs of the most insensitive lack of feeling. It is a genre of sacrifice to others. To each of these belongs *its own* time and *its own* place. Even so-called word painting in music cannot be dislodged from time and place, if it emphasizes a particularly striking word and enlivens daring decisiveness through the ways it is bound to and stimulates the power of nature like an invisible voice.[j] Playful and joyful music, too, has its value, for are not playfulness and pleasure our most lively and conscious reasons for being?

13. It would be a misunderstanding of all this to come to the conclusion that *the musical tone could never be separated from words and from gestures* to such a degree that they would have to accompany and translate every little step. It is, therefore, a burdensome accompaniment; what would a musical tone really aim to interpret with each note of the transformation through words or gestures? What we're being told is that the answer to that question is *thought*. *Sensations* only come about as if stammered out, expressing themselves more through what they are not than what they actually state. A prattling sensation becomes unbearable, as if the prattler even wants to overcome it and reveal that it is thus untrue. Musical tones may weave in and out of themselves, repeating and contradicting one another. The flight and return of these magical spirits is precisely the essence of art, which achieves its impact through movement. In contrast, words, which stumble all over each other, snatching at every stroke of the bow and whistling with every breath of air, are just so much meaningless chitchat of speech and music, particularly among slowly speaking peoples. Music, too, needs its freedom when it is by itself, as when the tongue speaks for itself. Song and speech do not require exactly the same mechanisms for

---

j. For his ideas on word painting, Herder draws on Gleichen 1791.

their production. Without words, purely in and of itself, music came to possess *its own* special type of art. Pan, who called forth Echo from his bamboo flute, did so without words, required no gestures. He was Pan, the one who summed up music and made known the music of the universe. Apollo, who invented the lyre at a moment when only the swan could hear him, was known as the founder of the chorus of muses because of this and the lyre. Orpheus moved Orcus[k] with the language of his string playing; the Eumenides[l] would never have listened to the words of a dying person.

For you who despise music itself without words, for you who has nothing to gain when music is wanting for text, you should keep your distance. Think of music as if it were a game, in which lively instruments, both with and without purpose, are practiced. For you who are musicians, however, designate your musical auditorium by adapting Plato's motto: "No one without the muse should enter here!"[m]

14. The long path of history reveals just how difficult it became for music to separate itself from its siblings, words and gesture, in order to establish itself as an art in and of itself. A convincing means all of its own was demanded, in order that music would gain its independence from all kinds of external assistance.

Among the Greeks music accompanied poesy, which it served, for the most part, only through recitative. It was able to contribute substantially to the manner of delivery in this way, but only as a servant in service to the poet. In dance, where music would appear to be the empress, it was the celebration, the social context, the form, and the movement of the human performers that commanded music. What helped to raise music up so that it, trusting in its own strength, was able to rise, borne by its own wings? What was that something that distinguished music from everything foreign, from everything we see before us, from dance movements, indeed from the accompaniment of the voice? *Devotion*. It is devotion that lifts human beings and a congregation of people above words and gesture, for then nothing remains for human feelings other than—musical tones. What does music not possess in such tones, in other words, in the sensations that are attached to them? What does music lack when it reaches this liberated high ground?

15. Devotion is blind to the person who is singing. The musical tones come from heaven, they resonate within the heart, and the heart itself sings

k. In Greek myth, the ruler of the underworld.

l. Greek deities who mobilized vengeance.

m. Herder refers here to Plato's sign over the entrance of the academy of mathematics in the Pythagorean style: "No one should enter here who understands nothing of geometry." *Kalligone* (1955 edition, ed. Begenau, 333; JGHW8, 818).

and plays. In this way, the musical tone from a string that has been set in motion or from small pipes into which one blows is able to resonate freely in the air, so that it is grasped by every sensitive being, and it resonates everywhere, renewing itself in the struggle against sustaining itself, able to communicate anew. Devotion arises in this way, borne by sound, pure and free, moving across the face of the earth, enjoying everything in the singular, in each tone sensing the harmony of all tones. In this way devotion sensitizes itself to every little dissonance, feeling in the narrow range of our few melodic styles and scales *all* vibrations, movements, modes, and accentuations of the spirit of the world, of the all-encompassing world. Might one therefore ask if music, through its inner efficacy, surpasses each art that expresses itself through the visible? It *must* surpass them, just as spirit surpasses the *body*, for music is spirit, related to the power of the innermost strength, that of *movement*. What cannot be made visible to the human will communicate to us in *its own* way and in its own way alone, revealing the world of that which is not visible. It speaks to us, moving us with true impact; we ourselves ... does anyone know how? ... sense this impact, without opposition, but with real power.

16. Every moment is *temporary* for this art, and so it must be, for it is precisely the ways in which it is *shorter* and *longer*, *stronger* and *weaker*, *more* and *less*, that produces its *meaning*, its *impression*. In its *arrival* and *departure*, in its *becoming* and *being*, therein lies the conquering strength of sound and its perception. In the ways this or that tone combines with others, in the ways tones rise and fall, disappear, or raise and renew themselves on the string stretched by harmony toward eternal, insoluble laws, therein lies my soul, my courage, my love and hope. In contrast, each of the visual arts, which must adhere to limited circumstances and gestures, indeed to local colors, even if it reveals everything at once, nonetheless can be only *slowly* understood, and because nothing visual can yield perfection, finally earns its *restitution*, while at the same time *outliving* itself. You effervescent spirits of the air, come with gentle tones and flee, move my heart and release me to an eternal longing, through you and to you.

17. At any rate, the quarrel about the *value* of the various arts, or about their relation to the nature of human beings, is always vacuous and worthless. Space cannot become time, nor time space. The visual cannot be made audible, nor the audible visual. Precisely because the arts exclude each other in their representation do they achieve their distinctiveness; they are never unified in human nature or at the center of our perception. Just how they can be enjoyed or ordered depends entirely on our taste, or even more, our rational sense of order. Just as an analogy between sound and color is imag-

ined to exist, so too can one respond to musical tones as colors and colors as musical tones. One can see pictures in music, and portraits in poetry, as the poet creates and paints with pastels. The arts themselves are innocent of what accrues to them from tastes that arise from later rationalization.

. . .

The "generally appropriate and necessary judgments arising from the critical power of judgment of the connections of the fine arts to one and the same product, and thus the comparison of the aesthetic value of the fine arts one to another," will not occupy us very long.[n] Is music to be regarded as a *"play of sound,* just as painting is regarded as an *art of color,* though the question remains open as to whether we are speaking of a fine art or an applied art (for example, in cooking or in *comedy)"*:[o] the critical observation should thus not serve to create further alienation, that music "without any real sense of meaning *through* pure emotions, from the outside, is produced, which is to say, *merely* ephemeral and more pleasure than culture is (that the play of thoughts, that which is produced secondarily, is merely the result of *similarly mechanical* association). Music is therefore judged *through* reason to have less value than any of the other fine arts. Accordingly, music requires, like *every* pleasure, *more frequent* change, and it does not sustain *extended* repetition without *producing* satisfaction." Contrary to all experience. Indeed, it is music among all the arts that most extensively lends itself to and sustains repetition; there is no other art in which one hears repetition so often. Simply putting *pitches in order,* that is, harmony, is tiring and must be tiring, because it is always the same, thus entirely familiar. *Real music,* however, that is, melody, the movement of the entire melodic passage, becomes more pleasant with each repetition; it rises even to the level of charm. We cannot listen often enough to the intimate passages that move us. How they echo, and we wish for their return without satisfaction, until we (so we imagine) absorb these passages and they become part of our soul. Pictures retreat from our consciousness and fade; musical tones accompany us as our most intimate friends, cheering us on and lifting us up, giving us pleasure and strength. "If one evaluates the value of the fine arts within culture, according to the ways they produce feeling, and measures the expansion of what they bequeath to the critique of perception, music occupies the lowest rung among the fine arts, because it *plays only with the most basic feelings."* Poor music, condemned to do only

n. Herder, *Über die menschliche Unsterblichkeit,* in JGHW8, 211–19.
o. Herder, *Tithon und Aurora,* in JGHW8, 222–27.

this; feeling without sensation that one hears only as a play of feelings in all music.

> —Do but note a wild and wanton herd
> Or race of youthful and unhandled colts
> Fetching mad bounds, bellowing and neighing loud—
> Which is the hot condition of their blood
> If they but hear perchance a trumpet sound
> Or any air of musik touch their ears,
> You shall perceive them make a mutual stand,
> Their savage eyes turn'd to a modest gaze
> By the sweet pow'r of musik. Therefore the Poet
> Did feign that Orpheus drew trees, stones and floods;
> Since nought so stockish, hard and full of rage
> But musik for the time *doth change his nature.*[p]

If one gathers, without any prejudice, the affects that melodies and songs invest in human feeling and have afforded to all collectives of human society, from the family to the nation, music would rise as a narrative of miraculous tales from the lowest rung to which it has been assigned to realize its relation to the *culture of humanity.* "The concepts of music come from *transitory* impressions; either they disappear entirely, or if they are deliberately repeated from the strength of imagination, they are more burdensome than unpleasant."[q] Poor music, which deliberately, again and again, becomes a burden! And a feeling, to which melodies, repeated again and again, though once lovely, now become a burden! Where do we find such circumstances? When we are dreaming, nothing sounds more heavenly than music; it exceeds in its loveliness all other images of beauty in our dreams. As we know so very well, it is music that we experience within ourselves that lifts us up from the earth at the very moment of death.

---

p. Shakespeare, *The Merchant of Venice*, act 5, scene 1.
q. Herder, *Über die menschliche Unsterblichkeit*, in JGHW8, 219.

Epilogue
Herder's Journey

> O, soul, what will happen to you when you depart this world? The narrow, firm, bounded center has disappeared as you flitter about in the air or swim upon the sea.... The world disappears from you ... it's disappeared from underneath you! ... What a new way of thinking! But it costs tears, repentance, departure from the old world, self-damnation!
> —JOHANN GOTTFRIED HERDER, *Journal meiner Reise im Jahr 1769*

THE WORLD DISAPPEARS

Journey provided Johann Gottfried Herder with one of the most pervasive metaphors for his own life, opening for him a path that would transform the grand intellectual narratives of his age. Herder embarked upon his life journeys from an early age in Eastern Europe—from his youth in rural Mohrungen to his studies in Königsberg and first employment as a pastor in Riga—and journey led him through the various stages of his career, from his early appointments to the years of relative stability in Weimar. He undertook journeys that were typical for an intellectual in the eighteenth century, notably his extended trip to Italy in 1788–89, meant to bring him into more direct contact with Europe's classical past (see the *Italienische Reise*, Herder 1988), but he also embarked on journeys that were uncharacteristic among his contemporaries, which drew him toward the more intimate possibilities of an unknown future. In the materiality of his writings and his ethnographic work, the journeys beyond the familiar world, those that led him to "a new way of thinking," framed his life and transformed it over its successive stages.

The chapters of the present book are among the most important records of the transformative journeys, for it was by design, not by chance, that the journeys left their mark on Herder's thought and work. The chapters in which there are annotations by Herder himself reveal a wide-ranging familiarity with travel literature in multiple languages, classical as well as modern. He uses a familiarity with travel literature to enhance the ethnographic sensibility of his observations, for example in his discussion of modern life in Palestine and the Levant as comparative context for the translations of the *Song of Songs* in chapter 3. Similarly, his knowledge of the Americas, Africa, and Indigenous peoples came from close readings of travel literature (see for example the closing songs in the anthology from *Volkslieder* in chapter 2). Herder's journeys, ethnographic and literary, are crucial to understanding the ways in which music and the all-important influences that charted his historiographic milestones reached Enlightenment Europe from elsewhere, accompanied by the differences that were transforming the shores of modernity. We have traveled with Herder on some of the most influential of his journeys through the pages of this book. The epilogue provides us with an opportunity to reflect upon the journeys again, to travel to the times and places in which Herder encountered song as a new way of thinking. In conclusion, we return to the beginning, the sea journey of 1769, as he realized that the world was disappearing from beneath him.

The 1769 sea journey afforded Herder the opportunity to strike out in search of an entirely new order. His *Journal meiner Reise im Jahr 1769* (Herder 1976) makes it clear that this search was intentional, for not only does he include observations from the voyage from Riga to Nantes in France, but he fills the pages with details for a grand educational plan to change learning and knowledge, an expansive school system that he needed first to imagine on the sea and then to establish upon his return to the shores of Europe. Herder fully recognized that journey by sea moves from the known to the unknown, and it is notable that he did not publish his reflections from 1769, even at a time in his career when he was publishing at an intense pace; he would have had no trouble interesting his Riga publisher, Johann Friedrich Hartknoch, in the *Journal*. It was only in 1846, more than a century after Herder's birth, that his son, Emil, would publish a complete version of the text. Its detailed plan for a universal history of humanity notwithstanding, the *Journal* remains symbolic of Herder's fragments, his movement to new areas, the inspiration of the moment, and the movement beyond into the unknown.

The 1769 voyage became an intellectual journey that was additionally a deliberate ethnographic and ontological move on Herder's part, a rerouting of Enlightenment teleology and historiography. Journey would become a fact of Herder's life, an intellectual aspiration even after his professional situation became more fixed after 1776. With the journey—if indeed also on the journey—his ethnographic move toward modern anthropology was fully launched (see Zammito 2002). Ethnographically, Herder sought new ideas: "My grand theme: humanity will not disappear if we open it to all possibilities! Until the genius of knowledge spreads across the entire world!

Epilogue: Herder's Journey / 263

Until universal history becomes education for the entire world" (Herder 1976, 17). Ontologically and philosophically, Herder sought a new system of education, the "natural knowledge of a new world" (ibid.). Religiously and historically, he believed his journey took him to the universal. Aesthetically and musically, he relished the diversity that would take him away from the fixed ideas of the past and into the heart, wherein music in all its diversity truly lived.

In *Song Loves the Masses* I have traced that journey and accompanied Herder on it in many ways. Herder began with the music from worlds he knew well, above all the music and sacred song of the Bible. With his ethnographic observations he turned to the vernacular music of the people close to him, especially in the Baltic lands. Chapter by chapter in the present book, Herder's musical journey expands, and it does so ethnographically. History gives way to ethnography. Song as object gives way to singing as subject. The exegetically established texts of music of the Bible open outward to the human agency of sacred song, not just in Judaism and Christianity, but in religious ritual and world religions such as Hinduism. Music moves from outside to inside, first to the heart and the soul, then beyond to the transcendent and the sublime.

Herder's musical journey as I have charted it here, like his sea journey, never fully brings him to the firm shores of an entirely new world. The *Journal* of his 1769 journey already contained the sketches of his metaphor for a historical *longue durée* that reflected the ages of a human being's life, and, notably, it is already clear that Herder left the final stages of adulthood, those preceding death, incomplete and their aesthetic realization inchoate. Whereas his anthropological and philosophical project was to trace the "culture of a nation to its perfection" (ibid., 20), the path toward eventual perfection required the intervention of a new way of thinking. Herder's intellectual journey followed a concept of history in which humanity developed increasingly toward perfection. There was an anthropological basis for this, namely the ways in which an understanding of diversity revealed that human societies were in certain fundamental ways the same. It is this basis, for example, that underlies the collections he published as *Volkslieder* and *Stimmen der Völker in Liedern* (see chapter 2). Cultural relativism was crucial to his thinking, and itself a shift from a strictly applied Christianity, with its implicit notion of European (and German) superiority. Perfection was no longer the privilege of European history alone. At the ethnographic and aesthetic confluence that Herder sought on his journey, music became deep and meaningful evidence for the universality of diversity: a perfection constituted of difference.

HERDER'S ETHNOGRAPHIC MOMENT

> If indeed the first human language was song, then it was the same song that stimulated the human organs and natural inclinations just as the nightingale's song stimulated it, the same as that generated from lungs in motion, which was indeed just that . . . our own language sounding.
>
> —JOHANN GOTTFRIED HERDER,
> *Abhandlung über den Ursprung der Sprache*

Music was critical to what was new and different on the journey of 1769. Music came to define a deeply personal moment, and it provided Herder a language with which to chart the journey toward perfection over the next decade, which is to say, in the writings on music, language, and nation during the 1770s (among them, chapters 1 through 4 and 8 in the present book). To understand the ethnographic, ontological, and aesthetic transformation in music, I return in this epilogue to Herder's journey—again—to give more complete meaning to its underlying and critical incompleteness as a life journey in which music came to represent a truly new way of thinking.

I begin biographically by asking, why 1769? First of all, the year was crucial in Herder's life. After serving for five years as a pastor, teacher, and public intellectual in Riga (today the capital of Latvia, in the eighteenth century a multicultural and cosmopolitan backwater), he decided to embark on a sea journey that would untether him from the stable and promising career he had successfully established. A product of the Baltic world of the Enlightenment, not least through his studies with Immanuel Kant and Johann Georg Hamann, Herder longed to set off for the world, which he did by climbing on a boat, journeying across and around the Baltic and North Seas, and then traveling to the heart of the West: France, Germany, and Italy (for his itinerary in his own hand, see fig. 17).

Second, 1769 brought with it an aesthetic transformation of considerable magnitude. The first three of his four *Kritische Wälder* (Critical Forests) began to appear in print (the fourth appeared posthumously much later), and Herder's ethnographic practices, as I should call them today, underwent a sea change (Gregory Moore's English translations of the first and fourth *Critical Forests* appear in Herder 2006). Growing up in the Baltic cultural region, Herder demonstrated a natural inclination toward several types of fieldwork. He was interested in local sacred musical practices, especially the oral-written interaction of Protestant hymnody in the Baltic region, a passion he had acquired from his father, who was a cantor, or church musician. He also traveled to rural areas of the Baltic region, collecting Lithuanian,

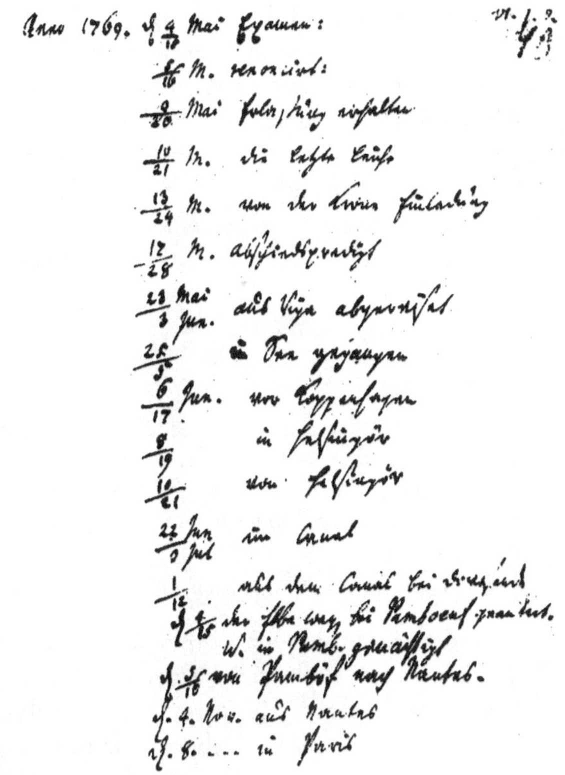

FIGURE 17. Itinerary from Herder's field notes of 1769, in his own hand. Source: Herder 1976, 5.

Latvian, Estonian, and Wendisch (roughly equivalent to modern Sorbian) traditions. In 1769 he turned outward as an ethnographer, consciously making his life's journey global. Michael Maurer argues that the sea journey began during a life crisis with several dimensions, personal and professional—basically that Herder needed to liberate himself from the provincial world of Riga and pursue a career as a writer, but that it was the sea journey itself that afforded the chance for an entirely new beginning for the "philosopher on the ship" (Maurer 2014, 39–48).

Third, Herder began to perceive his journey of 1769 as an ethnographic excursion into the world, that is, as fieldwork with global dimensions. He implemented several new forms of writing and representation, adapting them in order to encounter cultural difference and otherness, which increasingly became his primary concern. He began to recognize that he was not simply recording objects, but encountering complex historical forces, "streams" (*Ströme*), which included those of East and West (*Morgenland* and *Abendland*), but also a "third stream" that emanated outside of Europe and was beginning to wash over Europe (Herder 1769, 15–16). In 1769, traveling through the world, he began to document that "third stream." The experiences of the 1769 sea journey increasingly constituted a global moment, not just in Herder's life, but also in the much larger intellectual history of which ethnomusicology would become an important part. I turn now to the personal and intellectual journey that led to Herder's global moment in 1769.

HERDER'S ENCOUNTER

> For this purpose I wish to collect data about the history of every historical moment, each evoking a picture of its own use, function, custom, burdens, and pleasures. Accordingly I shall assemble everything I can, leading up to the present day, in order to put it to good use.
>
> —JOHANN GOTTFRIED HERDER, *Journal meiner Reise im Jahr 1769*

From the outset Herder meant his 1769 journey to release him from the Baltic world he had known so well through his youth and first professional undertakings. It is more than accurate to refer to the Baltic region of Herder's youth as a world, for it was precisely its concentrated complexity, coupled with and limited by its provincialism, that provided Herder with a lens capable of turning to the world he did not yet know but was eager to encounter. In the East Prussian lands of his youth, he had felt the pull of German history to the West, locally but also internationally once he had slid centrifugally into the East Prussian Hanseatic orbit of Königsberg. In the Russian Protectorate to which Riga and Latvia were allied, Herder sensed a different pull, to the East, relatively unknown to him yet possessing an aesthetic magic and attraction. The Baltic world, even more fundamentally, was crucial to the shaping of Herder's global epistemology because it was there that he became aware of local knowledge, in other words the culture of rural Lithuanians, Latvians, and Estonians, as well as the speakers of dialects of sundry Slavic and Germanic languages.

Critically, Herder expressed his awareness of local culture in his Baltic world through a vocabulary that mixed traditional Enlightenment themes with concepts that reached beyond the linguistic boundaries of a literary age to those he invested with ethnographic potential. There is, moreover, an uncertainty about the ways in which his writing expressed the local encounter, producing considerable slippage between and among his categories. There are moments in his early ethnographic writings especially when *Sitten* (customs), *Volk* (folk), and *Nation* (nation) are all the same, and other moments when they are vastly different. *Poesie* (poesy) might embrace poetry and song, but it might wedge its way into an expressive domain between the two. *Volkslied* sometimes insists on textual mooring, while at other times it casts itself into the more turbulent seas of oral tradition. The slippage between and among these distinctions, which we have followed throughout the present book, appears initially in his 1769 *Journal*, where the context is ethnographic for the first time.

When Herder sailed from Riga on the third of June 1769, he did not know where his travels would take him. Setting off into the unknown might seem quite remarkable for a teacher, pastor, scholar, and public intellectual of his achievement, but the truly essential point to keep in mind is that it was Herder himself who imagined the goal of his journey to be the unknown. He had just completed five years (1764 to 1769) in Riga, serving primarily as a schoolteacher, a position that had left him increasingly unfulfilled. He had also just completed his first major aesthetic project, the *Critical Forests*. Quite consciously, the journey he undertook in the summer of that year turned away from the safer shores of the world he knew, whose Enlightenment discourse network was familiar not only to Herder but also to the whole of German-speaking Europe through the philosophical writings and teachings produced by Kant and Hamann.

The "unknown," as I describe it in this epilogue, was also a product of Herder's ethnographic imagination, and it is that imagination that we encounter in his 1769 *Journal* and in the aesthetic writings that would mark the watershed years upon which he was embarking, leading directly into the musical writings of the 1770s (see chapters 1 through 4). In his journal he makes it clear that he understands the journey into the Baltic Sea as having no primary goal. When we consider maritime travel on the Baltic today, or for that matter around the northern coasts of Europe, it is rather difficult to recognize what might have been unknown about it, even in the late eighteenth century. We must remember, however, that for Herder, like many others who took to the seas in his day, the waters at any distance from shore were uncharted. Maps followed the shoreline, which is to say, the terrain that could be visibly perceived. In Herder's day there was, then, an important geographical and physical, even visible, distinction between the known and the unknown. In his *Journal* Herder further modulated that difference into cultural and historical distinctions. The teleology of the journey into the unknown, with its absence of a specific goal, also rerouted the path of history, opening for Herder the cultures of the "people without history" (Wolf 1982). His very awareness of this disentanglement from history not only found its way into his notebooks of the time, but was also fundamental to their structure and form, and beyond to their representation of an aesthetic of *Sturm und Drang* and a philosophy with global dimensions that sprang forth from the natural world of the sea (Herder 2002b, 5–6).

> And so it was that I became a philosopher on the ship, albeit a philosopher who had learned his lessons badly, with no books and instruments drawn from nature. Had I only known what kind of perspective one had while sitting under the ship's mast on the expanse of the ocean, philosophizing about the skies, the sun, the stars, the moon, the air, the wind, the sea, rain, streams, fish, and the seafloor. From all of this one can determine physics. A philosopher of nature: that should be your point of departure with the young people you teach! Take your place on the wide sea, and point out the fact and reality to a student, and do not use words to make everything clear, rather let the student clarify everything to himself. (Herder 1976, 13–14)

HERDER'S AESTHETIC MOMENT

The years leading up to Herder's ethnographic turn followed a path that had itself followed a sharp turn toward the aesthetic (for a discussion of Herder's seminal works in the early decades of modern aesthetics, see Moore 2006). The most concerted literary endeavors of the Riga years were the *Critical Forests*, four volumes that included the broad outlines of an aesthetic theory. In the early parts of the *Critical Forests* Herder's theory took shape as a series of responses to the emergence of aesthetics in the mid-eighteenth century as a distinctive, if not independent, field of philosophical and scientific inquiry (e.g., in the *Aesthetica* of Alexander Gottlieb Baumgarten [1714–1762]). The first three *Forests* were, in fact, responses to contemporary debates, especially those that swirled around Lessing's 1766 essay *Laocoön*, some of them polemic, even to the point of creating open conflict between Herder and those whose theories he assaulted rather directly (e.g., Christian Adolph Klotz [1738–1771]; see Kantzenbach 1970, 32–37). The fourth of the *Forests* marked yet a new departure, all in all, the sharpest turn yet toward a new aesthetic grounded in experience and demonstrating a theory of the arts generated from below. Completed in 1769, with fragments appearing in posthumously published philosophical writings from 1808 and 1810, the fourth *Forest* did not appear as a complete work until after Herder's lifetime, in 1846. It is not entirely clear why the

Epilogue: Herder's Journey / 269

volume was withheld from publication, for both before and after 1769 Herder worked closely with his Riga publisher, Hartknoch. What is clear, however, is that Herder used the opportunity of the final *Critical Forest* to rethink his aesthetic theory and resituate it in the human body.

If the posthumously published fourth *Critical Forest* of 1769 theorized an aesthetic of experience, it was the journey of 1769 that put theory into practice. In the *Journal* Herder openly embraced the spirit of experience, celebrating it for the new aesthetic domains into which it would take him. The experiences to which he consciously drew himself involved both humans (for instance with the sailors and others on the ship he boarded at Riga) and works of art (for example the Greek sculpture in the Mannheim Antikensaal; see *Sculpture*, Herder 2002b). Together, such experiences and projections of encounter found their way into what we would, in an age of anthropology, call field notes. He accounts for his aesthetic experiences in varied ways, often as fragments, but almost always as truncated notes, anecdotes, and smaller writings in his notebooks and in the 1769 *Journal*. The aesthetics of encounter would shape his thinking and writing through the 1770s and into the 1780s, when he would undergo another aesthetic turn, and when, specifically, his major aesthetic works were absorbed in a larger critique of philosophical writings from his era, for example Kant's *Critique of Judgment* in *Kalligone* (see chapter 9 in the present book).

From personal and philosophical perspectives, there can be no question that 1769 was a year of radical change in Herder's life, change that marked a paradigm shift of dramatic proportions. In his writings, particularly in the four volumes of *Critical Forests*, that shift underwent a formulation that we can understand as a culmination of his thinking in the formative years in East Prussia and Königsberg, and then matured during the five years in Riga, when his philosophical work reflected extensively on the German and English traditions. His philosophical reflections, moreover, found their focus in the *Critical Forests*, when his aesthetic theories began to depart from those of an earlier philosophical tradition—Leibniz and Wolff in Germany, Locke in England, and Condillac and Diderot in France—and from the generation of his own teachers, notably Kant and Hamann.

The departure into a full-blown aesthetic domain found its springboard in the mid-eighteenth-century work of Alexander Gottlieb Baumgarten, especially his *Meditationes philosophicae* of 1735 and *Aesthetica* of 1750 (English translations appear in Baumgarten 1954 and 1983). Like Baumgarten, Herder advocated the scientific basis for aesthetic understanding, which is to say, the philosophical analysis of knowledge gained through sensual experience. Herder departed from Baumgarten through his recognition of a distinction between knowledge obtained through senses that was more directly connected to thought and idea, hence reason, and knowledge that feeling and more sensual experience had generated. The senses, Herder argued in a philosophical fragment from the late 1760s, "On the Meaning of Feeling" (Zum Sinn des Gefühls), provide the direct point of contact between the human being and the world. Aesthetic response is possible because physical perception has first taken place. Placing Descartes behind him, Herder proclaims, "Ich fühle mich! Ich bin!" (I feel! I am!) (Herder 1877–1913, vol. 8, 96, and Herder 2002b, 9). An aesthetic based on physical experience, Herder came to recognize in the *Critical Forests* and other aesthetic works leading to 1769, necessarily required ethnographic encounter.

Seizing Baumgarten's argument but expanding upon it in several crucial ways, Herder launched his new aesthetic program. Whereas Baumgarten had undertaken a significant departure by recognizing that any aesthetic must account for all the five senses, Herder proceeded to advance several steps further. First, he argued in the *Critical Forests* that each of the five senses was different from the others, and that each was distinctive because of the ways in which perception took place. Painting, for example, required that the perceiver assemble experiences as spatial; poetry, in contrast, relied on temporal sequences. Second, Baumgarten interpreted perception as a top-down phenomenon, thus privileging the senses as the means whereby the fine arts are bounded by perception. Herder, in sharp contrast, attributed a physical basis to perception, a "physiology of the senses" (Herder 2002b, 9), which in turn refocused Herder's attention on the origins of the arts, for it was in the origins that the experience itself came into being. It is this path of perception and action that we encounter as the move from the external to the internal throughout the chapters of the present book.

Anthropologically, Herder draws himself closer to the point of conjunction between the ethnographic and aesthetic moments: the correlation of Herder's call for aesthetic encounter "from below" and the crucial role of origins (*Ursprung*) with cultural encounter. Jason Gaiger asks us not to underestimate the importance of the point of conjunction, "for if it can be shown that the different senses reveal the world to us in different ways, then aesthetics can begin where Herder believed it should: in an analysis of the physiological and imaginative capacities that we bring to bear in responding to and interpreting the world around us and of the distinctive ways in which we draw upon these capacities when considering works of art" (Gaiger in Herder 2002b, 11).

Once he had formulated a new aesthetic in 1769, which at once included music among the arts and then insisted on the distinctiveness of the ways in which humans perceive music, Herder had launched himself along a path that would require him to experience folk song through ethnographic encounter. Consistent with his treatment of the other arts, music required two different forms of perception. Painting, for example, required "seeing" and "looking," whereas sculpture was perceived through "seeing" and "touching." Musical perception relied on a distinction between "hearing" and "listening." Though the differences between these processes of perception may at first glance seem subtle, they are, in fact, quite profound. Most significantly, it is in the difference and the tension they reveal that we find the dynamic aesthetic movement "from below."

That tension and the concomitant aesthetic movement runs throughout Herder's writings from 1769 through the 1770s. They engender, for example, the persistent distinctions between "voice" (*Stimme*) and "hearing" (for instance the *Menge der Hörer* [masses of listeners] in the introduction to the second part of the *Volkslieder*; see chapter 2 in the present volume). They draw attention to the ears as organs of musical experience, implicitly and sometimes explicitly separating them from the mouth as the organ for the production of sound. Remarkably, Herder not only suggests a relation between sound and perception that presages modern sound studies, but also comes, in the late eighteenth century, very close to a musical ontology with clear overtones from Islamic and Jewish thought, notably the location of musical experience in *samāʿ* and *shema*, both of which distinguish between and then juxtapose "listening" and "hearing."

The more nuance he afforded the distinctive processes necessary for sensually perceiving music, the more Herder directed himself toward what he would in the coming decade call "folk songs." If music unfolded primarily through time, perception of music was necessarily at its most refined when it could operate temporally—in other words, when it could follow a succession of tones in time. What this meant, quite simply, was that melody *as aesthetic experience* claimed priority over harmony, polyphony, and other modes of perceiving sounds together and outside of time. It was for this aesthetic reason that Herder would take a step that was radical for an Enlightenment philosopher, namely, formulating an aesthetic of music from repertories that were melodic, indeed, where the experience of music was one in which the "voices of the people" (*Stimmen der Völker*) and the "masses of listeners" (*Menge der Hörer*) conjoined in the same temporal experience. It was for this aesthetic reason that Herder took an ethnographic turn that led him directly to the experience with folk song, the next stage of his ethnomusicological journey in the 1770s (chapters 1, 2, and 4).

HERDER'S ETHNOMUSICOLOGICAL EPIPHANY

> The stream of the centuries flows dark and murky for Germany. Here and there, the voice of the people, a song, a notable phrase, a rhyme managed to survive; usually, however, rather saturated, so that it was pulled back beneath the waves.
>
> —JOHANN GOTTFRIED HERDER, *Volkslieder*

During the years between 1769 and the publication of the volumes on and of folk songs in 1778/79, Herder was prolific as an author at the same time that he was traveling and garnering increasingly more diverse cultural experiences, and publishing some of his most influential early writings, not least among them his study of the origins of language (Herder 1772). His activities as a folk song collector were also developing systematically, both on the sea journey, during which he read a volume of Macpherson's Ossian songs, and after reaching France and then the German lands, where, notably, he and Johann Wolfgang von Goethe encountered and gathered folk songs in Alsace during a time both were in Strasbourg. By 1773 Herder had gathered enough folk songs, from oral traditions and from printed sources, that his manuscripts for anthologies of folk songs had already begun to assume coherent shape (see chapters 1 and 2). The anthology provided the comparative basis in 1773 for his first major essay devoted to folk song, the Ossian correspondence that provides the basis for chapter 4. The manuscript anthology thus already lent itself to the formulation of a theoretical framework for giving folk song temporal, historical dimensions and spatial, geographical dimensions. In the course of the next five years, Herder would both add songs to the manuscript and remove them, refining and refocusing, before publishing the folk songs together as an anthology whose dimensions had become distinctively global.

Drawing on the preparation of the works on folk song during his 1769 journey and published in the years that followed, *Song Loves the Masses* illustrates the ways in which these experiences and the writing they generated navigated the discursive space between an ethnographic moment and a global moment. That space was narrated and inscribed by the transformation of the empirical evidence gathered ethnographically in the field through a series of linked representational practices: from folk song or custom in oral tradition to field note; from field note to personal and reflexive narrative; from narrative to anthology of musical "works"; from anthology to a new ontology of world music. These linked representational practices, moreover, do not derive only or entirely from a top-down perspective; rather, it is the ethnographic experience, however inchoately, that generates them.

Despite the boldness of his journey in 1769, it is not the case that Herder reinvented himself as an anthropologist from one day to the next. John Zammito has reexamined the birth of anthropology at the transition from German Enlightenment to German Idealist philosophy in light of the intellectual exchange and competition between Herder and his Königsberg teacher, Kant (Zammito 2002). This transition amounts to what Zammito calls a "critical turn" toward anthropology, whereby he means also to assign an enormous importance to the emergence of a sweeping new intellectual epistemology, one in which the "popular" was to claim a radically different place by the end of the eighteenth century. For Kant, the "critical turn" took place during a period from 1762 to 1769, during which he moved away from large systematic projects and toward what is generally called "popular philosophy" (in German, both *Popularphilosophie* and *Schulphilosophie*). Michael Forster further applies this explanation of the context for Herder's writing style to the dominant role of a philosophy of language in his thought (Forster 2010). For Herder, according to Zammito, the "critical turn" began in 1769:

> I propose what Kant turned away from around 1769–1770 was in fact the path of a *popular philosopher*. In the preceding seven years, deeply troubled about the direction of traditional German school metaphysics, as well as about the role of the *Gelehrtenstand* in the project of Enlightenment, it is not unreasonable to suspect that Kant considered an alternative identity, that of the popular philosopher—a project that in fact Herder would take up in his stead (and even, I am suggesting, in his image). (Zammito 2002, 6; emphasis and parentheses in the original)

A shift in literary and discursive style was crucial for this critical turn of the 1760s, a shift that aimed to broaden the audience for philosophical and ethical speculation, but also to broaden—I should say, to reimagine—the presence of subjects and subjectivity in Enlightenment metaphysics. Driving the ethnographic moment was, therefore, the discourse of popular philosophy itself. The German philosophers of the mid-eighteenth century, especially Gotthold Ephraim Lessing and Moses Mendelssohn, as well as Johann Georg Sulzer and Thomas Abbt, were much more broadly concerned with the more international domains of Enlightenment philosophy, notably with English analytical philosophy and the engagement of French philosophy with nature. At the moment of his critical turn, Kant openly embraced the German philosophers of the *Hochaufklärung*, or High Enlightenment, above all their active integration of Jean-Jacques Rousseau's writings into a new program of public expression, or *Öffentlichkeit* (ibid., 10). As Zammito points out, it was precisely at the moment of Kant's most intense engagement with Rousseau that Herder was his student at the University of Königsberg. The teaching of that moment would not only be Kant's greatest legacy to Herder, but it would plant the fundamental seeds of disagreement that would increasingly lead to their parting of ways (ibid.). That disagreement also provided text and context for one of Herder's most ambitious essays on music aesthetics, which appeared in the 1800 *Kalligone* (chapter 9 in the present book). When they began to follow different paths, it was Herder who stayed the course toward anthropology, whereas Kant had put it behind him after the early 1770s. Herder would emerge, as Hans-Jürgen Schings has claimed, as the most important anthropologist of the late eighteenth century, "who as no other embodies the style of thought and the competence of an anthropologist" (Schings 1994, 5; see also Zammito 2002, 8).

During the 1770s the anthropological and the historical intersect in Herder's writings, linking the aesthetic writings in the *Critical Forests* with the more specifically musical writings in the folk song volumes. The key to that link lies in a work he published in 1774, *Auch eine Philosophie der Geschichte zur Bildung der Menschheit* (Yet Another Philosophy of History for the Education of Humanity) (Herder 1774). With this work Herder launched an open assault on the absolutism that had characterized the Enlightenment notion of universal history. Crucial to his program for a new historiography was an insistence that the histories of past cultures were encountered only within those cultures themselves, in their own time and terms, without imposing the values purportedly immanent in a universal history. Herder, instead, made the case that the encounter between a culture and its environment determined the shape of its practices and the course of its history. If this sounds like an open call for cultural relativism, it both was and was not. On one hand, Herder insisted that understanding a culture at historical and geographical distance from eighteenth-century Europe required understanding its own conditions. On the other, he stopped short of stripping history of teleology altogether, specifically the process of development toward increasing progress, even Rousseau's concept of *perfectibilité* (perfectibility; see Gaiger in Herder 2002b, 21). After 1774 Herder increasingly directed his historiographic journey toward the perfection in the final life stage of history, a perfection that was at once possible and impossible.

In the years that followed the 1774 *Yet Another Philosophy of History for the Education of Humanity* Herder revisited the aesthetic materials he had gathered in and around 1769, coupling them with the new concept of experience and sensation that was central to his anthropological program, and publishing them in his two most substantial works specifically devoted to the arts, the study of *Plastik*, or *Sculpture*, in 1776, and the volumes on folk song in 1778/79 (chapter 2 in the present volume). In both works we encounter a remarkably bold new anthropology, one that argues forcefully for the embodiment of the artistic experience, particularly in the visual and musical arts. It is through embodiment, moreover, that the arts acquire their potential to express something profoundly human, which is to say, potentially bound to the development and perfection of humanity as a whole. The shift to the human body thus is also a shift to a humanity that was globally, indeed, phylogenetically, conceived. On a much grander scale Herder is extending Enlightenment universalism to a globalization palpable in the aesthetic—and musical—experience. The first complete map of that globalization was to become the folk song project (chapter 2).

If we begin to look at Herder as an ethnographer, his writings on music start to tell entirely different tales from the field. First of all, his inscriptions of song no longer fulfill only the characteristics of a history predicated on text, the dissemination of which depends on literary technologies such as printing and translation. Second, Herder's collections of and essays on music cease to represent the types of nationalist rhetoric that prevailed in the nineteenth century, especially in Germany. German songs, indeed, appear in relatively small numbers. Third, we recognize that his writings on music have polysemic dimensions; in other words, they are meant to embrace different ontologies and epistemologies of music, especially folk song. Fourth, Herder is remarkable for the ways in which he recognizes how local knowledge realizes the global and vice versa, all the more because he recognizes the power of discourse networks, say, in a Latin Marian song that becomes a Sicilian sailors' song on its way to entering the canon of German Christmas songs as "O, du fröhliche" (see chapter 2, appendix, song 17, "An die Jungfrau Maria").

Herder's music aesthetics also possess many of the attributes of early Romantic notions of music's relation to experience. Citing Friedrich Schlegel, Berthold Hoeckner observes that Herder was perhaps the first writer to attempt to bring an epistemological whole into view through the parts, both individually and collectively. Schlegel noted that "it was Herder, who first knew to grasp a whole with an emphatic imagination and to express this feeling in words" (Schlegel 1958, vol. 3, 296; quoted in Hoeckner 2002, 5). I want to suggest, furthermore, that Herder's seminal epistemological focus on the relation between parts and wholes was born of his ethnomusicological epiphany, itself ineluctably connected to his global moment. We witness the epistemological refocusing in the representational forms that Herder began to employ in his aesthetic writings, beginning after 1769 and throughout the 1770s. Such forms appear in his earliest writings devoted to music and they sustain his approach to folk music, not least the use of fragments in the Ossian essay and in the folk song volumes. Critical to the approach to translation that I employ throughout the present book, these fragments themselves had even earlier origins, namely in the 1769 *Journal* (Herder 1769, 129).

Herder also sutures aesthetic and ethnographic modes of rhetoric, notably through the ethnographic tradition of juxtaposing diachronic and synchronic representation. Indeed, we can even say that the relation of the two editions of *Volkslieder* and *Stimmen der Völker in Liedern* was one of systematically presenting synchronic evidence in the 1778/79 edition to the diachronic historiography in the 1807 edition. The first edition begins with a section devoted to what he calls *Zeugnisse* ("witnesses," or "evidence") of folk song and then unfolds as an anthology with very sparse commentary on the songs themselves, intentionally allowing them to speak for themselves. The second edition, especially in the appendix with new songs from the Nordic region, Africa, and South America, intersperses extensive historical commentaries with the songs, and through this rhetorical ploy Herder uses folk song as a means of representing cultural and national history—that is, of narrating the diachronic (see chapter 2).

The addition of fragments to whole literary works (as in the addition of songs and commentaries on songs to the 1773/74 folk song manuscripts and after 1779 to subsequent publications on music) allowed him quite unsystematically to evoke a systematic view of a globalized and globalizing music culture. The commentary in the second edition of *Stimmen der Völker in Liedern* has particularly far-reaching global dimensions, and it draws attention to processes we today understand as globalization: encounter, colonialism, hybridity, change, exchange.

To what extent can one really make the claim that Herder's publications on music in the years following the 1769 journey also represent world music, which in turn might signal his own response to the global moment he had encountered in the waning years of the Enlightenment? In *Song Loves the Masses* I have employed many ways to interpret the evidence constituting the repertories he brought together as single works with multiple parts. Once again, it is important unequivocally to clarify what the *Volkslieder* are not: they are not primarily German folk songs, and they bear no resemblance to a nationalist collection, German or otherwise. It is clear in table 1 that German songs (thirty-eight) represent a rather small number of the total contents; there are almost as many songs in "Romance languages" (thirty), and there are substantially more in "English, Scottish,

TABLE 1. Statistical Representation of Repertories in *Volkslieder* (1778/79)

Origin	1773/74 Manuscript	1778/79 Published Version
English, Scottish, Gaelic		**53**
Percy's *Reliques*	14	24
Diverse collections	—	18
Shakespeare	12 (11)	8
Ossian	—	3
German		**38**
Folk songs, oral tradition	5	9
Folk songs, printed	9	6
Art songs, 16th–17th c.	1	13
Art songs, 18th c.	—	10
Romance		**30**
Spanish	—	18
French	—	5
Medieval Latin	—	3
Italian	—	3
Portuguese	—	1
Slavic (according to Herder's categories)		**15**
Lithuanian	2	8
Dalmatian (Morlakisch)	—	4
Latvian	2	2
Wendisch	1	1
Nordic		**14**
Old Nordic	5	10
Danish	—	4
"Old" (classical) languages		**6**
Greek	—	5
Latin	—	1
Other languages		**6**
Estonian	1	3
Sámi	2	2
Inuit	1	1

NOTE: Adapted from Rölleke 1975, 475–76

and Gaelic" (fifty-three). We also know that among the twenty-five songs and folk tales that Herder may have gathered for the 1807 edition—only three were from German sources, while the others noticeably pushed at the borders of Europe—he begins with an Estonian, Tatar, and Sicilian song. He extends his ethnographer's gaze and collector's reach far beyond Europe, locating a group of songs from Madagascar at the end, but closing with a song from Peru. Even when German repertories serve comparative ends, for example in his assessment of the Ossian songs, there is a noticeable absence of privilege assigned to them (see chapter 4 in the present volume).

The statistics that describe the 1773/74 manuscript and the 1778/79 publications, moreover, reveal the extent of Herder's ethnomusicological epiphany in other ways. Songs from Thomas Percy's *Reliques of Ancient English Poetry* (1765) and those from sixteenth- and seventeenth-century German art song appear in rather substantial numbers (twenty-four and thirteen), but so do Spanish songs (eighteen) and ones in Old Norse (ten). Significantly, in each of these cases, we witness repertories that Herder plumbed during the course of his lifetime and integrated into publications of all kinds, from the first German translation of the *Cid* epic (chapter 8) to essays on Nordic folklore.

Diversity of repertory and representation of world music characterize the folk song collections of 1778/79 in at least two other significant ways. First, Herder clearly feels himself ontologically unencumbered by the limitations of genre. The concept of *Volkslied* is expansive, and it should and does include different modes of musical production, different performance and representational practices, and more rather than fewer ontologies of music itself. He gathers songs from fieldwork, and he reproduces both songs from published collections that have entered a canon and those circulating in popular traditions, such as broadsides. Dialect songs in different variants find their way into the anthologies alongside songs transmitted in literary languages.

Second, Herder believes that world music must possess the cultural and temporal qualities of universal history. His collections reveal attention to history on many different levels. In effect, his "evidence"—his *Zeugnisse*—begins with Montaigne's reflections on Jean de Léry's Tupinamba songs, collected in the Bay of Rio de Janeiro in the mid-sixteenth century (de Léry 1578; for a superb English translation see de Léry 1990), and it closes in the 1807 edition with African and Andean songs, also the products of colonial contact (see chapter 2). Most significantly, history, as articulated through what he calls folk songs, functions in many different ways and follows the many courses of diverse epistemologies. Call his volumes what one will—

multicultural, multiethnic, multilingual—Herder used folk song to chart multiple courses for history, many of which looked very different from those familiar to the Enlightenment gaze (Bohlman 2013b).

RETURN VOYAGES

> It is a difficult thing to return with the concepts from all fields of scientific inquiry and with each word of all languages to the senses from which they arose, and yet this is exactly what is necessary for every science and every language.
> —JOHANN GOTTFRIED HERDER, *Journal meiner Reise im Jahr 1769*

Paradox and contradiction have consistently accompanied Herder over the two centuries since his death. With each anniversary and commemoration, with each attempt to draw him into the political issues of the moment, he returns as the chronicler of a different past and as the emblem for transformation to a new future. He has symbolized the politics of a conservative nationalism and the moral responsibility for a radical idealism. He is celebrated for his contributions to humanistic education in Germany and for his tolerance of intellectual traditions that arose from a universal humanism that developed at far reaches from Germany and the West. Some of his ideas return because they are malleable, while others remain at remote distance because they are rigid and inappropriate. In the twenty-first century Herder's journey has ironically assumed the form of multiple return routes, none of them fully realizing a return voyage.

Commemorations and anniversaries have sometimes been kind to Herder, sometimes not. The two hundredth anniversary of his birth, for example, fell in 1944, the penultimate year of World War II, at a moment when many Germans were realizing that the outcome of the war would not be in their favor. Herder had never been a favorite of fascist German scholarship, not least because of his long engagement with Jewish theology and theologians, and the attraction that his ideas on nationalism and its moral imperatives held for those beyond the borders of Germany. His role in the enlightened world of late eighteenth-century Weimar, which had been the political seat of interwar Germany, the Weimar Republic, also made him suspect.

By 1944, however, there was growing need for intellectual heroes from Germany's past, and Herder was a prime candidate (see the essays in Schneider 1994). Herder's ideas for a universal history, which had always passed through the Germany of Herder's own day, as we have seen throughout the chapters of this book, were conveniently rerouted back to Germany.

The *Volkslieder* project, which Herder had used to discover musical meaning beyond Europe, was seized as the foundation of Germany's expansion into the lands settled by Germans during earlier eras (see, e.g., Bohlman 2002). Folk song scholarship had accelerated, not diminished, during the war, and Herder was claimed repeatedly as its Nestor. A darker side of German nationalism had increasingly appropriated Herder during World War II, and in 1944, two centuries after his birth, he was accorded an official role by many that he would have himself rejected on all counts.

Commemorations and anniversaries in the East—Eastern Europe and East Germany—tell a different story entirely. Rather than a symbol of German nationalism, Herder serves as the champion of an Eastern Europe establishing its cultural and political independence from Central Europe. A "Herder Gesellschaft" had appeared in Riga already in 1921, and it was staking a claim again to the influences of the Enlightenment on the Baltic countries (after World War I under Soviet control) in which Herder had himself developed his early intellectual traditions, and where, as we saw in chapter 2, his first epiphany of folk song took place (see also Jaremko-Porter 2009). After World War II, surely also because of the celebrations of Herder during its final years, the shift of Herder scholarship to Eastern Europe intensified. Herder research institutes (in Marburg and elsewhere) dedicated themselves to Herder in the East. Herder commemorations in the German Democratic Republic had considerable visibility, and they produced a respectable body of scholarship, which was virtually unknown in the Federal Republic (for the commemorative volume of the 175th anniversary of his birth, see Akademie der Wissenschaften der DDR 1978). In the upper levels of East German schools, students with an outstanding understanding of the Russian language were awarded a "Johann Gottfried Herder Medal." The East German equivalent of the West German Goethe Institute bore Herder's name, before and after reunification. Herder awards and prizes from various cultural and academic foundations went to artists and scholars in Eastern Europe (for a more extensive list, see Maurer 2014). By the beginning of the twenty-first century, Herder had become *the* symbol for German intellectual politics in Eastern Europe, the region from which he had departed in 1769, never to return.

Herder reception in the late twentieth and early twenty-first centuries would seem to be a tale of two Herders. That designation, however, is an oversimplification, for it does little to account for the ironies and contradictions. It would be tempting to imagine, for example, that Herder the theologian would disappear from assessments of the Weimar pastor in the German Democratic Republic, in which public religion had little official support, but quite the opposite proved to be the case. Herder's writings on religion appeared in editions that were widely and inexpensively available throughout East Germany, and in the literary cultures of other East European countries (see, e.g., Schmidt 1956). The writings on music—folk music and music aesthetics—influenced folk music scholarship in West Germany, but had much less impact on ethnomusicology; in East Germany, the concepts of world music and universal history were widely influential across the disciplines of music scholarship (Bohlman 2010a).

The two Herders of twentieth- and twenty-first-century Herder reception notwithstanding, the trajectory of his 1769 journey—and the metaphors it spun out for him throughout his life—are easier to chart. Herder's goal was to travel from the known to the unknown, thus enriching the diversity of experiences that he could gather for a universal history of humanity. Schematically I might map this common trajectory of Herder's journey onto the many areas in which he worked in the following ways:

Religion Herder took Protestant Christianity as a point of departure, searching for what he understood as a basic human spirit (*Geist*) in religion. That spirit provided the context for Jewish and Christian biblical writings, as well as the ways in which these acquired aesthetic, literary, and musical dimensions. It was this spirit of religion that he sought in writings on Jewish texts as the historical foundations for poesy, for example in the *Vom Geist der ebräischen Poesie* (1787) and *Lieder der Liebe*, his translator's exploration of the *Song of Songs* (see the prologue and chapter 3 in the present volume). It was also the search for the spirit of religion that led him to an understanding of the universality of religion beyond the Abrahamic faiths, for example in his studies of Hinduism that have led some Indian scholars to refer to him as "the Brahman Herder" (Ghosh 1990).

Philosophy Herder embarked upon a philosophical path that was designed as much to provide possibilities for other philosophical systems as to be a systematic philosophy of his own. The openness of that philosophical journey is striking in the following summary by Michael Forster:

> Hegel's philosophy turns out to be an elaborate systematic extension of Herderian ideas (especially concerning God, the mind, and history); so too does Schleiermacher's (concerning God, the mind, interpretation, translation, and art); Nietzsche is strongly influenced by Herder (concerning the mind, history, and morals); so too is Dilthey (in his theory of the human sciences); J. S. Mill has important debts to Herder (in political philosophy); Goethe not only received his philosophical

outlook from Herder but was also transformed from being merely a clever but conventional poet into a great artist mainly through the early impact of Herder's ideas. (Forster in Herder 2002a, vii)

Language Language served as a port of embarkation for Herder in countless ways, not in small part because the core of his own thought may have been the philosophy of language. By the time of his 1772 essay on the origins of language, Herder was already extending ontological and epistemological import to speech, and he was clearly signaling his intent to develop his aesthetic approaches around language. The underlying role of language in song, and by extension music, is one of the most persistent themes in this book. Common to the repertory that fills the volumes of folk songs from 1774 and then 1778/79 is the role of language. Language provides a historical connection between songs through translation, and the aesthetic rules of imitation and creativity forge the processes that shape song from one historical moment to the next.

History Herder argues for a close relation between language as history and song as history. We witness this in the present book in the emphasis placed on epic, the genre of song that transmits history through oral tradition. It was epic that connected the Moses of the Pentateuch to Homer to Ossian to the *Cid*. The transition from oral to written tradition, moreover, was crucially historical for Herder, and it was essential for the ways in which the narratives of song—epic is a narrative genre—enter the human soul and shape the human spirit. In the bold strokes of Herder's historical writings, the perfection of the human spirit was idealized, while at the same time remaining open to the diverse possibilities of histories that lay outside the history of European civilization to which Herder repeatedly returned for comparison.

Politics Herder is a political writer, even when striving most consciously for an aesthetic equality across a universal history of humanity. Politics pervaded his own life, not least because he was always in service to the aristocracy, even when professionally positioned as a religious leader. In many ways Herder's constant search for more comfortable political shores reveals much about the shifting language with which he treats the nation. He does use the term "nation" (the same in German as in English) throughout his writings, but his use reflects different, and eventually complex, understandings of what a nation is. In the early stages of history, a nation was a loose bundle of language, literature, society, and religion. In Herder's own century, an age of revolution, the concept of nation described a political entity with a common culture, even when still inchoate, as in the case of the musical and literary Germany Herder sought to will into existence. Despite the degree to which the nation was changing in Herder's writings, the chapters of the present book reveal that music was increasingly critical for understanding its modern identities.

Music When music appears in *Journal meiner Reise im Jahr 1769*, it does not appear by itself, isolated from the other arts or as a separate pursuit for the students Herder envisaged for a world shaped by new experiences and gathered in a radically new educational system. In 1769, music continued to occupy the "outer" world for Herder, manifest in "tones" and "shapes" that together constitute objects. Largely unnamed at the time of Herder's journey, however, music would move to its "inner" subjectivity in the soul and the heart the moment Herder reached the end of the journey, at which time he would embark on the major musical projects of the 1770s. The tension between the external object and the internal subject of music remained central to Herder's thought for the rest of his life, remaining unresolved even in the writings on music from his final years, when it was unleashed from all that would bind it to the past, language, and nature, embarking once again on a journey to the transcendent and the sublime.

The tale of two Herders has also come to depend on the availability and accessibility of his writings. Herder editions—complete, selected, with specific disciplinary areas—have appeared at various times during the more than two hundred years since his death, but these reflect the intellectual history of which he has been a part in different ways, leaving him, in Michael Maurer's words, a *bekannter Unbekannter* (someone known for being unknown) (Maurer 2014, 18–20). New editions and translations would seem to rectify this situation, but they also seem not to resolve a persistent enigma expressed in the need to distinguish what people have thought Herder said from what he really said. It may well be the case that this "really" does not reduce to singular explanations and convenient conclusions. Rather, it remains the subject for a longer search—indeed, the journey that Herder himself set in motion. It is that journey, with its incomplete and rerouted return voyages, that has provided the metaphor connecting the chapters in *Song Loves the Masses*.

As he reaches the final pages of *Journal meiner Reise im Jahr 1769*, Herder expresses a growing anxiety about the return voyage, particularly the ways in which it would mean that he had to abandon his encounter with new ideas and retreat to shores that, though more familiar, would lead him finally toward atrophy at the final stages of life:

> As long as the mind, or the mirror of the soul, remains intimate and tender, is capable of absorbing each new image, with complete force, in all colors and nuances, with each truth, experience, and flexibility, we possess the tender and maturing youth of the soul! . . . There is more anxiety in the soul, however, even as it encounters new experiences in a different culture, for it returns also to revisit the old, which is already familiar. And this, too, is pleasing, the fruitfulness of encountering new ideas, just as the dependence on old friends is a sign of aging. (Herder 1769, 149)

We, too, return to the question of Herder's journey and why he chose not to publish his *Journal*, one of the seminal works of his early career and the intimate record of life-changing events. The *Journal* was itself a mirror of Herder's soul, just as it reflected all the new experiences that provided ethnographic and philosophical direction for his 1769 journey. In the course of the voyage, he laid the foundations of a world for which he would unceasingly search, knowing full well he would never land on its shores. From the beginning of Herder's life journey until its close, music, in all the universality of its diversity, would draw him increasingly toward those shores, dangerously, like a siren, and yet intimately, in the songs so beloved by humanity.

Notes

PROLOGUE

1. Herder's translation into the German, which appears in *Vom Geist der ebräischen Poesie* (1787), is as follows:

"GEFANGENSCHAFT IN BABEL"
DER 137. PSALM

An Babels Strömen saßen wir
und weinten, wenn wir an Zion dachten:
An ihren Weiden hingen unsre Harfen.

Zwar foderten daselbst, die uns gefangen hielten,
Lieder von uns;
unsre Dränger heischten von uns Freude:
"Der Zions-Lieder singet uns doch Eins!" –
Wie sollen wir singen Jehovahs Lied
in einem fremden Lande! –

Vergäß' ich dein, o Jerusalem;
so vergesse meiner die Rechte!
Es hange meine Jung' an meinem Gaum,
wenn ich nicht dein gedenke! –
wenn nicht Jerusalem allein
mein höchste Freude bleibt!

Gedenk' o Herr, gedenk der Töchter Edoms
am Unglücks-Tage Jerusalems,
da sie ausriefen: Reißet ein!
reißt ein bis auf den Grund!

Tochter Babels! Verwüstete!
Heil ihm, der dir vergilt!
der dir vergilt, was du an uns getan.
Heil ihm, der deine Säuglinge ergreift,
und wirft sie an den Fels.
(JGHW5 [1787], 1208–9)

CHAPTER 2

1. Herder's German translation of the epigraph from *Hamlet*, in which Laertes is speaking to his sister, Ophelia:

... Sind Veilchen in des Jahres Jugend, sind
Erstlinge der Natur, früh und nicht daurend,
Süß, aber bald dahin: Der Duft, die Blüthe
Von wenigen Minuten ...

2. Translations of Shakespeare into German multiplied during the mid-eighteenth century, with the first translation of his complete works, by Johann Joachim Eschenburg, appearing between 1775 and 1782, almost exactly at the time the folk song project was coalescing. Herder's contemporaries in Weimar, Friedrich Schiller and Johann Wolfgang von Goethe, were known on occasion as "the German Shakespeares." Among the German literary figures contributing to German translations were August Wilhelm von Schlegel and Ludwig Tieck.

3. The number of songs in individual books differs, and the figure of twenty-four as the projected contents remains approximate. The first two books of part 1, nonetheless, contain exactly twenty-four songs each. When Herder created his own translation into German of the Spanish *El Cid*, he divided the epic into seventy cantos, again approximating the division of the entire epic into three parts with twenty-four songs each (see chapter 8).

4. The most recent edition, for example, published for widespread reader distribution through the well-known Reclam house of Stuttgart and Leipzig, appeared with the title *"Stimmen der Völker in Liedern" / Volkslieder* (Herder 1975).

5. The contrast between *Volk* and *Völker* has a long history in the social sciences of the German-speaking lands, for example in the disciplinary designations of folklore as *Volkskunde* and anthropology as *Völkerkunde*.

CHAPTER 3

1. Although both the *Songs of Solomon* and the *Song of Songs* are common translations, I use the latter throughout the present chapter because it is closer to the Hebrew *Shir ha-shirim*. Herder's title, *Lieder der Liebe* (Love Songs), is his own invention.

CHAPTER 6

1. Herder speaks of the *gemeiner Mensch*, which glosses roughly as the "common man." "Common," used in this way, combines the sense of individuals sharing common culture, but also who are connected when culture and religion are most universal.
2. Published as the ninth volume in the modern collected writings (JGHW9/1, 547–55).
3. Interpretation of Herder as a theologian employed by religious institutions provides the substance of Schmidt 1956. See also the essay "Herder als Theologe," in JGHW9/1 (Bultmann and Zippert 1994, 861–78).
4. In the summer of 2015, as I write the present chapter, two important moral essays appeared in epistolary form: Pope Francis's encyclical on the environment and climate change in June, and Ta-Nehisi Coates's letter to his son about the difficulties of growing up black in contemporary American society, which appeared in July as an epistolary novel (Coates 2015). For the papal encyclical see http://w2.vatican.va/content/francesco/en/encyclicals/documents/papa-francesco_20150524_enciclica-laudato-si.html.
5. *Briefe zu Beförderung der Humanität*.

CHAPTER 7

1. The fourth and concluding chapter of *Über die Wirkung der Dichtkunst auf die Sitten der Völker in alten und neuen Zeiten* (JGHW4, 197–214). The essays originally appeared as a response to a question posed in 1777 for a competition by the Bavarian Academy of Sciences, "What Influences Did the Poetry of Ancient Times Have on the Customs of the People? What Influences Today?" Herder's essay was unanimously voted the winning entry, and he was awarded the medal and a sum of ten ducats on February 25, 1778.

CHAPTER 8

1. Editions of Herder's *Cid* used for chapter 8:

PRIMARY EDITION

Der Cid—Geschichte des Don Ruy Diaz, Grafen von Bivar, nach spanischen Romanzen. 1990. In Ulrich Gaier, ed. *Johann Gottfried Herder Werke*. Vol. 3, *Volkslieder, Übertragungen, Dichtungen*, 545–693. Frankfurt am Main: Deutscher Klassiker Verlag.

SECONDARY EDITIONS

de Escobar, Juan. 1605. *Historia del muy valeroso Cavallero Don Rodrigo de Bivar, el bravo Cid Campeador*. Lisbon.
Der Cid nach spanischen Romanzen besungen durch Herder. 1869. Berlin: G. Grote'sche Verlagsbuchhandlung.
Groth, Ernst, ed. 1920. *Der Cid nach spanischen Romanzen besungen von Johann Gottfried Herder*. Deutsche Schulausgaben 59. Bielefeld und Leipzig: Velhagen und Klafing.
Herder, Johann Gottfried von. 1894. *Der Cid: Geschichte des Don Ruy Diaz, Grafen von Bivar*. Edited by Rudolf Reichel. Freytags Schulausgaben classischer Werke für den deutschen Unterricht. Vienna and Prague: Verlag von F. Tempsky.
Schmidt, Julian, ed. 1868. *Der Cid: Nach spanischen Romanzen besungen durch Johann Gottfried von Herder*. Leipzig: F. A. Brockhaus.

Bibliography

HERDER EDITIONS

Ausgewählte Werke. 1884–1901. Edited by Bernhard Suphan. 5 vols. Berlin: Weidmann.
Herder: Ein Lesebuch für unsere Zeit. 1962. Edited by Wilhelm Dobbek. Lesebücher für unsere Zeit. Weimar: Volksverlag.
Herder/Goethe/Frisi/Möser: Von deutscher Art und Kunst. 1968. Edited by Hans Dietrich Irmscher. Stuttgart: Reclam.
Herder on Social and Political Culture. 1969. Translated and edited by F.M. Barnard. Cambridge, England: Cambridge University Press.
Herders Sämmtliche Werke. 1877–1913. Edited by Bernhard Suphan. 33 vols. Berlin: Weidmann.
Herders Volkslieder. 1885. Edited by Carl Redlich. Suphans Herder-Ausgabe. Auswahl. Berlin: Weidmann.
Johann Gottfried Herder, Journal meiner Reise im Jahr 1769. 1985. Illustrated by Johannes Lencker, Lorenz Stöer, and Wenzel Jamnitzer. Nördlingen: Delphi.
Johann Gottfried Herder: Werke in zehn Bänden. 1985–2000. Edited by Günter Arnold et al. 11 vols. Frankfurt am Main: Deutscher Klassiker Verlag. [Cited as JGHW in this book].
Kalligone. 1955. Edited by Heinz Begenau. Weimar: Hermann Böhlaus Nachfolger.
Lieder der Liebe: Die ältesten und schönsten aus Morgenlande, nebst vier und vierzig alten Minneliedern. 1992. Zurich: Manesse.
Philosophical Writings. 2002a. Translated and edited by Michael N. Forster. Cambridge Texts in the History of Philosophy. Cambridge, England: Cambridge University Press.
Sculpture: Some Observations on Shape and Form from Pygmalion's Creative Dream. 2002b. Edited and translated by Jason Gaiger. Chicago: University of Chicago Press.

Selected Writings on Aesthetics. 2006. Translated and edited by Gregory Moore. Princeton, NJ: Princeton University Press.
The Spirit of Hebrew Poetry. 1833. Translated by James Marsh. Burlington, VT: Edward Smith.
Sprachphilosophie: Ausgewählte Schriften. 1960. Edited by Erich Heintel. Philosophische Bibliothek 248. Hamburg: Felix Meiner.
Stimmen der Völker in Liedern and *Volkslieder*. 1975. Edited by Heinz Rölleke. Stuttgart: Reclam.
Stimmen der Völker in Liedern. 1807. Edited by Johann von Müller. 2nd edition of *Volkslieder* (1778/79). Tübingen: J. G. Cotta.

ADDITIONAL WORKS BY JOHANN GOTTFRIED HERDER CITED IN THE BOOK

1985 [1764]. *Versuch über das Sein*. In Ulrich Gaier, ed. *Johann Gottfried Herder Werke*. Vol. 1, *Johann Gottfried Herder: Frühe Schriften, 1764–1772*, 9–21. Frankfurt am Main: Deutscher Klassiker Verlag.

1985 [1764]. *Dithyrambische Rhapsodie über die Rhapsodie kabbalistischer Prose*. In Ulrich Gaier, ed. *Johann Gottfried Herder Werke*. Vol. 1, *Johann Gottfried Herder: Frühe Schriften, 1764–1772*, 30–39. Frankfurt am Main: Deutscher Klassiker Verlag.

1989 [1768–]. *Ideen zur Philosophie der Geschichte der Menschheit*. In Martin Bollacher, ed. *Johann Gottfried Herder Werke*. Vol. 6, *Herder: Ideen zur Philosophie der Geschichte der Menschheit*. Frankfurt am Main: Deutscher Klassiker Verlag.

1997 [1769]. *Journal meiner Reise im Jahr 1769*. In *Johann Gottfried Herder Werke*. Vol. 9/2, 9–126. Edited by Rainer Wisbert and Klaus Pradel. Frankfurt am Main: Deutscher Klassiker Verlag. Also: 1976 [1769]. *Journal meiner Reise im Jahr 1769*. Stuttgart: Reclam.

1772. *Abhandlung über den Ursprung der Sprache*. Berlin: Christian Friedrich Voß.

1774. *Auch eine Philosophie der Geschichte zur Bildung der Menschheit*. No place or publisher.

1778. *Lieder der Liebe: Die ältesten und schönsten aus Morgenlande, nebst vier und vierzig alten Minneliedern*. Leipzig: Weygandsche Buchhandlung.

1995 [1787]. *Vom Geist der ebräischen Poesie*. In Rudolf Smend, ed. *Johann Gottfried Herder Werke*. Vol. 5, *Schriften zum Alten Testament*, 661–1308. Frankfurt am Main: Deutscher Klassiker Verlag.

1988. *Italienische Reise: Briefe und Tagebuchaufzeichnungen, 1788–1789*. Edited and with commentary and an afterword by Albert Meier and Heide Hollmer. Munich: Deutscher Taschenbuch Verlag.

EDITIONS OF HERDER'S *CID*

de Escobar, Juan. 1605. *Historia del muy valeroso Cavallero Don Rodrigo de Bivar, el bravo Cid Campeador.* Lisbon.
Der Cid: Geschichte des Don Ruy Diaz, Grafen von Bivar. 1894. Edited by Rudolf Reichel. Freytags Schulausgaben classischer Werke für den deutschen Unterricht. Vienna and Prague: Verlag von F. Tempsky.
Der Cid—Geschichte des Don Ruy Diaz, Grafen von Bivar, nach spanischen Romanzen. 1990. In Ulrich Gaier, ed. *Johann Gottfried Herder Werke.* Vol. 3, *Volkslieder, Übertragungen, Dichtungen,* 545–693. Frankfurt am Main: Deutscher Klassiker Verlag.
Der Cid nach spanischen Romanzen besungen durch Herder. 1869. Berlin: G. Grote'sche Verlagsbuchhandlung.
Groth, Ernst, ed. 1920. *Der Cid nach spanischen Romanzen besungen von Johann Gottfried Herder.* Deutsche Schulausgaben 59. Bielefeld und Leipzig: Velhagen und Klafing.
Schmidt, Julian, ed. 1868. *Der Cid: Nach spanischen Romanzen besungen durch Johann Gottfried von Herder.* Leipzig: F.A. Brockhaus.

SECONDARY LITERATURE

Adam, Johannes. 1911. *Übersetzung und Glossar des altspanischen Poema del Cid.* Breslau: K.B. Hof- und Univ.–Buchdruckerei von Junge und Sohn.
Adler, Hans. 1990. *Die Prägnanz des Dunklen: Gnoseologie, Ästhetik, Geschichtsphilosophie bei J.G. Herder.* Studien zum achtzehnten Jahrhundert 13. Hamburg: Felix Meiner Verlag.
Adler, Hans, and Wulf Koepke, eds. 2009a. *A Companion to the Works of Johann Gottfried Herder.* Rochester: Camden House.
———. 2009b. "Introduction." In *A Companion to the Works of Johann Gottfried Herder,* 15–41. Rochester: Camden House.
Akademie der Wissenschaften der DDR, ed. 1978. *Johann Gottfried Herder: Zum 175. Todestag am 18. Dezember 1978.* Berlin: Akademie-Verlag.
Altschul, Nadia R. 2012. *Geographies of Philological Knowledge: Postcoloniality and the Transatlantic Epic.* Chicago: University of Chicago Press.
Andraschke, Peter, and Helmut Loos, eds. 2002. *Ideen und Ideale: Johann Gottfried Herder in Ost und West.* Reihe Litterae 103. Freiburg im Breisgau: Rombach.
Andruchowytsch, Juri, and Andrzej Stasiuk. 2004. *Mein Europa: Zwei Essays über das sogenannte Europa.* Translated by Sofia Onufriv and Martin Pollack. Frankfurt am Main: Suhrkamp.
Armistead, Samuel G., and Joseph H. Silverman. 1986. *Judeo-Spanish Ballads from Oral Tradition.* Vol. 1, *Epic Ballads.* Folk Literature of the Sephardic Jews 2. Berkeley: University of California Press.

Arnim, L. Achim von, and Clemens Brentano. 1806 and 1808. *Des Knaben Wunderhorn: Alte deutsche Lieder.* Heidelberg: Mohr und Zimmer.

Arnold, Günter, Kurt Kloocke, and Ernest A. Menze. 2009. "Herder's Reception and Influence." In *A Companion to the Works of Johann Gottfried Herder,* edited by Hans Adler and Wulf Koepke, 391–419. Rochester: Camden House.

d'Arvieux, Laurent. 1717. *Voyage dans la Palestine.* Paris: A. Cailleau.

Baildam, John D. 1999. *Paradisal Love: Johann Gottfried Herder and the Song of Songs.* Sheffield, England: Sheffield Academic Press.

Bakhtin, Mikhail M. 1981. *The Dialogical Imagination: Four Essays.* Translated by Michael Holquist and Caryl Emerson. Edited by Michael Holquist. Austin: University of Texas Press.

———. 1990. "Author and Hero in Aesthetic Activity." In *Art and Answerability: Early Philosophical Works by M. M. Bakhtin,* translated by Vadim Liapunov, edited by Michael Holquist and Vadim Liapunov, 4–256. Austin: University of Texas Press.

Barnard, F. M. 1969. "Introduction." In Johann Gottfried Herder, *Herder on Social and Political Culture,* translated and edited by F. M. Barnard, 3–60. Cambridge, England: Cambridge University Press.

———. 2003. *Herder on Nationality, Humanity, and History.* McGill-Queen's Studies in the History of Ideas. Montreal and Kingston: McGill-Queen's University Press.

Bartholin, Thomas. 1689. *Antiquitatum Danicarum de causis contemptae a Danis adhuc gentilibus mortis libri tres.* Copenhagen: Literis Joh. Phil. Bockenhoffer.

Barton, Simon, and Richard Fletcher. 2000. *The World of El-Cid: Chronicles of the Spanish Reconquest.* Manchester: Manchester University Press.

Baumgarten, Alexander. 1954. *Reflections on Poetry: Meditationes philosophicae de nonnullis ad poema pertinentibus.* Translated by Karl Aschenbrenner and William B. Holther. Berkeley: University of California Press.

———. 1983. *Theoretische Ästhetik: Die grundlegenden Abschnitte aus der "Aesthetica" (1750/1758).* Hamburg: Felix Meiner.

Becker, Max. 1996. *Narkotikum und Utopie: Musik-Konzepte in Empfindsamkeit und Romantik.* Musiksoziologie 1. Kassel: Bärenreiter.

Beissinger, Margaret, Jane Tylus, and Susanne Wofford, eds. 1999. *Epic Traditions in the Contemporary World: The Poetics of Community.* Berkeley: University of California Press.

Benjamin, Walter. 1963. *Ursprung des deutschen Trauerspiels.* Frankfurt am Main: Suhrkamp.

Bishop, Samuel. 1766. *Ferias poeticas: Carmina Anglicana elegiaci plerumque argumenti latine reddita.* London: D. Leach.

Blair, Hugh. 1763. *Critical Dissertation on the Poems of Ossian.* London: T. Becket and P. A. De Hondt.

Bodmer, Johann Jakob. 1781. *Altenglische und altschwäbische Balladen.* Zurich: n.p.

Bohlman, Philip V. 1988. *The Study of Folk Music in the Modern World.* Bloomington: Indiana University Press.

———. 1992. "Die Vorstellungen vom Judentum in der 'Schönen Jüdin.'" In *Deutsche Volkslieder mit ihren Melodien*, vol. 9, edited by Jürgen Dittmar und Wiegand Stief, 79–84. Freiburg im Breisgau: Deutsches Volksliedarchiv.

———. 2002. "Landscape–Region–Nation–Reich: German Folk Song in the Nexus of Nationalism." In *Music and German National Identity*, edited by Celia Applegate and Pamela Potter, 105–27. Chicago: University of Chicago Press.

———. 2004. *The Music of European Nationalism: Cultural Identity and Modern History*. 1st ed. World Music Series. Santa Barbara, CA: ABC-CLIO.

———. 2010a. "600 Jahre DDR–Musikgeschichte—am Beispiel deutscher Volkslieder demokratischen Charakters." In *Musikwissenschaft und Kalter Krieg—Das Beispiel DDR*, edited by Nina Noeske and Matthias Tischer, 79–95. Cologne: Böhlau.

———. 2010b. "Herder's Nineteenth Century." *Nineteenth-Century Music Review* 7 (1): 3–21.

———. 2011a. *Focus: Music, Nationalism, and the Making of the New Europe*. Rev. 2nd ed. Focus on World Music Series. New York: Routledge.

———. 2011b. "Translating Herder Translating: Cultural Translation and the Making of Modernity." In *The Oxford Handbook of the New Cultural History of Music*, edited by Jane F. Fulcher, 501–22. New York: Oxford University Press.

———. 2011c. "Stimmen der Lieder in Völkern: 'Musikalische Einheiten' in der Einheit der Nation." In *Musikalien des Übergangs: Festschrift für Gerlinde Haid anlässlich ihrer Emeritierung 2011*, edited by Ursula Hemetek, Evelyn Fink-Mennel, and Rudolf Pietsch, 67–82. Vienna: Böhlau.

———. 2012. "Found in Translation: Epic, Song, and the Discovery of the Mediterranean." *Journal of Mediterranean Studies* 21 (2): 219–34.

———, ed. 2013a. *The Cambridge History of World Music*. Cambridge, England: Cambridge University Press.

———. 2013b. "Johann Gottfried Herder and the Global Moment of World-Music History." In *The Cambridge History of World Music*, edited by Philip V. Bohlman, 255–76. Cambridge, England: Cambridge University Press.

———. 2017. *Wie sängen wir Seinen Gesang auf dem Boden der Fremde! Jüdische Musik zwischen Aschkenas und Moderne*. KlangKulturStudien. Berlin: LIT Verlag.

Bohlman, Philip V., and Otto Holzapfel. 2001. *The Folk Songs of Ashkenaz*. Middleton, WI: A-R Editions.

Bohlman, Philip V., and Nada Petković, eds. 2012. *Balkan Epic: Song, History, Modernity*. Europea: Ethnomusicologies and Modernities 11. Lanham, MD: Scarecrow.

Bollacher, Martin. 2003. "'Feines, scharfsinniges Volk, ein Wunder der Zeiten!'—Herders Verhältnis zum Judentum und zur jüdischen Welt." In *Hebräische Poesie und jüdischer Volksgeist: Die Wirkungsgeschichte von Johann Gottfried Herder im Judentum Mittel- und Osteuropas*, edited by Christoph Schulte, 17–33. Hildesheim: Georg Olms Verlag.

Borsche, Tilman, ed. 2006. *Herder im Spiegel der Zeiten: Verwerfungen der Rezeptionsgeschichte und Chancen einer Relektüre*. Munich: Wilhelm Fink.
Buber, Martin. 1962. *Die Schrift*. Vol. 4, *Die Schriftwerke*. Translated from Hebrew to German by Martin Buber. 6th ed. Stuttgart: Deutsche Bibelgesellschaft.
Buchanan, John Lanne. 1793. *Travels in the Western Hebrides, from 1782 to 1790*. London: Robinson and Debrett.
———. 1795. *Reisen durch die Westlichen Hebriden, während 1782 bis 1790*. Berlin: Maurer.
Buchholtz, Samuel. 1765. *Versuch einer Geschichte der Churmarck Brandenburg*. Berlin: n.p.
Bultmann, Christoph. 2009. "Herder's Biblical Studies." In *A Companion to the Works of Johann Gottfried Herder*, edited by Hans Adler and Wulf Koepke, 233–46. Rochester: Camden House.
Bultmann, Christoph, and Thomas Zippert. 1994. "Herder als Theologe." In JGHW9/1, 861–78.
Burke, James F. 1991. *Structures from the Trivium in the "Cantar de Mio Cid."* Toronto: University of Toronto Press.
Buth, Matthias. 2003. "Epilog, vor einem Krieg: Herder, die deutsche und die jüdische Kultur." In *Hebräische Poesie und jüdischer Volksgeist: Die Wirkungsgeschichte von Johann Gottfried Herder im Judentum Mittel- und Osteuropas*, edited by Christoph Schulte, 257–64. Hildesheim: Georg Olms Verlag.
Butler, Samuel. 1674–78. *Hubidras*. Parts 1 and 2. London: John Martyn and Henry Herringman.
Cancionero de romances. 1568. *Cancionero de romances, en que están recopilados la mayor parte de los romances Castellanos que hasta agora se han compuesto*. Antwerp: Philippo Nucio.
Catholic Encyclopedia. 2007. "El Cid." Accessed July 13, 2016. http://www.newadvent.org/cathen/03769a.htm.
Cesarotti, Melchiore. 1763. *Poesia di Ossian Figlio di Fingal antico Poeta Celtico ultimamente scoperte e tradotte in prosa Inglese da Jacopo Macpherson*. Padua: Appresso Giuseppo Comino.
de Charlevoix, Pierre François Xavier. 1744. *Histoire et déscription générale de la Nouvelle France*. Paris: P. F. Giffart.
Chasca, Edmund de. 1976. *The Poem of the Cid*. Boston: Twayne Publishers.
Cheesman, Tom. 2001. "The Turkish German Self: Displacing German-German Conflict in Oriental Street Ballads." In *Imagined States: Nationalism, Utopia, and Longing in Oral Cultures*, edited by Luisa Del Giudice and Gerald Porter, 136–63. Logan: Utah State University Press.
Clarke, H. Butler. 1897. *The Cid Campeador and the Waning of the Crescent in the West*. Heroes of the Nations. New York: G. P. Putnam's Sons.
Claudius, Matthias. 1778. "Puter puter Schneiderscherz." In *Voßscher Musenalmanach* (1778), 130. Berlin: Christian Friedrich Voss.
Clissold, Stephen. 1965. *In Search of the Cid*. London: Hodder and Stoughton.
Coates, Ta-Nehisi. 2015. *Between the World and Me*. New York: Spiegel and Grau.
Cohen, Hermann. 1912. *Ästhetik des reinen Gefühls*. Berlin: B. Cassirer.

Colden, Cadwallader. 1727. *The History of the Five Indian Nations Depending on the Province of New-York in America.* New York: William Bradford.
Constantine, Mary-Ann, and Gerald Porter. 2003. *Fragments and Meaning in Traditional Song: From the Blues to the Baltic.* British Academy Postdoctoral Fellowship Monograph. London: The British Academy.
Corneille, Pierre. 1931. *The Cid.* Translated by Paul Landis. In *Six Plays by Corneille and Racine.* Edited by Paul Landis. New York: The Modern Library.
Cornelius, Peter. 1865. "Ouverture zum lyrischen Drama, Der Cid." In *Der Cid.* Opera. London: Ernst Eulenburg.
Cranz, David. 1765. *Historie von Grönland.* Barby and Leipzig: H. D. Ebers.
Davis, Richard H. 2015. *The "Bhagavad Gita": A Biography.* Lives of Great Religious Books. Princeton, NJ: Princeton University Press.
Denis, Michael. 1772. *Lieder Sineds, des Barden.* Vienna: Johann Thomas Edlen von Trattnern.
Deyermond. A. D. 1968. *Epic Poetry and the Clergy: Studies on the "Mocedades de Rodrigo."* London: Tamesis Books.
Diamond, Beverley. 2008. *Native American Music in Eastern North America: Experiencing Music, Expressing Culture.* New York: Oxford University Press.
Dobbek, Wilhelm, ed. 1962. *Herder: Ein Lesebuch für unsere Zeit.* Weimar: Volksverlag.
Dohrn, Verena. 2003. "Bundistische und folkloristische Konzeptionen der Kulturnation—inspiriert von Johann Gottfried Herder." In *Hebräische Poesie und jüdischer Volksgeist: Die Wirkungsgeschichte von Johann Gottfried Herder im Judentum Mittel- und Osteuropas,* edited by Christoph Schulte, 167–79. Hildesheim: Georg Olms Verlag.
DuBois, Thomas A. 2006. *Lyric, Meaning, and Audience in the Oral Tradition of Northern Europe.* Notre Dame, IN: University of Notre Dame Press.
Duggan, Joseph J. 1989. *The "Cantar de mio Cid": Poetic Creation in Its Economic and Social Contexts.* Cambridge Studies in Medieval Literature 5. Cambridge, England: Cambridge University Press.
Duttenhofer, F. M. 1833. *Der Cid: Ein Romanzen-Kranz.* Stuttgart: F. C. Löflund und Söhne.
Eckhard, Johann Georg von. 1729. *Commentarii de rebus Franciae orientalis et episcopatus Wirceburgensis.* 2 vols. Würzburg: H. Engmann.
Falkenstein, Johann Heinrich von. 1739. *Civitatis Erffurtensis Historia.* Erfurt: Johann Wilhelm Ritschel.
Forster, Michael N. 2002. "Herder's Philosophy of Language, Interpretation, and Translation: Three Fundamental Principles." *Review of Metaphysics* 56: 323–56.
———. 2010. *After Herder: Philosophy of Language in the German Tradition.* Oxford: Oxford University Press.
Fugate, Joe K. 1966. *The Psychological Basis of Herder's Aesthetics.* Studies in Philosophy 10. The Hague: Mouton.
Funkenstein, Amos. 1993. *Perceptions of Jewish History.* Berkeley and Los Angeles: University of California Press.

Gaier, Ulrich. 1990. "Kommentar." In Ulrich Gaier. *Johann Gottfried Herder Werke*. Vol. 3. Frankfurt am Main: Deutscher Klassiker Verlag.

———. 2009. "Myth, Mythology, New Mythology." In *A Companion to the Works of Johann Gottfried Herder*, edited by Hans Adler and Wulf Koepke, 165–88. Rochester: Camden House.

Gärtner, Karl Christian, ed. 1744–57. *Neue Beiträge zum Vergnügen des Verstandes und des Witzes*. Bremen: N. Saurmann.

Gaskill, Howard. 1989. "German Ossianism: A Reappraisal." *German Life and Letters* 42: 329–41.

———, ed. 1991. *Ossian Revisited*. Edinburgh: Edinburgh University Press.

———. 1994. "Ossian in Europe." *Canadian Review of Comparative Literature* 21: 643–78.

———. 1996. "Herder, Ossian and the Celtic." In *Celticism*, edited by Terence Brown, 257–71. Amsterdam: Rodopi.

———. 2001. "'Aus der dritten Hand': Herder and His Annotators." *German Life and Letters* 54 (3): 210–18.

Gelbart, Matthew. 2007. *The Invention of "Folk Music" and "Art Music": Emerging Categories from Ossian to Wagner*. New Perspectives in Music History and Criticism. Cambridge, England: Cambridge University Press.

———. 2009. "'The Language of Music': Music as Historical Crucible for the Methodology of Folkloristics." *Ethnomusicology* 53 (2): 363–95.

Gerstenberg, Heinrich Wilhelm von. 1971 [1815]. *Vermischte Schriften*. 3 vols. in 2. Frankfurt am Main: Athenäum.

Ghosh, Pranabendra Nath. 1990. *Johann Gottfried Herder's Image of India*. Santiniketan, India: Visva-Bharati Research Publications.

Gillies, Alexander. 1933. *Herder und Ossian*. Neue Forschung, Arbeiten zur Geistesgeschichte der germanischen und romanischen Völker. Berlin: Junker und Dünnhaupt Verlag.

———. 1945. *Herder*. Oxford: B. Blackwell.

Giordanetti, Piero. 2005. *Kant und die Musik*. Würzburg: Königshausen und Neumann.

Giudice, Luisa Del, and Gerald Porter, eds. 2001. *Imagined States: Nationalism, Utopia, and Longing in Oral Cultures*. Logan: Utah State University Press.

Glafey, Adam F. 1568. *Kern der Geschichte des Chur- und Fürstlichen Hauses Sachsen-Altenburg*. Nuremberg: n.p.

Gleichen, Karl Heinrich von. 1791. *Metaphysische Kezereien oder Versuche über die verborgensten Gegenstände der Weltweisheit und ihre Grundursachen*. Regensburg: n.p.

Greif, Stefan. 2009. "Herder's Aesthetics and Poetics." In *A Companion to the Works of Johann Gottfried Herder*, edited by Hans Adler and Wulf Koepke, 165–88. Rochester: Camden House.

Gutsleff, Eberhard. 1732. *Kurzgefaßte Anweisung zur Esthnischen Sprache*. Halle: Orban.

Habermas, Jürgen. 1990. *Die Moderne, ein unvollendetes Projekt: Philosophisch-politische Aufsätze, 1977–1990*. Leipzig: Reclam.

HaCohen, Ruth. 2011. *The Music Libel against the Jews*. New Haven, CT: Yale University Press.
Häfner, Ralph. 1995. *Johann Gottfried Herders Kulturentstehungslehre: Studien zu den Quellen und zur Methode seines Geschichtsdenkens*. Studien zum achtzehnten Jahrhundert 19. Hamburg: Felix Meiner Verlag.
Hämel, Adalbert. 1910. *Der Cid im spanischen Drama des XVI. und XVII. Jahrhunderts*. Halle: Ehrhardt Karras.
Harder, Johann Jakob. 1764. *Untersuchung des Gottesdienstes, der Wissenschaften, Handwerke, Regierungsarten und Sitten der alten Letten, und ihrer Sprache (Gelehrte Beyträge zu den Rigischen Anzeigen)*. Riga: Hartknoch.
Harrán, Don. 1999. *Salamone Rossi: Jewish Musician in Late Renaissance Mantua*. Oxford: Oxford University Press.
Harries, Elizabeth Wanning. 1994. *The Unfinished Manner: Essays on the Fragment in the Later Eighteenth Century*. Charlottesville: University of Virginia Press.
Hasselquist, D. Friedrich. 1762. *Reise nach Palästina in den Jahren von 1749 bis 1752*. Rostock: J. C. Koppe.
Haym, Rudolf. 1958. *Herder*. 2 vols. Berlin: Aufbau-Verlag.
Heim, Johannes. 1766. *Hennebergische Chronik*. Meiningen: Hartmann.
Heinz, Marion, and Heinrich Clairmont. 2009. "Herder's Epistemology." In *A Companion to the Works of Johann Gottfried Herder*, edited by Hans Adler and Wulf Koepke, 43–64. Rochester: Camden House.
Heise, Jens. 1998. *Johann Gottfried Herder zur Einführung*. Zur Einführung. Hamburg: Junius Verlag.
Herder Yearbook: Publications of the International Herder Society. 1992–ongoing. Rochester: Camden House.
Hess, Jonathan M. 2002. *Germans, Jews and the Claims of Modernity*. New Haven, CT: Yale University Press.
Heupel, Georg Friedrich. 1693. *Dissertatio historico-philologica de Ulphila, seu versione IV. Evangelistarum Gothica*. Wittenberg: G. W. Kirchmajer.
Hickes, George. 1705. *Linguarum veterum septemtrionalium thesaurus grammatico-criticus et archaeologicus*. Oxford: Sheldonian Theatre.
Hippel, Theodor Gottlieb von. 1779. *Lebensläufe nach aufsteigender Linie*. Vol. 1. Berlin: C. F. Voss.
Hirschhausen, Ulrike von, and Jörn Leonhard, eds. 2001. *Nationalismen in Europa: West- und Osteuropa im Vergleich*. Göttingen: Wallstein.
Hoeckner, Berthold. 2002. *Programming the Absolute: Nineteenth-Century German Music and the Hermeneutics of the Moment*. Princeton, NJ: Princeton University Press.
Höfel, Johann. 1681. *Historisches Gesangbuch*. Schleusingen: Göbel.
Holt, Fabian. 2007. *Genre in Popular Music*. Chicago: University of Chicago Press.
Homer. 1778. *Homers Werke*. Edited by Johann Jakob Bodmer. Zurich: Bey Orell, Gessner, Füesslin und Compaignie.
Hupel, August Wilhelm. 1777. *Topographische Nachrichten von Lief- und Esthland*. Vol. 2. Riga: Hartknoch.

le Huray, Peter, and James Day, eds. 1981. *Music and Aesthetics in the Eighteenth and Early Nineteenth Centuries*. Cambridge, England: Cambridge University Press.

Irmscher, Hans Dietrich. 1998. "'Metakritik' und 'Kalligone.'" In *Schriften zu Literatur und Philosophie, 1792–1800*. Vol. 8, *Johann Gottfried Herder Werke*, edited by Hans Dietrich Irmscher, 1062–70. Frankfurt am Main: Deutscher Klassiker Verlag.

———. 1999. "Nachwort." In Johann Gottfried Herder, *Von deutscher Art und Kunst: Einige fliegende Blätter*, 163–96. Stuttgart: Reclam.

———. 2001. *Johann Gottfried Herder*. Stuttgart: Reclam.

Jaremko-Porter, Christina. 2009. "Johann Gottfried Herder and the Latvian Voice." PhD diss., University of Edinburgh.

Kant, Immanuel. 1781. *Kritik der reinen Vernunft*. Riga: Hartknoch.

———. 1790. *Kritik der Urteilskraft*. Berlin and Liepāja: Lagarde und Friederich.

Kantzenbach, Friedrich Wilhelm. 1970. *Johann Gottfried Herder in Selbstzeugnissen und Bilddokumenten*. Reinbek bei Hamburg: Rowohlt.

Karadžić, Vuk Stefanović. 1997. *Songs of the Serbian People: From the Collections of Vuk Karadžić*. Translated and edited by Milne Holton and Vasa D. Mihailovich. Pittsburgh: University of Pittsburgh Press.

Karnes, Kevin C. 2005. "A Garland of Songs for a Nation of Singers: An Episode in the History of Russia, the Herderian Tradition and the Rise of Baltic Nationalism." *Journal of the Royal Musical Association* 130: 197–235.

Kauffmann, Kai. 2007. "'Bilderrede': Zur Beziehung von Theorien des Sprachursprungs und einer Poetik des Orientalismus bei Rousseau und Herder." In *Orientdiskurse in der deutschen Literatur*, edited by Klaus-Michael Bogdal, 31–48. Bielefeld: Aisthesis Verlag.

Kayser, Wolfgang. 1945. *Die iberische Welt im Denken J. G. Herders*. Hamburg: C. Behre.

Kelch, Christian. 1695. *Liefländische Historia, oder kurtze und eigentliche Beschreibung der Denckwürdigsten Friedens- und Krieges-Geschichte, So sich theils vor, theils nach der Liefländer Bekehrung zum Christenthum, biß auffs Jahr 1689 begeben*. Frankfurt am Main and Leipzig: Mener.

Kessler, Martin. 2009. "Herder's Theology." In *A Companion to the Works of Johann Gottfried Herder*, edited by Hans Adler and Wulf Koepke, 247–75. Rochester: Camden House.

Keyser, Erich, ed. 1913. *Im Geiste Herders: Gesammelte Aufsätze zum 150. Todestage J. G. Herders*. Marburger Ostforschungen 1. Kitzingen am Main: Holzner-Verlag.

Kleist, Ewald Christian von. 1758. *Neue Gedichte*. Berlin: Christian Friedrich Voss.

Köhler, Reinhold. 1867. *Herders Cid und seine französische Quelle*. Leipzig: Vogel.

Kurzke, Hermann. 1990. *Hymnen und Lieder der Deutschen*. Mainz: Dietrich'sche Verlagsbuchhandlung.

Lacan, Jacques. 1989a. *Écrits: A Selection*. London: Routledge.

———. 1989b. "The Mirror Stage as Formative of the Function of the *I*." In *Écrits: A Selection*, 1–8. London: Routledge.

---. 1989c. "On a Question Preliminary to Any Possible Treatment of Psychosis." In *Écrits: A Selection*, 198–249. London: Routledge.
Lafitau, Joseph François. 1724. *Mœurs des sauvages amériquains comparées aux mœurs des premiers temps*. 2 vols. Paris: Saugrain et Hocherau.
Lamport, F. J. 1998. "Goethe, Ossian and Werther." In *From Gaelic to Romantic: Ossianic Translations*, edited by Fiona J. Stafford and Howard Gaskill, 97–106. Amsterdam: Rodopi.
Landis, Paul, ed. 1931. *Six Plays by Corneille and Racine*. New York: Modern Library.
Leibniz, Gottfried Wilhelm. 1962. *Werke*. Series 6, vol. 6. Edited by Deutsche Akademie der Wissenschaften zu Berlin. Berlin: Deutsche Akademie der Wissenschaften.
Leitzmann, Albert. 1916. *Histoire du Cid nach der Ausgabe von 1783*. Quellenschriften zur neueren deutschen Literatur 7. Halle a.S.: M. Niemeyer.
de Léry, Jean. 1578. *Histoire d'un voyage faict en la terre du Bresil*. La Rochelle: Antoine Chuppin.
---. 1990. *History of a Voyage to the Land of Brazil, Otherwise Called America*. Translated and edited by Janet Whatley. Berkeley: University of California Press.
Lessing, Johann Gottlieb. 1777. *Eclogae Regis Salomonis*. Leipzig: Dyk.
Letzner, Johann. 1596. *Dasselsche und Eimbeckische Chronica*. Erfurt: n.p.
Lied der Liebe. 2013. *Lied der Liebe: Das Hohelied im Deutschen Barock*. CD and booklet. Christophorus CHR 77378.
Lindenbrug, Erpold. 1706. *Scriptores rerum Germanicarum septentrionalium*. Hamburg: C. Liebe.
Lönnrot, Elias. 1967. *Kalevala: Das finnische Epos des Elias Lönnrot*. Translated by Lore Fromm and Hans Fromm. Munich: Carl Hanser Verlag.
---. 1999. *The Kalevala: An Epic Poem after Oral Tradition*. Translated by Keith Bosley. Oxford and New York: Oxford University Press.
Luther, Martin. 1661–64. *Alle deutschen Bücher und Schrifften des Doct. Martini. Lutheri*. 10 vols. Altenburg in Meissen: Fürstl. Sächs. Officin.
MacFarlane, Robert. 1769. *Temorae liber primus versibus latinis expressus*. London: T. Becket and P. A. De Hondt.
Mackensen, Karsten. 2000. *Simplizität: Genese und Wandel einer musikästhetischen Kategorie des 18. Jahrhunderts*. Musiksoziologie 8. Kassel: Bärenreiter.
Macpherson, James, ed. 1760. *Fragments of Ancient Poetry, Collected in the Highlands of Scotland and Translated from the Galic or Erse Language*. 1st and 2nd printings. Edinburgh: G. Hamilton and J. Balfour.
---. 1762. *Fingal: An Ancient Epic Poem, in Six Books, Together with Several Other Poems*. London: Thomas Becket and P. A. de Hondt.
---. 1763. *Temora, an Ancient Epic Poem, in Eight Books, Together with Several Other Poems, Composed by Ossian, the Son of Fingal, Translated from the Gaelic Language, by James Macpherson*. London: Thomas Becket and P. A. de Hondt.

———, ed. 1764a. *Fragmente der alten hochschottländischen Dichtkunst, nebst einigen andern Gedichten Ossians, eines schottischen Barden, aus dem Englischen übersetzt.* Translated by Johann Andreas Engelbrecht. Hamburg: Michael Christian Bock.

———, ed. 1764b. *Fingal: Ein Helden-Gedicht in sechs Büchern.* Hamburg und Leipzig: G.C. Grunds Wittive und Holle.

———. 1765a. *The Works of Ossian, the Son of Fingal.* 2 vols. London: T. Becket and P.A. Dehondt.

———. 1765b. *Dissertation Concerning the Poems of Ossian.* In James Macpherson, *The Works of Ossian.* London: T. Becket and P.A. Dehondt.

Manthey, Jürgen. 2005. *Königsberg: Geschichte einer Weltbürgerrepublik.* Munich: Carl Hanser Verlag.

Maurer, Michael. 2014. *Johann Gottfried Herder: Leben und Werk.* Cologne: Böhlau.

Meibom, Heinrich. 1688. *Scriptores rerum Germanicarum.* Part 3. Helmstedt: Hammius.

Meier, Mischa, ed. 2007. *Sie schufen Europa: Historische Portraits von Konstantin bis Karl dem Großen.* Munich: C.H. Beck.

Mencke, Johann B. 1728–30. *Scriptores rerum Germanicarum praecipue Saxonicarum.* 3 vols. Leipzig: Martini.

Mendelssohn, Moses. 1985 [1788]. *Das Hohelied.* In Werner Weinberg, ed., *Schriften zum Judentum 4,* 237–52. Günther Holzboog. Stuttgart-Bad Cannstatt: Friedrich Frommann Verlag.

———. 2006a. *Ästhetische Schriften.* Hamburg: Felix Meiner Verlag.

———. 2006b. "Über das Erhabene und Naïve in den schönen Wissenschaften." In Moses Mendelssohn, *Ästhetische Schriften,* 188–215. Hamburg: Felix Meiner Verlag.

Menges, Karl. 2009. "Particular Universals: Herder on National Literature, Popular Literature, and World Literature." In *A Companion to the Works of Johann Gottfried Herder,* edited by Hans Adler and Wulf Koepke, 189–213. Rochester: Camden House.

Meyer-Benfey, Heinrich. 1904. *Herder und Kant. Der deutsche Idealismus und seine Bedeutung für die Gegenwart.* Halle: Gebauer-Schwertshke Druckerei u. Verlag.

Miller, Johann Martin. 1777. *Siegwart: Eine Klostergeschichte.* Leipzig: Weygandsche Buchhandlung.

Montesquieu, Charles Louis de Secondat de. 1764. *Lettres persannes.* Amsterdam: Chez les Librairies associés.

Moore, Gregory. 2006. "Introduction." In Johann Gottfried Herder, *Selected Writings on Aesthetics,* 1–30. Princeton, NJ: Princeton University Press.

Morgan, Michael J. 1997. *Molyneux's Question: Vision, Touch, and the Philosophy of Perception.* Cambridge, England: Cambridge University Press.

Morrison, Toni. 1977. *Song of Solomon.* New York: Alfred A. Knopf.

Moser, Hugo, and Joseph Müller-Blattau. 1968. *Deutsche Lieder des Mittelalters.* Stuttgart: Klett.

Mueller-Vollmer, Kurt, ed. 1990. *Herder Today: Contributions from the International Herder Conference, November 5–8, 1987, Stanford, California.* Berlin: Walter de Gruyter.
Nicolai, Friedrich. 1775–76. *Das Leben und die Meinungen des herrn magister Sebaldus Nothanker.* 3 vols. Berlin and Stettin: F. Nicolai.
Nisbet, H. B. 1985. *German Aesthetic and Literary Criticism: Winckelmann, Lessing, Hamann, Herder, Schiller, Goethe.* Cambridge, England: Cambridge University Press.
Nobus, Dany. 2003. "Lacan's Science of the Subject: Between Linguistics and Topology." In *The Cambridge Companion to Lacan,* edited by Jean-Michel Rabaté, 50–68. Cambridge, England: Cambridge University Press.
Noverre, Jean Georges. 1769. *Briefe über die Tanzkunst und über die Ballette.* Hamburg and Bremen: J. H. Cramer.
Nufer, Wolfgang. 1929. *Herders Ideen zur Verbindung von Poesie, Musik und Tanz.* Germanische Studien 74. Berlin: Verlag von Emil Eberling.
Otto, Regine. 1992. "Nachwort." In Johann Gottfried Herder, *Lieder der Liebe: Die ältesten und schönsten aus Morgenlande, nebst vier und vierzig alten Minneliedern,* 168–75. Zurich: Manesse.
———, ed. 1996. *Nationen und Kulturen: Zum 250. Geburtstag Johann Gottfried Herders.* Würzburg: Königshausen und Neumann.
Pelli, Moshe. 2003. "'These Are the Great Words of the Great Pundit, Scholar and Poet Herder . . .': Herder and the Hebrew Haskalah." In *Hebräische Poesie und jüdischer Volksgeist: Die Wirkungsgeschichte von Johann Gottfried Herder im Judentum Mittel- und Osteuropas,* edited by Christoph Schulte, 107–24. Hildesheim: Georg Olm Verlag.
Percy, Thomas. 1765. *Reliques of Ancient English Poetry, Consisting of Old Heroic Ballads, Songs, and Other Pieces of Our Earlier Poets (Chiefly of the Lyric Kind) Together with Some Few of Later Date.* London: J. Dodsley.
Péres de Hita, Ginez. 1647. *Historia de los vandos de los Zegries, y Abencerrages, cavalleros moros de Granad, de las civiles guerras.* Barcelona: S. deCormellas.
Peringer de Peringskiöld, Johann. 1710–19. *Monumenta Sveo-Gothica.* Stockholm: Olavus Enaeus.
Pomarius, Johannes [Johann Baumgart]. 1589. *Chronik der Sachsen und Niedersachsen.* Magdeburg: Johann Francken.
Powell, Brian. 1983. *Epic and Chronicle: The "Poema de mio Cid" and the "Crónica de veinte reyes."* London: Modern Humanities Research Association.
Ramnarine, Tina K. 2003. *Ilmatar's Inspirations: Nationalism, Globalization, and the Changing Soundscapes of Finnish Folk Music.* Chicago: University of Chicago Press.
Regis, Gottlob. 1842. *Das Liederbuch von Cid, nach der bis jetzt volltsändigsten, Keller'schen Ausgabe verdeutscht.* Stuttgart and Tübingen: J. G. Gotta'scher Verlag.
Reinhard, Johann Paul. 1760–63. *Beyträge zur Historie Franckenlandes.* 3 vols. Bayreuth: Lübeck.

Ricoeur, Paul. 1992. *Oneself as Another.* Translated by Kathleen Blamey. Chicago: University of Chicago Press.

Riley, Matthew. 2004. *Musical Listening in the German Enlightenment: Attention, Wonder and Astonishment.* Aldershot: Ashgate.

Robscheit, Hellmuth. 1956. "Herder als Ausleger des Alten Testamentes (dargestellt an seiner Schrift 'Vom Geist der Ebräischen Poesie')." In *Herder im geistlichen Amt: Untersuchungen, Quellen, Dokumente,* edited by Eva Schmidt, 39–53. Leipzig: Koehler und Amelang.

Rogers, Robert. 1765. *A Concise Account of North America.* London: J. Millan.

Rollin, Charles. 1726–28. *De manière et d'étudier les belles-lettres.* 4 vols. Paris: J. Estienne.

Rosen, Charles. 1998. *Romantic Poets, Critics, and Other Madmen.* Cambridge, MA: Harvard University Press.

Rosenzweig, Franz. 1926. *Zweistromland: Kleinere Schriften zur Religion und Philosophie.* Berlin: Philo Verlag.

Ruhig, Philipp. 1747. *Litauisch-Deutsches und Deutsch-Litauisches Lexicon: Nebst einer historischen Betrachtung der Litauischen Sprache.* Königsberg: Hartung.

———. 1748. *Betrachtung der litauischen Sprache in ihrem Ursprung, Wesen und Eigenschaften,* in *Litthauisch-deutsches und deutsch-litthauisches Lexikon.* Königsberg: J.H. Hartung.

Sauder, Gerhard. 2009. "Herder's Poetic Works, His Translations, and His Views on Poetry." In *A Companion to the Works of Johann Gottfried Herder,* edited by Hans Adler and Wulf Koepke, 305–30. Rochester: Camden House.

Scheffer, Johannes. 1673. *Lapponia, id est Regionis Lapponum et gentis nova et verissima descriptio.* Frankfurt am Main: M. Hallervorden.

Schilter, Johannes. 1726–28. *Thesaurus antiquitatum teutonicarum, ecclesiasticarum, civilium, litterarum.* 2 vols. Ulm: D. Bartholomæi und filii.

Schings, Hans-Jürgen, ed. 1994. *Der ganze Mensch: Anthropologie und Literatur im 18. Jahrhundert.* Stuttgart: Metzler.

Schlegel, Friedrich. 1958. *Kritische-Schlegel-Ausgabe.* Edited by Ernst Behler, Jean-Jacques Anstett, and Hans Eichner. Munich: F. Schöningh.

Schmidt, Eva, ed. 1956. *Herder im geistlichen Amt: Untersuchungen, Quellen, Dokumente.* Leipzig: Koehler und Amelang.

Schneider, Jost, ed. 1994. *Herder im "Dritten Reich."* Bielefeld: Aisthesis Verlag.

Schoeps, Julius H. 2003. "Das kollektive jüdische Bewußtsein: J.G. Herders Volksgeistlehre und der Zionismus." In *Hebräische Poesie und jüdischer Volksgeist: Die Wirkungsgeschichte von Johann Gottfried Herder im Judentum Mittel- und Osteuropas,* edited by Christoph Schulte, 181–89. Hildesheim: Georg Olms Verlag.

Schorch, Grit. 2003. "Das Erhabene und die Dichtkunst der Hebräer: Transformationen eines ästhetischen Konzepts bei Lowth, Mendelssohn und Herder." In *Hebräische Poesie und jüdischer Volksgeist: Die Wirkungsgeschichte von Johann Gottfried Herder im Judentum Mittel- und Osteuropas,* edited by Christoph Schulte, 67–92. Hildesheim: Georg Olms Verlag.

Schöttgen, Christian, and Georg Christian Kreisig. 1733. *Diplomatische und curieuse Nachlese der Historie von Obersachsen*. 12 vols. Dresden: Hekel.

Schulte, Christoph, ed. 2003. *Hebräische Poesie und jüdischer Volksgeist: Die Wirkungsgeschichte von Johann Gottfried Herder im Judentum Mittel- und Osteuropas*. Haskala: Wissenschaftliche Abhandlungen 28. Hildesheim: Georg Olms Verlag.

Seckendorff, Siegmund von. 1779. *Volks- und andere Lieder, mit Begleitung des Forte piano*. Weimar: Hoffmann.

Shaw, Thomas. 1765. *Reisen, oder, Anmerkungen verschiedene Theile der Barbarey und der Levante betreffend*. Leipzig: B.C. Breitkopf und Sohn.

Siegismund von Seckendorf, Karl Friedrich. 1779. *Volks- und andere Lieder, mit Begleitung des Forte piano*. Vol. 1. Weimar: Hoffmann.

Sikka, Sonia. 2011. *Herder on Humanity and Cultural Difference*. Cambridge, England: Cambridge University Press.

Singer, Rüdiger. 2006. *"Nachgesang": Ein Konzept Herders, entwickelt an "Ossian," der Popular Ballad und der frühen Kunstballade*. Würzburg: Königshausen und Neumann.

Slenczka, Reinhard. 2004. *Humanität und Nation: Europäische Gemeinschaft im Leben und Denken von Johann Gottfried Herder*. Neuendettelsau: Freimund-Verlag.

Šmidchens, Guntis. 1996. "A Baltic Music: The Folklore Movement in Lithuania, Latvia, and Estonia, 1968–1991." PhD diss., Indiana University.

Smith, Colin. 1983. *The Making of the "Poema de mio Cid."* Cambridge, England: Cambridge University Press.

Smith, John. 1781. *Gallische Alterthümer oder eine Sammlung alter Gedichte aus dem Gallischen des Ullin, Ossian, Orran von John Smith ins Engländische und aus diesem ins Deutsche übersetzt*. Translated by C.F. Weisse. Leipzig: Weidmanns Erben und Reich.

———, ed. 1787. *Sean Dana*. Edinburgh: Charles Eliot.

Sorkin, David. 1996. *Moses Mendelssohn and the Religious Enlightenment*. Berkeley: University of California Press.

———. 2000. *The Berlin Haskalah and German Religious Thought: Orphans of Knowledge*. London: Vallentine Mitchell.

———. 2008. *The Religious Enlightenment: Protestants, Jews, and Catholics from London to Vienna*. Princeton, NJ: Princeton University Press.

Spalding, Johann Joachim. 1780. *Neues Gesangbuch zum gottesdienstlichen Gebrauch in den königlichen preußischen Landen*. Berlin: Voss.

Spangenberg, Cyriacus. 1755. *Hennebergische Chronica*. Meiningen: Scheidemantel.

Stafford, Fiona J. 1988. *The Sublime Savage: James Macpherson and the Poems of Ossian*. Edinburgh: Edinburgh University Press.

Stafford, Fiona J., and Howard Gaskill, eds. 1998. *From Gaelic to Romantic: Ossianic Translations*. Amsterdam: Rodopi.

Steinberg, Michael P. 2004. *Listening to Reason: Culture, Subjectivity, and Nineteenth-Century Music*. Princeton, NJ: Princeton University Press.

Steinhäuser, Theodor. 1956. "Herder als Pfarrer." In *Herder im geistlichen Amt: Untersuchungen, Quellen, Dokumente*, edited by Eva Schmidt, 13–25. Leipzig: Koehler und Amelang.

Stollberg, Arne. 2006. *Ohr und Auge—Klang und Form: Facetten einer musikästhetischen Dichotomie bei Johann Gottfried Herder, Richard Wagner und Franz Schreker*. Beihefte zum Archiv für Musikwissenschaft 58. Stuttgart: F. Steiner.

Stowe, David. 2016. *Song of Exile: The Enduring Mystery of Psalm 137*. New York: Oxford University Press.

Taruskin, Richard. 1997. *Defining Russia Musically: Historical and Hermeneutical Essays*. Princeton, NJ: Princeton University Press.

Thévenot, Jean de. 1689. *Voyages de Mr de Thévenot tant en Europe, Asie et Afrique, divisez en trois parties*. Paris: Angot.

Thomas, Downing A. 1995. *Music and the Origins of Language: Theories from the French Enlightenment*. New Perspectives in Music History and Criticism. Cambridge, England: Cambridge University Press.

Timberlake, Henry. 1765. *The Memoirs of Lieutenant H. T., Who Accompanied the Three Indians to England in the Year 1762*. London: [Henry Timberlake].

Timm, Hermann, ed. 1982. *Das Hohe Lied Salomos: Nachdichtungen und Übersetzungen aus sieben Jahrhunderten*. Frankfurt am Main: Insel.

Trabant, Jürgen. 2009. "Herder and Language." In *A Companion to the Works of Johann Gottfried Herder*, edited by Hans Adler and Wulf Koepke, 117–39. Rochester: Camden House.

Trevor-Roper, Hugh. 1983. "The Invention of Tradition: The Highland Tradition of Scotland." In *The Invention of Tradition*, edited by Eric Hobsbawm and Terence Ranger, 15–41. Cambridge, England: Cambridge University Press.

Trumpener, Katie. 1997. *Bardic Nationalism: The Romantic Novel and the British Empire*. Princeton, NJ: Princeton University Press.

d'Urfey, Thomas. 1712. *Wit and Mirth: Or Pills to Purge Melancholy; Being a Collection of the Best Merry Ballads and Songs, Old and New*. Vol. 2. London: J. Tonson.

de la Vega, Garcilaso. 1704. *Histoire des Yncas rois du Peru etc. Traduite de l'Espagnol de l'Ynca Garcilasso de la Vega, par J. Baudoin*. Amsterdam: Gerard Kuyper.

Verelius, Olof, ed. 1672. *Hervarar-Saga på gammal götska med Olai Vereli uttolkning och notis*. Uppsala: Henricus Curio.

Voegelin, Anton Salomon. 1879. *Herders Cid, die französische und die spanische Quellen*. Heilbronn: Gebr. Henninger.

Wagner, Fritz. 1960. *Herders Homerbild, seine Wurzeln und Wirkungen*. PhD diss., University of Cologne.

Weber, Friedrich Christian. 1744. *Das veränderte Rußland*. Vol. 1. Frankfurt am Main and Leipzig: N. Förster.

Weissberg, Liliane. 2003. "Ortswechsel: Hannah Arendts Suche nach dem 'asiatischen Volk.'" In *Hebräische Poesie und jüdischer Volksgeist: Die Wirkungsgeschichte von Johann Gottfried Herder im Judentum Mittel- und*

Osteuropas, edited by Christoph Schulte, 247–56. Hildesheim: Georg Olms Verlag.
Weiße, Christian Felix. 1769. *Neue Bibliothek der schönen Wissenschaften und der freien Künste*. Vol. 9. Leipzig: J.G. Dyck.
Wiedebach, Hartwig. 2003. "Herders 'Humanität' in Hermann Cohens Ästhetik und im Begriff der Nationalität." In *Hebräische Poesie und jüdischer Volksgeist: Die Wirkungsgeschichte von Johann Gottfried Herder im Judentum Mittel- und Osteuropas*, edited by Christoph Schulte, 193–210. Hildesheim: Georg Olms Verlag.
Wieland, Christoph Martin. 1762–66. *Prosaübersetzung von 22 Dramen Shakespeares*. In *Shakespeares theatralische Werke*. 8 vols. Zurich: Orell, Geßner und Comp.
Wiese, Benno von. 1939. *Herder: Grundzüge seines Weltbildes*. Meyers kleine Handbücher 19. Leipzig: Bibliographisches Institut.
Wolf, Eric R. 1982. *Europe and the People without History*. Berkeley: University of California Press.
Wolfhagen, Tilemann Elhen von. 1875. *Die Limburger Chronik*. Marburg: N.G. Elwert'sche Verlagsbuchhandlung.
Wood, Robert. 1769. *An Essay on the Original Genius of Homer*. London: n.p.
Wormius, Olaus [Olaf Worm]. 1636. *Danica litteratura antiquissima, vulgo gothica dicta*. Copenhagen: Georg Holst.
———. 1651. *Runica, seu danica litteratura antiquissima*. Copenhagen: Martzan et Holst.
Young, Edward. 1743. *The Complaint, or Night-Thoughts on Life, Death, and Immortality*. London: R. Dodsley.
Young, Matthew. 1784. *Ancient Gaelic Poems, Respecting the Race of the Fians, Collected in the Highlands of Scotland in the Year 1784*. Dublin: George Bonham.
Zammito, John H. 2002. *Kant, Herder, and the Birth of Anthropology*. Chicago: University of Chicago Press.
Zaremba, Michael. 2002. *Johann Gottfried Herder—Prediger der Humanität: Eine Biografie*. Cologne: Böhlau.
Ziegengeist, Gerhard, Helmut Graßhoff, and Ulf Lehmann, eds. 1978. *Johann Gottfried Herder: Zur Herder-Rezeption in Ost- und Südosteuropa*. Slawistische Studien und Texte. Berlin: Akademie-Verlag.
Zollikofer, Georg Joachim. 1766. *Neues Gesangbuch oder Sammlung der besten geistlichen Lieder bey dem öffentlichen Gottesdienst*. Leipzig: Weidmanns Erben und Reich.

Index

Aachen, 56
"Abendlied" / "Evening Song," 96–97
Abildgaard, Nicolai Abraham, 142
Abrahamic faiths, 8, 281
Adler, Israel, xii
Aeschylus, 53
aesthetics, xiv–xv, 2, 5–6, 10, 12, 43, 46, 48–49, 107–8, 135, 139, 187–88, 190, 201, 246–49, 258, 267–71, 274–76, 281
Africa, 72, 276
afterlife, 105
al-Andalus, 8, 75, 221, 223–24, 238
allegory, 13, 45, 106, 188, 222
Alsace, 74, 272
Alte Volkslieder, xix, 5, 21–44, 46, 72, 136, 203
"altfranzösisches Sonnet, ein" / "A Sonnet in Old French," 90
American Musicological Society, xii
Ampanani, 100–2
"Ampanani" / "Ampanani," 102
"An die Jungfrau Maria" / "To the Virgin Mary," 98–99, 275
"An sein Mädchen" / "To His Child," 104
ancient and modern, 137, 227
Annäherung, 13, 15, 106
"Ans Rennthier" / "To the Reindeer," 82–83
anthology, xvii, xx, 5, 21–23, 45, 47, 60, 71, 73–74, 88, 96, 100, 104, 144, 168, 173, 188, 195, 202, 262, 272, 276, 278
anthropology, xiv–xv, 5–6, 8, 47–48, 201, 247–48, 252, 262, 269, 273–75
antiquity, xvii–xviii, 14, 27, 131, 164, 201–2, 209, 221
anti-Semitism, 8
Apollo, 146, 207, 209, 216, 256
architecture, 136, 249
Aristotle, 51, 190
Arjuna, 1–5
Arnim, Ludwig Achim von, 46
art, visual. See painting
arts (as general category), 202, 204, 247–50, 258, 270–71, 275, 283
Asia, 106
authenticity, xx, 47–48, 51, 140, 145, 175

Babylon, 1, 12, 16, 194, 285n1, 286prologuen1
Bach, Johann Christian, 14–15
bagpipe, 64–65
Baildam, John, 106
ballad, 8–9, 23–24, 33, 46, 72–73, 79, 94, 137, 144–45, 154, 158, 224–26
Baltic region, 5, 37, 263–64, 266–67, 280
bard, 26–27, 29, 54, 72, 92, 140, 142, 146, 148, 150, 157, 159, 168, 174, 203, 215, 217–18
Baroque, 14

307

Baumgarten, Alexander Gottlieb, 268–70
Benjamin, Walter, 3
Be-reshit, 1
Berlin, xii
Bhagavad Gita, 105–6
Bible, xvii, 1, 5, 10, 16, 57, 96, 106, 108, 110, 166, 191–94, 197, 263
Bode, 136
Bohlman, Andrea F., xiii
Bohlman, Benjamin, xiii
Bohlman, Christine Wilkie, xiii
Bohlman, Philip V., 26, 44–74, 105–11, 135, 140, 168, 172, 186, 190, 201, 205, 221, 228, 246, 249
Brahms, Johannes, 46, 90, 138, 158
Brentano, Clemens, 46
"Briefwechsel über Ossian und die Lieder alter Völker," 135–67, 187, 272
Brunswick, 56
Brussels, 57
Buber, Martin, 16
Buchanan, John, 171, 183–84

Canada, 148
canon, 105, 221, 275
canto, 226–27, 237
Catalus, 53
Charlemagne, 21, 26, 174
Child ballad, 77, 138, 154
chorus, 50, 53, 64, 127, 166, 182, 230, 248, 253–54
Christ, 13, 167, 216
Christianity, 2, 16–17, 105, 220, 223, 236, 263, 281
church (as religious institution), xviii, 13, 53, 187, 192
Cid (eponymous hero in El Cid), 223–25, 228–45
Cid, der (as translated epic by Johann Gottfried Herder), xvii–xix, 7–9, 75, 105–6, 139, 210, 221–45, 278, 282, 286chap2n3, 287chap8n1
civilization, 34, 40
Claudius, Matthias, 72, 96
Codex Manesse, 27–28, 60, 215
Cohen, Hermann, 16

collective (as social group), xiii, 47–48, 187, 202, 259
colonialism, 227, 276
community, xiii
comparative musicology, 24, 252
composition, 61, 193, 209
contrafact, 13
"Correspondence about Ossian and the Songs of Ancient Peoples." See "Briefwechsel über Ossian und die Lieder alter Völker"
Cremmerdamm, 56
cultural relativism, 8, 263, 274
culture, 25, 38, 43, 47–48, 50, 106, 149, 151, 160, 186, 201–4, 219, 258–59, 263, 266–67, 274, 283–84, 287chap6n1
customs, xviii, 26–27, 37–38, 43, 100, 149, 151, 202–3, 206, 208–12, 214–20

Damascus, 124
dance: as form of the arts, 52–53, 100, 127, 165, 248, 252–54, 256; folk, 54, 151, 184
Denis, Michael, 33, 92, 137–38, 140–41, 143, 145, 147–49, 157–59, 173, 183
Des Knaben Wunderhorn, 46, 57
Descartes, René, 270
Deutsches Volksliedarchiv, xii
dialect, 28, 33, 72–73, 175, 188, 266, 278
diaspora, 8, 16
Díaz, Rodrigo. See Cid
difference, xx, 17, 25, 73, 106–8, 110, 262–63, 265, 267
discourse, 22–23, 48, 267
diversity, xx
Don Ruy Diaz. See Cid
drama, 179, 206, 254
"drey Fragen, die" / "The Three Questions," 77–79
Dundes, Alan, xii

East. See Orient
East Germany. See German Democratic Republic

East Prussia, 3
Eastern Europe, xi
Edda, 137, 144, 147, 160
"Edward, Edward," 23, 46, 137, 154–58
Egypt, 12
eighteenth century, xiv–xv, xviii, xx, 2, 22–23, 48, 63, 94, 168, 186–87, 202, 246, 248, 250, 261, 264, 267–68, 271, 273, 279, 286chap2n2
empire, xiv
encounter, 17, 25, 137, 139, 171, 218, 265–67, 269–71, 274, 283
England, xviii, 148–49, 211–12, 269
Enlightenment, 3, 5, 8, 13, 15, 17, 21, 23, 25, 44, 47, 89, 106–8, 135, 137–38, 168, 174, 201, 207, 221, 224–25, 227, 246–47, 262, 264, 266–67, 271, 273–76, 279–80
epic: as narrative genre of folk song, xv, xviii, 3, 7–10, 17, 24, 29, 45, 48, 51, 54, 73, 92, 105–6, 136–41, 147, 159, 168–71, 173–75, 178–79, 188, 196, 210–11, 221–27, 278, 282; Balkan, 83, 225
epistemology, 38, 48, 248, 266, 273, 278, 282
Erfurt, 55–56
"Erinnerung des Gesanges der Vorzeit" / "Remembering the Song of the Days of Old," 92–93
"Erlkönig," 94
"Erlkönigs Tochter" / "The Elf King's Daughter," 94
Estonia, 62–65
ethics, 6, 43, 201, 246
ethnography, 5, 8, 139, 261, 263, 270
ethnomusicology, xi–xii, 2–3, 5, 16–17, 266, 281
Europe: as larger cultural and geographic area, xii, 5, 8, 16, 42, 72, 79, 137, 204, 206, 220–21, 223–24, 227, 261–62, 266, 274, 278, 280; Central, 280; Eastern, 261, 280; Northern, 47, 82, 92, 138, 160–61, 220, 267
everyday, 48, 105

exegesis, biblical, xvii–xviii, 10, 107–8, 110

fairy tale, 28, 38, 51, 79, 131, 164, 219
fascism, 49
fieldwork, 264–65
Fingal, 145, 147, 150–51, 159, 168–70, 173–76, 178–80, 185
Fingal. See Fingal
Five Nations, 148
folk (as national collective), 30, 34, 44, 48, 51, 68, 203, 216, 219, 232. See also Volk
folk song project, 44–104, 275
folk tale, 51, 278
folksinger, 53, 58
Folk Song. See Volkslieder
Forster, Michael, 273, 281
fragment, xv, xix, 4, 10, 22, 45–46, 54, 59, 107–8, 110, 131, 135–67, 173, 175, 188, 204, 221, 269, 276
France, 5, 139, 149, 210, 262, 264, 269, 272
Francis, Mary, xiii
Freiburg im Breisgau, xii
Frisi, Paolo, 136

Gaiger, Jason, 270
genre, 22, 24, 45, 53, 60, 72–73, 135, 138, 167, 186, 188, 190, 213–14, 220–23, 255, 278
German Democratic Republic, 280–81
German idealism, 46, 273, 279
Germany, xii, xviii, 5, 22, 28, 31, 54, 98, 139–40, 150, 194–95, 201, 203, 215–17, 264, 269, 272, 275, 279–80, 283
Gesang, xviii, 4, 47
gesture, 252–57
Goethe, Johann Wolfgang von, 15, 72, 93–94, 106, 136, 217, 272, 281, 286chap2n2
Greece, 45, 178, 180
Greenland, 68, 92
Grimm, Wilhelm, 94
Grubenhagen, 56

"Hagestolze, der" / "The Confirmed Bachelor," 97–98
Hamann, Johann Georg, 4, 106, 192, 264, 267, 269
Hamburg, 136
Hamlet, 44–45, 87, 212, 286chap2n1
Handel, George Frideric, 186, 188, 196–97, 217, 254
harmony, 165, 252, 257, 258, 271
harp, 51–53, 93, 159, 178, 207, 285n1
Hartknoch, Johann Friedrich, 246, 262, 269
Haskala, 8, 13, 15
hemistich, xix
Hempach, 56
Herder, Emil, 262
Herder, Johann Gottfried, xi–xvii, xix–xx, 1–8, 10–11, 13, 15–17, 21–26, 44–49, 69, 71–72, 74–75, 79, 82–83, 87–90, 93–94, 96, 100, 104–11, 131, 135–36, 138–40, 144, 147, 149–50, 152–54, 156–58, 160, 168–69, 171–72, 175, 177, 183, 186–88, 190, 192, 194, 196–97, 201–3, 205, 207, 209–10, 212–13, 215–17, 219, 221–28, 237, 246–50, 252, 255, 258–59, 261–84, 285n1, 287chap7n1
Herder, Karoline, 47, 71, 105, 225
Hinduism, xvii, 2, 263, 281
historiography, 3, 225, 262, 274, 276
history: cultural, 25, 276; European, 224, 263; general, 7, 9–10, 12, 21, 25, 30, 38, 45, 48, 51, 59, 110, 136, 145, 149, 168, 171–72, 174, 177, 179, 188, 221–23, 247, 256, 263, 267–68, 275, 279, 282; German, 32, 266; global, 2; intellectual, xv, xix, 3, 16–17, 201–2, 248, 266, 283; Jewish, 7, 16; literary, 202–3; music, 49; national, 21–43, 169, 276; natural, 37–38; of ideas, 3, 7, 17, 23; of religion, 17; of song, 70; political, 203; reception, xx, 2, 17, 45, 221; universal, xv, 262–63, 274, 278–79, 281–82; world, 37
Hoeckner, Berthold, 275
Holzapfel, Otto, xii
Homer, 9, 39, 45, 51–53, 139, 150, 168–70, 172–75, 177–81, 188, 219, 224, 282
"Homer and Ossian." See "Homer und Ossian"
"Homer und Ossian," 136, 168–85
Horace, 39–40
Horton, Jennie, xiii
humanism, 16, 38, 248, 279
humanity, 34, 36, 96, 129, 149, 211, 248, 250, 259, 262, 275, 281–82, 284
humankind, 7, 43, 97, 172, 182, 186
hymn, 165, 188, 190–91, 264
hymnbook, 186

Iberia, 223, 226
Iceland, 144, 147
icon, 39
imitation, 33, 206
improvisation, 65–66
in-betweenness, 135, 137
India, xi, 10
Indigenous people, 43, 106, 138, 149, 158, 262
"Influence of Poetry on the Customs of Modernity, the." See "Wirkung der Dichtkunst auf die Sitten neuerer Zeiten"
intertextuality, xvii
intimacy, 106–7, 114, 180, 193, 221, 258, 284
Ireland, 174, 211
Islam, 223
Israel, xi–xii, 12, 107, 117, 126, 204
Italy, 45, 205–6, 261, 264

Jerusalem, xii, 13–14, 63, 112–15, 117, 121–22, 125, 128, 174, 216, 219, 285n1
Jewish Music Research Centre, xii
Journal meiner Reise im Jahr 1769, 7, 37, 261–63, 266–67, 269, 276, 279, 283–84
Judaism, 2, 6, 263
"Judentochter, die" / "The Jewish Daughter," 79–81. See also "Jüdin, die"
"Jüdin, die," 23. See also

"Judentochter, die" / "The Jewish Daughter"

Kalligone, 246–49, 269, 274
Kant, Immanuel, 3–4, 246–47, 249, 264, 267, 269, 273–74
Khan, Zuha, xiii
"Klaggesang von der edlen Frau des Asan-Aga" / "Lament of the Noble Wife of Hassan Aga," 73, 83–87
Kleist, Ewald Jürgen Georg von, 141, 217
Klopstock, Friedrich Gottlieb, 141, 147, 159, 165, 183, 196, 217
"Klosterlied" / "Cloister Song," 91
"König, der" / "The King," 100
"König im Krieg, der" / "The King at War," 100–1
Königsberg, 4, 106, 192, 246, 261, 266, 269, 273–74
Kosovo, 83
Krishna, 1–5, 106
Kritische Wälder, 5

labor, 48
Lacan, Jacques, 17
Laertes, 45
lament, 68–69, 182–83, 185
landscape, folk song, xi, xv
language, 21–24, 26–27, 29, 32, 36–38, 40, 43, 50–51, 53, 58, 62, 66–68, 114, 116, 119, 126, 135, 138–40, 142, 148–49, 151, 168–69, 175–76, 182, 184, 191–95, 202, 205, 209–10, 225, 240, 248, 254, 261, 264, 266, 272, 278, 280, 282
Latin America, 222, 262. See also South America
Latvia, 63–68, 264, 266
Lebanon, 13, 107, 117–18, 122–24, 129, 131
legend, 174, 181
Leibniz, Gottfried Wilhelm, 43
Leipzig, 13, 56, 71
Lessing, Ephraim Gotthold, 8, 56, 268, 273
Levant, 261

Lied, xviii, 47
"Lied vom Fischer, das" / "The Fisherman's Song," 89
"Lied vom jungen Grafen, das" / "The Song of the Young Count," 74–75
Lieder der Liebe, xv, xviii, 13, 16, 105–32, 281, 286chap3n1. See also Song of Songs
Limburg, 55–56
Lisbon, 225
literature, 38, 137, 149, 170, 201–2, 208–9, 217, 261–62, 282
Lithuania, 3, 68
liturgy, xvii, 192
Lucretius, 53
lullaby, 104, 116
Luther, Martin, 15, 57, 59, 106, 108, 110, 128, 188, 194–96
Lycurgus, 150

Macpherson, James, 92, 137, 139, 141, 145, 149–50, 157, 168–71, 175–77, 179, 272
Madagascar, 99–100, 278
Magdeburg, 55
Mantua, 110
masses, 50, 53, 186, 193, 206, 271
materiality, 34
Maurer, Michael, 265, 283
Meistersinger, 29, 57, 59
melody, 40, 46, 53, 59, 61–62, 146, 154, 165, 176, 182, 192, 195–96, 252, 258–59, 271
Mendelssohn, Moses, 8, 14–15, 110, 273
Messiah, 186–88, 196–97, 217
metaphor, 8, 16, 23, 69, 107, 138, 169, 261, 263, 281, 283
meter, 64, 165, 208, 226, 252
Middle Ages, 79, 210, 215, 227
Middle East, xi, 15, 27
Milan, 79, 81
minnesinger, xvii, 15, 27–28, 58, 110
minstrel, 29, 159
missionary, 25
modernity, xiii, 171, 201–3, 222
Mohrungen, 3, 261

Moors, 76–77, 206, 230–31, 235, 238–39, 241–43
"Morgengesang im Kriege" / "Morning Song during War," 81–82
Möser, Justus, 137
Moses, 9, 12, 191, 282
Müller, Johann von, 47, 71
muses, 53, 166, 209, 216, 218–19, 256
music: art, 248; as ontological subject, xiv–xv, xvii, 44–105, 135, 167–68, 171, 186–87, 190, 192–93, 196, 201, 203, 208, 226, 246–59, 263–64, 271, 283; church, 57, 166, 196; folk, xi–xii, 248, 276, 281; Gaelic, 184; sacred, 186–88, 192; secular, 186; world, 17, 25, 44, 71–72, 222, 272, 278, 281
musical thought, xvi–xvii, 2
musicology, 47
myth, 7, 9, 38, 40, 43, 107, 160, 171, 221, 223–24
mythology, 40, 176, 203, 207, 219

Nantes, 262
narrative, xv, xix, 10, 24, 33, 46, 72, 79, 105, 107–8, 110, 148, 166, 168, 179, 221–26, 228, 259, 261, 272, 282
nation, xiv, xviii, xx, 2–3, 5, 7–10, 21–25, 28–31, 36, 45, 48, 53, 67, 116, 135–67, 169, 177–78, 180–81, 183, 191, 199, 202–4, 206, 209, 211–12, 214–15, 217, 220–21, 226–27, 259, 263–64, 267, 282–83
nationalism: age of, 221; sense of belonging to a nation, xiii, xvi, 2–3, 5, 7, 10, 17, 44–73, 168–69, 201, 203, 222, 226–27, 279–80
nature, 24, 34, 36, 39–40, 42, 43, 127, 129, 135, 165, 169, 248, 251–53, 257, 268
Nettl, Bruno, xi
New Testament, 5
Nibelungen, 137
nineteenth century, 23–24, 45–46, 48, 73, 105, 135, 137–38, 154, 226, 246–47, 275
North Africa, 223
North America, xviii, 69, 148, 219, 262

North Sea, 5, 264
Norway, 144
Nuremburg, 56, 60

object, xviii, 201, 263
ode, 42
"Odins Höllenfahrt" / "Odin's Journey into Hell," 160–63
Odyssey, 45
"On Music." See "Von Musik"
ontology, xviii, 2, 12, 19, 23, 48–49, 203, 248, 271–72, 282
organ, 192
Orient, 50, 111, 113–16, 119–20, 127, 129–31, 172
orientalism, 13, 106–7
origins, 3, 6, 21, 25, 32, 47, 217, 246, 270, 272, 276, 282
Orpheus, 39
Ossian, xv, xix–xx, 9, 22, 27, 33, 39–40, 46, 72, 92, 135–71, 173–83, 185, 188, 216, 218, 224, 276, 282
otherness, 24–25, 223, 227, 265
Ottoman Empire, 83

painting, 107, 135, 167–68, 201, 249–50, 258, 270–71
Palestine, 261
Paris, 194, 211, 215
Parny, Évariste Desiré de Forges, Vicomte de, 99
parody, 57
Pavia, 59
Pentateuch. See Torah
Percy, Thomas, 28–30, 72, 79, 81, 144, 148, 154, 156, 278
Peru, 278
Petkovi, Nada, 83
phenomenology, 2
philosopher, xvii
philosophy: general, xiv, 4, 6, 36, 149, 207–8, 210, 247, 268, 273, 281; moral, 187; of language, xvii, 6, 248, 273, 282; popular, 273
Pietsch, Rudolf, xii
Pindar, 53, 191, 215
Plato, 173, 190, 219, 256

poesy, 10, 12, 24, 29, 33, 43, 50–52, 59, 66–67, 69, 100, 135, 137, 166, 177, 190–91, 194, 201–3, 209–12, 215, 226, 249, 256, 267
poet, 208, 210–14, 216–17, 259
poetics, 6, 8, 10, 12, 43, 166
poetry: as aesthetic practice: 26–30, 38, 40, 43, 51, 54, 58, 65–66, 94, 100, 110, 136–37, 141, 146, 166–68, 173–76, 178, 180, 183, 190–91, 201–2, 204–11, 213–14, 216–20, 222, 227, 258, 267, 270; pedagogical, 191–92
Poland, 150
Polivka, Raina, xiii
politics, 10, 43, 149, 282
prose, 190–91, 210, 228
prosody, 165
Protestantism, 105
psalm, 1, 3, 16, 105, 126, 165, 172, 182
Psalm 137, 1–2, 10, 16
psalmody, 10
Pythagoras, 173

Qur'an, 39

Ramler, Karl Wilhelm, 166
Red Sea, 127
redemption, 186, 189
Regenstein Library, xiii
Reinking, Francisco, xiii
religion, xvii, 5, 36, 48, 105–6, 186, 192, 195, 203, 207, 215, 219, 280–82
Reliques of Ancient English Poetry, 148, 154, 156, 278
Renaissance, 108, 110, 203–4
repertory, 23, 47, 59, 83, 106–7, 188, 225, 271, 278, 282
repetition, 69, 258
representation, 37–38, 169, 226, 265, 276
Rg Veda, 6, 10
rhyme, 66, 69, 193, 208, 212–13
rhythm, 148, 151–52, 157, 226, 249, 252
Riga, 4–5, 7, 135, 139, 149, 246, 261–62, 264, 266–69, 280
Ritual, 48

Roganovi, Boro, 83
Rom, 79
romance (as Spanish- and French-language song genre), 8–9, 33, 72, 75, 144, 224–28
Romanesque, 27
Romanticism, 135, 138, 168, 227, 246
Rome, 220
"Röschen auf der Heide" / "Heidenröslein," 93–94
Rosenzweig, Franz, 16
Rossi, Salamone, 14, 110
Rousseau, Jean-Jacques, 8, 149, 273–74
Russia, 98

sacred body, 105
saga, 27
Saint Augustine, 14
Sámi, 42, 69, 82, 138, 152–54
Sanskrit, 6, 10
Sappho, 40–43, 172
Saxony, 28, 56, 194
Scandinavia, 147
Schings, Hans-Jürgen, 274
Schlegel, Friedrich, 275
Schubert, Franz, 93–94, 138, 154
Scotland, 140, 169, 176, 178
sculpture, 249, 275
self and other, xi, 1, 17, 25, 48, 107, 227
selfness, 24–25
seventeenth century, 202, 278
"Shakespear" / "Shakespeare," 87–88
Shakespeare, William, 22–23, 25, 29–30, 44–45, 72, 87–88, 136, 142–43, 211–12, 259, 286chap2n2
Shiloah, Amnon, xii
Shir ha-shirim, 13–16, 106, 108, 110, 286chap3n1
Shulamit, 115, 123, 127
Silcher, Friedrich, 93
singer, 33, 51, 54, 61, 69, 137, 141–42, 144, 150, 154, 159, 178, 181, 208, 218, 221, 223
singing, xvii, 60, 148, 176, 185–86, 189, 203, 263
sixteenth century, 56, 278
Skalds, 48, 54, 72, 144

Solomon (King), 13, 105, 107, 112, 117, 126, 130–31, 172
song: ancient, 160; art, 46, 48, 94, 278; as ontological subject, xv, 1, 8, 10, 12, 17, 21, 24, 29–30, 38, 40, 43–45, 48, 50, 52–53, 57, 59–62, 69, 105–6, 108, 119, 122, 126–27, 135, 137–38, 141, 147, 151, 165, 169, 171, 178, 180, 182–84, 189–90, 192–95, 204, 226, 235, 248, 153, 255–56, 259, 262, 264, 267, 272, 275, 284; as object, 45–47; as subject, 45–47; Christian, 195; folk, xi–xii, xv, xvii, 3, 5, 7, 12–13, 17, 21–43, 55, 74–104, 108, 135, 137, 139, 141, 144, 157, 168, 181, 188, 201–2, 222, 224–26, 271–72, 274, 279–80, 282. See also Volkslied; German, 275; Indigenous, 149; Irish, 174; Jewish, xii; love, 33, 40–42, 60, 69, 120, 154; national, 2, 13, 146; Nordic, 22, 24, 34, 48, 72, 94, 144, 147, 150, 278; Norse. See song, Nordic; Ossian, 171, 176–77, 272, 278; patriotic, 27; sacred, 2, 12, 56, 186–97, 263; Scottish, 137, 168, 176, 184; secular, 56; street, 33, 66; urban, 66
songbook, 57, 59, 192–94, 196
Song of Songs, xv, xvii–xviii, 13, 15, 59, 106–8, 111, 139, 262, 281, 286chap3n1. See also Lieder der Liebe. See also Shir ha-shirim
Songs of Solomon. See Song of Songs
Sophocles, 53
soteriology, 105
sound, 250–52, 254, 257–58
South America, xviii, 72, 276. See also Latin America
Spain, 45, 206, 235, 243
Stimmen der Völker in Liedern, xv, 13, 44–104, 158, 263, 276, 286chap2n4
Strasbourg, 135, 194, 272
Sturm und Drang, 135, 138, 268
subject, xviii, 165, 189, 201, 263, 273
subjectivity, xiii, 48, 273, 283
sublime, 1, 3, 15, 47, 186–89, 191–92, 197, 246–48, 263, 283
Suphan, Bernhard, xv

Tanach, 5, 10
Tantalus, 53
Temora, 173, 176, 178–79
theater. See drama
Theological Writings. See Theologische Schriften
Theologische Schriften, 186, 190–97
theology, xiv, 48, 110, 187, 196, 279
thirteenth century, 90
thought, musical, 17, 188
Thuringia, 91
"Todtenklage, um des Königs Sohn" / "Lament for the King's Son," 101
tonality, 59
Torah, 12, 21, 282
tradition: as transmitted culture, 38, 43; oral, 27, 47, 91–94, 105, 169, 223, 226, 267, 272, 282; written, 23, 27, 94, 105, 169, 223, 226, 282
transcendence, 44, 122, 246–47, 263
translation, xiv–xv, xvii–xx, 1–2, 7–8, 13, 15–16, 22–23, 25, 45, 52–53, 60, 66, 68, 71–72, 74, 88, 92–93, 98, 100, 105–8, 110, 119, 130, 137–40, 145, 156, 163–64, 168–69, 173–74, 188, 221, 224–27, 275–76, 278, 283, 286chap2n1
transmission, oral. See tradition, oral
"Trauet den Weissen nicht" / "Have No Pity for the White People," 101–2
Tübingen, 71
twentieth century, 42, 44, 226, 280
twenty-first century, 187, 280

Ulysses, 52, 174
United States, 148
universalism, 16, 23, 49, 248, 250, 263, 275, 284
University of California, Berkeley, xii
University of California Press, xii–xiii
University of Chicago, xiii
University of Illinois at Urbana-Champaign, xi
d'Urfey, Thomas, 72

Valencia, 223–24, 235, 237–39, 241–42
variant, 57, 61, 105

Venice, 206
Vienna, xii, 206
Viking, 150
voice, 179, 182, 188, 201, 208, 253–54, 271
Volk, xvii–xviii, 10, 24, 47–48, 186, 202, 267, 286chap2n5. See also folk, the
Volkslied, xi, 89, 141, 157, 224, 267, 278. See also song, folk
Volkslieder (as book by Johann Gottfried Herder), xiv, xix, 5, 13, 44–104, 139, 147, 151, 154, 160, 188, 202, 212, 225, 262–63, 271–72, 276–77, 280, 286chap2n4
Voltaire, François-Marie Arouet, 149, 210–11
Vom Geist der ebräischen Poesie, xv, 2, 10–12, 16, 281, 285n1
Von deutscher Art und Kunst, 57, 93, 135–37, 163
"Von Musik," 246–59
vox populi, 47

Weimar, 5, 35, 135, 187, 194, 196, 246, 261, 279–80, 286chap2n2
Weise, 60
Westbrook, Lindsey, xiii
Western Europe, 47
Weygandsche Buchhandlung, 13, 71
Winters, Christopher, xiii
"Wirkung der Dichtkunst auf die Sitten neuerer Zeiten," 201–20, 287chap7n1
Wirkungsgeschichte. See history, intellectual
Withey, Lynne, xiii

yoiking, 82

"Zaid und Zaida" / "Zaid and Zaida," 75–77
Zammito, John, 273
"Zanhar und Niang" / "Zanhar and Niang," 102
Zion, 1, 117, 285n1
Zweistromland, 16–17

www.ingramcontent.com/pod-product-compliance
Lightning Source LLC
Chambersburg PA
CBHW021336230426
43666CB00006B/313